English Grammar and Composition

THIRD COURSE

English Grammar and Composition

THIRD COURSE

JOHN E. WARRINER

MARY E. WHITTEN

FRANCIS GRIFFITH

HARCOURT BRACE JOVANOVICH, INC.

New York   Chicago   San Francisco   Atlanta   Dallas

THE SERIES:

English Grammar and Composition: First Course
English Grammar and Composition: Second Course
English Grammar and Composition: Third Course
English Grammar and Composition: Fourth Course
English Grammar and Composition: Fifth Course
English Grammar and Composition: Complete Course

Test booklet and teacher's manual for each title above

CORRELATED BOOKS OF MODELS FOR WRITING:
Composition: Models and Exercises A
Composition: Models and Exercises B
Composition: Models and Exercises C
Composition: Models and Exercises D
Composition: Models and Exercises E
Advanced Composition: A Book of Models for Writing

AUTHORS: John E. Warriner has taught English for 32 years, in junior and senior high schools and in college. He is also a coauthor of the *English Workshop* series. Mary E. Whitten, in addition to teaching English in teachers colleges, including a course entitled "Methods of Teaching English in the High School," has had several years' experience teaching and supervising the English program in grades 8–12 in Texas and Oklahoma schools. She is coauthor of *English Workshop*, Fourth Edition, Grade 9; *Harbrace College Handbook*, Sixth Edition; and *College English: The First Year*, Fifth Edition. Francis Griffith, who holds a doctor's degree in education from Columbia University and includes in his experience advanced courses from the National University of Ireland, was for many years Chairman of English and Speech in a Brooklyn, New York, high school.

ISBN 0-15-311931-4

Preface

In presentation and content *English Grammar and Composition, Third Course*, has been planned specifically to help students at that point in their English education when they need to clinch those fundamental skills to which they have already been introduced but which they have not quite mastered. Whether used at the end of a junior high sequence or at the beginning of the senior high school, *Third Course* occupies a pivotal position. It clinches fundamentals at the same time that it gives the student a taste of the kinds of work he will encounter in the next few years. Its goals are review and preparation. The authors believe that thoroughness is more important than variety and that rigorous training in the basic aspects of good writing and speaking is more appropriate than superficial exposure to everything that can possibly pass as English. To further these ends, *Third Course*, while more limited in scope than succeeding books in the series, aims at mastery of fundamentals.

The teaching of writing, as all experienced teachers know, presents special problems. The intractability of the written word, the class load, the demands made upon the student's time and energies by his other subjects are necessarily more familiar to the English teacher than to his many critics. Nevertheless, the English teacher must accept the primary responsibility for teaching competence in writing. To acquit himself of it successfully he must make use of all the help he can. Specifically, he must have a textbook that provides needed materials in a form convenient for teaching.

No textbook can pretend to do the whole job of teaching composition. Students learn to write by writing, not by memorizing precepts. The writing they do must be read and commented upon by the teacher. Nor will students be helped much by reading that composition is really an easy and pleasant pastime—something they would really enjoy as much as games and gossip if only they would give it a try. A student with the intelligence to write a satisfactory paper will not believe in such nonsense for long. Effective communication in writing is difficult to learn and difficult to teach, and a textbook does no one any service by pretending otherwise. On the other hand, a textbook can help the teacher by providing the right materials at the right time. It can help the student by giving him clear instructions and examples in a form that will be useful both when he is studying a skill in class and when he has need to review it in the course of his own writing. *Third Course* does not claim to make the teaching of writing simple; it does attempt to make the job manageable.

Like the others in the *English Grammar and Composition* series, this textbook has a serious and businesslike approach to language skills. Fringe areas of English give way to fundamentals. Engaging "motivational" essays and pictures are sacrificed for additional teaching materials. Providing the motivation for learning, essential to all teaching, is considered the prerogative of the teacher, not the textbook. The textbook serves as a clear statement of the subject matter to be taught and a collection of teaching materials to enforce the learning.

In preparing this latest edition, the authors have carefully maintained the basic character of a series that received wide acceptance in its previous edition. The book is organized in subject matter units: grammar, usage, composition, aids to good English (library, dictionary, vocabulary), speaking and listening, and mechanics (capitalization, punctuation, spelling, and manuscript form). The instructional and practice materials in any one area will thus be found in the same chapter or group of chapters, not distributed throughout the text. The advantage of this arrangement is twofold. First, it permits the teacher to teach any chapter or group of chapters as an independent unit, concentrating on one skill at a time. This independence of chapters and parts makes the book flexible enough for immediate adaptation to any course of study. The teacher may teach the chapters in any sequence. The *Teacher's Manual* contains a suggested sequence in the form of a recommended course of study. Since the book is arranged according to subject matter units rather than as a consecutive series of lessons, no teacher should teach it straight through from cover to cover.

A second advantage of the subject matter arrangement is that it greatly enhances the book's value as a reference tool. The student learns quickly in which part of his text he will find help in punctuation, for example, or in answering a specific usage problem or in understanding a grammar term. He can turn easily to the information he wants.

Grammar

The grammar taught in the *English Grammar and Composition* series is traditional grammar. Although linguistic research shows us that our Latin-based traditional grammar does not provide the most accurate possible description of our language, a new and specifically English grammar based on linguistic research has not yet been clearly enough stated for general use in the schools. Until such a new grammar is fully developed, teachers must continue to use the grammar they have in teaching usage and composition. It is not too soon, however, for interested teachers to begin experimenting with linguistic concepts in the classroom. Indeed, until many more teachers engage in such experiments, the arguments for and against linguistic methods must be inconclusive. Teachers inclined to experiment with linguistic concepts will find twelve carefully worked out lesson plans on structural grammar in the *Teacher's Manual*.

As in the earlier editions, diagraming is included for those who find it a helpful means to understanding the grammatical structure of the sentence. Teachers who do not wish to teach diagramming will find that the diagrams may be easily passed over.

Usage

The usage chapters teach students to avoid in their speaking and writing the most common pitfalls in usage. Outmoded distinctions (*shall, will*) have been abandoned, and the customs of current usage (*It's me*) have been recognized. While liberal in attitude, the book is not unrealistically permissive. The usage taught is the usage expected of educated people—standard English. The final chapter in the usage section (Chapter 9, "Glossary of Usage") is an alphabetically arranged list of common usage problems not covered in Chapters 5–8. Teachers will wish to take their students through this chapter early in the year. Students will find it convenient for reference at any time.

Sentence Structure and Composition

The seven chapters in these two parts make it possible for teachers to meet the current demand for more emphasis on composition skills. The first two chapters, "Writing Complete Sentences" and "Achieving Sentence Variety," continue and expand instruction begun in these subjects in the earlier books of the series. The chapters "Writing Paragraphs" and "Writing Compositions" emphasize the planning and writing of interesting, clear, and coherent compositions. The teaching of composition is always concrete, never vague. It is bolstered by many examples and models.

Teachers know the effectiveness of models in the teaching of composition. *Third Course* contains models of paragraphs, the long composition, friendly and business letters, narratives, and the summary and the report. However, the amount of space a general text can devote to reproduction of space-consuming models is limited. To provide teachers with additional models of good writing in handy form, a companion series of texts, *Composition: Models and Exercises*, has been prepared, intended for use with the *English Grammar and Composition* series. In approximately two hundred pages, the book presents dozens of carefully selected models by professional writers, showing how to write all types of discourse. Each model illustrates an important teaching point. It is followed by a helpful analysis and a number of writing assignments.

Aids to Good English

In this section the authors have grouped three chapters: "The Library," "The Dictionary," and "Vocabulary." As the library more and more assumes its proper position at the center of the instructional program, students need to learn the resources it provides and the most efficient means of using these resources. The extent to which a student will need instruction in the efficient use of the dictionary, by all odds his most important reference book, will depend on his past experience. For those who need such instruction, Chapter 18 will give a sound understanding of the kinds of dictionaries, the wealth of information to be found in a dictionary, and training in the interpretation of the dictionary symbols for etymology, meaning, and pronunciation.

Makers of college entrance examinations and the standard tests of student potential long ago discovered that one of the most reliable criteria is the student's vocabulary. For this reason, if for no other, teachers recognize the practical importance of making their students word-conscious and of helping them to enlarge their vocabulary. Every book in the *English Grammar and Composition* series has a chapter on vocabulary development. Chapter 19 and the Supplement (pages 599–620) are part of this program. Chapter 19 explains the various ways in which we acquire new words and the importance of precision in word selection; it gives the student valuable experience in word analysis (prefixes, roots, suffixes) as well as in etymology. A word list of three hundred and sixty words constitutes a year's program in vocabulary study. The Supplement gives the student practice in choosing appropriate words for his compositions. Connotation as well as denotation is emphasized.

Speaking and Listening

While the emphasis in *Third Course* is on written English, the book does not neglect spoken English. The usage chapters, with their oral drills and quick-response exercises, help the student to correct his speech. The two chapters in Part Six, "Speaking Before Groups" and "Listening," help him to become an effective speaker before a group and an effective listener in a group. Often neglected in the classroom, public speaking is nevertheless a subject in which students need the security which practice in school can provide. Listening skills, in an age of radio, television, and school and college lectures, always need sharpening.

Mechanics

Part Seven embraces chapters in capitalization, punctuation, spelling, and manuscript form. The capitalization and punctuation chapters present the rules commonly followed by today's writers. Abundant practical exercises are provided. Equally important is the clear arrangement of rules, which enables the student to look up on his own the answer to any problem a pupil at this level is likely to encounter in these areas.

Chapter 28 states the most widely used spelling rules and supplies lists of commonly confused homonyms and of frequently misspelled words which, like the word list in the vocabulary chapter, may be made the basis for lessons throughout the year.

Although Chapter 29, "Manuscript Form," comes near the end of the book, it should be taught in connection with the year's first written assignment because it deals with practical matters of theme writing such as margins, penmanship and neatness, the use of abbreviations, the writing of numbers, and standard correction symbols.

English Grammar and Composition, *Third Course*, employs the same clean-cut format used in the previous editions, with a second color for important rules, an open page, and tab keys for quick reference. Every effort has been made to make the texts as easy to use as they are reliable in content.

A separate booklet of tests—one test for each testable chapter—may be ordered from the publisher at a small cost. The tests were prepared by Mr. Orville Palmer of the Educational Testing Service. Teachers will find them a great time-saver in evaluating their students and a help in motivation. Students respect printed tests.

A *Teacher's Manual* is available from the publisher. The *Teacher's Manual* presents a recommended sequence of chapters ("Suggested Course of Study") for schools that do not have one of their own, a page-by-page discussion of the text with helpful suggestions for the teacher, a section on motivation and classroom procedures in the teaching of composition, a number of sample lesson plans of special value for beginning teachers, and answers for all exercises in the text and in the separate test booklet.

J. W.

ACKNOWLEDGMENTS   The authors and publishers wish to acknowledge the valuable assistance given by many teachers who contributed in many ways to the preparation of this series. Special thanks are due to Mr. Henry Aronson, International School of The Hague, Netherlands; Dr. John Arscott, Coordinator, Senior Division, West Essex High School, North Caldwell, New Jersey; Mrs. Margaret R. Bonney, Lexington High School, Lexington, Massachusetts; Mrs. Louise Brock, Tuckahoe Junior High School, Richmond, Virginia; Mrs. Kenneth Brown, Hand Junior High School, Columbia, South Carolina; Mr. Lewis Browne, Myers Park High School, Charlotte, North Carolina; Mrs. Margaret Christianson, Point Loma High School, San Diego, California; Mr. W. Griffith Couser, Melrose High School, Melrose, Massachusetts; Miss Jean E. Crabtree, Garden City Senior High School, Garden City, New York; Mr. Peter Evarts, Assistant to the Director, Teacher Education Program, Oakland University, Rochester, Michigan; Miss Anna Fort, Deal Junior High School, Washington, D.C.; Mrs. Betty Gray, Abington Junior High School, Abington, Pennsylvania; Mrs. Helen Hiller, Former Chairman of English Department, Macomb's Junior High School, Bronx, New York; Mr. Robert U. Jameson, The Haverford School, Haverford, Pennsylvania; Mr. Raymond Kavanagh, Levittown Memorial High School, Levittown, New York; Mrs. Gladys Kronsagen, Glenbard Township High School, Glen Ellyn, Illinois; Miss Alice Liberto, Miami Edison Junior High School, Miami, Florida; Mrs. Archibald McClure, John Adams High School, South Bend, Indiana; Mrs. Ruth McKinney, A. C. Flora High School, Columbia, South Carolina; Miss Rita Morgan, James Madison High School, Vienna, Virginia; Miss Geraldine Oliver, Fairview High School, Dayton, Ohio; Mr. Orville Palmer, Educational Testing Service, Princeton, New Jersey; Mrs. Helen Slonin, Baldwin Junior High School, Baldwin, New York; Miss Julia Tygart, Miami Edison Junior High School, Miami, Florida; Mr. Arthur Weisbach, Summit High School, Summit, New Jersey.

Contents

xiii

SUPPLEMENT

English Grammar and Composition

THIRD COURSE

PART ONE

Grammar

CHAPTER 1

The Parts of Speech

The Work That Words Do

As you speak or write, you express your thoughts in words. Sometimes you may use only one word, such as *Quiet!* or *Hello*. Usually, however, you use groups of words that make statements, ask questions, or give instructions or directions. Every word you speak or write has a definite use in expressing a thought or idea. The way the word is used determines what *part of speech* that word is. There are eight parts of speech:

nouns	verbs	conjunctions
pronouns	adverbs	interjections
adjectives	prepositions	

As you study this chapter, learn to recognize the parts of speech, the eight ways that words work for you as you communicate your thoughts and ideas to others.

THE NOUN

Perhaps the words most frequently used are those by which we identify someone or something. These labels, or name words, are called nouns.

3

1a. A *noun* names a person, place, thing, or idea.

Persons	Celia, Mr. Tompkins, postman, women, Americans
Places	Chicago, Alaska, Europe, Bryant Park, kitchen, suburbs
Things	money, poem, pencils, airplanes, merry-go-round
Ideas	perfection, strength, happiness, obedience, liberty

● EXERCISE 1. Copy each of the following words on your paper. After each, tell whether it names a person, a place, a thing, or an idea. If the word does not name, write *not a noun*.

1. novelist	8. silly	15. Midwest
2. biscuits	9. Canadians	16. advertise
3. sharpen	10. patriotism	17. supposedly
4. sharpener	11. believe	18. faith
5. gratitude	12. belief	19. Santa Claus
6. gratify	13. across	20. joy
7. loses	14. for	

Common and Proper Nouns

There are two classes of nouns, *proper nouns* and *common nouns*. A proper noun names a particular person, place, or thing and is always capitalized. A common noun names any one of a group of persons, places, or things and is not capitalized.

COMMON NOUNS	PROPER NOUNS
inventor	Thomas A. Edison, Eli Whitney, Eastman
man	Mr. Jones, Dr. Smith, Professor Brown, William
city	Boston, Des Moines, Salt Lake City
school	Lincoln High School, Harvard University
state	Georgia, Tennessee, Utah, Pennsylvania
river	Mississippi River, Colorado River
month	January, April, August, November

● EXERCISE 2. There are fifty nouns in the following paragraph. As you list the nouns on your paper, circle all the proper nouns. A name is counted as one noun, even if it has more than one part.

1. In our living language, proper nouns occasionally change to common nouns. 2. Losing significance as names of particular people, these words become names for a general class of things. 3. For example, during the nineteenth century, Samuel A. Maverick was unique among ranchers in Texas. 4. Maverick did not regularly brand his calves. 5. Therefore, cattlemen on neighboring ranches began to call any unbranded, stray yearling a "Maverick." 6. For these cattlemen, a *maverick* soon became a common name for a certain kind of calf, and now *maverick* is standard English for any unbranded animal or motherless calf. 7. Many other words have similar origins. 8. The term *pasteurization* is derived from Louis Pasteur, and *mesmerism* comes from F. A. Mesmer. 9. From John L. McAdam, a Scottish engineer, comes the word *macadam*, referring to a pavement made of crushed stones. 10. Once used exclusively as names of particular people, *silhouette*, *macintosh*, and *watt* have undergone similar changes and no longer begin with capital letters.

● EXERCISE 3. Study the nouns listed below. In class, be prepared to (1) identify each noun as a common or a proper noun, and (2) if the noun is a common noun, name a corresponding proper noun; if the noun is proper, name a corresponding common noun. Remember that capitalization is one of the signals of a proper noun.

1. girl	6. town	11. college	16. holiday
2. day	7. lake	12. church	17. teacher
3. Iowa	8. actor	13. Italy	18. Memphis
4. sea	9. king	14. Broadway	19. language
5. Poe	10. song	15. Uncle George	20. islands

Compound Nouns

By now, you have probably noticed that two or more words may be used as a single noun. In the examples below rule 1a on page 4, you find *postman* and *Mr. Tompkins* in the list of persons, *Bryant Park* in the list of places, and

1a

merry-go-round in the list of things. These word groups are called *compound nouns*.

As you see, the parts of a compound noun may be written as one word, as two or more words, or may be hyphenated. Here are some more compound nouns.

EXAMPLES   housekeeper, basketball, drugstore, schoolteacher
            commander in chief, tennis ball, home economics
            father-in-law, baby-sitter, great-grandfather

If you are in doubt as to how to write a compound noun, you should consult your dictionary. Some dictionaries may give two correct forms for a word; for example, you may find *vice-president* written also without the hyphen. As a rule, it is wise to use the form the dictionary gives first.

THE PRONOUN

1b. A *pronoun* is a word used in place of one or more nouns.

One way to refer to something is to use the noun that names it. We usually have to do this to make clear what we mean. However, once we have made clear the identity of the person or thing we are talking about, we can make other references without having to give the name each time.

EXAMPLE   Harry looked into the billfold and found **it** empty.

It would be awkward and unnecessary to repeat *billfold* in the last part of this sentence. The pronoun *it* does the job better by simply taking the place of the noun *billfold*.

In the following sentences a number of different pronouns are used. Notice that they all take the place of a noun in just the way that *it* does in the example above.

EXAMPLES   Where is Anne? **She** said **she** was coming right home.
            [The pronoun *she*, used twice, takes the place of
            Anne in the second sentence.]

            The principal and Mr. Gates said **they** would come.
            [The pronoun *they* takes the place of two nouns:
            principal and *Mr. Gates*.]

As these examples show, pronouns almost always refer to a word mentioned earlier. This noun on which the pronoun depends for its meaning is called the antecedent, which simply means "something going before." In the following examples, the arrows point from the pronouns to their antecedents.

EXAMPLES   Jack read the **letter** again and then tore **it** up.

The judge informed the **twins** that **they** had won the contest.

Nan has **her** own way of doing things.

Personal Pronouns

The pronouns that have appeared in the examples so far are called *personal* pronouns. In this use, *personal* does not have its common meaning of "private or having to do with a person." Instead it refers to one of the three possible ways of making statements: The person speaking can talk about himself (first person) or he can talk about the person to whom he is speaking (second person) or he can talk about anyone or anything else (third person). The few pronouns in English that have different forms to show person are called *personal pronouns*.

PERSONAL PRONOUNS

	SINGULAR	PLURAL
First person (the person speaking)	I, my,[1] mine, me	we, our, ours, us
Second person (the person spoken to)	you, your, yours	you, your, yours
Third person (some other person or thing)	he, his, him she, her, hers it, its	they, their, theirs, them

[1] The possessive forms *my*, *your*, *her*, etc., are called pronouns in this book. (See page 10.)

1b

Other Commonly Used Pronouns

Here are some other kinds of pronouns that you will encounter as you study this textbook:

REFLEXIVE PRONOUNS   (the *–self, –selves* forms of the personal pronouns)

myself	ourselves
yourself	yourselves
himself, herself, itself	themselves

◆ NOTE   Never write or say *hisself* or *theirselves*.

RELATIVE PRONOUNS   (used to introduce adjective clauses; see pages 96–97)

who	whom	whose	which	that

INTERROGATIVE PRONOUNS   (used in questions)

Who . . .?	Whose . . .?	What . . .?
Whom . . .?	Which . . .?	

DEMONSTRATIVE PRONOUNS   (used to point out a specific person or thing)

this	that	these	those

INDEFINITE PRONOUNS   (not referring to a definite person or thing; frequently used without antecedents)

all	each	more	one
another	either	most	other
any	everybody	much	several
anybody	everyone	neither	some
anyone	everything	nobody	somebody
anything	few	none	someone
both	many	no one	

● EXERCISE 4.   Number 1–20 on your paper. List in order the twenty pronouns in the following sentences. After each pronoun, write the noun to which it refers.

1. Angela keeps an interesting notebook; in this, she writes down the favorite sayings of her teachers.

2. One of the first entries is a quotation of Mr. Adams, her speech teacher: "Speech is a mirror of the mind."

3. Another quotes Miss Dugan, who once said, "A person should never use a word he cannot pronounce or spell. The word is not his to use, for it does not belong to him."
4. Some of the best advice, however, comes from Coach Morris: "Suppose the opposing players are too strong for the home team. Since they are four touchdowns ahead of us, we cannot hope to beat them. My advice is to fight even harder than before. Every boy should say to himself, 'If I must fall, I will fall forward.'"

● **EXERCISE 5.** Copy the following paragraph, and fill in the twenty blanks with appropriate pronouns. Do not write in this book.

—— main objection to mystery stories is the effect that —— have on —— peace of mind. When reading —— of ——, —— imagine that —— is in the closet or just outside the window. Whether the author chooses to have a victim poisoned or to have —— strangled, —— always has —— murdered. In a story that —— read recently, a murderer overpowers a millionaire, twisting and bruising —— body and casting —— into the cage of a gorilla. Unlike ——, Helen, —— likes mystery stories as a means for escape, particularly enjoys reading —— just before —— goes to sleep. —— favorite stories include —— —— cause terrible nightmares.

THE ADJECTIVE

Sometimes we wish to describe, or make more definite, a noun or pronoun we use. We then *modify* the word by using an adjective.

1c. An *adjective* modifies a noun or a pronoun.

To *modify* a word means to describe the word or to make its meaning more definite. An adjective modifies a noun or a pronoun by answering one of these questions: *What kind? Which one? How many?* Notice how the bold-faced adjectives on the following page answer these questions about the nouns modified.

1c

WHAT KIND?	WHICH ONE?	HOW MANY?
white car	**this** road	**one** minute
nylon rope	**last** week	**three** boys
wise man	**the first** day	**few** people
big desk	**the other** man	**several** days

Pronoun or Adjective?

Notice that in the phrases above, *one*, *this*, *other*, *few*, and *several*—words which may also be used as pronouns—are adjectives, because they modify the nouns in the phrases rather than take the place of the nouns.

The words *my*, *your*, *his*, *her*, *its*, *our*, and *their* are called pronouns throughout this book; they are the *possessive* forms of personal pronouns, showing ownership. Some teachers, however, prefer to think of these words as adjectives because they tell *Which one?* about nouns: *his* sister, *your* book, *our* team, *their* tents. Often they are called *pronominal adjectives*.

Nouns Used as Adjectives

Sometimes you will find nouns used as adjectives.

NOUNS	NOUNS USED AS ADJECTIVES
large **table**	**table** leg
expensive **dinner**	**dinner** table
next **Sunday**	**Sunday** dinner

Notice in the last example above that a proper noun, *Sunday*, is used as an adjective. Here are some other proper nouns used as adjectives:

Florida coast	**Thanksgiving** turkey
Norway pine	**March** wind

When you find a noun used as an adjective, your teacher may prefer that you call it an adjective. If so, proper nouns used as adjectives will be called *proper adjectives*. In any exercises you do, follow your teacher's directions in labeling nouns used as adjectives.

Articles

The most frequently used adjectives are *a, an,* and *the.* These little words are usually called *articles.*

A and *an* are indefinite articles; they refer to one of a general group.

EXAMPLES A teacher arrived.
An automobile went by.
We waited an hour.

A is used before words beginning with a consonant sound; *an* is used before words beginning with a vowel sound. Notice in the third example above that *an* is used before a noun beginning with the consonant *h,* because the *h* in *hour* is not pronounced. *Hour* is pronounced as if it began with a vowel (like *our*). Remember that the *sound* of the noun, not the spelling, determines which indefinite article will be used.

The is a definite article. It indicates that the noun refers to someone or something in particular.

EXAMPLES The teacher arrived.
The automobile went by.
The hour for our departure finally arrived.

Adjectives in Sentences

In all the examples you have seen so far, the adjective comes before the noun modified. This is the usual position.

Mrs. Russell gave each boy here hot tea and apple pie.

The ancient, battered manuscript was found in the desk.

Sometimes, however, adjectives follow the word they modify.

Magazines, old and dusty, cluttered his desk.

Other words may separate an adjective from the noun or pronoun modified.

Felix seemed **unhappy.** He was not **mischievous.**

Courageous in battle, he deserved his medals.

● EXERCISE 6.   Copy the following sentences onto your paper, and fill in the blanks with adjectives. (Do not use articles.) Answer the questions *What kind? Which one? How many?* Draw an arrow from each adjective to the noun or pronoun modified.

1. —— cowboys wore —— boots and —— hats.
2. The —— buildings looked ——.
3. At the zoo we saw —— birds, —— monkeys, and —— snakes.
4. —— and ——, she flounced down the hall.
5. At —— o'clock, the —— travelers fretted beneath the —— sun.
6. Pine trees, —— and ——, dotted the horizon.
7. Since the package was ——, he became ——.
8. After a —— day, we arrived home, —— and ——.
9. Not —— of high places, she climbed the mountain to watch the sunset, which was ——.
10. As they saw the —— lightning and heard the —— thunder, the boys, though —— and ——, pretended to be ——.

● EXERCISE 7.   Except for articles, the sentences below contain no adjectives. Using a separate sheet of paper, revise the sentences by supplying interesting adjectives to modify the nouns or pronouns. Underline the adjectives.

1. Winds uprooted trees and leveled houses.
2. All during the night in the forest, the boys heard noises, cries of birds and beasts.
3. Without money, I strolled down the midway at the fair and watched the crowds at the booths and on the rides.
4. Everybody at the party received a gift, such as candy, jewelry, soap, or a book.
5. At the end of the program, when the hero swaggered forth with a gun to meet the villain on the sands of the desert, a tube burned out and spread a blanket of snow across the screen.

● EXERCISE 8.   Look for adjectives as you read a news-paper or a magazine. Find a section containing at least twenty adjectives, not counting articles. Clip it out and paste it onto your paper. Underline the adjectives.

● REVIEW EXERCISE A.   List on your paper the *italicized* words in the following sentences. Before each word, write the number of its sentence, and after the word, write whether it is a noun, pronoun, or an adjective.

EXAMPLE   1. *This* article tells about Shakespeare's *life*.
          1. *This, adjective*
          1. *life, noun*

1. Recently many *schools* paid *tribute* to William Shakespeare.
2. *Shakespeare*, the most *famous* playwright of *all* time, was born in Stratford-on-Avon in 1564.
3. He was baptized in the *small* church at Stratford shortly after *his* birth.
4. *He* was buried in the *same* church.
5. On the stone above his grave, *you* can find an inscription which places a *curse* upon *anyone* who moves his bones.
6. Out of *respect* for his wish or because of fear of his curse, *nobody* has disturbed the grave.
7. *This* explains why his body was never moved to Westminster Abbey, where many *other English* writers are buried.
8. In addition to the church, the visitor in *Stratford* can see the house in *which* Shakespeare was born.
9. *One* can walk through the home of the *parents* of Anne Hathaway, the *woman* whom Shakespeare married.
10. Inside the thatched-roofed cottage a person can see a very *uncomfortable* bench on which Shakespeare and *Anne* may have sat when he called on *her*.
11. At *one* time visitors could also see the *large* house which Shakespeare bought for *himself* and his *family*.
12. When he retired from the *theater*, he lived there, and there he also died.
13. Unfortunately, the house was destroyed by a *later* owner *who* did not want to pay taxes on *it*.

THE VERB

A noun or a pronoun, no matter how many modifiers it may have, cannot make a sentence. The noun or pronoun must act in some way, or something must be said about it. The part of speech that performs this function is the *verb.*

1d. A *verb* is a word that expresses action or otherwise helps to make a statement.

Action Verbs

Words such as *do, come, go,* and *write* are action verbs. Sometimes action verbs express an action that cannot be seen: *believe, remember, know, think,* and *understand.*

● EXERCISE 9. Make a list of twenty action verbs not including those listed above. Include and underline at least five verbs that express an action that cannot be seen.

There are two large classes of action verbs—transitive and intransitive. A verb is *transitive* when the action it expresses is directed toward a person or thing named in the sentence.

EXAMPLES The bride **cut** the cake. [The action of the verb *cut* is directed toward *cake.* The verb is transitive.]

Amy finally **sent** the letter.

In these examples the action passes from the doer—the subject—to the receiver of the action. Words that receive the action of a transitive verb are called *objects.*

A verb is intransitive when it expresses a simple action (or helps to make a statement) without reference to an object.[1] The following sentences contain intransitive verbs.

EXAMPLES This morning I **overslept.**

The children **behaved** badly.

The train **arrived** on time.

[1] Linking verbs (*be, seem, appear,* etc.) are usually considered to be *intransitive verbs.*

The same verb may be transitive in one sentence and intransitive in another. A verb that can take an object is often used intransitively when the emphasis is on the action rather than the person or thing affected by it.

EXAMPLES John **speaks** French. [transitive]
John **speaks** fluently. [intransitive]

The speaker **answered** many questions. [transitive]
The speaker **answered** angrily. [intransitive]

● EXERCISE 10.   Some of the action verbs in the following sentences are transitive and some are intransitive. Write the verb of each sentence after the proper number and label it as a dictionary would—*v.t.* for transitive, *v.i.* for intransitive.

1. The contest judges selected a winner.
2. Lawyers sometimes charge high fees for their advice.
3. The army retreated to a stronger position.
4. The club finally voted funds for the picnic.
5. The best of friends sometimes quarrel.
6. At the last moment, Cinderella remembered her Fairy Godmother's warning.
7. The rain lasted all afternoon.
8. Mary practices every day for an hour.
9. On the opening night of the class play, Charlie forgot his lines.
10. During vacation, time passes rapidly.
11. Last week our scout troop took an overnight hike.
12. On sunny days we walk to school.

Linking Verbs

Some verbs help to make a statement, not by expressing an action but by serving as a link between two words. These verbs are called *linking verbs* or *state-of-being verbs*.

The most commonly used linking verbs are forms of the verb *be*. You should become thoroughly familiar with the verbs listed at the top of the next page.

1d

be	shall be	should be
being	will be	would be
am	has been	can be
is	have been	could be
are	had been	should have been
was	shall have been	would have been
were	will have been	could have been

Any verb ending in *be* or *been* is a form of the verb *be*. Here are some other frequently used linking verbs:

appear	grow	seem	stay
become	look	smell	taste
feel	remain	sound	turn

Notice in the following sentences how each verb is a link between the words on either side of it. The word that follows the linking verb fills out or completes the meaning of the verb and refers to the word preceding the verb.

The sum of two and four **is** six. [sum = six]
Roger **could have been** a mechanic. [Roger = mechanic]
That barbecue **smells** good. [good barbecue]
The light **remained** red. [red light]

◆ NOTE   Many of the linking verbs listed above can be used as action (nonlinking) verbs as well.

The movie star **appeared** in a play.
The cook **tasted** the soup.

Even *be* is not always a linking verb. It may be followed by only an adverb: I was *there*.[1] To be a linking verb, the verb must be followed by a word that names or describes the subject.

● EXERCISE 11.   Copy the following sentences, and fill in the blanks with linking verbs. Use a different verb for each blank.

1. My dog's name —— Jim Dandy.
2. I —— bad.
3. Pine trees —— tall.
4. He —— a good Samaritan.
5. Did she eventually —— a teacher or a nurse?
6. My face —— red.

[1] See pages 19–22 for a discussion of adverbs.

7. All morning the baby —— quiet.
8. This soup —— good.
9. Paul —— lucky.
10. At sea, exactly what —— a dead reckoning?

● EXERCISE 12. Using the linking verb given in italics, change each word group below to a sentence. Underline the linked words.

EXAMPLES 1. *became* one impatient clerk
        1. *One <u>clerk</u> became <u>impatient</u>.*

        2. *is* Mr. Alford, our family doctor
        2. *<u>Mr. Alford</u> is our family <u>doctor</u>.*

1. *was*   the lukewarm coffee
2. *had been*   Alfred Daniels, a man of integrity
3. *looks*   the frightened animal
4. *grew*   the restless audience
5. *tastes*   that bitter medicine
6. *is*   Louise, the editor of our yearbook
7. *remained* the calm lake
8. *seems*   their odd behavior
9. *may become* one daughter, a famous pianist
10. *looks*   that expensive watch

● EXERCISE 13. Write a sentence using each of the following nouns with an action verb. Then write another sentence using the same noun with a linking verb.

EXAMPLE 1. sister
        1. *My sister bought a round tablecloth.* [action verb]
          My sister is a backseat driver. [linking verb]

1. brother
2. Connie
3. tornadoes
4. policeman
5. actress
6. spiders

Verb Phrases

Parts of the verb *be* may serve another function besides that of linking verb. They may be used as *helping verbs* (sometimes called *auxiliary verbs*) in *verb phrases*. A *phrase* is a group of related words. A verb phrase consists of a main verb preceded by one or more helping verbs. Besides all forms of the verb *be*, helping verbs include the following:

has	can	might
have	may	must
had	should	do
shall	would	did
will	could	does

These helping verbs work together with main verbs as a unit. The helping verbs are in bold-faced type in the following examples.

is leaving	**may** become	**might have** remained
had seemed	**should** move	**must have** thought
shall be going	**could** jump	**does** sing

Sometimes the parts of a verb phrase are interrupted by other parts of speech.

EXAMPLES   She **had** evidently **been thinking** of that.

Your book **may** not **have been stolen** after all.

They **should** certainly **be arriving** any minute.

Parts of verb phrases are often separated in questions.

EXAMPLES   **Did** you **see** the film?

Can his sister **help** us?

Has the boy next door **been introduced** to you?

● EXERCISE 14. Find and list on your paper the verbs and verb phrases in the following paragraph. Be sure to include all helping verbs, especially when the parts of the verb phrase are separated by other words.

EXAMPLE   1. As our teacher has often observed, such things as a star, a cross, or a flag can be symbolic.

1. *has observed*
   can be

1. In history class yesterday we were discussing the fasces, a symbol of authority used in ancient Rome. 2. After Mr. King had described the fasces, which was carried by officers in front of the magistrates, he explained its symbolism. 3. "First," Mr. King said, "you will probably notice the ax, a reminder of the king's power of execution. 4. Rebels might defy the king, but

they might also 'get the ax.' 5. Next, you may notice the bundle of rods which are held together by a strap. 6. Many men who had broken Roman laws had been whipped with rods, and the fasces was a reminder to these offenders: such punishment would be used again if necessary." 7. After these remarks, when the class was comparing the fasces with other symbols, Mr. King interrupted with a question. 8. "Do you know how or where or why Americans have used the fasces as a symbol?" 9. Since we could not even guess the answer, he quickly took a dime from his pocket and showed it to us. 10. "This 1942 dime," Mr. King explained, "bears the fasces; for Americans it has long been a symbol of unity."

THE ADVERB

You know that nouns. and pronouns are modified by adjectives. Verbs and adjectives may have modifiers, too, and their modifiers are called *adverbs*. Adverbs may also modify other adverbs.

1e. An *adverb* is a word used to modify a verb, an adjective, or another adverb.

Adverbs Modifying Verbs

Sometimes an adverb modifies (qualifies or adds to the meaning of) a verb. Study the adverbs in bold-faced type below. Notice that they modify verbs by answering one of these questions: *Where? When? How? To what extent (how long or how much)?*

WHERE?	WHEN?
I moved **forward**.	I moved **immediately**.
Sleep **here**.	Sleep **later**.
Did you go **there**?	Did you go **daily**?

HOW?	TO WHAT EXTENT?
I **gladly** moved.	I **barely** moved.
Sleep **well**.	He **scarcely** sleeps.
Did you go **quietly**?	Did you go **far**?

1e

Adverbs may precede or may follow the verbs they modify, and they sometimes interrupt the parts of a verb phrase. Adverbs may also introduce questions.

EXAMPLE   **How** on earth will we **ever** finish our work on time? [The adverb *how* modifies the verb phrase *will finish*. Notice, too, the adverb *ever*, which interrupts the verb phrase and also modifies it.]

● EXERCISE 15.   Number your paper 1–10. After the appropriate number, write an adverb to fill each blank in the sentence. Following each adverb, write what the adverb tells: *where* the action was done, *when* the action was done, *how* it was done, or *to what extent* it was done.

1. Play ——.
2. I can swim ——.
3. Mr. Thomas —— changes his opinions.
4. Does your brother drive ——?
5. Around the campfire we —— sang cowboy ballads.
6. They did —— win ——.
7. I —— want to send letters, but I —— like to get them.
8. Could he sing ——?
9. The dog jumped —— and barked ——.
10. He sighed —— as he —— waited for a telephone ring.

● EXERCISE 16.   Write ten sentences describing an incident at a ball game, in the classroom, or at a party. Use at least ten adverbs modifying verbs. Underline the adverbs, and draw arrows from them to the verbs they modify.

Adverbs Modifying Adjectives

Sometimes an adverb modifies an adjective.

EXAMPLES   Glenn is an **unusually** good quarterback [The adjective *good* modifies the noun *quarterback*. The adverb *unusually*, telling "how good," modifies *good*.]

During the burglary our dog was **strangely** silent. [The adverb *strangely* modifies the adjective *silent*, which in turn modifies the noun *dog*.]

Probably the most frequently used adverbs are *too* and *very*. In fact, these words are overworked. Try to avoid overusing them in speaking and particularly in writing; find more precise adverbs to take their place.

● EXERCISE 17.   Give one adverb modifier for each of the italicized adjectives below. Use a different adverb in each item; do not use *too* or *very*.

1. a *clever* remark
2. *beautiful* girls
3. an *easy* test
4. *dangerous* waters
5. a *sharp* blade
6. Tony seemed *happy*.
7. My allowance is *small*.
8. Irving became *sick*.
9. Had Clara been *rude*?
10. The problem was *difficult*.

● EXERCISE 18.   Find and list the ten adverbs that modify adjectives in the following sentences. After each adverb, give the adjective modified.

1. Considering its quality, I thought the dress surprisingly inexpensive.
2. The most powerful swimmers are the only ones who can manage the river currents.
3. The highway patrol warned drivers about the extremely slippery roads.
4. The stunted pine tree looked very familiar to the scouts.
5. The scoutmaster remained exceptionally calm under the circumstances.
6. He seemed quite confident that they would eventually find the campsite again.
7. Holmes soon realized that he was dealing with a fiendishly clever adversary.
8. The magician made the trick seem quite easy.
9. The legislators' decision to cut their own salaries was entirely unexpected.
10. Jeff was very unhappy to find three beady eyes peering at him from the darkness.

Adverbs Modifying Other Adverbs

Sometimes an adverb modifies another adverb. Notice in the first column on page 22 that each italicized adverb modifies a verb or an adjective. In the second column each added word in bold-faced type is an adverb that modifies the italicized adverb.

EXAMPLES

Roy is *always* hungry.   Roy is **almost** *always* hungry.

They had met *before*.   They had met **long** *before*.

He saw it *recently*.   He saw it **rather** *recently*.

● EXERCISE 19.   Find and list the ten adverbs that modify other adverbs in the following sentences. After each adverb, give the adverb modified.

1. Designs for the new supersonic airliner have developed rather slowly.
2. My brother stayed somewhat longer in high school than most students.
3. Sam reached the meeting too late to hear the complete discussion.
4. If you handle this material very carefully, you will be in no danger.
5. To our surprise, Father took the news quite calmly.
6. Fairly recently he abruptly changed his views.
7. We all finally agreed that Joe had done extremely well.
8. Lately it seems that each generation wants to travel more rapidly than the preceding generation.
9. Arguments on both sides were most cleverly presented.
10. Although they are extremely young, these students measure up surprisingly well.

Forms of Adverbs

You have probably noticed that many adverbs end in *–ly.* You should remember, however, that many adjectives also end in *–ly:* the *daily* newspaper, an *early* train, an *only* child, his *untimely* death, a *friendly* person. Moreover, words like *now, then, far, wide, fast, high, already, somewhat, not,* and *right,* which are often used as adverbs, do not end in *–ly.* In order to identify a word as an adverb, do not depend entirely upon the ending. Instead, ask yourself: Does this word modify a verb, an adjective, or another adverb? Does it tell *when, where, how,* or *to what extent?*

● EXERCISE 20. Number your paper 1–30, and list after the proper number the adverbs in each sentence. After each adverb, write the word or expression it modifies. Be able to tell whether the word or expression modified is a verb, an adjective, or another adverb.

1. People who travel abroad usually visit the Tower of London.
2. The Tower, which was first built by William the Conqueror, is one of the most famous landmarks in London.
3. The Tower formerly served as a fortress, and it is still garrisoned today.
4. A special ceremony called "The Ceremony of the Keys" is performed nightly.
5. The three gates of the Tower are securely locked by the Chief Warder, and an escort is especially detailed for the ceremony.
6. The Chief Warder and his escort promptly report to the front of the Tower.
7. The sentry immediately challenges the men: "Halt! Who comes there?"
8. The Chief Warder quickly responds, "The Keys."
9. The sentry then asks, "Whose keys?" and the Warder replies distinctly, "Queen Elizabeth's Keys."
10. The Chief Warder then calls solemnly, "God preserve Queen Elizabeth."
11. And all the guards respond together, "Amen."
12. Finally the Chief Warder carries the keys to the Queen's House, and they remain there for the night.
13. The Ceremony of the Keys is not the only pageantry associated with the Tower.
14. Royal salutes are often fired from the Tower in recognition of particularly important occasions.
15. At the coronation of a king or queen, a sixty-two-gun salute is traditionally fired.
16. A royal birth is appropriately proclaimed by a forty-one-

gun salute; a forty-one-gun salute is fired if the sovereign is there for the opening of Parliament.

17. The oldest residents of the Tower of London are the ravens; they have probably always been at the Tower.

18. Legend claims that the Tower will fall if the ravens ever leave.

19. So that ravens are always there in the Tower, the guards clip their wings.

20. The ravens are not unhappy; their needs are well supplied by the weekly allowance which they receive from the state.

21. Visitors to the Tower of London always enjoy seeing the ravens, the various ceremonies, and the gaily dressed sentries.

22. Children are especially excited by the Beefeaters, the famous yeomen of the royal guard, who patiently pose for pictures.

23. If one carefully investigates the Tower, he can really feel that he has gone back in time.

24. The Tower, which is actually composed of several buildings, constantly reminds the British of their history.

25. The Bloody Tower was supposedly the scene of the murder of two young princes, Edward V and the Duke of York.

26. Sir Walter Raleigh was imprisoned in this same tower for approximately twelve years.

27. The White Tower, the oldest part of the fortress, was the part built by William the Conqueror, and it is now used as a museum of armor.

28. Here one can see the armor worn by the kings of England throughout history.

29. Swords, guns, and other weapons are also displayed in the White Tower.

30. It is not surprising that the Tower is one of the most frequented tourist attractions in the world.

THE PREPOSITION

Certain words function in a sentence as relaters. That is, they relate nouns and pronouns to other nouns and pronouns, to verbs, or to modifiers. These words are called *prepositions.*

1f. A *preposition* is a word that shows the relationship of a noun or a pronoun to some other word in the sentence.

The relationship shown by the preposition is an important one. In the examples below, the prepositions in bold-faced type make a great difference in meaning as they relate *house* to *walked* and *him* to *book*.

I walked **to** the house.   The book **by** him is new.
I walked **around** the house.   The book **about** him is new.
I walked **through** the house.   The book **for** him is new.

The following words are commonly used as prepositions. You should study the list and learn to recognize the words.

COMMONLY USED PREPOSITIONS

aboard	beyond	out
about	but (meaning *except*)	over
above	by	past
across	concerning	since
after	down	through
against	during	throughout
along	except	till
among	for	to
around	from	toward
at	in	under
before	inside	underneath
behind	into	until
below	like	up
beneath	near	upon
beside	of	with
besides	off	within
between	on	without

◆ NOTE Many words in the list above can also be adverbs. To distinguish between adverbs and prepositions, ask yourself whether the word relates a following noun or pronoun to a word that precedes. Compare the following:

Look **around**. [adverb]
Look **around** the corner. [preposition]

There are also compound prepositions, having more than one word. Here are some that are frequently used.

COMPOUND PREPOSITIONS

according to	in addition to	on account of
as to	in front of	out of
aside from	in place of	owing to
because of	in spite of	prior to
by means of	instead of	

The preposition and the noun or pronoun that follows combine to form a *prepositional phrase* (For a discussion of prepositional phrases, see page 70.)

● EXERCISE 21.   Number your paper 1–10. Write in order after the proper number appropriate prepositions to fill the blanks.

1. Recently I have learned a great many facts —— animals.
2. A whale cannot stay —— the water long because he must breathe air.
3. Though a whale may live a hundred years, a horse is old —— the age —— thirty, and a dog usually dies before it reaches twenty.
4. The deafness —— insects may surprise you.
5. —— their blindness, bats depend greatly —— their voices and ears.
6. Equipped —— a type —— radar, a blind bat squeaks —— a high pitch, listens —— the echo, and detects and dodges obstacles.
7. The ears —— both bats and dogs can detect sounds that cannot be heard —— human ears.
8. Owls may see rays —— light which are invisible —— human eyes.
9. It is, —— course, a tragedy when a man loses an arm or a leg —— an automobile accident.
10. Yet, if —— chance a starfish should lose arms, new arms would grow; if one type —— flatworm should get its head chopped off, it would —— time grow a new head.

THE CONJUNCTION

1g. A *conjunction* joins words or groups of words.

There are three kinds of conjunctions: *coordinating* conjunctions, *correlative* conjunctions, and *subordinating* conjunctions. Since you will study subordinating conjunctions in connection with subordinate clauses in Chapter 3, at present you need to concern yourself only with the first two kinds of conjunctions:

COORDINATING CONJUNCTIONS	CORRELATIVE CONJUNCTIONS
and	both . . . and
but	not only . . . but also
or	either . . . or
nor	neither . . . nor
for	whether . . . or
yet	

Coordinating conjunctions may join single words, or they may join groups of words. They always connect items of the same kind:

EXAMPLES baseball **and** tennis [two nouns]
at home **or** in the library [two prepositional phrases]
Kate has arrived, **for** I saw her in the garden. [two complete ideas]

◆ NOTE *For* is a conjunction only when it means "because." Otherwise it is a preposition.

We waited for a long time, **for** the bus was late. [*For* means "because."]

We waited a long time **for** the bus. [*For* is a preposition.]

Correlative conjunctions also connect items of the same kind. However, unlike coordinating conjunctions, correlatives are always used in pairs.

1g

EXAMPLES   **Both** Sue **and** Jack entertained the class. [two nouns]

The freshmen asked **not only** for a big celebration **but also** for a special holiday. [two prepositional phrases]

Either you must wash the dishes, **or** you will have to clean the bedroom. [two complete ideas]

● EXERCISE 22.   Number your paper 1–10. Write all the correlative and coordinating conjunctions from the same sentence after the corresponding number on your paper. (Separate the conjunctions by commas.) Be prepared to tell whether they are correlative or coordinating conjunctions.

EXAMPLE   1. Both his father and he played football in high school and in college.
    1. *both—and, and*

1. I have fished in the Colorado River many times, but I never catch any fish.
2. Not only have I tried live bait, but I have also used artificial lures.
3. Whether I go early in the morning or late in the afternoon, the fish either aren't hungry or won't eat.
4. Using both worms and minnows, I have fished for perch and bass, but I have usually caught turtles or eels.
5. The postman told me last winter that my poor luck was caused neither by my lack of skill nor by my choice of the wrong bait.
6. He advised me to fish at either Lake Travis or Marshall Creek, for there, he said, the fish are more plentiful.
7. He also suggested that I buy a spinning reel and a special kind of lure.
8. I saved my money and bought both the reel and the lure, for I was determined to make a big catch.
9. January 2 was very cold, but I decided to try my luck at Lake Travis; I caught nothing.
10. An old man and his companion told me that my new lure was made only for white bass and should be used only in early spring; the man started to tell me a different way to catch fish, but I didn't stay to listen.

THE INTERJECTION

Sometimes we use a word like *Ouch! Whew! Ahem!* or *Well!* to show anger, surprise, or some other sudden emotion. These words are called *interjections.*

1h. An *interjection* **is an exclamatory word that expresses emotion. It has no grammatical relation to the rest of the sentence.**

Interjections are not connectives or modifiers. Since they are unrelated to other words in the sentence, they are set off from the rest of the sentence. They are usually followed by an exclamation point. Sometimes, however, when the exclamation is mild, the interjection may be followed by a comma.

EXAMPLES **Ugh!** The milk tastes sour.
Yippee! We won!
Wow! It worked.
Well, forget it.
Oh, all right.

DETERMINING PARTS OF SPEECH

It is easy to identify a word like *oh* as an interjection. However, the part of speech of a word is not always so simply determined. You must see how the word is used in the sentence.

1i. **What part of speech a word is depends upon how the word is used.**

The same word may be used as different parts of speech.

EXAMPLES 1. The quarterback made a first **down.** [noun]
2. He made a small **down** payment. [adjective]
3. You must **down** the spoonful of medicine. [verb]
4. She glanced **down.** [adverb]
5. She glanced **down** the hall. [preposition]

1
h-i

To determine what part of speech *down* is in each case, you must read the entire sentence. That is, you must study the *context* of the word—how the word is used in the sentence. From the context, you can identify the part of speech that *down* is.

The following summary will help you identify parts of speech in context:

Summary

RULE	PART OF SPEECH	USE	EXAMPLES
1a	noun	names	**Martha** likes **fish.**
1b	pronoun	takes the place of a noun	**You** and **I** must change **this.**
1c	adjective	modifies a noun or a pronoun	What a **hot** day! They were **angry.**
1d	verb	shows action or helps to make a statement	They **played** and **sang.** He **is** a senior.
1e	adverb	modifies a verb, an adjective, or another adverb	We **soon** quit. I am **very** sad. It happened **quite** suddenly.
1f	preposition	relates a noun or a pronoun to another word	Two **of** the gifts **under** the Christmas tree had my name **on** them.
1g	conjunction	joins words	Ed **or** Joe lost.
1h	interjection	expresses strong emotion	**Wow! Ouch! Oh,** I don't mind.

● EXERCISE 23.   Number 1–20 on your paper. Study the use of each italicized word in the following sentences. Place beside the proper number the part of speech of the italicized word. **Be able** to justify your answer by giving the *use* of the word in the sentence. Use the following abbreviations:

n.	noun	*adv.*	adverb
pron.	pronoun	*prep.*	preposition
v.	verb	*conj.*	conjunction
adj.	adjective	*interj.*	interjection

1. *Light* the oven now.
2. A *light* rain fell.
3. A red *light* flashed.
4. Cars whizzed *by*.
5. Dad went *by* air.
6. Look *up*.
7. Sail *up* the river.
8. Can you *top* that?
9. Lock the *top* drawer.
10. We climbed to the *top*.
11. *Shoo!* Get out of here!
12. I *shooed* the hen away.
13. *That* looks beautiful.
14. *That* cat is smart.
15. He did it *for* you.
16. I slept, *for* I was tired.
17. We must soon *part*.
18. One *part* is missing.
19. It may *snow* tonight.
20. We saw *snow* there.

● EXERCISE 24. Write twenty short sentences. Use each of the following words as two different parts of speech. Underline the word, and give its part of speech in parentheses after the sentence.

EXAMPLE 1. on
    1. *We drove <u>on</u>. (adverb)*
       I sat <u>on</u> his hat. (preposition)

1. off	3. over	5. near	7. out	9. above
2. run	4. like	6. ride	8. love	10. paint

● REVIEW EXERCISE B. Number 1–33. After each number, give the part of speech of the italicized word following that number in the paragraph below. Be able to explain its use in the sentence.

(1) *One* of the most (2) *popular* animal fables is a story (3) *about* an owl who (4) *becomes* a god (5) *to* his fellow creatures. Because the owl can see in the (6) *dark* (7) *and* can (8) *answer* questions with a few pet phrases, the (9) *other* animals decide (10) *he* is the wisest creature in the world. They (11) *follow* in his footsteps and (12) *mimic* his (13) *every* action. When he bumps (14) *into* a tree, they (15) *do* the same. And when he staggers down the

(16) *middle* of the highway, they follow his (17) *lead*. They do (18) *not* realize that their (19) *idol* cannot see (20) *during* the daytime. Because the owl fails to see a truck that (21) *is* approaching, he marches (22) *straight* ahead, and the animals follow (23) *behind* him, thinking that he is (24) *very* (25) *brave* and that he will protect them from (26) *harm*. Naturally the owl is (27) *no* help to them when they are in the path of a fast-moving truck. The truck proves (28) *beyond* question that the owl (29) *is* (30) *not* a god, but (31) *this* lesson comes too (32) *late*. The (33) *foolish* animals are all killed by the truck. They followed a leader without regard for his weaknesses.

The Parts of a Sentence

Subject, Predicate, Complement

As you study this chapter and do the exercises in it, you will become familiar with the structure of a sentence. You will learn how a given part of speech functions as part of a sentence—how a noun functions as a subject or a complement, for example. You will then be able to develop or fortify your "sentence sense." This means that you will learn to recognize what a sentence is and how its parts fit together to communicate a complete thought. This understanding of sentence structure will help you to speak and to write more effectively.

In your everyday conversations, you frequently do not use complete sentences. You might say something like the following:

No more ice cream for me.
So long.

Your meaning here is perfectly clear. In *written* English, however, you should express your ideas in clear, complete sentences.

EXAMPLE To everyone's surprise, Jack firmly announced that he had finally had enough ice cream.

THE SENTENCE

Although you use sentences constantly in speaking and writing, you may not be able to say exactly what a sentence is.

2a. *A sentence* is a group of words expressing a complete thought.

As the basic unit of written expression, a sentence must express a complete thought.

SENTENCE	The great door was open.
NOT A SENTENCE	the great door of the auditorium
SENTENCE	The crowd rushed in.
NOT A SENTENCE	the crowd outside the building
SENTENCE	Where were the police?
NOT A SENTENCE	before the police arrived

If a group of words does not express a complete thought, it is a *fragment*, or piece of a sentence, not a sentence.

FRAGMENTS	popcorn and drinks
	from daylight until dark
	the leader of the Boy Scouts
	talking in his sleep again

These groups of words can become sentences only when other words are added to make the thoughts complete:

SENTENCES	I sell popcorn and drinks at the stadium.
	Mother often works from daylight until dark.
	Bert Neal is the leader of the Boy Scouts.
	Larry was talking in his sleep again.

● EXERCISE 1. Number 1–20 on your paper. Decide whether each group of words is a sentence or only a fragment. If the word group is a sentence, write *S* after the proper number. If the word group is a fragment, change it to a sentence by adding one or more words to make the thought complete, and write the sentence. As you turn the fragments into sentences, remember to begin the first word with a capital letter and to insert a mark of punctuation after the last word.

1. tomorrow or the next day
2. obviously fishing for compliments
3. shall I cross the stage slowly
4. the driver of the other car
5. last week I found
6. two home runs in the first inning
7. it runs on regular gasoline
8. going faster than forty miles an hour
9. three horses, two cows, and a pig
10. before class and during the lunch hour
11. then in he walked
12. across the street we saw
13. a gallon of strawberry ice cream
14. awaited the postman
15. the twins would have liked
16. without saying a word
17. the boys painted the garage
18. a car painted orange and white
19. this needs a dash of salt
20. clouds floating across the moon

SUBJECT AND PREDICATE

2b. A sentence consists of two parts: the *subject* and the *predicate*. The *subject* of the sentence is that part about which something is being said. The *predicate* is that part which says something about the subject.

In the following examples, the subjects are separated from the predicates by vertical lines.

Seagulls | were flying around the pier.
The members of the club | arrived.
The lead in the operetta | is my sister.

2
a-b

As you see, the subject and the predicate may be only one word, or they may be more than one word.

In the previous examples, the words to the left of the vertical line make up the *complete subject*. The words to the right of the vertical line make up the *complete predicate*. Often, however, the subject can be in the middle of or at the end of a sentence. Notice the complete subjects, which are in bold-faced type, in the examples below.

On rainy mornings, is **your bus** usually late?
In the desk were **the red pencils.**
Do **your parents** mind your getting home late?

● EXERCISE 2.   Number your paper 1–10. After the corresponding number on your paper, write the complete subject of each sentence.

1. A big animal does not necessarily have a big brain.
2. The rhinoceros, one of the world's largest animals, is also one of the world's most stupid creatures.
3. His big, bulky body makes him a fearsome sight.
4. He is, nevertheless, less dangerous than the water buffalo and the elephant.
5. This remnant from an earlier period of time is actually a pitiful creature.
6. Jutting from his upper lip is a large, heavy horn.
7. All other mammals have horns in more appropriate locations.
8. Doesn't he charge at the slightest disturbance?
9. His eyesight is very poor, however.
10. Swarms of bloodsucking parasites crawl all over his back.

● EXERCISE 3.   Add complete predicates to the following complete subjects to make complete sentences.

1. they
2. honesty
3. his nickname
4. good intentions
5. my best friend
6. all kinds of fireworks
7. a lantern and a hatchet
8. a basket of peaches
9. one boy near me
10. a trip to Utah or Ohio

The Simple Subject

Within the complete subject, every sentence has a *simple subject*.

2c. **The *simple subject* is the main word or group of words in the complete subject.**

To distinguish the simple subject from the complete subject, you select the most important word in the complete subject. This word names the person, place, thing, or idea being talked about.

EXAMPLE   Successful businessmen budget their time wisely.
Complete subject   Successful businessmen
Simple subject   businessmen

EXAMPLE   The cruel King John of England was forced to sign the Magna Charta.
Complete subject   The cruel King John of England
Simple subject   King John

◆ NOTE   Compound nouns, such as *King John* in the second example, are considered one noun.

From the examples above, you can see that the complete subject consists of the simple subject and all the words that belong with it. Adjectives and prepositional phrases (*cruel, of England*) that modify the simple subject are thus included in the complete subject.

Hereafter in this book, the term *subject*, when used in connection with the sentence, refers to the simple subject, unless otherwise indicated.

● EXERCISE 4.   On a separate sheet of paper, fill in each of the following blanks with a subject plus any other words needed to complete the thought.

1. —— may soon wither.
2. —— will rearrange the furniture.
3. —— is an interesting conversationalist.
4. Had —— eaten a green persimmon?

2c

5. —— scooted over to the curb.
6. —— glittered in the moonlight.
7. —— flippantly tossed a coin to the beggar.
8. Next in line was ——.
9. Lying beside the wrecked car was ——.
10. On the other side of the fence stood ——.

The Simple Predicate

2d. The *simple predicate*, or *verb*, is the main word or group of words within the complete predicate.

The essential word (or words) in the complete predicate is always the simple predicate, usually referred to as the *verb*. The other words in the complete predicate may affect the meaning of the verb in various ways, often by making it more definite, but it is the verb that is essential in completing the statement.

EXAMPLE   The rescue team scaled the steep mountainside with agonizing slowness. [Complete predicate: *scaled the steep mountainside with agonizing slowness.* Verb: *scaled.*]

The simple predicate may consist of a single verb or of a verb phrase. In the latter, the verb will be more than one word: *will sing, has been broken, may have been trying,* etc.

When you are asked to pick out the simple predicate in a sentence, be sure to include all parts of a verb phrase. In doing so, keep in mind the various helping verbs that are commonly used as parts of verb phrases: *shall, will, has, have, had, do, does, did, may, might, can, could, should, would, am, is, are, was, were, be,* and *been.*

Study the following examples, noticing the difference between the complete predicate and the verb.

EXAMPLE   Mollie had obediently scrubbed the dingy walls.
Complete predicate   had obediently scrubbed the dingy walls
Verb   had scrubbed

EXAMPLE   My father was sleeping on an army cot.
Complete predicate   was sleeping on an army cot
Verb   was sleeping

Hereafter throughout this book, the word *verb* will be used to refer to the simple predicate, unless otherwise indicated.

● EXERCISE 5.   Make two columns on your paper. Label one of them *Complete predicate* and the other *Verb*. From the following sentences, copy the complete predicates and the verbs in the appropriate columns. If you find a verb phrase, be sure to include all helpers.

1. Many writers' first novels are autobiographical.
2. *Look Homeward, Angel*, the first novel of Thomas Wolfe, was written about his early life in Asheville, North Carolina.
3. In the novel appear the people and scenes of Wolfe's youth.
4. His mother, father, and brother Ben will always be remembered because of Wolfe's book.
5. The boyhood home of Wolfe is still standing in Asheville.
6. The house and its furnishings are carefully described by Wolfe in *Look Homeward, Angel*.
7. A trip to the Asheville library supplies one with many facts about Wolfe.
8. In the library can be found all the newspaper clippings about Wolfe's life and works.
9. At first an outcast in Asheville, Wolfe was later revered by the town's citizens.
10. The whole town mourned the early death of its most famous son.

● EXERCISE 6.   Now that you have learned about subjects and predicates, you should be able to distinguish sentences from fragments more easily. Remembering that a sentence must have a subject and a predicate, revise the following fragments to make the thoughts complete.

1. my bruised toes
2. food for the puppies
3. seems unnecessary
4. a wasp on the back of your neck

2d

5. flashing neon signs
6. rolled down the mountainside
7. dropped thirty degrees during the night
8. a capsized canoe
9. completely destroyed the old building
10. soared high above the dark clouds

Finding the Subject

The best way to find the subject of a sentence is to find the verb first. After you have found the verb, ask "Who?" or "What?" in connection with the verb.

EXAMPLES   There we can wade across the Mississippi River. [The verb is *can wade*. Who can wade? The answer is *we*, the subject.]

Around the bend came a freight train. [The verb is *came*. What came? The *train* came; therefore, *train* is the subject.]

The road to the lake has big holes in it. [The verb is *has*. What has? *Road* is the subject.]

● EXERCISE 7.   Find the subject of each of the following sentences by first finding the verb and then by asking "Who?" or "What?" in front of the verb. After numbering 1–10, list on your paper each verb and its subject. Be sure to include all parts of a verb phrase.

1. Many men have produced great works of art in spite of serious handicaps.
2. Ludwig van Beethoven was one such man.
3. Certainly deafness is a horrible affliction for a musician.
4. Symptoms of his coming deafness first appeared during Beethoven's late twenties.
5. In the beginning, the musician could only feel sorry for himself.
6. His anger at his fate was directed at his friends and associates.
7. In time, though, the rage within him subsided.
8. Courage in the face of seeming destruction became the driving force in his life and a central theme of his music.

9. From the dying man came an appropriate gesture.
10. The fifty-six-year-old composer raised a clenched fist at the storm raging outside his home.

2e. The subject of a verb is never in a prepositional phrase.

You will remember that a prepositional phrase begins with a preposition and ends with a noun or a pronoun: *to the bank, by the door, in the picture, of a book, on the floor, after class, at intermission, for them, except him.* (For a full discussion of prepositional phrases, see page 70.) Since the prepositional phrase contains a noun or a pronoun, and since it often comes before the verb, you may make the mistake of thinking that the noun following a preposition is the subject.

EXAMPLE   **One of the boys** helped us.

When you ask "Who helped?" you may be tempted to answer, "Boys helped." But on second thought you realize that the sentence does not say the *boys helped;* it says only *one* of the boys *helped.* The fact is that a word in a prepositional phrase is never the subject. *Boys* is in the phrase *of the boys*.

Prepositional phrases can be especially misleading when the subject follows the verb.

EXAMPLE   **In the middle of the lake** is a small island.

Neither *middle* nor *lake* can be the subject because each word is part of a prepositional phrase. The subject of *is* has to be *island.*

● EXERCISE 8.   Copy the following sentences onto your paper. Cross out each of the prepositional phrases. Underline each verb twice and its subject once.

1. That house near the railroad tracks is my home.
2. Mr. Ayres of the Federal Investment Company sold it to us last month.

2 e

3. Everything about the house except its location is very satisfactory.
4. Every hour or so trains of all shapes and sizes roar through our backyard.
5. The vibrations of the heavy freight trains cause the most damage.
6. Sometimes a picture on the living-room wall crashes to the floor.
7. The oven door of the gas range habitually snaps open.
8. Yesterday at breakfast, a piece of plaster from the ceiling fell into Dad's coffee.
9. The thunderous clanking of the trains completely absorbs the sound of our television.
10. Each of the advertisers on the screen moves his lips rapidly without saying a thing.

The Subject in an Unusual Position

Sentences which ask questions and sentences which begin with *there* or *here* have a word order that places the subject in an unusual position.

Sentences That Ask Questions

Questions often begin with a verb or with a verb helper. They also frequently begin with words such as *what*, *when*, *where*, *how*, or *why*. Either way, the subject ordinarily *follows* the verb or verb helper.

EXAMPLES   How is **she** now?

Does the **novel** have a happy ending?

In questions that begin with a helping verb, like the second example above, the subject always comes between the helper and the main verb. You can also find the subject by turning the question into a statement, finding the verb, and asking "Who?" or "What?" in front of the verb.

EXAMPLES   Was the door open? *becomes* The door was open. [What was open? *Door*.]

Did he tell you the news? *becomes* He did tell you the news. [Who did tell? *He*.]

Sentences Beginning with <u>There</u>

There is never the subject of a sentence, except when spoken of as a word, as in this sentence. However, this word often appears in the place before a verb where we would expect to find a subject. *There* can be used to get a sentence started when the real subject comes after the verb. In this use, *there* is called an *expletive*. (The verb and its subject are labeled for you in the sentences below.)

EXAMPLES
          V   S
      There is a log cabin in the clearing.

          V   S
      There are oranges in the refrigerator.

To find the subject in such a sentence, omit *there* and ask "Who?" or "What?" before the verb.

There is someone in the phone booth. [Who *is*? Someone. Therefore, *someone* is the subject.]

With *there* omitted, these sentences read as follows:

A log cabin is in the clearing.
Oranges are in the refrigerator.
Someone is in the phone booth.

● EXERCISE 9. Numbering your paper 1–20, list the subjects and verbs in the following sentences after the proper numbers. Write subjects first, verbs second.

1. There are many questions on American history in my book.
2. Naturally, there are answers, too.
3. Under whose flag did Columbus sail?
4. Where is Plymouth Rock?
5. How much do you know about the Lost Colony?
6. What does "squatter's rights" mean?
7. In what state did most of the early Dutch colonists settle?
8. Was there dissension among settlers in Massachusetts?
9. What kinds of schools did the colonists' children attend?
10. How did one travel in colonial America?
11. Were there any sports?
12. When were the famous Salem witch trials?
13. Why did such a tragedy occur?

14. Can you name the three oldest colleges in America?
15. Were there many great American writers during the Colonial period?
16. For what inventions is Benjamin Franklin remembered?
17. Why were the colonists dissatisfied with England?
18. How did the Americans proclaim their independence?
19. Did all of the colonists fight against England?
20. How many of the leaders of the Revolution can you identify?

The Understood Subject

In a request or a command, the subject of a sentence is usually not stated. In such sentences, the person spoken to is understood to be the subject.

EXAMPLES   Please close the door.
            Listen carefully to these instructions.

In the first sentence, a request, *who* is to close the door? *You* are—that is, the person spoken to. In the second sentence, a command, *who* is to listen? Again, *you* are. In each sentence, then, *you* is the understood subject.

Sometimes a request or command will include a name.

EXAMPLES   **Phyllis,** please close the door.
            Listen carefully to these instructions, **students.**

Neither *Phyllis* nor *students* is the subject of its sentence. These words are called nouns of *direct address*. They *identify* the person spoken to. *You*, however, is still the understood subject of each sentence.

Phyllis, (you) please close the door.

Compound Subjects

2f. A *compound subject* consists of two or more subjects joined by a conjunction and having the same verb.

The conjunctions most commonly used to connect the words of a compound subject are *and* and *or*. Study the sentences at the top of the next page.

EXAMPLES   **Myra** poured the punch. [Who poured the punch? Myra poured it. *Myra* is the simple subject.]

          Myra and **Hazel** poured the punch. [Who poured the punch? Myra poured it. Hazel poured it. *Myra* and *Hazel*, then, form the compound subject.]

When more than two words are included in the compound subject, the conjunction is generally used only between the last two words. Also, the words are separated by commas.

EXAMPLE   Myra, Hazel, **and** Pamela poured the punch. [Compound subject: *Myra, Hazel, Pamela*]

Correlative conjunctions may be used with compound subjects.

EXAMPLE   **Either** Myra **or** Hazel poured the punch. [Compound subject: *Myra, Hazel*]

● EXERCISE 10.   Number your paper 1–10. Find and list the compound subjects as well as the verbs in the following sentences.

EXAMPLE   1. Broken mirrors and black cats are often associated with bad luck.
           1. *mirrors, cats—are associated*

1. Volcanoes and earthquakes are destructive natural phenomena.
2. The hero of the novel and a boy in my class have similar personalities.
3. Venus, Juno, and Minerva were three famous Roman goddesses.
4. Do you or he know the origin of the word *bedlam*?
5. *Frankenstein* and *Dracula* were both written during the nineteenth century.
6. Either a raven or a crow is the team's mascot.
7. Into the room strode Natty Bumppo and his Indian companion.
8. There have always been optimists and pessimists.
9. Both poets and kings are buried in Westminster Abbey.
10. Where are the dictionaries and other reference books located?

2f

Compound Verbs

2g. A *compound verb* consists of two or more verbs joined by a conjunction and having the same subject.

The following sentences show how verbs may be compound:

EXAMPLES   Don **went** to the counter and **ordered** a lemonade.
We **searched** the attic but **found** nothing.
The children **skated, rode** bicycles, and **played** hopscotch.
Father **will rent** or **sell** the house.

Notice in the last sentence that the helping verb *will* is not repeated before *sell*, though it is understood: Father *will rent* or *will sell* the house. In compound verbs consisting of verb phrases, the helper may or may not be repeated before the second verb if the helper is the same for both verbs. Often the helper is not repeated when there is a correlative conjunction:

EXAMPLE   I **will** not only **scrub** the floor but also **wax** it.

● EXERCISE 11.   After numbering 1–10, make a list of the compound verbs in these sentences. Be sure to include verb helpers.

1. Stop, look, and whistle.
2. During class Walter stretched, yawned, and sighed.
3. At the rodeo Vaughan leaped upon the wild steer and stayed on him for four full minutes.
4. Must you always worry or complain?
5. My hound can bark, sit up, or lie down.
6. Pauline can neither sing nor dance.
7. Between two and three o'clock I will either be studying in Room 17 or be reading in the library.
8. Can you type a letter or take shorthand?
9. Many men from Tennessee fought and died at the Alamo.
10. The ball lingered for a few seconds on the edge of the basket and then dropped through for a score.

Both the subject and the verb may be compound.

EXAMPLES   The **boys** and **girls** | **played** games and **sang** songs.
Either **Howard** or **Francis** | **will rent** the tape re-
corder and **reserve** the auditorium. [Notice that with
the second verb, *reserve*, the helper *will* is understood.]

● REVIEW EXERCISE A.   Try to make a perfect score on
this exercise, which is a mastery test on subjects and verbs.
After you have copied the sentences below, your job is
this:

1. Cross out all prepositional phrases so that you can
   isolate the verb and the subject.
2. Cross out a *here* or *there* at the beginning of a sentence,
   thus eliminating these words as possible subjects.
3. Underscore all verbs twice; be sure to include all helpers
   and all parts of a compound verb.
4. Underscore all subjects once; be sure to underscore all
   parts of a compound subject.

EXAMPLES   1. ~~During the last ten years,~~ *ballads* *have become* very
   popular.
   2. ~~There~~ are individual *singers* and group *singers* ~~on~~
   ~~folk music programs.~~

1. There are many reasons for the popularity of ballads.
2. Ballads tell simple stories and create strong moods.
3. In ballads people live, work, love, and die.
4. The words of ballads were written by common people and
   therefore relate the concerns of common people.
5. In one ballad can be heard a jilted lover's complaints.
6. In another is found the lament of a mother for her dead son.
7. The death of a dog and the heroism of a coal miner are
   related in still other ballads.
8. How can anyone resist the appeal of such simple tales?
9. Everyone at some time or other has felt the emotions of the
   characters in ballads.
10. Here, then, are some of the reasons for the phenomenal
    success of ballads during the last few years.

2g

DIAGRAMING SENTENCES

In order to write good sentences, you should have in your mind a clear picture of the ways in which sentences are built. Many students find that they can understand a sentence better when they use a diagram. The diagram is a quick picture of how the various parts of a sentence fit together and how the words are related.

Diagraming the Subject and the Verb

A diagram begins with a straight horizontal line. This line is for the main parts of the sentence. Crossing it approximately in the center is a short vertical line. This vertical line divides the complete subject from the complete predicate. On the horizontal line the simple subject is placed to the left of the vertical line, the verb to the right of it.

PATTERN

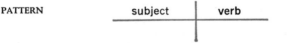

EXAMPLE   Students voted.

If the sentence has an understood subject, place *you* in parentheses on the subject line.

EXAMPLE   Hurry!

Nouns of direct address are placed on a separate horizontal line above the understood subject.

EXAMPLE   Jump, **Rover!**

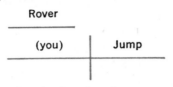

The expletive *there* is also placed on a separate horizontal line. (Modifiers have been omitted from the following diagram.)

EXAMPLE   **There** are three birds in the tree.

When the sentence has a compound subject, diagram it as in the following example. Notice the position of the coordinating conjunction on the dotted line.

EXAMPLE   **Arthur** and **Lewis** are studying.

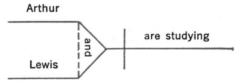

If the verb is compound, it is diagramed in this way:

EXAMPLE   We **live** and **learn.**

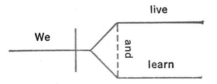

A sentence with both a compound subject and a compound verb is diagramed in this way:

EXAMPLE   **Students** and **teachers shouted** and **waved.**

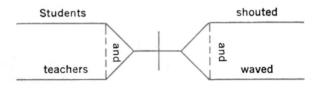

Notice how a compound verb is diagramed when the helping verb is not repeated:

EXAMPLE   They **were screaming** and **crying.**

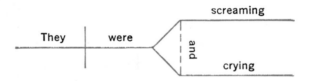

Since *were* is the helper for both *screaming* and *crying*, it is placed on the horizontal line, and the conjunction *and* joins the main verbs *screaming* and *crying*.

Sometimes parts of a compound subject or a compound verb will be joined by correlative conjunctions. Correlatives are diagramed like this:

EXAMPLE   **Both** Miriam **and** Ernest can **not only** sing **but also** dance.

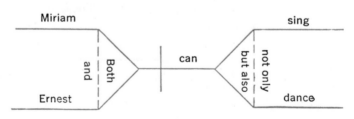

● EXERCISE 12.   Diagram the following sentences.

1. Vesuvius erupted.
2. Look, Roland!
3. James and he are sleeping.
4. Indians fought and died.
5. Both Ellen and Brenda have finished and gone.

Diagraming Adjectives and Adverbs

Adjectives modify nouns or pronouns, and adverbs modify verbs, adjectives, or other adverbs. Both adjectives and adverbs are written on slanted lines connected to the words they modify.

PATTERN

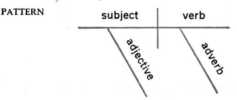

EXAMPLE   **Our new** sofa has **not** arrived.

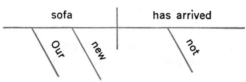

An adverb that modifies an adjective or an adverb is placed on a line connected to the adjective or adverb modified, as follows:

EXAMPLE   That **extremely** lazy dog **almost** never barks.

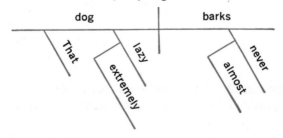

Notice the position of the modifiers in the following example:

EXAMPLE   **Tomorrow** Charlotte and **her** mother will write or will telephone.

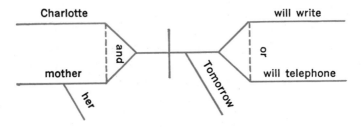

Her modifies only one part of the compound subject: *mother*. *Tomorrow* modifies both parts of the compound verb: *will write* and *will telephone*. Where would *will* have been placed in the diagram if it had not been repeated before *telephone*?

When a conjunction joins two modifiers, it is diagramed as in this example:

EXAMPLE   The French **and** German dancers twirled rapidly **and** extremely gracefully.

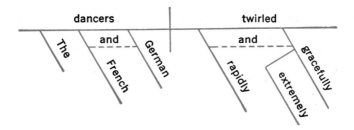

● EXERCISE 13.   Diagrams for the following sentences have been provided for you. Copy them on your paper, and fill them in correctly.

1. Each boy listened attentively.

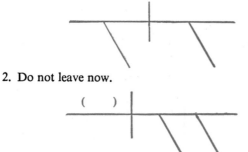

2. Do not leave now.

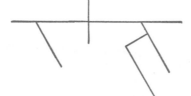

3. The scouts arose very early.

4. An extremely interesting book nearly always sells.

5. The big airliner landed safely and quite smoothly.

● REVIEW EXERCISE B.   Diagram each of the following sentences.

1. Lowell and Tom win occasionally.
2. There were many unpopular and seemingly senseless regulations.
3. Rosalie graciously smiled and bowed.
4. There was much hubbub.
5. The fire flickered weakly and then died.
6. Father and Uncle Edmund are hammering and sawing enthusiastically.
7. Menacingly the white and red horse snorted and stamped.
8. Here come Dr. Bradford and his somewhat chubby wife.
9. Sit quietly and concentrate hard.
10. Both Elise and her brother can read and write rather well.

● REVIEW EXERCISE C.   Write five separate sentences, using an example of each of the following; underline what is asked for.

EXAMPLE   1. a prepositional phrase
                1. *We ate at the drugstore.*

1. a verb phrase
2. a compound verb
3. a compound subject
4. an understood subject
5. an adverb modifying an adjective

COMPLEMENTS

Every sentence has a *base*. This base may be compared to the backbone of an animal or to the main framework of a building. It is that part of the sentence on which are suspended all other parts. A sentence base may consist of only the subject and the verb; for many sentences nothing else is needed.

EXAMPLES   Flowers died.

                One boy from Oklahoma was yodeling.

Frequently the sentence base will have not only a subject and a verb but also a completer, or *complement*.

2h. A *complement* completes the meaning begun by the subject and the verb.

It is possible for a group of words to have a subject and a verb and not express a complete thought. Notice how the following word groups need other words to complete their meaning.

EXAMPLES   Those clothes look
                    He may become
                    I said

If you add words to complete the meaning, the sentences will make sense.

EXAMPLES   Those clothes look **clean.**
                    He may become **an engineer.**
                    I said **that.**

The words *clean*, *engineer*, and *that* are complements; they complete the thought of the sentence. The complement may be a noun, a pronoun, or an adjective.

Study the structure of these sentences. The base of each sentence—subject, verb, complement—is labeled.

EXAMPLES
$$\overset{s}{\text{A stranger}} \overset{v}{\text{approached}} \overset{c}{\text{me.}}$$

$$\overset{s}{\text{The man}} \text{ in the moon } \overset{v}{\text{looks}} \overset{c}{\text{friendly.}}$$

$$\text{At that time } \overset{s}{\text{labor}} \overset{v}{\text{was}} \text{ very } \overset{c}{\text{cheap.}}$$

$$\overset{s}{\text{Tony}} \overset{v}{\text{will be}} \text{ a } \overset{c}{\text{doctor.}}$$

$$\overset{s}{\text{A recording}} \overset{v}{\text{provided}} \text{ background } \overset{c}{\text{music.}}$$

The complement is never in a prepositional phrase. Look at these sentences:

EXAMPLES   Later he consulted the other students.
                    Later he consulted with the other students.

2h

In the first sentence, *students* is the complement. In the second sentence, *students* is the object of the preposition *with;* the prepositional phrase *with the other students* modifies the verb *consulted.*

● EXERCISE 14.   Complete the meaning of the following sentences by adding a complement to each.

1. Sheila unraveled
2. I usually look
3. Tomorrow we will see
4. Your father seems
5. A girl in the back row raised
6. Yesterday in history class I answered
7. Shall we punish
8. A stitch in time saves
9. At the end of the act, Kenneth lowered
10. The word *integrity* means

● EXERCISE 15.   Write five sentences using the following sentence bases. Do not be satisfied with adding only one or two words. Make *interesting* sentences.

Subject	*Verb*	*Complement*
1. underdogs	upset	champions
2. impact	shattered	glass
3. girls	feel	responsible
4. men	desire	peace
5. recreation	can become	work

● EXERCISE 16.   Make three columns on your paper. Label the first *subject*, the second *verb*, and the third *complement*. Find the base of each sentence and enter the parts in the appropriate column.

1. The history of the English stage is very interesting.
2. In the beginning the Church gave plays for instruction.
3. The stories of early English drama were usually biblical ones.
4. Frolicsome actors, however, eventually became too irreverent for religious purposes.

5. Clergymen then recommended the abolition of acting within the Church.

6. At the same time, they encouraged the development of moral themes in drama outside the Church.

7. The actors presented their plays on wagons in the open air.

8. The top of the wagon soon became a convenient place for "heaven."

9. There the "angels" in the play could address the "sinners" on earth below.

10. In Shakespeare's time, the upper stage was an important part of the theater.

11. It was especially useful for eavesdroppers.

12. Shakespeare used the upper stage for the famous balcony scene in *Romeo and Juliet.*

● EXERCISE 17. Using each word in the list below as a complement, write ten sentences. Underscore the subject once, the verb twice, and the complement three times.

EXAMPLE 1. glint
     1. *Thomas then noticed the glint in Susan's eye.*

1. gun
2. bellboy
3. groceries
4. pilot
5. shrewd

6. sluggish
7. fable
8. clown
9. skeleton
10. inevitable

The Subject Complement

2i. A *subject complement* is a noun, pronoun, or adjective that follows a linking verb.[1] It describes or explains the simple subject.

EXAMPLES   Mark Twain's real name was **Clemens.**
            I remained **silent.**

In the first sentence, the complement *Clemens* explains the subject *name.* In the second, the complement *silent* describes the subject *I.*

[1] Linking verbs are discussed on page 15.

2i

(1) A *predicate nominative* is one kind of subject complement. It is a noun or pronoun that explains or identifies the subject of the sentence.

EXAMPLES Kevin will be my **partner.**
The heroine is **she.**
That building is a **school.**

(2) A *predicate adjective* is another kind of subject complement. It is an adjective that modifies the subject of the sentence.

EXAMPLES That dog looks **sick.** [sick dog]
The candy is too **sweet.** [sweet candy]
She seemed **content.** [content she]

Subject complements may be compound.

EXAMPLES The class officers are **Lynn** and **Charles.** [compound predicate nominatives]
The puppies are **healthy** and **happy.** [compound predicate adjectives]

● EXERCISE 18.   In the sentences of Exercise 16 (p. 56) there are six subject complements. List them on your paper. After each noun or pronoun, write *predicate nominative;* after each adjective, *predicate adjective.*

● EXERCISE 19.   Read the following groups of words aloud, making sentences by using nouns, pronouns, or adjectives as subject complements. Use five compound complements. Tell whether each complement is a predicate nominative or a predicate adjective.

1. Detours are often
2. This is
3. Mr. White seemed
4. They may be
5. The berries taste
6. Were they
7. The shark appears
8. The river looks
9. Cecil had been
10. Does he feel

Objects

Objects are complements that do not refer to the subject.

EXAMPLE   Alan swallowed a watermelon seed.

In this sentence, the object *seed* does not explain or describe the subject *Alan*, and *swallowed* is an action verb rather than a linking verb.

There are two kinds of objects: the *direct object* and the *indirect object*. Neither is ever in a prepositional phrase.

2j. The *direct object* of the verb is a noun or pronoun that receives the action of the verb or shows the result of the action. It answers the question "What?" or "Whom?" after an action verb.

EXAMPLES   Herbert hit **Mortimer** on the jaw.
            Her essay won a **prize**.

In the first sentence, *Mortimer* receives the action expressed by the verb *hit* and tells *whom* Herbert hit; therefore, *Mortimer* is the direct object. In the second sentence, *prize* names the result of the action expressed by the verb *won* and tells *what* her essay won; *prize* is the direct object.

As you study the following sentences, observe that each object answers the question "Whom?" or "What?" after an action verb.

   S   V   O
Vivian moved furniture.

    S   V   O
Sarcasm annoys me.

 S   V   O
We were singing songs.

     S   V   O
The police were expecting trouble.

2j

60 *The Parts of a Sentence*

● EXERCISE 20. Number your paper 1–10 and write after the appropriate number the direct object for each sentence.

1. This article gives many interesting facts about libraries.
2. Alexandria, in Egypt, had the most famous library of ancient times.
3. This library contained a large collection of ancient plays and works of philosophy.
4. The Roman emperor Augustus founded two public libraries.
5. Fire later destroyed these buildings.
6. Readers could not take books from either the Roman libraries or the library in Alexandria.
7. The monastery library of the Middle Ages first introduced the idea of a circulating library.
8. In the sixth century, everyone in the Benedictine monasteries borrowed a book for daily reading.
9. Today, the United States has over six thousand circulating libraries.
10. Readers borrow millions of books from them every year.

● EXERCISE 21. There are twenty direct objects in the following quotations. Number your paper 1–14 and write the direct objects after the appropriate numbers. Naturally, some sentences contain two direct objects.

1. Mind moves matter.—VERGIL
2. God helps them that help themselves.—BENJAMIN FRANKLIN
3. Study the past, if you would divine the future.—CONFUCIUS
4. You can never plan the future by the past.—EDMUND BURKE
5. A merry heart maketh a cheerful countenance.—PROVERBS XV, 13
6. Answer a fool according to his folly.—PROVERBS XXVI, 5
7. The man who makes no mistakes does not usually make anything.—BISHOP W. C. MAGEE
8. Love rules his kingdom without a sword.—ITALIAN PROVERB
9. A generous heart repairs a slanderous tongue.—HOMER
10. He that will not command his thoughts . . . will soon lose the command of his actions.—THOMAS WILSON
11. Time sees and hears all and will all reveal.—SOPHOCLES

12. The happiest person is the person who thinks the most interesting thoughts.—TIMOTHY DWIGHT
13. Patch grief with proverbs.—WILLIAM SHAKESPEARE
14. The wise make proverbs and fools repeat them.

—ISAAC DISRAELI

2k. The *indirect object* of the verb is a noun or pronoun that precedes the direct object and usually tells "to whom" or "for whom" (or "to what" or "for what") the action of the verb is done.

DIRECT OBJECTS	Ted mailed several **postcards.**
	Mother may broil a **steak.**
INDIRECT OBJECTS	Ted mailed **Marjorie** several postcards.
	Mother may broil **me** a steak.

In the sentences above, *postcards* and *steak* are direct objects answering the question "What?" after action verbs. Ted mailed postcards *to whom? Marjorie*, the answer, is an indirect object. Mother may broil a steak *for whom? Me* is the indirect object.

The indirect objects in the sentences below are bold-faced. Each tells *to whom* or *for whom* something is done.

EXAMPLES	He showed **her** the lantern.
	The doctor gave **Mother** good advice.
	I bought **him** a new baseball.
	My cousin left **Dennis** a message.

If the word *to* or *for* is used, the word following it is part of a prepositional phrase, not an indirect object.

PREPOSITIONAL PHRASES	I sold tickets **to the girls.**
	Kathy saved some cake **for me.**
INDIRECT OBJECTS	I sold the **girls** tickets.
	Kathy saved **me** some cake.

2k

Both direct and indirect objects may be compound.

EXAMPLES   Donna showed **snapshots** and **slides.** [compound direct object]

Donna showed **Dorothy** and **me** some pictures. [compound indirect object]

● EXERCISE 22.   Number your paper 1–10, and list the indirect and direct objects in the following sentences. After each, write in parentheses *i.o.* (for indirect object) or *d.o.* (for direct object). You will not find an indirect object in every sentence.

1. According to Greek mythology, Daedalus, a famous artist and inventor, built the King of Crete a mysterious building known as the labyrinth.
2. The complicated passageways of this building give us our word for "a confusing maze of possibilities."
3. After the completion of the labyrinth, the King imprisoned Daedalus and his son, whose name was Icarus.
4. In order to escape, Daedalus made Icarus and himself wings out of feathers and beeswax.
5. He gave Icarus careful instructions not to fly too near the sun.
6. But Icarus soon forgot his father's advice.
7. He flew too high, and the hot sun melted the wax in the wings.
8. Daedalus used his wings wisely and reached Sicily in safety.
9. Mythology tells us many other stories of Daedalus' fabulous inventions.
10. Even today, the name Daedalus suggests almost superhuman ingenuity.

Diagraming Complements

As a part of the sentence base, the subject complement is placed on the horizontal line with the subject and verb. It comes after the verb. A line *slanting toward the subject*, drawn upward from the horizontal line, separates the subject complement from the verb.

PATTERN

| subject | verb | subject complement |

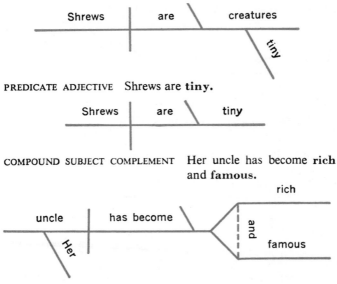

PREDICATE NOMINATIVE   Shrews are tiny **creatures.**

PREDICATE ADJECTIVE   Shrews are **tiny.**

COMPOUND SUBJECT COMPLEMENT   Her uncle has become **rich** and **famous.**

● EXERCISE 23.   Diagram the following sentences.

1. Superstitions are illogical beliefs.
2. A black cat is a bad sign.
3. A broken mirror remains an unlucky omen.
4. Such notions seem both childish and foolish.
5. Superstitious beliefs are still common.

The *direct object* is diagramed in much the same manner as the predicate nominative. The only difference is that the line separating the direct object from the verb is vertical, not slanting.

PATTERN

subject	verb	direct object

EXAMPLE   Everyone played **games.**

Everyone	played	games

The compound direct object is diagramed in this way:

EXAMPLE   They sell **bicycles** and **sleds.**

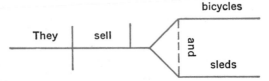

The *indirect object* is diagramed on a horizontal line beneath the verb.

EXAMPLE   Randy tossed **Elmer** an apple.

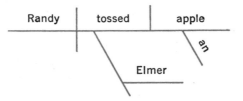

Note that the slanting line from the verb extends slightly below the horizontal line for the indirect object.

The compound indirect object is diagramed in this way:

EXAMPLE   Ray gave the **dogs** and **cats** some hamburger.

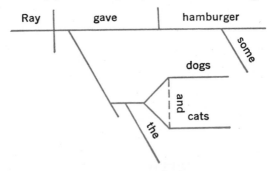

● EXERCISE 24.   Diagram the following sentences.

1. The traitor sold the enemy important secrets.
2. Mr. Sievers gave the team and the fans a memorable lesson.

3. Who will lend us a tent and a canoe?
4. Charles gave us a confident wave.
5. The storekeeper paid the other employees and me our wages and a bonus.

● REVIEW EXERCISE D. Number your paper 1–50, and list the italicized words in the passage below. Identify each word, using one of the following abbreviations:

s.	subject	*p.a.*	predicate adjective
v.	verb	*d.o.*	direct object
p.n.	predicate nominative	*i.o.*	indirect object

(1) *Many* of Edgar Allan Poe's stories do not deal with horror or terror. Not (2) *all* of his main characters are ghosts or (3) *devils.* Poe has written many comic (4) *tales.* For instance, "The Business Man" or "Loss of Breath" (5) *gives* the (6) *reader* a (7) *chance* for hearty laughter.

In "The Business Man" is a particularly funny (8) *character.* He (9) *is* extremely (10) *shrewd* and makes money by outwitting the other fellow. This "Peter Profit" (11) *entered* the "organ-grinding" business. First, however, he opened his organ and (12) *gave* (13) *it* several hard (14) *licks* with a hammer. Then the (15) *noise* of the organ (16) *sounded* (17) *terrible.* Under the windows of his victims, the little (18) *man* with an eye for business played his (19) *organ* until the annoyed listeners paid him to hush. This (20) *business*, however, gave the hero a (21) *headache.* He (22) *changed* (23) *jobs.* He (24) *became* more (25) *ambitious.* His next venture (26) *was* cat growing. Soon (27) *cats* of all kinds (28) *were running* all over the neighborhood. Finally, the (29) *citizens* in the community (30) *made* an (31) *agreement.* They (32) *would give* the (33) *owner* of the cats money so that he would shut down his business. (34) *This*, of course, (35) *was* exactly the (36) *idea!* The (37) *hero* of this tale (38) *considers* many other schemes for getting rich in a hurry.

In "Loss of Breath" is another amusing (39) *character.* The (40) *author* saw the (41) *humor* of the expression, "I've lost my breath." He (42) *based* a (43) *story* on it. The main (44) *character* in "Loss of Breath" (45) *is* (46) *Mr. Lackobreath.* Angry with his wife, he (47) *argues* furiously and loses his breath. Then the unhappy husband begins a long (48) *search* for his lost breath. Finally he finds it. On the very day of the argument, a (49) *man* by the name of Mr. Windenough had "caught his breath." The end of the story is a happy (50) *one.*

CLASSIFYING SENTENCES BY PURPOSE

Sentences may be classified according to the kinds of messages they express. This method of classifying, which distinguishes between questions, statements, commands or requests, and exclamations, reflects the purpose of the speaker or writer.

21. Sentences may be classified as *declarative, imperative, interrogative,* or *exclamatory.*

(1) A *declarative* sentence makes a statement.

Declarative sentences make assertions or state ideas without expecting a reply. Most sentences are declarative. All declarative sentences are followed by periods.

EXAMPLES   George Eliot's real name was Mary Ann Evans.
Bubble gum can contain insoluble plastics.

(2) An *imperative* sentence gives a command or makes a request.

A command or a request has the understood subject *you.* Like the declarative sentence, the imperative sentence is usually followed by a period. Very strong commands, however, may take an exclamation point.

EXAMPLES   Go to the storm cellar now.
Be courteous to other drivers.
Run!

(3) An *interrogative* sentence asks a question.

To *interrogate* means to "ask." An interrogative sentence is followed by a question mark.

EXAMPLES   Wasn't the joke funny?
Why didn't the pony express riders carry guns?

(4) An *exclamatory* sentence expresses strong feeling. It exclaims.

An exclamatory sentence is always followed by an exclamation point.

EXAMPLES   Oh, my! How time flies!
What hope a rainbow brings after a storm!

● EXERCISE 25.   Classify each of the following sentences according to its purpose. After numbering 1–10, write *declarative*, *imperative*, *interrogative*, or *exclamatory* after the corresponding number on your paper.

1. Wasn't that an exciting ending to our ball game?
2. The bases were loaded, and Raymond was next at bat.
3. What a tense moment!
4. Would he strike out as usual, or would he make a miraculous hit?
5. After rubbing his hands in the sand, Raymond took a firm grip on the bat.
6. I'll knock this one to the west side of Kalamazoo!
7. Stand back out of my way.
8. The ball was low, fast, tricky.
9. Crack! The ball whizzed past the fielders and then crashed into a window a half block away!
10. When an angry face appeared at the broken window, all the players quickly scampered out of sight—except Raymond, who took plenty of time to enjoy his walk to home plate before going over to make friends with the window's owner.

● EXERCISE 26.   Copy the last word of each of the following sentences, and then give the correct mark of punctuation. Classify each sentence as imperative, declarative, interrogative, or exclamatory.

EXAMPLE   1. Pilot fish live in warm waters
           1. *waters. declarative*

1. Have you ever seen a pilot fish
2. What an odd answer that is
3. Stop your chatter about a horsefly and a catfish

2 1

4. Where are pilot fish found
5. You can seldom find them at a market
6. A pilot fish is one of the most interesting fish in the sea
7. Name a few facts, and tell a few legends about this fish
8. To ancient tribes, the pilot fish was a sacred animal
9. What curious companions pilot fish and sharks are
10. How did the pilot fish get its name

The Phrase

Prepositional and Verbal Phrases, Appositive Phrases

In Chapter 1 you learned that two or more words (for example, *will be playing*, *were laughing*, *has done*) may be used as a verb, a single part of speech. Such a word group is called a *verb phrase*.

A word group may also be used as an adjective, an adverb, or a noun. You have already learned something about *prepositional phrases*. In this chapter, you will study prepositional phrases in greater detail, and you will learn about other kinds of phrases.

3a. A *phrase* is a group of related words that is used as a single part of speech and does not contain a verb and its subject.

EXAMPLES   **will be trying** [verb phrase; no subject]

between you and me [prepositional phrase; no subject or verb]

If a group of words has a subject *and* a verb, then the group of words is not a phrase.

EXAMPLES   **We bought** a new car. [a subject and a verb; *we* is the subject of *bought*]

after **he had left** [a subject and a verb; *he* is the subject of *had left*]

69

● EXERCISE 1.   Study the following groups of words and decide whether or not each group is a phrase. After numbering from 1–10, write *p.* for *phrase* or *n.p.* for *not a phrase* after the appropriate number.

1. was running
2. when she finally arrived
3. for Andrew and Tim
4. will be completing
5. of the story

6. because Joyce won
7. after you go
8. has been ironed
9. in the deep water
10. if the bell rings

PREPOSITIONAL PHRASES

3b. A *prepositional phrase* is a group of words beginning with a preposition and ending with a noun or pronoun.

In the following examples of prepositional phrases, the prepositions are bold-faced.

in front of our house
like them
during the night

Some prepositions are made up of more than one word, like *in front of* in the first example. Notice that an article or other modifier often appears in the prepositional phrase: the first example contains *our;* the third, *the.*

3c. The noun or pronoun that ends the prepositional phrase is the *object* of the preposition that begins the phrase.

The prepositional phrases in the following sentence are in bold-faced type.

Of the stars near the earth, Sirius is the brightest.

Here *stars* is the object of the preposition *of.* How is *earth* used? What preposition does it follow?

Like other sentence parts, objects of prepositions may be compound.

EXAMPLES   Michael sat **between Elaine and me.** [Both *Elaine* and *me* are objects of the preposition *between.*]

We drove **to Sterling Park and North Star Lake.** [Both *Sterling Park* and *North Star Lake* are objects of the preposition *to.*]

Main Street runs **in front of the school and the church.** [The preposition *in front of* has a compound object, *school* and *church.*]

Do not be misled by a modifier coming after the noun or pronoun in a prepositional phrase; the noun or pronoun is still the object.

EXAMPLE   Mother and Dad strolled **through the park** yesterday. [The object of the preposition *through* is *park; yesterday* is an adverb telling *when* and modifying the verb *strolled.*]

● EXERCISE 2.   List in order the twenty prepositions in these sentences. After each preposition, write its object. Indicate the number of the sentence from which each preposition and its object are taken. You may wish to refer to the list of prepositions on page 25.

EXAMPLE   1. The oracles played an important role in the history of ancient Greece.

1. *in—history*
   of—Greece

1. One of the most famous oracles in Greece was the Delphic oracle.
2. It was located in Apollo's temple at Delphi.
3. The temple, supposedly the center of the earth, was a religious shrine for all Greece.
4. The temple's priestess inhaled vapors which rose from a chasm, and then she went into a trance.
5. During the trance she delivered messages from Apollo.
6. Often the pronouncements by the oracle were misleading and caused much misfortune.

3
b-c

7. Croesus undertook an expedition against the Persians on the strength of the oracle's prediction.
8. The oracle foretold that he would destroy a great empire through such an expedition.
9. After the encounter with the Persians, he realized that the oracle meant *his* kingdom, not the Persians'.
10. Because of predictions like this one, the term *Delphian* is sometimes applied to an ambiguous statement.

The Adjective Phrase

Prepositional phrases are used in sentences mainly as adjectives and adverbs. Prepositional phrases used as adjectives are called *adjective phrases*.

EXAMPLE   We **of the freshman class** are planning a television program **about our city government.**

The prepositional phrase *of the freshman class* is used as an adjective modifying the pronoun *we. About our city government* is also used as an adjective because it modifies the noun *program.*

Study the following pairs of sentences. Notice that the nouns used as adjectives may easily be converted to objects of prepositions in adjective phrases.

NOUNS USED AS ADJECTIVES	ADJECTIVE PHRASES
The **car** key is lost.	The key **to the car** is lost.
The **Miami** and **Houston** teams won.	The teams **from Miami and Houston** won.
Those are **cowboy** boots.	Those are boots **for cowboys.**

Unlike a one-word adjective, which usually precedes the word it modifies, an adjective phrase always follows the noun or pronoun it modifies.

More than one prepositional phrase may modify the same word.

EXAMPLE   The picture **of him in the newspaper** was not flattering. [The prepositional phrases *of him* and *in the newspaper* both modify the noun *picture.*]

A prepositional phrase may also modify the object of another prepositional phrase.

EXAMPLE   The books **on the shelf of my closet** were all birth-day gifts. [The phrase *on the shelf* modifies the noun *books. Shelf* is the object of the preposition *on.* The phrase *of my closet* modifies *shelf.*]

● EXERCISE 3.   Revise the following sentences by using adjective phrases in place of the italicized nouns used as adjectives. Be sure you can tell which word each phrase modifies.

1. Amy Patchell has several *opera* tickets.
2. The paper prints *school* news only.
3. I have bought some *cat* food.
4. We admired his *rose* garden.
5. The *hall* lamp is broken.
6. I need a new *typewriter* ribbon.
7. It was a melancholy *November* day.
8. The jeweler showed us a lovely *platinum* and *pearl* necklace. (*one phrase*)
9. The rain helped the *Indiana corn* crop. (*two phrases*)
10. Newcomers need a *Charleston city* map. (*two phrases*)

The Adverb Phrase

When a prepositional phrase is used as an adverb to tell *when, where, how, how much,* or *how far,* it is called an *adverb phrase.*

EXAMPLES   I dived **into the water.** [The adverb phrase *into the water* tells *where* I dived.]

The train arrived **at noon.** [The adverb phrase *at noon* tells *when* the train arrived.]

We accepted the invitation **with pleasure.** [The adverb phrase *with pleasure* tells *how* we accepted the invitation.]

Martin missed the target **by a foot.** [*By a foot* is an adverb phrase telling *how far* Martin missed the target.]

In the previous examples, the adverb phrases all modify verbs. An adverb phrase may also modify an adjective or an adverb.

EXAMPLES   Dad smilingly tells Mother he is unlucky **at cards** but lucky **in love.** [The adverb phrase *at cards* modifies the adjective *unlucky; in love*, another adverb phrase, modifies the adjective *lucky*.]

I will see you later **in the day.** [*In the day* is an adverb phrase modifying the adverb *later*.]

Unlike adjective phrases, which always follow the words they modify, an adverb phrase may appear at various places in a sentence.

Like adjective phrases, more than one adverb phrase may modify the same word.

EXAMPLE   **On Saturday** my father worked **in the garden.** [The adverb phrases *on Saturday* and *in the garden* both modify the verb *worked*. The first phrase tells *when* my father worked; the second phrase tells *where* he worked. Notice that the first phrase precedes the word it modifies; the second phrase follows it.]

● EXERCISE 4. Number 1–10 on your paper. List the prepositional phrases used as adverbs in each sentence. There may be more than one in a sentence. After each adverb phrase, write the word it modifies.

1. Yesterday, many citizens of Chicago suffered from the heat.
2. In the morning, my friends and I drove to Lincoln Park.
3. At noon, we ate our big picnic lunch with gusto.
4. Later in the day, we walked around the park.
5. An unusual monument stands near the picnic grounds.
6. This monument shows humanity as it marches through time.
7. In Rockefeller Center I once saw another artist's concept of time.
8. Three men are painted on the ceiling; they represent Past, Present, and Future.
9. Wherever you stand in the room, Past's eyes are turned away from you; Future's eyes look outward and upward.
10. The eyes of Present, however, look straight at you.

Diagraming Prepositional Phrases

The preposition is placed on a slanting line leading down from the word that the phrase modifies. Its object is placed on a horizontal line connected to the slanting line.

EXAMPLES **By chance,** a peasant uncovered a wall **of ancient Pompeii.** [adverb phrase modifying the verb; adjective phrase modifying the direct object]

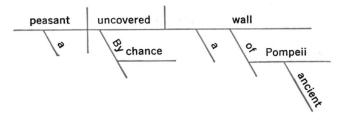

We will leave early **in the morning.** [adverb phrase modifying an adverb]

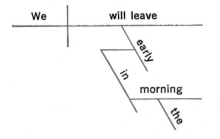

We strolled **down the hill** and **across the bridge.** [two phrases modifying the same word]

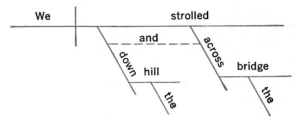

Father bought tickets **for Mother, my brothers, and me.** [compound object of preposition]

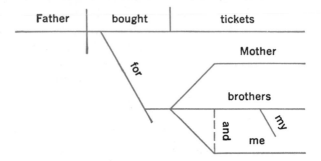

Show your tickets to the guard **at the door.** [phrase modifying the object of another preposition]

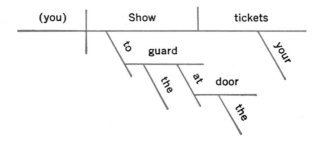

● EXERCISE 5.   Diagram the following sentences.

1. I have read many books by Arthur Conan Doyle about Sherlock Holmes.
2. Dr. Watson is the friend of the famous detective.
3. One story about Holmes and Watson appears in our literature textbook.
4. The story contains many clues to the solution of the mystery.
5. I was delighted with the outcome of the story.
6. Dozens of stories about Holmes are available in the school library.
7. Books of detective stories and other mysteries are on the second shelf.
8. Early in the afternoon, I went to the library.

9. The librarian took from her desk a new edition of one of Doyle's books.
10. She placed it in the display case in front of the window.

● REVIEW EXERCISE A. There are twenty-five prepositional phrases in the following sentences. Number 1–9 on your paper. List the prepositional phrases in each sentence; and after each, write how the phrase is used—as an adjective or an adverb.

EXAMPLE   1. His glass of milk was not filled to the brim.
   1. *of milk—adj.*
      to the brim—adv.

1. During the last week in May, our club will adjourn for the summer.
2. Find at once a better place for those books.
3. In history class, we are studying the causes of the French and Indian War.
4. Johnny crawled from the bush and dashed into the house.
5. Which one of these books contains the rest of the stories by Hawthorne?
6. In June, some of the teachers in our school will attend the meeting in Washington.
7. Two of the plays in the summer series will be presented on Saturday night in the school auditorium.
8. During the summer, will you be in town for the plays?
9. The town of Madison is eager for more schools.

VERBALS AND VERBAL PHRASES

Verbals are forms of verbs that are used as other parts of speech. These words are really two parts of speech in one. Verbals are formed from verbs and function very much like verbs; they may be modified by adverbs and may have complements. They are, however, used as other parts of speech.

There are three kinds of verbals: *participles*, *gerunds*, and *infinitives*.

The Participle

3d. **A** *participle* **is a verb form used as an ad-jective.**

The participle is part verb and part adjective. It might be called a "verbal adjective."

EXAMPLES   **Leaping** the fence, the great cat surprised me.
Defeated teams should congratulate the winners.
Moving quickly, he intercepted the pass.

Leaping is part verb because it carries the action of the verb *leap*. It is also part adjective because it modifies the noun *cat—leaping cat*. *Defeated*, formed from the verb *defeat*, modifies the noun *teams*. *Moving*, formed from the verb *move*, modifies the pronoun *he*. Verb forms used as adjectives, *leaping*, *defeated*, and *moving* are participles.

There are two kinds of participles: *present participles* and *past participles*.

(1) *Present participles* **consist of the plain form of the verb plus** *–ing*.[1]

EXAMPLES   The **crying** baby hid under the table.
Pointing at me, the teacher snapped a question.

In the first example, *crying* (formed by adding *–ing* to the verb *cry*) is a present participle modifying the noun *baby*. In the second, the present participle *pointing* (consisting of the plain form of the verb *point* plus *–ing*) modifies the noun *teacher—pointing teacher*. Verb forms used as adjectives, *crying* and *pointing* are participles.

Although participles are formed from verbs, they are not used to stand alone as verbs. A participle may, however, be used with a helping verb to form a verb phrase:

The baby **was crying.**

The teacher **had been pointing** at me.

When a participle is used in a verb phrase, it is considered as part of the verb, not as an adjective.

[1] The plain form of the verb is the infinitive form. See pages 131–32.

(2) *Past participles* usually consist of the plain form of the verb plus -*d* or -*ed*. Others are irregularly formed.[1]

EXAMPLES   The **frightened** and **embarrassed** actor missed his cue. [The past participles *frightened* and *embarrassed* modify the noun *actor*.]

The survivor, visibly **shaken** by his long ordeal, shuddered at the sight of the huge crowd. [The past participle *shaken* modifies the noun *survivor—shaken survivor*.]

Like a present participle, a past participle can also be part of a verb phrase. Just as in the case of the present participle, a past participle used in a verb phrase is considered as part of the verb, not as an adjective.

EXAMPLES   He **had finished** the assignment by that time.

I **was warned** that the movie was extremely dull.

● EXERCISE 6.   Number 1–10 on your paper. List the participles used as adjectives in the following sentences, and after each participle write the noun or pronoun modified.

1. The prancing horses were loudly applauded by the delighted audience.
2. The colorful flags, waving in the breeze, brightened the gloomy day.
3. Swaggering and boasting, he made us extremely angry.
4. The game scheduled for tonight has been postponed because of rain.
5. Leaving the field, the happy player rushed to his parents sitting in the bleachers.
6. Rain pattering on the roof made an eerie sound.
7. We thought the banging shutter upstairs was someone walking in the attic.
8. Painfully sunburned, I vowed never to be so careless again.
9. Terrified by the big dog, Fluffy yowled and hissed.
10. The platoon of soldiers, marching in step, crossed the field to the stirring music of the military band.

3d

[1] See the discussion of irregular verbs on pages 133–35.

● EXERCISE 7.   Condense each of the following pairs of sentences into one sentence by using a participle. You may use a present or a past participle, as appropriate. Underline the participle in each of your sentences. Punctuate your sentences correctly.

EXAMPLE   1. Leon ate watermelon. We saw him.
          1. *We saw Leon <u>eating</u> watermelon.*
          2. Mildred accepted the Citizenship Award. She was smiling happily.
          2. *<u>Smiling</u> happily, Mildred accepted the Citizenship Award.*
     or *<u>Accepting</u> the Citizenship Award, Mildred was smiling happily.*

1. Rick was pleased by her invitation. He accepted it immediately.
2. The telephone in the next apartment was ringing insistently. It annoyed me.
3. I was startled by the sudden noise. I leaped out of bed.
4. The escaped convict hid in the bushes. The policeman arrested him.
5. We were challenged by Mr. Cole's remarks. We resolved not to fail again.
6. I heard the news on the radio this morning. It is depressing.
7. The long pass was caught by Gordon. It meant victory for our team.
8. The enemy troops were defeated in the battle. They retreated across the bridge.
9. I scorched my best dress with a hot iron. I had to throw it away.
10. The car sped down the narrow road. It barely missed a pedestrian.

The Participial Phrase

A participle may be modified by an adverb or by a prepositional phrase, and it may have a complement. These related words combine with the participle in a *participial phrase*.

3e. A *participial phrase* consists of a participle and its related words, such as modifiers and complements, all of which act together as an adjective.

The participial phrase in each of the following sentences is in bold-faced type. An arrow points to the noun or pronoun that the phrase modifies.

EXAMPLES **Outwitting the hounds,** the raccoon easily escaped. [participle with object *hounds*]

I saw him fishing contentedly. [participle with adverb modifier *contentedly*]

Tackled on the one-foot line, he fumbled the ball. [participle with prepositional phrase modifier *on the one-foot line*]

Wildly cheering for the team, we celebrated the victory. [Notice that *wildly*, which precedes the participle and modifies it, is included in the phrase.]

A participial phrase should be placed very close to the word it modifies. Otherwise the phrase may appear to modify another word, and the sentence may not make sense.[1]

POOR The clerk handed the gift box to the customer tied with red ribbon. [The placement of the modifier calls up a silly picture. The gift box, not the customer, is tied with ribbon.]

IMPROVED The clerk handed the customer the gift box tied with red ribbon.

● EXERCISE 8. Use the following participial phrases in sentences of your own. Be sure to place each phrase very close to the noun or pronoun it modifies, and to punctuate the phrases correctly.

[1] The punctuation of participial phrases is discussed on pages 504–06 and 509. The participle as a dangling modifier is discussed on pages 180–82.

3 e

EXAMPLE   1. balancing a book on his head
            1. *Balancing a book on his head, Larry walked the*
               tightrope.

1. expressing his approval
2. blaming me for the accident
3. buried on the bank of the river
4. pointing to the referee
5. acting like a bashful chipmunk
6. left alone in the dark
7. swallowing the sandwich in large bites
8. puzzled by his sarcastic remarks
9. trained to respect authority
10. holding medicine in one hand and the kitten in the other

The Gerund

3f. **A** *gerund* **is a verb form used as a noun.**

A participle is part verb and part adjective. A *gerund* is part verb and part noun. It is formed by adding *–ing* to the plain form of the verb. Like nouns, gerunds are used as subjects, predicate nominatives, direct objects, or objects of prepositions.

EXAMPLES   **Walking** is good exercise. [subject]
            My hobby is **sewing.** [predicate nominative]
            Gardner enjoys **reading.** [direct object]
            That is used for **drilling.** [object of preposition]

Like nouns, gerunds may be modified by adjectives and adjective phrases.

EXAMPLES   We listened to the **beautiful** singing **of the glee**
            club. [The adjective *beautiful* and the adjective
            phrase *of the glee club* modify the gerund *singing.*
            Singing is used as the object of the preposition *to.*]

            The **gentle** ringing **of the church bells** wakes me
            every morning. [Both the adjective *gentle* and the
            adjective phrase *of the church bells* modify the gerund
            ringing, which is the subject of the sentence.]

Like verbs, gerunds may also be modified by adverbs and adverb phrases.

EXAMPLES Basking **quietly in the sun** is my favorite summer pastime. [The gerund *basking*, used as the subject of the sentence, is modified by the adverb *quietly* and also by the adverb phrase *in the sun*, which tells *where*.]

Brandywine enjoys galloping **briskly on a cold morning**. [The gerund *galloping*, which is the direct object of the sentence, is modified by the adverb *briskly* and also by the adverb phrase *on a cold morning*, which tells *when*.]

Gerunds, like present participles, end in *–ing*. To be a gerund, a verbal must be used as a noun In the following sentence, there are three words ending in *–ing*, but only one of them is a gerund.

EXAMPLE **Ignoring** the ranger's advice, Clem was **planning** to go on with his **hunting**.

Ignoring is a present participle modifying *Clem*, and *planning* is part of the verb phrase *was planning*. Only *hunting*, used as object of the preposition *with*, is a gerund.

● EXERCISE 9. After you have listed each gerund in the sentences below, write how each is used: subject, predicate nominative, direct object, or object of preposition.

1. His whistling attracted my attention.
2. By studying, you can raise your grades.
3. One requirement is thinking.
4. The booing violates basic rules of courtesy.
5. Frowning, Dad discouraged our quarreling.
6. Abner's favorite sport is fishing.
7. Before eating, we sat on the lawn and watched the frolicking puppies.
8. Yesterday, Mr. Paulson was discussing flying.
9. One of Steve's bad habits is boasting.
10. Without knocking, the hurrying boy opened the door.

3f

The Gerund Phrase

3g. A *gerund phrase* consists of a gerund together with its complements and modifiers, all of which act together as a noun.

EXAMPLES **The loud knocking by the courier** awakened the porter. [The gerund phrase is used as the subject of the sentence. The gerund *knocking* is modified by the article *the*, the adjective *loud*, and the prepositional phrase *by the courier*. Notice that modifiers preceding the gerund are included in the gerund phrase.]

I dislike **talking loudly in the corridor.** [The gerund phrase is used as the object of the verb *dislike*. The gerund *talking* is modified by the adverb *loudly* and by the prepositional phrase *in the corridor*.]

His favorite pastime is **telling us his troubles.** [The gerund phrase is used as predicate nominative. The gerund *telling* has a direct object, *troubles*, and an indirect object, *us*.]

We were disturbed by **her constant chattering.** [The gerund phrase is used as the object of the preposition. The two modifiers preceding the gerund *chattering* are included in the gerund phrase.]

◆ NOTE   In the last example above, the gerund is preceded by the possessive pronoun *her*. Whenever a noun or pronoun comes before a gerund, the possessive form should be used.

EXAMPLES   We were disturbed by **Joan's** constant chattering.
I dislike **your** teasing the little boy.

● EXERCISE 10.   Write five sentences, following the directions given. Underline the gerund phrase in each of your sentences.

EXAMPLE   1. Use *writing* as the subject of the sentence. Include an adjective modifying the gerund.
    1. *Effective writing is a major part of our English course.*

1. Use *shouting* as the subject. Include an adjective phrase modifying the gerund.
2. Use *playing* as the direct object of the sentence. Include a direct object of the gerund.
3. Use *telling* as the object of a preposition. Include in the gerund phrase a direct object and an indirect object of *telling*.
4. Use *arguing* as the predicate nominative. Include an adverb and an adverb phrase modifying the gerund.
5. Use *speaking* as a gerund in any way you choose. Include in the gerund phrase a possessive pronoun and a participle.

The Infinitive

3h. An *infinitive* is a verb form, usually preceded by *to*, that is used as a *noun, adjective,* or *adverb*.

An infinitive consists of the plain form of the verb, usually preceded by *to*. It can be used as a noun, an adjective, or an adverb. Carefully study the following examples.

Infinitives used as nouns: **To forget** is **to forgive.** [*To forget* is the subject of the sentence; *to forgive* is the predicate nominative.]

Libby offered **to help** in any way except **to wash** dishes. [*To help* is the object of the verb *offered; to wash* is the object of the preposition *except*.]

Infinitives used as adjectives: The man **to watch** is the quarterback. [*To watch* modifies *man*.]

That was a day **to remember.** [*To remember* modifies *day*.]

Infinitives used as adverbs: The senator rose **to speak.** [*To speak* modifies the verb *rose*.]

Eager **to please,** my dog obeyed my command. [*To please* modifies the adjective *eager*.]

◆ NOTE   *To* plus a noun or pronoun (*to town, to him, to the store*) is a prepositional phrase, not an infinitive. An infinitive is always the first principal part of the verb.

3
g-h

The Infinitive Phrase

3i. An *infinitive phrase* consists of an infinitive together with its complements and modifiers.[1]

Infinitive phrases, like infinitives alone, can be used as adjectives, adverbs, or nouns.

EXAMPLES   **To interrupt a speaker abruptly** is impolite. [The infinitive phrase is used as a noun, as the subject of the sentence. The infinitive has an object, *speaker*, and is modified by the adverb *abruptly*.]

We had hoped **to leave at noon.** [The infinitive phrase is used as a noun—the object of *had hoped*. The infinitive is modified by the phrase *at noon*.]

He is the person **to see about the job.** [The infinitive phrase is used as an adjective modifying the predicate nominative *person*. The infinitive is modified by the adverbial prepositional phrase *about the job*.]

They were glad **to hear an answer.** [The infinitive phrase is used as an adverb modifying the predicate adjective *glad*. The infinitive has a direct object, *answer*.]

The Infinitive with "to" Omitted

Sometimes the *to* of the infinitive will be omitted in a sentence. This frequently occurs after such verbs as *see*, *hear*, *feel*, *watch*, *help*, *know*, *dare*, *need*, *make*, *let*, and *please*.

EXAMPLES   Did you see the team **play** yesterday?
Cathy did not dare **tell** us the bad news.
We have done everything except **wash** the dishes.

[1] Unlike the other verbals, an infinitive may have a subject: I wanted him to help me with my algebra. [*Him* is the subject of the infinitive *to help*. The infinitive, together with its subject, complements, and modifiers, is sometimes called an *infinitive clause*.]

● EXERCISE 11. Make a list of the infinitives or infinitive phrases in the following sentences. After each one, give its use: *noun*, *adjective*, or *adverb*.

1. To give advice is easy.
2. We had hoped to solve the problem.
3. Nelson plans to go.
4. I went to the gymnasium to find him.
5. One way to keep a secret is to forget it.
6. They dared discuss his brother's nomination.
7. We hope to be leaving immediately after school.
8. The best way to have a friend is to be one.
9. Phil and Claude helped move the couch.
10. The door is not easy to open.

● EXERCISE 12. Write five sentences, following the directions given below. Underline each infinitive phrase.

1. Use *to play* as a direct object.
2. Use *to ask* as an adjective, with a phrase modifier.
3. Use *to show* as an adverb modifying an adjective.
4. Use *to write* as the subject of a sentence. Include a direct object of the infinitive.
5. Use *to think* in any way you choose. Then write how you used it: *noun—direct object, adverb modifying the verb*, etc.

Diagraming Verbals and Verbal Phrases

Participial phrases are diagramed as follows:

EXAMPLE **Carrying a large package,** the messenger stumbled through the door.

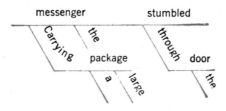

3i

Gerunds and gerund phrases are diagramed this way:

EXAMPLE   **Being unaware of the traffic regulations** is no
excuse for **breaking the law at any time.** [Gerund
phrases used as subject and as object of preposition.
The first gerund has a subject complement (*unaware*);
the second one has a direct object (*law*) and an
adverb prepositional phrase modifier (*at any time*).]

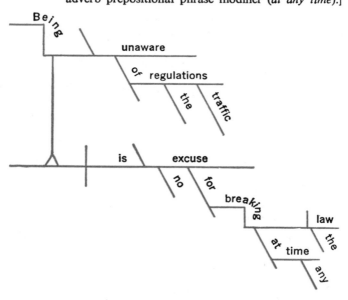

Infinitives and infinitive phrases used as modifiers are
diagramed like prepositional phrases.

EXAMPLE   We are going **to see the parade.** [Infinitive phrase
used as adverb. The infinitive has an object, *parade*.]

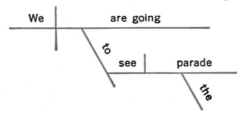

Infinitives used as nouns are diagramed as follows:

EXAMPLE   **To enlist in the Peace Corps** is his present plan.

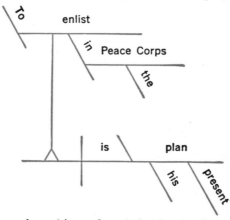

Notice how the subject of an infinitive is diagramed and how the infinitive is diagramed when *to* is omitted:

EXAMPLE   My father helped me **wash** the car.

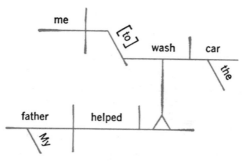

● EXERCISE 13.   Diagram the following sentences.

1. Playing the radio at night may disturb our neighbors.
2. Hearing our footsteps, the dog ran to greet us.
3. To reach the fifth floor, take the other stairs.
4. After hearing her assembly speech, I decided to become a teacher.
5. The man digging in the quarry helped us find our baseball.

APPOSITIVES AND APPOSITIVE PHRASES

Sometimes a noun or pronoun will be followed immediately by another noun or pronoun that identifies or explains it.

EXAMPLE   My sister **Cynthia** is a senior.

In this sentence, the noun *Cynthia* tells *which* sister. *Cynthia* is said to be *in apposition with* the word *sister*. *Cynthia* in this sentence is called an *appositive*.

3j. An *appositive* is a noun or pronoun that follows another noun or pronoun to identify or explain it.

EXAMPLE   Jimmy, a star **athlete,** will surely go to college.

Like any noun or pronoun, an appositive may have adjective and adjective phrase modifiers. If it does, it is called an *appositive phrase*.

3k. An *appositive phrase* is made up of the appositive and its modifiers.

In the following sentences the appositives and appositive phrases are in bold-faced type.

EXAMPLES   Our mathematics teacher, **Mr. Franklin,** also coaches our football team, **the Williamstown Wildcats.**

Gene Simpson, **the captain of the team,** received an award, **an engraved bronze trophy.**

◆ NOTE   Occasionally the appositive phrase precedes the noun or pronoun explained.

EXAMPLES   **A man of integrity,** Mr. Aldrich never cheats anyone.

The adviser for our school paper, Mr. Frank is always there after school.

Appositives and appositive phrases are usually set off by commas, unless the appositive is a single word closely related to the preceding word. The comma is always used when the word to which the appositive refers is a proper noun.

EXAMPLES   Dr. Reed, the man sitting in the front row, is my dentist.

His son Clint is my classmate.

Judith, his daughter, is a senior in college.

In diagraming, place the appositive in parentheses after the word with which it is in apposition.

EXAMPLE   Our honored guest, **the author of the book,** is a friend of Mr. Sutherland, **our mayor.**

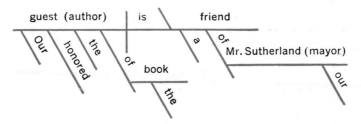

● EXERCISE 14.   List on your paper the appositive phrases in each of the following sentences. Underline the appositive in each phrase, and be sure that you know the word to which each appositive refers.

1. Our school has a dramatic club, the Masquers.
2. Miss Harlow, my English teacher, is adviser for the Masquers.
3. Members of the club, mostly freshmen, planned an assembly program.
4. The program was presented on Friday, the day of our monthly meeting.
5. Duncan Bradley, the program chairman, introduced Mr. Wilson, director of the summer theater in Burnsville.
6. From Rebecca Bryant, president of the Masquers, Mr. Wilson received our Achievement Award, a scroll signed by all club members.
7. After the program, Mr. Wilson was interviewed by Lucille Grant, editor of *Insights,* our school newspaper.

3
j-k

● Review exercise B.   There are twenty verbals and five appositives in the following sentences. After numbering 1–12, list the verbals and appositives in each sentence. After each, write in parentheses what the word is.

example   1. After reading the quotation beginning with "a rose by any other name," I decided to discuss the importance of a person's name, his designating title.

      1. *reading* (*gerund*)
        beginning (*participle*)
        discuss (*infinitive*)
        designating (*participle*)
        title (*appositive*)

1. Having Hepzibah Schleirbeck for a name, I have gone through life as a kind of handicapped person, a truly unfortunate soul.
2. Knowing that my name is unusual, I am patient with strangers.
3. After all, pronouncing or spelling Hepzibah Schleirbeck is not easy.
4. One day Margaret, my favorite cousin, excited by a new family car, tried to tell me about it by making a long-distance telephone call from Castleburg, her hometown.
5. Not remembering my number, she spelled my name over and over again for the operator, a woman of unusual patience.
6. Finally exhausted by efforts to understand, the operator remarked, "It seems to me the number would be easier to remember than the name."
7. When I am calling my dentist, Dr. Johnson, I sometimes get a quick appointment by changing my name to Mary Brown or Jane Jones.
8. Occasionally, however, I forget to answer to Mary or Jane.
9. When this happens, the embarrassed dentist looks at me strangely.
10. He seems to think I'm a criminal using an alias.
11. I must find another way to change my name.
12. My one desire is to marry a man named John Smith.

The Clause

Independent and Subordinate Clauses

Like a phrase, a clause is a word group used as a part of a sentence. The difference is that a clause contains a verb and its subject, while a phrase does not.

4a. A *clause* is a group of words that contains a verb and its subject and is used as part of a sentence.

Although every clause has a subject and verb, not all clauses express a complete thought. Those that do are called *independent clauses*. Such clauses could be written as separate sentences. We think of them as clauses when they are joined with one or more additional clauses in a single larger sentence. Clauses that do not make complete sense by themselves are called *subordinate clauses*. Subordinate clauses do the job of nouns, adjectives, or adverbs just as phrases do. In this chapter you will become better acquainted with both kinds of clauses.

KINDS OF CLAUSES

4b. An *independent* (or *main*) *clause* expresses a complete thought and can stand by itself.

We said that an independent clause could be written as a separate sentence. To see how this works out, consider the following example, in which the independent clauses are underlined:

EXAMPLE   Mr. Lacy cut pieces of stained glass with a diamond wheel, and his partner put the pieces together with wax and lead.

Each clause has its own subject and verb and expresses a complete thought. In this example, the clauses are joined by a comma and the coordinating conjunction *and.* They could also be written with a semicolon between them:

Mr. Lacy cut pieces of stained glass with a diamond wheel; his partner put the pieces together with wax and lead.

or as separate sentences:

Mr. Lacy cut pieces of stained glass with a diamond wheel. His partner put the pieces together with wax and lead.

4c. A *subordinate* (or *dependent*) *clause* does not express a complete thought and cannot stand alone.

Subordinate means "lesser in rank or importance." Subordinate clauses (also called *dependent* clauses) are so described because they need an independent clause to complete their meaning.

SUBORDINATE CLAUSES   before the bell rings
because he is proud
after it stopped raining

These clauses sound incomplete to our ears because we know the subordinate part they play in sentences. Notice that the reason they sound incomplete is not that something is missing in the clause.

Just the reverse is true, for by omitting the first word we can make each of these subordinate clauses into complete sentences: *before the bell rings* becomes *The bell rings.* Most subordinate clauses are introduced by a word like *when, if, until, because,* etc., that makes them subordinate. When we hear a clause that starts with one of these words, we know that there has to be at least one more clause in the sentence, and that at least one of the other clauses must be an independent clause.

● EXERCISE 1.   Number your paper 1–10. Identify each clause in italics by writing either *independent* or *subordinate* after the corresponding number.

1. *When my family went to New York last summer,* we visited the Theodore Roosevelt museum.
2. *The museum has been established in the house* where Roosevelt was born.
3. It is located on the basement floor of Roosevelt's birthplace, *which is on East Twentieth Street.*
4. *The museum contains books, letters, and documents* that pertain to Roosevelt's public life.
5. There are mounted heads of animals, a stuffed lion, and zebra skins from the days *when Roosevelt was big-game hunting in Africa.*
6. *Because Roosevelt was once a cowboy,* there are also branding irons and chaps.
7. Before Theodore Roosevelt became President, *he gained fame in the Spanish-American War.*
8. During that war he led the Rough Riders, *who made the famous charge up San Juan Hill.*
9. Trophies *that commemorate Roosevelt's war exploits* abound in the museum.
10. *The Roosevelt Memorial Association,* which established the museum, *charges a nominal admission fee to visitors.*

THE USES OF SUBORDINATE CLAUSES

Subordinate clauses, like phrases, function in sentences as single parts of speech. A subordinate clause can be used as an adjective, an adverb, or a noun, thus enabling us to express ideas that are difficult or impossible to state with single-word nouns and modifiers alone.

4c

The Adjective Clause

4d. An *adjective clause* is a subordinate clause used as an adjective to modify a noun or pronoun.

In the following sentences the arrow points to the noun or pronoun that each adjective clause modifies.

EXAMPLES   In the case at school is the trophy that Patsy won.

Smog, which is fog and smoke, blanketed the city.

The adjective clause follows the word it modifies, and it is sometimes set off by commas and sometimes not. Commas should be used unless the clause answers the question "Which one?" in which case no commas are used. In the first example, the clause *that Patsy won* tells *which* trophy; no comma is used. In the second example, the clause *which is fog and smoke* does not tell *which* smog. It merely describes smog. The clause is therefore set off by commas. (See page 504, rule 23i.)

Relative Pronouns

Adjective clauses are generally introduced by *relative pronouns*. The relative pronouns are *who, whom, whose, which,* and *that.* They are called *relative* because they *relate* the adjective clause to the word that the clause modifies. In Chapter 1, you learned that the noun to which a pronoun refers is the *antecedent* of the pronoun. The noun or pronoun modified by the adjective clause, then, is the antecedent of the relative pronoun that introduces the clause.

Besides introducing the adjective clause, the relative pronoun has a function in the clause.

EXAMPLES   Yvonne, who lives in Iowa, quickly learned Southern customs. [The relative pronoun *who* relates the adjective clause to *Yvonne. Who* is used as the subject of the adjective clause.]

Mrs. Daly recommended the book **that I am reading.** [*Book*, the word that the clause modifies, is the antecedent of the relative pronoun *that*. The pronoun is used as the direct object in the adjective clause.]

Here is the letter **for which I have been searching.** [The relative pronoun *which* is the object of the preposition *for* and relates the adjective clause to the pronoun's antecedent *letter*.]

The paroled prisoner visited the man **whose car he had stolen.** [The relative pronoun *whose* shows the relationship of the clause to *man*. *Man* is the antecedent of *whose*.]

Frequently the relative pronoun in the clause will be omitted. The pronoun is understood and will still have a function in the clause.

EXAMPLE   This is the dress **I want.** [The relative pronoun *that* is understood. This is the dress *that* I want. The pronoun relates the adjective clause to *dress* and is used as the direct object in the adjective clause.]

Occasionally an adjective clause will be introduced by an adverb.

EXAMPLES   Across the street is the house **where I was born.**
Midnight is the hour **when ghosts walk abroad.**

● EXERCISE 2.   After the proper number, list the adjective clause from the corresponding sentence, underlining the relative pronoun that introduces the clause. Then list the antecedent of the relative pronoun after the clause.

EXAMPLE   1. People who want to learn languages must discipline themselves to study every day.
1. *who* want to learn languages—*People*

1. Students who read a great deal usually do well in composition.
2. Some of the paintings that were hanging at the student exhibition sold for twenty-five dollars or more.

4 d

3. Mercury, who served as the messenger for the gods, wore a pair of winged sandals.
4. The man whom he has been chasing is only the henchman of the "big man."
5. Will the man whose car is parked in the driveway please report to the information booth?

● EXERCISE 3. Number your paper 1–5. Follow the directions for Exercise 2.

1. Galileo is usually remembered as the scientist who invented the telescope.
2. His telescope helped to prove the theory of Copernicus, who believed the sun, not the earth, to be the center of the solar system.
3. With his telescope Galileo studied the Milky Way and discovered a fact that startled many people: the Milky Way is made up of an infinite number of stars.
4. Galileo's discovery threatened the thinking of those men who believed man to be the center of the universe.
5. After his discovery was made known, many men whom Galileo had considered his friends avoided him.

● EXERCISE 4. Write ten sentences using subordinate clauses as adjectives. Draw an arrow from each adjective clause to the noun or pronoun it modifies.

● EXERCISE 5. These groups of sentences are choppy and babyish. Revise them by using adjective clauses to make each pair of sentences one long sentence. Remember that the clause should be placed close to the word it modifies.

EXAMPLES 1. He does not have "a right to his own opinion." He knows nothing about the topic.

1. *He who knows nothing about the topic does not have "a right to his own opinion."*

2. The test covered yesterday's assignment. I did well on it.

2. *I did well on the test that covered yesterday's assignment.*

1. My cousin enjoys practical jokes. He put pepper into my popcorn.
2. Father prefers a worm fence. It has zigzagging rails.
3. The horse once belonged to my grandfather. It has a broken leg.
4. The dress is too large for me. It may fit Marian.
5. Manley drove the new red convertible. The car led the parade.
6. I fell madly in love with the artist. He lives next door.
7. I stumbled over the scooter. It was lying on the sidewalk.
8. My father paid over a hundred dollars for the chair. It was once owned by the first governor of the state.
9. A monkey lost its temper. It began throwing rocks at us.
10. The tall man coaches our football team. I introduced him to you at the picnic.

The Adverb Clause

4e. An *adverb clause* is a subordinate clause that modifies a verb, an adjective, or an adverb.

An adverb clause tells *how*, *when*, *where*, *why*, *how much*, or *under what condition* the action of the main verb takes place.

EXAMPLES　**Before the game started,** Bryan and I ate lunch in the stadium. [The adverb clause *Before the game started* tells when Bryan and I ate lunch.]

Because she felt dizzy, Paula sat down for a while. [*Because she felt dizzy* tells why Paula sat down.]

I will attend the wedding **if it takes place on Saturday.** [*If it takes place on Saturday* tells under what condition I will attend the wedding.]

The adverb clauses in the examples above modify verbs. Adverb clauses may also modify adjectives or adverbs.

EXAMPLES　I am glad **that you are coming.** [The adverb clause modifies the adjective *glad*, telling why I am glad.]

4 e

My brother slept later **than I did.** [The adverb clause modifies the adverb *later*, telling how much later my brother slept.]

Subordinating Conjunctions

Adverb clauses are introduced by *subordinating conjunctions*. You should become thoroughly familiar with these words.

SUBORDINATING CONJUNCTIONS

after	before	unless
although	if	until
as	in order that	when
as if	since	whenever
as long as	so that	where
as soon as	than	wherever
because	though	while

◆ NOTE   Remember that *after*, *before*, *since*, *until*, and *as* may also be used as prepositions.

● EXERCISE 6.   After numbering 1–10, write the subordinating conjunction and the last word of each adverb clause in the following sentences; then write what the clause tells: *when, where, how, why, how much, under what condition?* A sentence may have more than one adverb clause. (Notice that introductory adverb clauses are usually set off by commas.)

EXAMPLES   1. If you will take my advice, you can be the death of a party.
1. *If—advice   under what condition*
2. You can easily follow my instructions because they are clear and simple.
2. *because—simple   why*

1. If you wish to be the death of a party, do these things.
2. When another person is speaking, interrupt him.
3. As soon as he starts telling a joke, you can steal his thunder by giving away the punch line.
4. You can then act as if his joke wasn't funny.

5. Later you can change the subject so that you can brag about yourself.
6. While you are talking about your heroic deeds or keen intelligence, emphasize many uninteresting details.
7. Before you describe saving a child's life, make yourself out to be nobler than anyone else is.
8. Whenever the occasion arises, you should complain to your hostess and criticize her guests.
9. Unless you monopolize every conversation, you won't be a professional "party pooper."
10. Enjoy yourself as you crowd others off the floor, because you will probably never be invited again.

● EXERCISE 7.   Write ten sentences of your own, using the following subordinate clauses as adverbs.

EXAMPLE   1. as the strangers talked
            1. *As the strangers talked, the icy distance between them gradually melted.*

1. although I am not a Sherlock Holmes
2. while the cab driver was honking the horn impatiently
3. as soon as we had finished eating
4. if he should hit a home run now
5. unless my father changes his mind
6. so that it will be a complete surprise
7. if the concrete has too much water in it
8. as if he had just seen a monster from Mars
9. after you add the eggs to the mixture
10. when he was leaving the theater

The Noun Clause

4f. A *noun clause* is a subordinate clause used as a noun.

A noun clause may be used as a subject, a complement (predicate nominative, direct object, indirect object), or the object of a preposition.

4f

Study the structure of the following sentences.

NOUNS	NOUN CLAUSES
Subject His **words** surprised me.	**What he said** surprised me.
Predicate nominative The champion will be the best **fighter**.	The champion will be **whoever fights best**.
Direct object She knows our **secret**.	She knows **what our secret is**.
Indirect object They give each **arrival** a name tag.	They give **whoever comes** a name tag.
Object of preposition She often sends flowers to sick **people**.	She often sends flowers to **whoever is sick**.

Noun clauses are usually introduced by *that, what, whatever, who, whoever, whom,* and *whomever.*

EXAMPLES   We could not tell **who he was.** [The introductory word *who* is the predicate nominative in the noun clause—*he was who.*]

Tell us **whom you saw.** [The introductory word is the direct object of the noun clause—*you saw whom.*]

She thought **that** I knew. [The introductory word *that* has no other function in the clause.]

● EXERCISE 8.   List on your paper the first and the last word of each noun clause in these sentences. Then tell how the noun clause is used: *subject, predicate nominative, direct object, indirect object,* or *object of a preposition.* (You will not find noun clauses in every sentence.)

EXAMPLE   1. You can never accurately predict what will happen at a rodeo.
        1. *what—rodeo   direct object*

1. What I like at a rodeo is the excitement.
2. My cousin Lynn often tells stories about what he has done at rodeos.
3. He will give whoever is interested an exciting account of his adventures.

4. In Arizona all the other cowboys knew that "Five Minutes till Midnight" was too dangerous a horse to ride.
5. That he had the courage to ride the wild horse was what Lynn wanted to prove to everyone.
6. The tense crowd watched Lynn as he jumped upon the back of the horse that no cowboy had ever ridden before.
7. He won the prize money for what he did; he stayed on the bucking horse until the whistle blew.
8. Upon hearing the whistle, Lynn knew that he had won.
9. The second that Lynn relaxed, however, the angry stallion tossed him high into the air.
10. Whoever saw Lynn sail through space that day will never forget how he turned a flip in mid-air and then landed safely on his feet.

Diagraming Subordinate Clauses

In a diagram, an adjective clause is joined to the word it modifies by a dotted line leading from the relative pronoun to the modified word, that is, to the antecedent of the relative pronoun.

EXAMPLES The movie **that we saw yesterday** won the Academy Award.

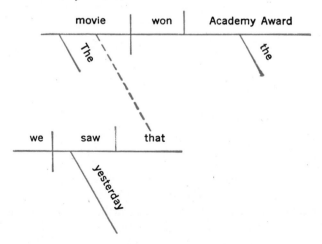

He is the man **from whom we bought the decorations.**

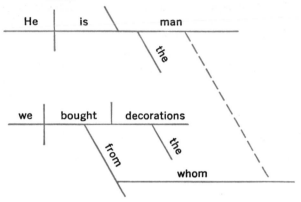

In diagraming an adverb clause, place the subordinating conjunction that introduces the clause on a dotted line leading from the verb in the adverb clause to the word the clause modifies.

EXAMPLE   **Before we leave the party,** we must thank the hostess.

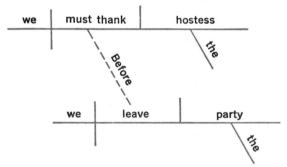

How a noun clause is diagramed depends upon its use in the sentence. It also depends on whether or not the introductory word has a specific function in the noun clause. Study the examples on the next page.

EXAMPLES **What you believe** is important to me. [The noun clause is used as the subject of the independent clause. The introductory word *what* is the direct object in the noun clause.]

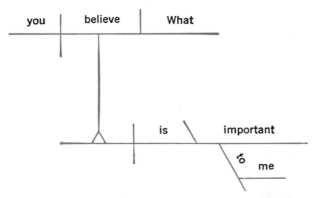

Columbus knew **that the world was round.** [The noun clause is the direct object of the independent clause. The word *that* has no function in the noun clause except as an introductory word.]

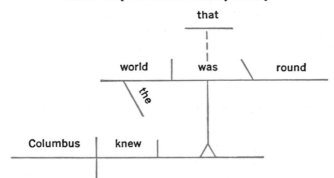

● EXERCISE 9. Diagram the following sentences.

1. What Catherine saw at Monticello was extremely interesting to all of us.
2. Monticello, which was the home of Thomas Jefferson, is located near Charlottesville, Virginia.

3. If you visit Monticello, you will see many fascinating devices that Jefferson invented.
4. The inventions that particularly interested Catherine were two dumbwaiters that ran between the dining room and the cellar.
5. If I ever visit my cousin who lives in Virginia, I know that we will go to Monticello.

SENTENCES CLASSIFIED ACCORDING TO STRUCTURE

In Chapter 2, you learned that sentences are classified according to *type* as declarative, imperative, interrogative, or exclamatory. Sentences may also be classified according to *structure*.

4g. Classified according to structure, there are four kinds of sentences; *simple*, *compound*, *complex*, and *compound-complex*.

(1) A *simple sentence* has one independent clause and no subordinate clauses. It has only one subject and one verb, although both may be compound.

EXAMPLE   George Vancouver was exploring the Northwest.

(2) A *compound sentence* has two or more independent clauses but no subordinate clauses.

In effect, a compound sentence consists of two or more simple sentences joined by a comma and a coordinating conjunction or by a semicolon.

EXAMPLE In 1792 Vancouver discovered a channel, and he gave it an unusual name.

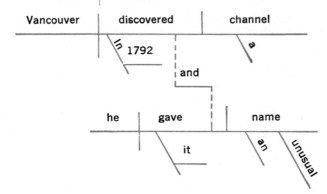

◆ NOTE If the compound sentence has a semicolon and no conjunction, place a straight dotted line between the two verbs.

(3) A *complex sentence* has one independent clause and one or more subordinate clauses.

EXAMPLE He originally thought that the channel was a harbor. [Here the subordinate clause is the direct object of the independent clause.]

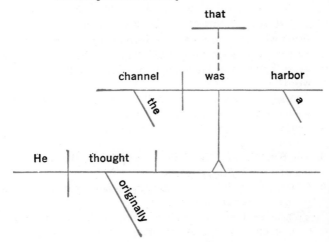

4g

(4) A *compound-complex sentence* contains two or more independent clauses and one or more subordinate clauses.

EXAMPLE   Since it was not a harbor, Vancouver had been deceived, and Deception Pass became its name.

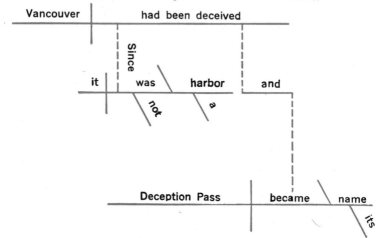

● EXERCISE 10.   After numbering 1–10, classify the following sentences according to structure. Be sure that you can identify all subordinate and independent clauses.

1. From what language does the word *chauffeur* come?
2. Perhaps you correctly guessed that *chauffeur* is a French word, but do you know anything about the history of the word?
3. Actually, *chauffeur* is originally derived from the Latin word *calefacere*, which means "to make hot."
4. During its early history, the automobile was often a steam-driven vehicle.
5. The French teased the professional driver of the car by calling him a *chauffeur*, or stoker.
6. Of course, the chauffeur is no longer a fireman or stoker, but the name has remained with him.
7. You can see that the original meaning of *chauffeur* has something in common with the meaning of the verb *chafe*.

8. The *chafing* dish is used for heating food at a table, and so it, too, is related to the original meaning of *chauffeur*.
9. When you trace the histories of words, you often make surprising discoveries.
10. Words that you never thought were related in any way turn out to have common origins.

● EXERCISE 11. Diagram the following sentences.

1. Tonight I am going to a concert with my parents, but I would prefer to play chess with you.
2. When he saw the accident, he shouted for help and then telephoned the police.
3. Twenty seniors in the graduating class will be attending college, and twelve of them have received scholarships.
4. Leaving for school, I knew that it would rain today; yet I did not carry my umbrella.
5. When my sister practices her singing lessons, Muff curls on the piano bench and purrs; but when I play my trumpet, that cat yowls and hides under the sofa.

● REVIEW EXERCISE A. Number your paper 1-10. Decide whether each *italicized* clause below functions as an adjective, an adverb, or a noun, and write *adjective*, *adverb*, or *noun* after the proper number. If the clause is used as an adjective or adverb, write the word(s) the clause modifies. If it is used as a noun, write *subj.* for subject, *d.o.* for direct object, *p.n.* for predicate nominative, or *o.p.* for object of a preposition.

(1) *As I watched the river yesterday,* I decided (2) *that I would analyze the moods of streams and oceans.* I believe (3) *that each body of water has its own personality.* (4) *When high winds push them forward,* ocean waves crash angrily against the shore (5) *as though they are jealous of the earth's stability.* This must be evident to (6) *whoever has been on a beach.*

Unlike the turbulent oceans, the streams (7) *which frolic through the ravines of the Rockies* are gay. (8) *That they use the earth as a playground* seems certain to me.

(9) *Because oceans and streams really aren't human,* I am imagining things. Men like Matthew Arnold, however, have written poems (10) *that describe the melancholy sea.*

● REVIEW EXERCISE B.   Diagram the following sentences.

1. Everyone knows who Alan Shepard is.
2. This astronaut wrote an exciting article that appears in our literature book.
3. He described his historic flight, which was the first trip into space by an American.
4. Because he had trained beforehand, the flight seemed familiar.
5. At one point the capsule in which Shepard was riding began to vibrate.
6. Shepard knew what caused the vibration.
7. It occurred when the capsule passed through the zone of maximum pressure.
8. The vibration was somewhat heavier than Shepard had expected.
9. Finally it stopped, and the flight continued on schedule.
10. Shepard said that he felt fine after his flight, and he praised the many hard-working men who had contributed to his outstanding success.

PART TWO

Usage

CHAPTER 5

Agreement

Subject and Verb,
Pronoun and Antecedent

Certain words that are closely related in sentences have matching forms. Subjects and verbs have this kind of close relationship, as do pronouns and their antecedents. When such words are correctly matched, we say that they *agree* grammatically. Have you ever heard someone say, "He don't," or "One of the girls forgot their book"? Each of these errors shows lack of agreement, the first one between subject and verb and the second one between a pronoun and its antecedent.

One way in which two words can agree with each other grammatically is in *number*. Number indicates whether the word refers to one person or thing, or to more than one.

5a. When a word refers to one person or thing, it is *singular* in number. When a word refers to more than one, it is *plural* in number.

Nouns and pronouns have number. The following nouns and pronouns are singular because they name or refer to only one person or thing: *hunter, child, it, story.* The following are plural because they refer to more than one: *hunters, children, they, stories.*

112

● EXERCISE 1. Number 1–20 in a column on your paper. After each number, write whether the word is *singular* or *plural*.

1. dentist	6. each	11. his	16. woman
2. dentists	7. both	12. our	17. months
3. someone	8. these	13. several	18. its
4. their	9. this	14. foot	19. cities
5. gallon	10. mile	15. foreman	20. dollars

AGREEMENT OF SUBJECT AND VERB

Verbs have number, too. In order to speak and write correctly, you must make verbs agree with their subjects.

5b. A verb agrees with its subject in number.

(1) Singular subjects take singular verbs.

EXAMPLES   My **brother knows** the answer. [The singular verb *knows* agrees with the singular subject *brother*.]

A **girl** in my class **sings** in the city chorus. [The singular verb *sings* agrees with the singular subject *girl*.]

(2) Plural subjects take plural verbs.

EXAMPLES   My **brothers know** the answer.

Many **girls** in my class **sing** in the city chorus.

The plural subjects *brothers* and *girls* take the plural verbs *know* and *sing*.

Generally, nouns ending in *s* are plural (*brothers*, *girls*), but verbs ending in *s* are singular (*knows*, *sings*). Since the form of the verb used with the singular pronouns *I* and *you* is regularly the same as the plural form, agreement in number presents problems mainly in the third person forms.

	SINGULAR	PLURAL
First person	I work	We work
Second person	You work	You work
Third person	He works	They work

5
a-b

● EXERCISE 2.　Number your paper 1–10. Write the verb in parentheses that agrees with the subject.

1. several (has, have)
2. postmen (arrives, arrive)
3. everyone (tries, try)
4. you (was, were)
5. both (is, are)

6. no one (seems, seem)
7. few (does, do)
8. either (looks, look)
9. anyone (reads, read)
10. it (gives, give)

5c. The number of the subject is not changed by a phrase following the subject.

Remember that a verb agrees in number with its subject, not with the object of a preposition. *The subject is never part of a prepositional phrase.*

EXAMPLES　One of the kites **has** caught in a tree.

The **ring** set with rubies **was** stolen from the jeweler's window.

Compound prepositions such as *together with*, *in addition to*, and *along with* following the subject do not affect the number of the subject.

EXAMPLES　**Alvin,** together with his sisters, **has** been taking voice lessons.

Charles, along with Jack and Dan, **was** elected to the Student Council.

● EXERCISE 3.　*Oral Drill.* Repeat each of the following sentences, stressing the italicized words.

1. Many *facts* in this textbook *are* important.
2. A *knowledge* of rules *helps* you use English correctly.
3. *Errors* in verb usage *are* particularly noticeable.
4. Correct *spelling*, in addition to usage of verbs, *is* essential to good writing.
5. *Men* in the business world *look* for correct English in a letter of application.
6. A *letter* with many mistakes *does* not make a good impression.

7. My *father*, along with two other officials, often *hires* applicants.

8. *One* of my friends *hopes* to work for Father's company.

9. Not *one* of the employers, however, *was* pleased with my friend's letter of application.

10. "Every *man* in my office *uses* good English," commented my father.

● EXERCISE 4. Number your paper 1–10. Write after the corresponding number the subject of each sentence. After the subject, write the verb in parentheses that agrees with it.

EXAMPLE 1. The girls in my class (has, have) arranged a display.
　　　　　1. *girls—have*

1. Cells in your brain (needs, need) oxygen.

2. Our boys, in position at the line of scrimmage, (was, were) awaiting the snap of the pigskin.

3. The first sight of Broadway, with its flashing lights and bright colors, (impresses, impress) a visitor.

4. A change in the rules often (confuses, confuse) the spectators.

5. The silence inside the Carlsbad Caverns (is, are) awe-inspiring.

6. The colors in the room (seems, seem) to flow into one another.

7. The cars on this expressway (travels, travel) at a high rate of speed.

8. John, as well as some of the other club members, (plans, plan) to ask the speaker questions.

9. Beams of colored light (passes, pass) through a prism without producing a rainbow pattern.

10. As each one of you students (knows, know), your reports will be due on Friday.

5d. The following pronouns are singular: *each, either, neither, one, everyone, everybody, no one, nobody, anyone, anybody, someone, somebody.*

Read the following sentences aloud, stressing the subjects and verbs in bold-faced type.

5
c-d

EXAMPLES   **Each** of these sounds **causes** drowsiness. [each one causes]

Neither of the boys **is** right. [neither one is]

Either of the dresses **is** appropriate. [either one is]

Everyone in the class **has** read the novel.

Someone in the choir **was** whistling softly.

Note that the first word in each of the example sentences is followed by a phrase. The object of the preposition in each of the first three sentences is plural: *sounds, answers, dresses.* There is a natural tendency to make the verb agree with these words rather than with its subject. However, since each of the five sentences has a singular pronoun as subject, each verb is also singular.

5e. **The following pronouns are plural:** *several, few, both, many.*

Study the use of subjects and verbs in these sentences. Read the sentences aloud.

EXAMPLES   **Few** of the students **have** failed the test.

Several of these plants **are** poisonous.

Many in the group often **ask** questions.

Were both of the problems difficult?

5f. **The pronouns** *some, all, most, any,* **and** *none* **may be either singular or plural.**

Some, all, and *most* are singular when they refer to a quantity of something and plural when they refer to a number of things thought of individually.

EXAMPLES   **Some** of the food **was** eaten.

Some of the apples **were** eaten.

All of the furniture **looks** comfortable.

All of the chairs **look** comfortable.

Most of the class **likes** *Great Expectations.*

Most of the students **like** *Great Expectations.*

The words *any* and *none* are singular if the speaker is thinking of each item individually and plural if he is thinking of several things as a group.

EXAMPLES **Any** of these boys **is** qualified. [*Any one* is qualified.]
Any of these boys **are** qualified. [*All* are qualified.]
None of the bushels **was** full. [*Not one* was full.]
None of the bushels **were** full. [*No bushels* were full.]

● EXERCISE 5. This exercise covers rules 5d, 5e, and 5f. Number your paper 1–10. Write the subject of each sentence on your paper. Select the correct verb, and write it after the subject.

1. Many of us actually (likes, like) long books.
2. Some of the children (seems, seem) shy.
3. Somebody in the audience (was, were) snoring.
4. Each of us (tries, try) to outdo the other.
5. Both of my parents (has, have) red hair.
6. Few of the pies (was, were) left after the sale.
7. Sometimes everyone in the office (works, work) late.
8. Nobody in my family (is, are) able to remember telephone numbers and addresses.
9. (Has, have) all of the senators returned?
10. (Does, do) either of the students need money to buy decorations?

● REVIEW EXERCISE A. Number your paper 1–20. Read each sentence aloud. If the verb agrees with the subject, write a plus (+) on your paper after the corresponding number. If the verb does not agree with the subject, write a zero (0).

1. One of the cabinets contain the club's banner, account books, and membership rolls.
2. Each of the hostesses are standing in the doorway.
3. Do the new uniforms for the band include majorette costumes?
4. Sometimes a leak in the gas pipes is hard to find.
5. The bridges on Highway 34 are extremely narrow.

5
e-f

6. The numbers on the license plate was covered with mud.
7. Yesterday you was asking me about camp.
8. Every one of the clerks have to punch the time clock.
9. One of his assistants answer the telephone.
10. Our assignment for the next two days cover events during the American Revolution.
11. Some of these pictures in the family album show how hair styles change.
12. A bag of golf clubs, as well as two tennis rackets, stand in the corner of the closet.
13. Most of us now agree to these plans.
14. Each of the farmers use modern machines.
15. Some of the salt in these shakers is damp.
16. A carton of cold drinks was in the refrigerator.
17. Neither of the hurdles look easy.
18. Does each of the girls play the piano?
19. Both of the hedges needs trimming.
20. Rupert, together with other school newspaper editors, are attending the Scholastic Press Association Convention.

The Compound Subject

5g. Subjects joined by *and* take a plural verb.

The following compound subjects joined by *and* name more than one person or thing and must take plural verbs:

Leon and **Roger** **were** nudging me forward. [Two persons were.]

Poetry and **prose** **differ** in form. [Two things differ.]

If a compound subject names only one person or thing, then the verb must be singular:

The secretary and treasurer plans to resign. [One person plans.]

Ham and eggs is a good breakfast dish. [The one combination is.]

In the sentences above, the compound subjects are thought of as units (one person, one dish) and are naturally singular.

5h. **Singular subjects joined by *or* or *nor* take a singular verb.**

EXAMPLES   Every Saturday, **Gail** or **Evelyn takes** the wash to the Laundromat. [Either Gail or Evelyn takes the wash, not both.]

Neither the **customer** nor the **clerk is** always right. [Neither one is always right.]

● EXERCISE 6.   Number your paper 1–10. Then rewrite the sentences below according to these instructions. If the sentence has a compound subject joined by *and*, change the conjunction to *or*, and make the necessary change in the number of the verb. If the sentence has a compound subject joined by *or*, change the conjunction to *and*, and make the necessary change in the number of the verb.

EXAMPLES   1. A dog and a cat are tearing up the paper.
        1. *A dog or a cat is tearing up the paper.*
        2. My father or his friend has finished the plans for the house.
        2. *My father and his friend have finished the plans for the house.*

1. Ned and Lawrence have gone to the science fair.
2. Your jacket and your coat are at the cleaners.
3. The girl and her mother are telling fortunes for the National Honor Society's booth at the school fair.
4. The house on the hill and the cottage in the valley are for sale.
5. *The Last of the Mohicans* or *The Mayor of Casterbridge* has been assigned.
6. Jane or Mary has prepared the punch.
7. Each week a poem and an essay appear in the school newspaper.
8. Rain or snow has been predicted for tomorrow.
9. Venus and Mars do not seem far away when one considers the distance from the earth to the nearest star.
10. The car in front of us and the car parked on the wrong side of the street are to blame for the accident.

5i. When a singular subject and a plural subject are joined by *or* or *nor*, the verb agrees with the subject nearer the verb.

ACCEPTABLE Neither the singers nor the **accompanist has** memorized the music.

ACCEPTABLE Neither the accompanist nor the **singers have** memorized the music.

Because of awkwardness, these constructions should usually be avoided.

BETTER The music has not been memorized by either the singers or the accompanist.

● REVIEW EXERCISE B. *Oral Drill.* Read each of the following sentences aloud several times.

1. The *plants* in the window box *need* watering.
2. A *can* of mixed nuts *is* on the coffee table.
3. *You were* asleep.
4. *Chester* and *Sarah are* distantly related.
5. *Reading* or *writing* letters *is* better than watching TV.
6. *Neither* of you *believes* us.
7. *Several* of these pests *annoy* the wild deer.
8. Every *one* of you *knows* Jack.
9. Either *Henry* or *Carl has* brought the records.
10. Neither *Polly* nor *Doris likes* ghost stories.

● REVIEW EXERCISE C. Rewrite each of the following sentences, (1) following the directions in parentheses and (2) changing the number of the verb to agree with the subject if necessary.

EXAMPLE 1. The boys have finished delivering the newspapers. (Change *The boys* to *Each of the boys.*)

    1. *Each of the boys has finished delivering the newspapers.*

1. My sister is planning to attend summer school. (Change *sister* to *sisters.*)
2. Have Sylvia and Margie asked to go with us? (Change *and* to *or.*)

3. Nobody in our town intends to participate in the ceremony. (Change *Nobody* to *Many*.)
4. My grandmother, as well as my mother, hopes to see our play. (Change *grandmother* to *grandparents*.)
5. Most of the money was contributed by children in grammar school. (Change *money* to *quarters*.)
6. Neither the students nor the teacher has found the missing book. (Change *Neither the students nor the teacher* to *Neither the teacher nor the students*.)
7. The president and the vice-president have promised to address the meeting. (Change *president and the vice-president* to *secretary and treasurer*.)
8. Some of the workers spend too much time in the snack bar. (Change *Some* to *One*.)
9. The children playing with the puppies do not want to go home. (Change *children* to *child*.)
10. Few of my questions were answered to my satisfaction. (Change *Few* to *Neither*.)

Other Problems in Agreement

5j. *Don't* and *doesn't* must agree with their subjects.

Don't and *doesn't* are contractions—two words combined into one by omitting one or more letters. *Don't* is the contraction for "do not," *doesn't* for "does not."

With the subjects *I* and *you* and with plural subjects, use *don't* (*do not*).

EXAMPLES   I **don't** cook.   They **don't** protest.
You **don't** mean it.   These **don't** fit.
We **don't** help.   Girls **don't** understand me.

With other subjects, use the singular *doesn't* (*does not*).

EXAMPLES   He **doesn't** cook.   One **doesn't** protest.
She **doesn't** mean it.   This **doesn't** fit.
It **doesn't** help.   Sue **doesn't** understand me.

5
i-j

The errors in the use of *don't* and *doesn't* are usually made when *don't* is incorrectly used with *it*, *he*, or *she*. Remember always to use *doesn't* with these singular subjects.

● EXERCISE 7.   *Oral Drill.* Read these sentences aloud.

1. It doesn't matter now.
2. This doesn't bother me.
3. Harry doesn't frighten easily.
4. One doesn't brag when he loses.
5. He doesn't ever sleep late.
6. Doesn't she live here?
7. Doesn't that amuse you?

● EXERCISE 8.   After numbering your paper 1–10, write the correct form (*doesn't* or *don't*) for each sentence below.

1. This —— influence me.
2. —— he like sour pickles?
3. No, he ——.
4. These —— suit me.
5. It —— look much like rain.
6. One of them —— expect to win.
7. They —— intend to go.
8. —— Edmund have a birthday soon?
9. —— either of them want a piece of pie?
10. Margie and Beth —— like to wear hats and gloves.

5k. Collective nouns may be either singular or plural.

Collective nouns are singular in form, but they name a *group* of persons or things.

group	committee	club	family
flock	herd	swarm	public
jury	army	audience	assembly
class	team	faculty	fleet

Collective nouns are used with plural verbs when the speaker or writer is referring to the individual parts or members of the group acting separately. They are used with singular verbs when the statement refers to the group acting together as a unit.

EXAMPLES   The jury **was** ready to announce its decision. [*Jury* is thought of as a unit.]

The jury **were** arguing among themselves. [*Jury* is thought of as individuals.]

◆ USAGE NOTE   Be sure that any pronoun referring to the collective noun has the same number as the noun (*its* in the first example above, *themselves* in the second).

● EXERCISE 9.   Select five collective nouns and write five pairs of sentences showing clearly how the nouns you choose may be either singular or plural.

EXAMPLE   1. *The class has elected its officers.*
              The class have finished their projects.

5 l. **A verb agrees with its subject, not its predicate nominative.**

When the subject and the predicate nominative are of different numbers, you should always remember that *the verb agrees with the subject.*

RIGHT   Traffic **jams are** one problem of commuters.

RIGHT   One **problem** of commuters **is** traffic jams.

5m. **When the subject follows the verb as in sentences beginning with *there* and *here* and in questions, be careful to determine the subject and make sure that the verb agrees with it.**

Each subject below agrees with its verb.

EXAMPLES   Here **is** a letter for you.
              Here **are** two letters for you.
              There **is** my friend now.
              There **are** my friends now.
              Where **is** Edith? Where **is** **Donald?**
              Where **are** Edith and **Donald?**

5
k-m

In conversations we frequently use contractions such as *here's*, *there's*, *where's*, *how's*, *what's*, *when's*, and the like. Since each of these includes the contracted form of *is*, do not use one of these contractions unless a singular subject follows it.

WRONG   There's many old magazines in the attic.

RIGHT   There **are** many old **magazines** in the attic.

RIGHT   There**'s** an **attic** filled with old magazines.

5n. Words stating amount are usually singular.

A word or group of words stating an amount of money, time, weight, or measurement is usually considered as one item and takes a singular verb.

EXAMPLES   **Ten dollars is** a high price for sneakers.
              Eight days was the time allotted.
              Two thirds of the food **was** eaten.

Sometimes, however, the amount is thought of as individual pieces or parts. If so, a plural verb is used.

EXAMPLES   **Ten** of the **dollars are** his.
              Seven of the **days were** spent rehearsing.
              Two thirds of the **doughnuts were** eaten.

5o. The title of a work of art, literature, or music, even when plural in form, takes a singular verb.

In the following sentences, notice that each title takes a singular verb, since it is only one work of art.

EXAMPLES   *Great Expectations* **is** one of my favorite novels. [one book]

              Peace and Plenty, by George Inness, **hangs** in the Metropolitan Museum. [one painting]

              The Pirates of Penzance **was** presented by the Dramatic Club and the Glee Club. [one operetta]

5p. *Every* or *many a* before a subject calls for a singular verb.

EXAMPLES   **Every** student and teacher in our school **has** contributed to the scholarship fund.

Many a member of the armed forces **has** given his life for our country.

5q. A few nouns, although plural in form, take a singular verb.

Some nouns, although they end in *s*, are considered singular in meaning. The word *news* is a common example; the singular verb is used.

The **news** of the astronaut's successful flight **was** exciting.

Names of certain diseases also end in *s* but are singular nouns: *measles, mumps, rickets.*

Mumps has prevented my little sister's attendance at kindergarten.

Words ending in *–ics* are generally used with a singular verb: *athletics, mathematics, physics, civics, economics, politics, ethics.*

Physics is my most difficult subject.

● REVIEW EXERCISE D. *Oral Drill.* Repeat each of the following sentences, stressing the italicized words.

1. *The Prince and the Pauper is* not so well known as Mark Twain's other books, but I found it delightful.
2. His chief *worry is* his increasing *debts.*
3. *Many a* man, woman, and child in Communist China *does* not have enough food.
4. Do you feel that *athletics is* overemphasized in your school?
5. *Where are* my *skates?*
6. My *family plans* to take *its* vacation in August.
7. My *family plan* to take *their* vacation in August.
8. *Are there* any *objections?*
9. *Romeo and Juliet is* a play, a ballet, and a movie.
10. *Two weeks is* enough time to complete the project.

5
n-q

● REVIEW EXERCISE E.   Number your paper 1–20. Choose the correct verb in parentheses, and write it after the appropriate number.

1. Clem, as well as Archie, (thinks, think) that women should not be allowed to vote.
2. "Snow White and the Seven Dwarfs" (is, are) a children's story which was made into a delightful movie by Walt Disney.
3. Fifteen pounds (is, are) a lot of weight to lose.
4. I simply cannot study when there (is, are) radios, record players, or television sets blaring.
5. Measles (is, are) common among children in the primary grades.
6. Taxes (is, are) a major problem facing the governor.
7. Not one of the boys (intends, intend) to help us with the decorations.
8. The basketball team (was, were) handicapped by injuries in its last game.
9. (Does, Do) either of them think that the membership rules should be changed?
10. In every detective story, there (is, are) usually a motive, suspects, clues, and discovery and punishment.
11. Ulysses S. Grant, along with Zachary Taylor, (was, were) probably better as a general than as a President.
12. Every student in the city schools (is, are) going to take the examination.
13. The actor's jovial manner and his ability to ad-lib (adds, add) to the merriment.
14. Neither the captain nor the coach (plans, plan) to attend the pep rally.
15. Both of a fly's big eyes (contains, contain) hundreds of little eyes.
16. According to Aristotle, nobody except malicious people (rejoices, rejoice) at the misfortunes of others.
17. *The King and I* (was, were) the first Broadway show I saw.
18. When I am on the stage, neither my memory nor my voice (is, are) reliable.
19. Why (doesn't, don't) that tall boy play basketball?
20. A few of us (has, have) a perfect attendance record.

AGREEMENT OF PRONOUN AND ANTECEDENT

You learned in Chapter 1 that the word to which a pronoun refers is called its *antecedent*. (For example, in the preceding sentence, *pronoun* is the antecedent of *its*.) There should always be agreement between the pronoun and its antecedent.

5r. **A pronoun agrees with its antecedent in number and gender.**

A few singular personal pronouns have forms that indicate the gender of the antecedent. *He*, *his*, and *him* are used if the antecedent is masculine. *She*, *her*, and *hers* are used if the antecedent is feminine. *It* and *its* are used if the antecedent is neither masculine nor feminine.

Study the following sentences, noticing how pronouns and antecedents agree in number and gender.

EXAMPLES **Marguerite** showed **her** paintings yesterday.
Today **Clarence** will make **his** report.
My **term paper** has as **its** subject "Two Distinguished American Poets."

When the antecedent of a personal pronoun is another kind of pronoun, it is often necessary to look in a phrase following the antecedent to determine gender.

EXAMPLES **One** of the **girls** in our group has cooked **her** own breakfast.
Each of the **forest rangers** performed **his** duties admirably.

Sometimes the antecedent may be either masculine or feminine; sometimes it may be both. In such cases, use the masculine form of the personal pronoun.

EXAMPLES **A person** can choose **his** friends but not always **his** relatives.
Every one of the **parents** is interested in **his** own child.

5r

(1) Use a singular pronoun to refer to *each, either, neither, one, everyone, everybody, no one, nobody, anyone, anybody, someone,* or *somebody*.

EXAMPLES   Each of the actors forgot his lines.

One of the birds built its nest there.

Notice in the sentences above that a prepositional phrase does not alter the number of the antecedent. The antecedent is singular in each sentence, and a singular pronoun (*he, she, him, her, it,* or *its*) must be used for agreement.

EXCEPTION   Sometimes the meaning of the antecedents *everyone* and *everybody* is clearly plural. In such cases the plural pronoun should be used.

ABSURD   Everyone moaned when he saw the fumble.

BETTER   Everyone moaned when they saw the fumble.

(2) Two or more singular antecedents joined by *or* or *nor* should be referred to by a singular pronoun.

EXAMPLES   Neither **Eugene nor Roy** blamed **himself.**

Just then **Bill or Bruce** cleared **his** throat.

◆ USAGE NOTE   You will find that Rules (1) and (2) are often ignored in conversation; nevertheless, they should be followed in writing.

(3) Two or more antecedents joined by *and* should be referred to by a plural pronoun.

EXAMPLES   **Diana and Grace** were giggling because **they** knew a secret.

Edna and Peter made up **their** own minds.

● EXERCISE 10.   Number your paper 1–10. First, copy the antecedents for each blank in the following sentences; then, for each blank, write a pronoun that will agree with its antecedent.

1. A person should not expect too much from —— friends.
2. The postman brought Jack and Ray the books that —— had ordered.

3. Norma or Polly will stay after school so that —— can help decorate the room.
4. Several of the convicts refused to eat —— food.
5. Each of the seals caught the fish that were thrown to ——.
6. Both of the boys forgot —— promises.
7. Everyone needs —— own fountain pen.
8. Neither apologized for —— blunder.
9. Each of the players looked unhappy because —— had failed the coach.
10. When Susan sees someone that she knows, she always stops and talks to ——.

● EXERCISE 11. Most of the following sentences contain errors in agreement of pronoun and antecedent. Number your paper 1–10. If the sentence is correct, write *C* after the corresponding number. If there is an error in agreement, write the correct form of the pronoun so that it will agree with its antecedent.

1. One of my aunts takes a great deal of pride in her furniture.
2. Knowing this, nobody in our family puts their feet on chairs or sits on beds at Aunt Mary's house.
3. One of her brothers used to think they could be an exception to the rule.
4. Uncle Charlie would often come home late at night, undress in the darkness, and then dive into his bed, nearly knocking every slat out of their place.
5. Each of these plunges left their mark on the rickety bed.
6. At first, both Aunt Mary and my mother offered their advice to Uncle Charlie and asked him to take better care of the furniture.
7. Anybody else in my family would have mended their ways, but not Uncle Charlie; he needed discipline, not advice.
8. Late one night there was a loud crash, and everyone ran out of their rooms to see what was wrong.
9. Not one of the family could believe their eyes! Lying in the middle of the floor was Uncle Charlie, groaning loudly.
10. If anybody ever asks you why Uncle Charlie suddenly reformed, tell them that one day Aunt Mary merely decided to rearrange her furniture.

● REVIEW EXERCISE F. In the sentences below, if the verbs agree with their subjects and the pronouns with their antecedents, write *C* (for *correct*) after the appropriate number. If the verb does not agree with its subject, or if a pronoun does not agree with its antecedent, write the correct form of the verb or the pronoun after the proper number.

1. Nearly everybody in our crowd collect things. 2. Some of my friends collect stamps, and a few save old coins. 3. One of the girls keep locks of hair clipped from the heads of various friends. 4. Every lock in the collection are put in a small envelope and pasted in a book. 5. Bill Reeves and his two brothers have a collection of old baseball pictures, made as long ago as the 1920's. 6. It seems that almost all of my classmates are always adding to a collection of one kind or another. 7. Each of these friends is proud of his varied assortment.

8. Jack Thompson, however, don't collect anything. 9. One of his favorite pastimes is just watching things—like lizards or birds. 10. If someone goes with Jack on a Saturday walk through the woods, Jack doesn't say much to them. 11. He is too busy watching one of the birds build their nest.

12. Not one of my friends, however, like to read about things ⁕ as much as I do. 13. Instead of collecting old bottles or watching robins, I learn about things in other lands. 14. Several of my friends says I read too much *about* doing things without *doing* anything. 15. Each book, as well as every magazine, teaches me far more than some of my friends are willing to admit. 16. For me, the habits of elephants in Africa or of kangaroos in Australia makes interesting reading.

17. In Australia there's many kinds of birds. 18. One of the most interesting birds is the kookaburra. 19. Neither Jack nor Bill knows about the kookaburra, which doesn't live in America. 20. Every one of these birds laugh. 21. It don't chirp, sing, or call as other birds do. 22. Several of them often get together on a fence, and then one of them starts cackling. 23. Quickly the others on the fence add their voices to the chorus. 24. Each bird seems to be enjoying a joke all their own. 25. Any person passing by will notice the noise, and they will soon burst out laughing, too.

The Correct Use of Verbs

Principal Parts, Regular and Irregular Verbs

The most frequent errors in usage occur when verb forms are used incorrectly. You may hear someone say, "He has spoke," "He swum," "The glasses were broke," or "The book is laying on the table." Although people quite naturally associate usage errors with lack of education, a person who makes such errors is not necessarily uneducated. Possibly he is just not thinking about what he is saying.

THE PRINCIPAL PARTS OF VERBS

The four basic forms of a verb are called the *principal parts* of the verb.

6a. The four principal parts of a verb are the *infinitive*, the *present participle*, the *past*, and the *past participle*.

The four principal parts of the verb *do*, for example, are *do* (infinitive), *doing* (present participle), *did* (past), and *done* (past participle).

6a

EXAMPLES   I **do** my homework after supper.
I am **doing** my homework now.
I **did** my homework this morning.
I have **done** my homework.

Notice that the forms of the present participle and past participle are used with helping verbs—*am, is, are, has, have, had,* etc.

Regular Verbs

6b. A verb that forms its past and past participle forms by adding *–d* or *–ed* to the first principal part (infinitive) is a *regular verb.*[1]

INFINITIVE	PRESENT PARTICIPLE	PAST	PAST PARTICIPLE
use	using	used	(have) used
suppose	supposing	supposed	(have) supposed
experience	experiencing	experienced	(have) experienced
risk	risking	risked	(have) risked
ask	asking	asked	(have) asked
dust	dusting	dusted	(have) dusted

You will observe that the present participle of many regular verbs ending in *–e* drops the *–e* before adding *–ing*.

The first principal part (infinitive) of a regular verb presents no usage problems. Errors do occur, however, in the choice of the past and the past participle forms. Do not carelessly omit the *–d* or *–ed* of the past or past participle of regular verbs like those listed above.

WRONG   Later Elbert ask the teacher.
RIGHT   Later Elbert **asked** the teacher.

WRONG   He is suppose to be there early.
RIGHT   He is **supposed** to be there early.

WRONG   We use to ride our bicycles.
RIGHT   We **used** to ride our bicycles.

[1] A few regular verbs have an alternate past form ending in *–t*; for example, the past form of *burn* may be *burned* or *burnt*.

You can avoid other mistakes with regular verbs by correcting faulty spelling and pronunciation of words like *attacked* and *drowned*.

WRONG   Athens was attackted by Sparta.
RIGHT   Athens was **attacked** by Sparta.

WRONG   Fortunately nobody had drownded.
RIGHT   Fortunately nobody had **drowned.**

● EXERCISE 1. *Oral Drill.* Read each sentence aloud, stressing the correct pronunciation of the italicized verb.

1. Bertha *used* to be shy.
2. Eugene *asked* a few questions.
3. Why has this *happened?*
4. Several were *drowned.*
5. Firemen *risked* their lives.
6. Are we *supposed* to help?
7. Donald is *experienced.*
8. The product is well *advertised.*
9. The satire *attacked* tyranny.
10. They were *surprised* to see us.
11. She *dusted* the table.
12. They *basked* in the sun.

Irregular Verbs

6c. **A verb that forms its past and past participle in some other way than a regular verb is an** *irregular verb.*

Irregular verbs form their past and past participle in various ways: by changing the vowel, by changing consonants, by adding *–en*, or by making no change at all.

INFINITIVE	PAST	PAST PARTICIPLE
begin	began	(have) begun
bring	brought	(have) brought
put	put	(have) put

6
b-c

IRREGULAR VERBS FREQUENTLY MISUSED

INFINITIVE	PRESENT PARTICIPLE	PAST	PAST PARTICIPLE
begin	beginning	began	(have) begun
blow	blowing	blew	(have) blown
break	breaking	broke	(have) broken
bring	bringing	brought	(have) brought
burst	bursting	burst	(have) burst
choose	choosing	chose	(have) chosen
come	coming	came	(have) come
do	doing	did	(have) done
drive	driving	drove	(have) driven
eat	eating	ate	(have) eaten
fall	falling	fell	(have) fallen
freeze	freezing	froze	(have) frozen
give	giving	gave	(have) given
go	going	went	(have) gone
know	knowing	knew	(have) known
ride	riding	rode	(have) ridden
ring	ringing	rang	(have) rung
run	running	ran	(have) run
see	seeing	saw	(have) seen
shrink	shrinking	shrank	(have) shrunk
speak	speaking	spoke	(have) spoken
steal	stealing	stole	(have) stolen
swim	swimming	swam	(have) swum
take	taking	took	(have) taken
throw	throwing	threw	(have) thrown
write	writing	wrote	(have) written

Since so many English verbs are regular, we naturally tend to make some irregular verbs follow the same pattern. However, you should avoid such forms as *throwed*, *knowed*, *bursted*, or *blowed*, which are regarded as substandard. If you are in doubt about the parts of a verb, consult your dictionary, which lists the principal parts of irregular verbs.

Remember that the present participle and past participle forms, when used as main verbs (simple predicates) in sentences, always require helping verbs. The present participle is used with forms of the verb *be: am taking, was throwing.* The past participle is used with *have, has,* or *had: have broken, had chosen;* or with a form of *be: was chosen.* When you memorize the principal parts of a verb, you need not worry about the present participle, which always ends in *–ing,* but you will help yourself if you always include *have* with the past participle. As you repeat principal parts, say, for example: *do, did, have done* or *see, saw, have seen.*

WRONG   I already seen that movie.

RIGHT   I **have** already seen that movie.

● EXERCISE 2.   Your teacher may dictate to you the first principal part of the irregular verbs listed on page 134. Study the list so that you can write from memory the other principal parts of each verb. Place *have* before the past participle.

● EXERCISE 3.   Number your paper 1–20. If the first principal part is given, change it to the past form. If the past form is given, change it to the past participle. Write *have* before the past participle form.

EXAMPLES   1. give
             1. *gave*
             2. wrote
             2. *have written*

1. do	6. know	11. choose	16. shrank
2. began	7. spoke	12. broke	17. ran
3. see	8. stole	13. drink	18. ring
4. rode	9. blew	14. drove	19. fell
5. went	10. bring	15. froze	20. swim

● EXERCISE 4.   Number 1–20. Choose the correct one of the two verbs in parentheses, and write it after the corresponding number on your paper. When your paper has been corrected, read each sentence aloud several times, stressing the correct verb.

1. Have you ever (saw, seen) the Grand Canyon?
2. Glowing in the darkness, the lantern fish had (came, come) to the surface.

3. I (drank, drunk) a cup of hot chocolate.
4. Has the nine o'clock bell already (rang, rung)?
5. The pressure of the water (bursted, burst) the pipes.
6. Dad (give, gave) me a lecture on the problems of the tobacco grower.
7. The clanking under the hood (began, begun) to grow louder.
8. Kathleen (did, done) all that she could to help me.
9. In a matter of seconds, the hot water had (froze, frozen).
10. No one has ever (rode, ridden) that colt before.
11. I have never (drove, driven) a car in town before.
12. Yesterday I (swam, swum) to the other side of the lake.
13. The sweater had (shrank, shrunk) when it was washed.
14. Has it (began, begun) to rain?
15. We (brung, brought) our lunches all last week.
16. He had (wrote, written) something in the sand.
17. Have they all (went, gone) swimming already?
18. For fourteen years, I (drank, drunk) a glass of milk every morning.
19. Suddenly the package (bursted, burst) open.
20. Has Mr. Crane actually (gave, given) us permission to go?

● EXERCISE 5.   Write two original sentences using correctly each verb that you missed in Exercise 4. Use the form of the verb that you missed. After your sentences have been checked for accuracy, read the sentences aloud until you feel that you have mastered the troublesome verbs.

● EXERCISE 6.   *Oral Drill.* Read each of the following sentences *aloud* three times, stressing the correct verbs.

1. He *asked* us to go with him.
2. How long *have* you *known* her?
3. They *have broken* the lock.
4. One balloon *burst.*
5. My uncle *came* to see us yesterday.
6. I *had begun* to worry.
7. I *saw* him yesterday.
8. Then the bell *rang.*
9. She *has written* the invitations.
10. He *brought* his first-aid kit.

● REVIEW EXERCISE A. Number your paper 1–50. Write the correct form (past or past participle) of the verb given at the beginning of each sentence.

1. *swim* Avery had —— in deep water before.
2. *break* The windshield was ——.
3. *run* Everyone —— as fast as he could.
4. *attack* Grasshoppers have —— the crops.
5. *eat* Has Bernard —— breakfast?
6. *write* Have you —— to your grandmother?
7. *bring* Anna —— a raincoat yesterday.
8. *give* After I explained, he —— me another chance.
9. *steal* A bear had —— into our tent.
10. *burst* The pile of brush —— into flames.
11. *drink* Emma sat down and —— her tea.
12. *use* When I was a child, I —— to dig tunnels.
13. *do* She —— her best yesterday.
14. *give* Father has —— us some suggestions.
15. *know* We have —— about the test for some time.
16. *risk* The policeman —— his life in last night's chase.
17. *ring* The bell —— an hour ago.
18. *run* Last year, Mr. Evans —— for mayor.
19. *break* The champion has —— the record.
20. *speak* Has anyone —— to you about me?
21. *drive* Have you —— one of the new cars?
22. *choose* Have they —— a leader?
23. *fall* You might have —— over the edge.
24. *go* He has —— after groceries.
25. *speak* The principal has —— to me about it.
26. *ride* That dude has never —— a horse.
27. *begin* It has —— to clear in the north.
28. *come* I noticed that he —— in late this morning.
29. *ring* Has the bell ——?
30. *happen* Has this —— before?
31. *see* Last night I —— him at the drugstore.
32. *take* Since I had —— my rifle along, we looked for deer as we hiked through the woods.
33. *fall* A child has —— from the ledge.
34. *climb* Has he —— the ladder of fame?

35. *go*   I was sure Suellen had —— riding.
36. *freeze* Many of the peach trees have —— during the cold weather.
37. *throw*   I should have —— to second base.
38. *freeze* Had the lake ever —— so early before?
39. *throw*   I —— his letters away when he left.
40. *write*   Janet will have —— me by then.
41. *see*   I have —— the President in person.
42. *ask*   She —— for a dog for her birthday last year.
43. *swim*   Have you ever —— here before?
44. *swim*   I —— here last summer.
45. *shrink* Had that material —— in the washing?
46. *choose* By the end of next week, we will have —— our class officers.
47. *blow*   Yesterday the wind —— with gale force.
48. *take*   I haven't —— the test yet.
49. *write*   He had —— down the wrong address.
50. *drown*   The number of people who —— last summer is alarmingly high.

● REVIEW EXERCISE B. Number your paper 1–20. Read each of the following sentences aloud. If a sentence is correct, write *C* after the proper number. If the form of a verb is wrong, write the correct verb form after the appropriate number.

1. The ball that begun the game was thrown out onto the playing field by the President of the United States.
2. The swimmer ask how far she had swum.
3. When the bag burst, all the candy inside fell to the floor.
4. Everyone feared that the man had drownded, but three days later he appeared in a neighboring town.
5. After the golfer had sunk his last putt, everyone ran up to congratulate him on his victory.
6. The fort was attackted at a time when it was least prepared to defend itself.
7. Both rain and hail fell before the football game, so that the players seemed to be slipping rather than running up the field.

8. Someone drunk the bottle of Coke I was saving.
9. The women were so drenched during the sudden storm that their knit dresses shrank.
10. When the bottle was broke, a message from a shipwrecked crew was found inside.
11. Somerset Maugham, a twentieth-century novelist, has often wrote about his own experiences.
12. Harpies were mythical winged creatures who were suppose to have the bodies of birds and the faces of women.
13. According to legend, many knights had risk their lives while they were searching for the Holy Grail, the cup which was used at the Last Supper.
14. After Satan in *Paradise Lost* had cautiously swum, crawled, and flew through Chaos, he reached the ladder extending from Heaven to Earth.
15. Beowulf drunk deeply from the mead cup after defeating Grendel.
16. Roland had not rode far before he came across an old man who warned him not to seek the Dark Tower.
17. When the death bell rung for her lover, Barbara Allan knew that it was also ringing for her.
18. The Green Knight, who come dressed entirely in green, challenged one of King Arthur's men. "I dare you to cut off my head with an ax."
19. According to the ancients, Atlantis, an island that supposedly lay west of the Pillars of Hercules, had sunk to the bottom of the ocean.
20. Romeo had chose to die rather than live without Juliet.

Tense

We speak of the time expressed by a verb as the *tense* of the verb. Every verb has six tenses: the *present tense*, the *past tense*, the *future tense*, the *present perfect tense*, the *past perfect tense*, and the *future perfect tense*. The tenses are formed from the principal parts.

Study the list of the six tense forms of *fly* on the next page. Giving all the forms of a verb in this way is called *conjugating* the verb; the list is called a *conjugation*.

CONJUGATION OF <u>FLY</u>

PRESENT TENSE

Singular	*Plural*
I fly	we fly
you fly	you fly
he flies	they fly

PAST TENSE

Singular	*Plural*
I flew	we flew
you flew	you flew
he flew	they flew

FUTURE TENSE

Singular	*Plural*
I will (shall) fly	we will (shall) fly
you will fly	you will fly
he will fly	they will fly

PRESENT PERFECT TENSE

Singular	*Plural*
I have flown	we have flown
you have flown	you have flown
he has flown	they have flown

PAST PERFECT TENSE

Singular	*Plural*
I had flown	we had flown
you had flown	you had flown
he had flown	they had flown

FUTURE PERFECT TENSE

Singular	*Plural*
I will (shall) have flown	we will (shall) have flown
you will have flown	you will have flown
he will have flown	they will have flown

Each of the six tenses has an additional form called the *progressive form*, which expresses continuing action. It consists of a form of the verb *be* plus the present participle of the verb. The progressive forms of *fly* follow.

Present Progressive   am, are, is flying
Past Progressive   was, were flying
Future Progressive   will (shall) be flying
Present Perfect Progressive   has, have been flying
Past Perfect Progressive   had been flying
Future Perfect Progressive   will (shall) have been flying

Remember: the progressive is not a separate tense but an additional form of each of the six tenses in the conjugation.

Consistency of Tense

6d. **Do not change needlessly from one tense to another.**

When writing about events in the past, choose verbs in the past tense. Do not suddenly shift, without reason, to the present. Similarly, if action takes place in the present, do not use verbs in the past tense unnecessarily.

WRONG   Chris grabbed his coat and rushes out. [The verb *grabbed* is past tense; *rushes* is present tense.]

RIGHT   Chris **grabbed** his coat and **rushed** out. [Both *grabbed* and *rushed* are in the past tense.]

WRONG   When Mrs. Ford cried, she wins the argument. [*Cried* is past tense, and *wins* is present.]

RIGHT   When Mrs. Ford **cries,** she **wins** the argument. [The verbs are both in the present tense.]

or   When Mrs. Ford **cried,** she **won** the argument. [Both verbs are in the past tense.]

The perfect tenses are mainly used in expressing action that has been completed, or finished. When one thing happened before something else, the perfect tense form shows the relation.

WRONG   I immediately felt sorry that I spoke so harshly. [Since *felt* is past tense and the speaking preceded it, the verb should be *had spoken*, not *spoke*.]

RIGHT   I immediately felt sorry that I **had spoken** so harshly.

6d

● EXERCISE 7. Rewrite the following paragraph, eliminating the needless changes of tense. First decide whether the paragraph should be told in the present or past tense. Then you will need to change the tense of many of the verbs to achieve consistency.

It all started as soon as I came home from school. I am in my room, and I have planned to study for two hours. It was about five o'clock. To my surprise, Nick Palmer decided to drop by. He dashes into the house, slams the door behind him, and yells for me. What he wanted is a hunting companion. He has seen a flock of ducks on Dawson's pond. Reaching for my gun, I become excited about racing out to the pond. Imagine our dismay when we arrived and find that Mr. Dawson has put out a dozen decoys. He is hoping to lure some real ducks within shooting range.

ACTIVE AND PASSIVE VOICE

A verb is said to be in the *active* voice when it expresses an action performed by its subject. A verb is in the *passive* voice when the action it expresses is performed *upon* its subject.

ACTIVE VOICE   The manager hired us. [The subject performs the action.]

PASSIVE VOICE   We were hired by the manager. [The subject receives the action.]

Only transitive verbs—those that can take objects—can be used in the passive voice. Compare the subjects of the following related sentences:

ACTIVE   The judge^s carefully instructed the jury.^o

PASSIVE   The jury^s was carefully instructed by the judge.

Notice that the object of the active sentence has become the subject of the passive one. The subject of the active sentence is expressed in the passive sentence only in a prepositional phrase. In fact, it can be omitted from the passive sentence altogether.

PASSIVE The jury was carefully instructed.

The verb in a passive sentence is always a verb phrase that includes a form of the verb *be* and the past participle of the main verb. If other helping verbs appear in the active sentence, they must also be included in the passive. Here are some more examples of related active and passive sentences:

ACTIVE Charles Dickens **wrote** *David Copperfield*.

PASSIVE *David Copperfield* **was written** by Charles Dickens.

ACTIVE Someone **has stolen** my watch.

PASSIVE My watch **has been stolen**.

The passive voice puts the emphasis on the person or thing receiving the action rather than upon the one performing it. It is often used in situations in which the speaker does not know or does not wish to say who performed the action (as in the last example above). Although useful for these purposes, the passive construction can easily be overused. A succession of passive sentences has a weak and awkward sound and should be avoided.

● EXERCISE 8. Number from 1–10. After the appropriate number, indicate whether each of the following sentences is active or passive.

1. The whole club elects the chairman.
2. A terrible accident has been prevented by George's quick thinking.
3. The leading role was played brilliantly by an understudy.
4. The book was unfavorably reviewed by the critics.
5. A newsboy recognized the public enemy.
6. At first, the prophet's advice was ignored.
7. The hostess usually invites the guests.

8. Children of many different countries play that game.
9. The rumors of a revolution were denied by the dictator.
10. He was then quickly driven to the airport by his bodyguard.

● EXERCISE 9.   Change the active verbs in the sentences in Exercise 8 to passives, and the passive verbs to active ones.

EXAMPLE   1. Anne wrote the skit.

1. *The skit was written by Anne.*

SPECIAL PROBLEMS WITH VERBS

Lie and Lay

The verb *lie* means "to rest" or "to recline," "to remain in a lying position." Its principal parts are *lie, lying, lay, (have) lain*. The verb *lie* never takes an object.

The verb *lay* means "to put" or "to place (something)." Its principal parts are *lay, laying, laid, (have) laid*. These forms may have objects (receivers of the action).

INFINITIVE	PRESENT PARTICIPLE	PAST	PAST PARTICIPLE
lie (to rest)	lying	lay	(have) lain
lay (to put)	laying	laid	(have) laid

Study these examples of the use of the verb *lie*, meaning "to rest" or "to recline."

Occasionally I **lie** down.
The letter is **lying** on the desk.
Yesterday Bennett **lay** on the sand.
How long have you **lain** here?

Notice how the following examples of the use of the verb *lay* differ from those above. In the sentences below, each verb means "to put" or "to place (something)."

Lay the boards down.
I was **laying** the letter on the desk.
Yesterday Bennett **laid** these towels on the sand.
Have you **laid** your work aside?

● EXERCISE 10. *Oral Drill*. Read each of the following sentences aloud several times. In the light of the information just given, be able to explain why the verb is correct.

1. I foolishly *laid* the matches near the open fire.
2. Yesterday I *lay* too long in the hot sun.
3. A lighted cigar *was lying* in the ash tray.
4. Father *was laying* the cigars on the table.
5. Diane *laid* the cushion on the floor.
6. The cushion *lay* there while she dusted the chair.
7. The rake and hoe *have lain* in the yard for days.
8. The men *have laid* the foundations.
9. His interests *lie* elsewhere.
10. Yesterday I *laid* the scissors on the machine, and they are probably *lying* there now.

● EXERCISE 11. After numbering 1–10, write the correct form of the proper verb (*lie—lay*) for each of these sentences. Make a perfect score by referring to the forms on page 144 if necessary.

1. An old mine used to —— at the foot of the mountain.
2. He —— his glasses aside and frowned.
3. I shall —— down for a few minutes.
4. She had —— on the divan before.
5. The baby was still —— quietly in his cradle.
6. The woman —— the baby in his cradle an hour ago.
7. Is the newspaper —— in the rain?
8. No, I have —— the paper near the fire to dry.
9. Last summer my dog often —— in his doghouse.
10. —— down, Snoopy.

● EXERCISE 12. Complete the explanation of the correct usage of *lie* and *lay* by filling in the blanks below with the right form of each verb. Use a separate sheet of paper, and number your answers correctly.

The verb (1) —— means "to put" or "to place (something)." The present participle of *lay* is (2) ——. The past and the past participle have the same form, which is (3) ——. The infinitive form is (4) ——.

The verb (5) —— means "to rest" or "to recline." The present participle of *lie* is (6) ——. The past form of *lie* is (7) ——, and the past participle is (8) ——.

The verb (9) ——, with all of its forms, never has an object; however, the forms of (10) —— may have objects.

Sit and Set

The verb *sit* means "to rest in an upright, sitting position." The principal parts of *sit* are *sit*, *sitting*, *sat*, (*have*) *sat*.

The verb *set* means "to put," "to place (something)." The principal parts of *set* are *set*, *setting*, *set*, (*have*) *set*.

INFINITIVE	PRESENT PARTICIPLE	PAST	PAST PARTICIPLE
sit (to rest)	sitting	sat	(have) sat
set (to put)	setting	set	(have) set

Study the following examples:

Sit down.   Vases sit on the shelf.
Set that down.   I set them on the shelf.

You will have little difficulty using these verbs correctly if you will remember two facts about them: (1) Like *lie*, the verb *sit* means "to be in a certain position." It almost never has an object. (2) Like *lay*, the verb *set* means "to put (something)." It may take an object. *Set* does not change to form the past or the past participle. Whenever you mean "to place" or "to put," use *set*.[1]

● EXERCISE 13. *Oral Drill.* Read the sentences below aloud several times. Think of the *meaning* of the verbs, and do not go on to other exercises until you feel that you know the right uses of *sit* and *set*.

1. I usually *sit* close to the stove.
2. I *set* the chair close to the wall.
3. Faye *was sitting* beside Keith.

[1] There are several uses of the verb *set* which do not mean "to put" or "to place"; for example: "The sun *sets*," "Hens *set* on eggs," "*set* one's watch," "*set* a speed record," "*set* out to do something."

4. Faye *was setting* the canned goods on the shelf.
5. Don't just *sit* there; *set* the dishes in the sink.
6. The grapes *are sitting* on the coffee table.
7. Where *was* he *setting* it?
8. I *have* never *sat* in this rocker before.
9. I *have* never *set* aside enough money for a trip.
10. Charles *sat* down and *set* the picture on the easel.

● EXERCISE 14.   Number 1–10 on your paper. Fill the blanks in the following sentences with a correct form of *sit* or *set*, whichever is required by the meaning.

1. Have you —— the flowers in the sunshine?
2. Will Mr. Davis —— at the head of the table?
3. I was —— on the steps.
4. I was —— the lamp beside the sofa.
5. Father has been —— out some tomato plants.
6. Yesterday Katherine —— near James.
7. The excited children will not —— still.
8. His old car is still —— in the garage.
9. We had —— there an hour.
10. Has Vernon —— in the front row all year?

Rise and Raise

The verb *rise* means "to go in an upward direction." Its principal parts are *rise, rising, rose, (have) risen*. Like *lie* the verb *rise* never has an object.

The verb *raise* means "to move something in an upward direction." Its principal parts are *raise, raising, raised, (have) raised*. Like *lay* and *set, raise* may take an object.

INFINITIVE	PRESENT PARTICIPLE	PAST	PAST PARTICIPLE
rise (to go up)	rising	rose	(have) risen
raise (to move something up)	raising	raised	(have) raised

You **should rise** early.
Who **will raise** the flag?
Prices **rose**.
Grocers **raised** prices.

● EXERCISE 15.   *Oral Drill.* Repeat each of the following sentences aloud three times, stressing the italicized verbs and thinking of the *meaning* of the sentence.

1. The sun *has* already *risen.*
2. I *raised* my hand.
3. The river *rises* in the spring.
4. My family *rises* early.
5. We *raise* our voices.
6. The man *rose* from his chair.
7. The man *raised* his eyebrow.
8. By noon the fog had *risen.*
9. When should the flag be *raised?*

● EXERCISE 16.   Number 1–10, and write the correct form of *rise* or *raise* for each of the following blanks.

1. The prisoner will —— and face the jury.
2. Last week, the committee —— no objections.
3. When will the moon ——?
4. Has the legislature —— taxes?
5. The biscuits have ——.
6. The curtain will —— at eight thirty.
7. Todd will —— the curtain.
8. The price of coffee has —— steadily.
9. When the President entered the room, all the reporters ——.
10. Mr. Henly had —— to speak.

● REVIEW EXERCISE C.   Correctly use each of the following as verbs in a sentence.

1. rise	5. was lying	9. has been rising
2. raised	6. was laying	10. had lain
3. have sat	7. will sit	
4. have set	8. has been setting	

● REVIEW EXERCISE D.   *Oral Drill.* Answer the following questions in complete sentences by choosing correct verb forms.

1. Do you lie or lay down for a nap?
2. Does the temperature rise or raise?

3. Have the guests sat or set down?
4. Have they lain or laid the foundation for the building?
5. Had the team's morale risen or raised?
6. Has a picture been sitting or setting on the table?
7. Was the rug lying or laying near the fire?
8. Was Wally lying or laying the rug near the fire?

● REVIEW EXERCISE E. Number your paper 1–20. Choose the correct verb in parentheses, and write it after the proper number.

1. (Lie, Lay) the magazine on the coffee table.
2. The magazine is (lying, laying) on the coffee table.
3. Scott (sat, set) the birdcage in the backyard.
4. The cage (sits, sets) in the backyard.
5. Sam (rose, raised) from his chair and went to the door.
6. The kite was swiftly (rising, raising) skyward.
7. He (lay, laid) on the bank and looked at the stars.
8. Has Mother (lain, laid) down yet?
9. The paper is (lying, laying) on the sidewalk.
10. The river is (rising, raising) steadily.
11. We were (sitting, setting) on a large rock.
12. A hand-painted vase (sits, sets) on the mantelpiece.
13. She had already (lain, laid) the cloth on the table.
14. (Sit, Set) down and talk for a while.
15. I (lay, laid) the keys there a few minutes ago.
16. The main pipes (lay, laid) under the floor.
17. A rope was (lying, laying) near the saddle.
18. The sun is (rising, raising) now.
19. Had you (sat, set) on his hat?
20. (Lying, Laying) in the top drawer was the necklace.

● REVIEW EXERCISE F. Correctly use each of the following verbs in brief sentences. Supply appropriate helping verbs if needed.

1. set	6. drunk	11. chose	16. rode
2. laid	7. shrank	12. begun	17. rang
3. rose	8. raised	13. went	18. fell
4. give	9. lying	14. seen	19. lain
5. done	10. laying	15. wrote	20. burst

● Review exercise G.   Number your paper 1–25. After
the number of the corresponding sentence, write the correct
form of the verb given at the beginning of the sentence.
In some cases you will have to add *have, has,* or *had.*

1. *rise, raise*   When the ship came within firing range, a pirate
    flag was ——.

2. *ask*   The telephone interviewer —— the people she
    called who their favorite comedian was.

3. *lie, lay*   The men —— aside all personal feelings and
    tried to find a solution to their common problem.

4. *take*   The editor had —— all responsibility for the
    story in the newspaper.

5. *read*   I was halfway through the assignment before I
    realized that I —— it the day before.

6. *swim*   While we were lowering sail, a group of native
    boys —— out to our boat.

7. *choose*   He —— his words carefully when he spoke to
    the chairman.

8. *suppose*   The captured sailor —— that the captain of the
    pirates would make him walk the plank.

9. *lie, lay*   Very tired, he —— on the bank of the river and
    waited for his friends.

10. *see*   How could the thief be so sure that no one ——
    him?

11. *know*   My friend —— that he had been tricked after
    he had waited thirty minutes for the rest of the
    guests to arrive.

12. *begin*   Men have —— to explore the polar regions ex-
    tensively.

13. *sit, set*   After the children had —— still for fifteen
    minutes, they began to squirm.

14. *choose*   The employer has —— his men carefully and has
    assigned them to appropriate jobs.

15. *burst*   The monkeys —— out of their cages and headed
    for the forest.

16. *take*   As the country began to look more and more
    unfamiliar, we began to sense that we —— a
    wrong turn miles before.

17. *use*   Until the medical supplies arrived, the men —— their shirts for bandages.

18. *rise, raise* Some writers of ghost tales like to create people who have —— from the dead.

19. *break*   Records in track and field are —— every year.

20. *shrink*   Either I have grown a lot since last spring, or else this suit has ——.

21. *write*   Did you know that *Frankenstein* was —— by a woman?

22. *lie, lay*   For centuries minerals and other natural resources on the ocean's floor have —— untouched by man.

23. *come*   As usual, Jerry —— rushing up to me and slapped me hard on the back.

24. *sink*   The *Merrimack* had —— several ships before she was met by the *Monitor*, the Union's vessel.

25. *give*   The crazed and fiendish hunter —— the man whom he intended to capture a day's head start.

● REVIEW EXERCISE H.   Number 1–25 in a column on your paper. Read each of the following sentences aloud, and determine whether the verbs are correct or incorrect. If the sentence is correct, write a plus sign (+) after the corresponding number. If a verb in a sentence is wrong, write a zero (0) after the proper number. Be prepared to give the correct verb form for each sentence that you label 0. Some sentences may have more then one incorrect verb.

1. I use to want a pet monkey all my own. 2. About a year ago, I set in the park for hours and watch the antics of the caged monkeys. 3. Since I've took care of Corky, though, I haven't had the slightest desire to have a monkey.

4. Alex, my friend who owns the monkey, ask me to keep Corky for six hours. 5. Since I was very pleased about keeping a real monkey all afternoon, Alex brung Corky over early one Saturday. 6. About one o'clock, after Alex had went on his way, I made friends with the monkey. 7. For a while we chose to play in the yard.

8. The trouble began when I went into the house to lie down for a nap. 9. As soon as Corky saw me laying on the bed,

he started to think of mischief. 10. I seen that he was not ready to settle down. 11. Suddenly he jump upon a chair, raised his arms, grabbed the pictures on the wall, and began to throw them at me. 12. I sat up and warned Corky to behave. 13. After rising from my bed, I tied the scoundrel to the leg of the bed.

14. After I had lain down again, I busted out laughing at his angry chattering. 15. No harm had been done; none of the picture frames were broken. 16. Soon, however, Corky thought of a new way to annoy me; his chain give him enough freedom to climb upon the high bedstead. 17. After sitting there quietly for an instant, he jump and hard, right onto the middle of my stomach. 18. I howled, "You've went too far, Corky!" 19. Defiantly putting his hands over his ears, Corky begun to bounce up and down on the bed as though celebrating a major victory.

20. After he had attack me, I no longer wanted him around. 21. Picking him up, I set him outside on the back porch. 22. Then I gave him some peanuts and went back to lie down. 23. I had to bribe him because I knowed that I couldn't teach him any manners.

24. When Alex finally come for Corky, I was never so happy to get rid of a guest. 25. After what he done, I won't ever invite that monkey—or any other monkey—to my house again.

The Correct Use of Pronouns

Nominative and Objective Uses

Nouns and pronouns have *case*. The case of a noun or pronoun depends upon the word's use in the sentence. In English, there are three cases: *nominative*, *objective*, and *possessive*.

Choosing the correct case form for a noun is no problem, since the form remains the same in the nominative and objective cases.

EXAMPLE   The **girl** [nominative] blamed another **girl** [objective].

Only in the possessive case does a noun change its form, usually by adding an apostrophe and an *s*.

EXAMPLE   One **girl's** handbag matched another **girl's** shoes.

Personal pronouns, however, have various case forms. In the following sentence, for example, the pronouns in bold-faced type all refer to the same person. They have three different forms because of their different uses.

EXAMPLE   **I** [nominative] do not think that **my** [possessive] big brother understands **me** [objective].

You can avoid using pronouns incorrectly by learning the case forms of pronouns and how they are used in sentences.

THE CASE FORMS OF PERSONAL PRONOUNS

Study the following list of personal pronouns, noticing the changes in form.

PERSONAL PRONOUNS

NOMINATIVE CASE	OBJECTIVE CASE	POSSESSIVE CASE
Singular		
I	me	my, mine
you	you	your, yours
he, she, it	him, her, it	his, her, hers, its
Plural		
we	us	our, ours
you	you	your, yours
they	them	their, theirs

As you see, *you* and *it* have the same form in the nominative and the objective case. You may therefore ignore them in your study of correct pronoun usage. Only the following pronouns have different nominative and objective forms. Memorize both lists.

NOMINATIVE CASE	OBJECTIVE CASE
I	me
he	him
she	her
we	us
they	them

● EXERCISE 1.   Number your paper 1–10. If the pronoun is in the nominative case, write the corresponding objective case pronoun; if it is in the objective case, write the corresponding nominative case pronoun.

1. they
2. him
3. me
4. we
5. she
6. he
7. I
8. them
9. us
10. her

THE NOMINATIVE CASE

7a. The subject of a verb is in the nominative case.

EXAMPLES He and I performed an experiment.
We students are planning a hobo party.
She was delighted that they came.

In the first sentence, *He* and *I* are subjects of the verb *performed.* In the second, *We* is the subject of *are planning.* In the third, *She* is the subject of *was delighted; they* is the subject of *came,* the verb in the subordinate clause.

Most errors in the use of pronouns as subjects are made when the subject is compound, particularly when both parts of the compound subject are pronouns.

RIGHT He and they passed the test.

You can often avoid using the incorrect form by trying each pronoun separately with the verb. Of course you would never say *Him passed the test* or *Them passed the test.*

He passed the test. They passed the test.
He and they passed the test.

Sometimes a pronoun will have a noun appositive.[1]

We students have volunteered to count ballots.

You can arrive at the correct form for the pronoun in such sentences by reading the sentence without the noun appositive: *We have volunteered to count ballots.*

Sometimes the pronouns *we* and *they* sound awkward when used as parts of a compound subject. In such instances, it is often advisable to restate the sentence.

AWKWARD We and they hope to sit together at the game.
BETTER We hope to sit with them at the game.

● EXERCISE 2. *Oral Drill.* Read each sentence aloud, stressing the correct italicized pronouns.

[1] For the definition of an appositive, see page 90.

7a

1. *We* boys built a pyramid of snowballs.
2. *She* and her brother are planning a trip to the mountains.
3. Why do you and *she* quarrel?
4. May *he* and *I* be partners?
5. Can you or *he* do twenty-five push-ups?
6. Where are Willy and *they?*
7. My brother and *I* knew that he would crash the party.
8. *We* girls learned that Ben and *she* were engaged.
9. Both *he* and *she* understood that *we* students needed to rest.
10. It was decided that *he* and *I* had tied.

● EXERCISE 3.   Number 1–10 on your paper. List the pronouns that are used as subjects in the following sentences. Do not include *you.*

1. In yesterday's game, we halfbacks ran effective interference.
2. Neither he nor Al has promised anything.
3. I hope that you and I can go to camp this summer.
4. Why did you and she refuse our invitation?
5. We think that you and they will enjoy the play.
6. Either you or I must take Pat to the zoo tomorrow.
7. Do you know why she and I were late?
8. We two have been neighbors since childhood.
9. Both Bob and he were tardy.
10. Both he and I enjoyed preparing the report.

● EXERCISE 4.   Use the following as subjects in sentences of your own.

1. he and I
2. Harvey and we
3. we amateurs
4. you and I
5. Jane and he

6. her parents and she
7. Mary, Nell, and they
8. she and my best friend
9. they and their escorts
10. you girls and we boys

7b. A predicate nominative is in the nominative case.

A predicate nominative is a noun or pronoun that follows a linking verb and explains or identifies the subject of the sentence (see pages 57–58). A pronoun used as a predicate nominative always follows a form of the verb *be* or verb phrases ending in *be* or *been*.

EXAMPLES   This is **he.**
             It may be **she.**
             It should have been **they.**

◆ USAGE NOTE   Listening to conversations, you will often hear educated people say, "It's me." Although *I*, not *me*, is the nominative case pronoun, the usage of educated people has made *It's me* acceptable English. Either *It's me* or *It's I* is correct. Similar expressions such as *That's him* or *Could it have been her?* (in which the rule calls for *he* and *she*) may be considered as acceptable in speaking, but you should avoid them in writing.

As you do the following exercises, follow the rule for written English: *A predicate nominative is in the nominative case.*

● EXERCISE 5.   Number 1–10 on your paper. Complete the following sentences by adding pronouns in the nominative case used as predicate nominatives. Write each pronoun after the corresponding number on your paper. Don't use *you* or *it;* use a variety of pronouns.

1. This is ———.
2. Are you ———?
3. That was ———.
4. Those are ———.
5. Can it be ———?
6. It can't be ———.
7. It is ———.
8. It might be ———.
9. Was that ———?
10. I knew it was ———.

THE OBJECTIVE CASE

The following pronouns are in the objective case:

me	us
him, her	them

These pronouns are used as objects: direct objects, indirect objects, objects of prepositions. (Review pages 59, 61, and 70.)

7b

7c. The direct object of a verb is in the objective case.

RIGHT   Clyde thanked **her**. [*Clyde* is the subject of the verb *thanked*. Clyde thanked *whom?* The answer is *her*, which is the direct object of *thanked*.]

WRONG Dad's story surprised Miles and I. [*I* is a nominative case pronoun and should not be used as direct object of the verb.]

RIGHT   Dad's story surprised Miles and **me**.

When the object is compound, try each pronoun object separately as you learned to do with compound subjects. "Dad's story surprised I" is obviously incorrect. Hence, "Dad's story surprised Miles and I" is also wrong.

WRONG He helped we boys with our homework.

RIGHT   He helped **us** boys with our homework.

● EXERCISE 6. *Oral Drill*. Recite each of the following sentences aloud, stressing the correct italicized pronouns. After you become familiar with the right sound of pronouns, your ear will tell you which pronoun is correct.

1. The postman disappointed Bill and *me*.
2. Ethel did not invite *us* boys.
3. The magician's tricks amazed their teacher and *them*.
4. Van often imitates Caroline and *her*.
5. Won't you believe *us* girls?
6. Have you seen *her* or *him* lately?
7. A lost child was following *her* and *me*.
8. Did Mr. Cass take Willis and *them* to the banquet?
9. Julia said that she recognized *him* and *me* at once.
10. Did you call *them* or *us?*

● EXERCISE 7. Number 1–10 on your paper. Supply appropriate pronouns for the blanks in these sentences. Use a variety of pronouns. (Do not use *you* or *it*.) After you have checked the exercise, read each sentence aloud.

1. Fog enveloped Allen and ——.
2. Will you oppose —— or ——?
3. Johnny loves both —— and ——.
4. Can't you trust Aline and ——?

5. Aline and —— you cannot trust!
6. I found Nancy and —— hard at work.
7. We watched Clay and ——.
8. Greg took Janet and —— to the game.
9. Now he needs you and —— more than ever.
10. That dress fits both Hilda and ——.

7d. The indirect object of the verb is in the objective case.

As you have already learned, an indirect object tells *to whom* or *for whom* something is done. (See pages 61–62.) Pronouns used as indirect objects are in the objective case: *me, him, her, us, them.*

EXAMPLES   The teacher paid **her** a compliment.
Polly sent **me** some photographs.

● EXERCISE 8.   *Oral Drill.* Recite each of the following sentences aloud, stressing the correct italicized pronouns.

1. Nora knitted Roy and *me* a sweater.
2. Show Ruth and *her* your ring.
3. They will bring you and *him* some pamphlets.
4. Will you please fix Tim and *me* some lunch?
5. Mrs. Carter handed *him* and *her* questionnaires.
6. Our parents gave *us* boys permission to go.
7. The principal told *him* and *me* the news.
8. Did Howard buy *him* and *her* what I suggested?
9. Send Bob and *me* a postcard from New York.
10. Tell Jack and *me* what you told your parents and *them*.

● REVIEW EXERCISE A.   Number 1–25. Write after the proper number the correct pronoun in parentheses. Be prepared to give the use of each pronoun in the sentence.

1. Where have you and (she, her) been?
2. (He, Him) and (I, me) have been to the fair.
3. (We, Us) boys spent hours looking at free displays.
4. One of the guides showed (we, us) boys the telephone room.
5. He told Angus and (I, me) about the unusual telephones.
6. You and (she, her) can't guess what happened.

7
c-d

7. After (we, us) boys had said a few words into a telephone, our own voices came back over the wire.

8. This really surprised (he, him) and (I, me).

9. I heard my own voice say, "Jay Jones? Oh, this is (he, him)."

10. Angus heard his voice boomerang, "(She, Her) and (they, them) aren't here just now. Will you leave (they, them) and (she, her) a message?"

11. Angus and (I, me) then found another free display.

12. A girl named Sarah showed Angus and (I, me) all kinds of candies.

13. (She, Her) and her sister were advertising powdered sugar.

14. We asked Sarah and (she, her) for a sample of their candy.

15. Then they gave (we, us) boys two large sacks full of fudge.

16. (They, Them) and the other people at the fair seemed to enjoy their work.

17. Have you and (she, her) ever seen their "House of Magic"?

18. (Him, He) and (I, me) were horrified by the severed head of Charles I.

19. Of course, (they, them) and (we, us) knew that it was only a piece of wax.

20. After all, as we have told you and (she, her), we were in the "House of Magic."

21. A clown and his dwarf singled out (we, us) boys to tease.

22. Seeing my white sweater, the clown and (he, him) scooted over to me.

23. (He, Him) and his dwarf kept waving very big fountain pens in the air.

24. When they squirted black ink all over my white sweater, you can imagine how worried Angus and (I, me) were.

25. In a matter of seconds, however, (we, us) boys watched the magic ink disappear before our eyes.

7e. The object of a preposition is in the objective case.

A prepositional phrase begins with a preposition (see the list on page 25) and ends with a noun or pronoun. The final word in a prepositional phrase is the *object of the preposition* that begins the phrase. When the object of a preposition is a pronoun, you must be careful to use the objective case. The words in bold-faced type below are objects of prepositions.

to me	before **her**	for **them**
by **him**	beyond **us**	

Errors in usage often occur when the object of a preposition is compound. Again, you can usually tell the correct pronouns by trying each one separately in the prepositional phrase.

EXAMPLES   toward Rachel and **her**   with **you** and **them**
except Suzanne and **us**   of Henry and **him**

● EXERCISE 9.   *Oral Drill.* Read each of the following sentences aloud, stressing the italicized words.

1. *Beside* Jess and *me* sat Mr. Ellis.
2. I wrote notes *to* his brother and *him*.
3. The boldness *of* Mark and *them* startled Lee.
4. *Between* you and *me*, she is worried about *him*.
5. Dr. Williams rode in the car *in front of us* students.
6. She was very rude *to them* and *me*.
7. The man was walking *toward* Dale and *her*.
8. With the help *of* Chester and *him*, we can soon finish.
9. Discuss your plans *with her* and *them*.
10. Did you sit *near him* and *her* in assembly?

● EXERCISE 10.   Number 1–10 on your paper. If the sentence is correct, write *C*. If there are pronoun errors, write the prepositional phrase, correcting the pronoun forms.

EXAMPLES   1. Did you go with Marty and them?
           1. *C*

          2. I sent copies of the report to both Mac and she.
           2. *to both Mac and her*

1. Nobody but Julie and me volunteered.
2. Everyone slept except Barry and I.
3. Like he and us, she has the flu.

7e

4. I have received no word from Jack or she.
5. Mr. Welch pointed toward we boys.
6. In front of Betty and him stood Ella.
7. Shall we eat supper with Karen and them?
8. Teddy, like you and I, dislikes tea.
9. In addition to her and me, Oscar will serve on the committee.
10. Between you and I, Sylvia cannot keep a secret.

◆ USAGE NOTE   Pronouns used in apposition are in the same case as the word to which they refer.

EXAMPLES   The committee members, **he, she,** and **I,** made our report. [Since *members* is the subject of the sentence, the pronouns in apposition with it (*he, she, I*) must be in the nominative case.]

The report was made by the committee members, **him, her,** and me. [Since *members* is the object of the preposition *by*, the appositives must be in the objective case.]

The master of ceremonies introduced the cocaptains, Bill and **me.** [Since *cocaptains* is the direct object of *introduced*, the pronoun *me*, which is in apposition to *cocaptains*, must be in the objective case.]

● REVIEW EXERCISE B.   Number your paper 1–18. Choose the correct pronoun in parentheses, and write it after the proper number. Two sentences have two sets of parentheses.

1. What do you and (he, him) know about it?
2. I don't think it was (they, them).
3. Was it Ellen or (she, her) that won the game?
4. No one told Fred and (I, me) about the test.
5. You must have been talking to Bob and (he, him).
6. He hired (we, us) boys for the job.
7. I planned to go to the game with Cindy and (she, her).
8. (He, Him) and (I, me) did our homework together.
9. When are you expecting your family and (they, them)?
10. Miss Kay said that (we, us) students were not polite.
11. Dick and (I, me) were asked to prepare a report.
12. The winner was probably George or (he, him).
13. Is the gift for Jean or (she, her)?

14. I don't know Howard and (he, him) very well.
15. If you and (she, her) are on time, we'll be surprised.
16. He would not believe either the teacher or (we, us) students.
17. You asked (he, him) and (I, me) for our opinion.
18. This argument is strictly between Joe and (I, me).

SPECIAL PRONOUN PROBLEMS

There are two kinds of problems you will frequently run across. One is the choice between *who* and *whom;* the other is which pronoun to use in an incomplete construction.

Who and Whom

The pronoun *who* also has different forms in the nominative and the objective cases. *Who* is the nominative form; the objective form is *whom*. Similarly, *whoever* is nominative; *whomever* is objective.

◆ USAGE NOTE   In spoken English, the use of *whom* is becoming less common. In fact, when you are speaking, you may correctly begin any question with *who* regardless of the grammar of the sentence.

In written English, however, you should distinguish between *who* and *whom*. *Who* is used as subject or predicate nominative, and *whom* is used as an object.

Often *who* or *whom* will appear in subordinate clauses—in adjective clauses or noun clauses.

7f. The use of *who* or *whom* in a subordinate clause is determined by the pronoun's function in the clause.

When you are deciding whether to use *who* or *whom* in a subordinate clause, follow these steps:

1. Pick out the subordinate clause.
2. Decide how the pronoun is used in the clause—as subject, predicate nominative, object of the verb, or object of a preposition.

7f

3. Determine the case of the pronoun according to the usual rules.

4. Select the correct form of the pronoun.

PROBLEM	Samoset was the Indian chief (who, whom) welcomed the Pilgrims.
Step 1	The subordinate clause is (*who, whom*) *welcomed the Pilgrims.*
Step 2	In this clause, the pronoun is the subject of the verb *welcomed.*
Step 3	Since it is the subject of the verb, the pronoun is in the nominative case.
Step 4	The nominative form is *who.*
SOLUTION	Samoset was the Indian chief *who* welcomed the Pilgrims.

PROBLEM	Do you know (who, whom) she is?
Step 1	The subordinate clause is (*who, whom*) *she is.*
Step 2	In this clause, the subject is *she*, the verb is *is*, and the pronoun is the predicate nominative: *she is* (*who, whom*).
Step 3	As predicate nominative, the pronoun is in the nominative case.
Step 4	The nominative form is *who.*
SOLUTION	Do you know *who* she is?

PROBLEM	I voted for Margaret, (who, whom) my friends recommended.
Step 1	The subordinate clause is (*who, whom*) *my friends recommended.*
Step 2	In this clause, the subject is *friends;* the verb is *recommended.* The pronoun is the object of the verb: *my friends recommended* (*who, whom*).
Step 3	The object of a verb is in the objective case.
Step 4	The objective form is *whom.*
SOLUTION	I voted for Margaret, *whom* my friends recommended.

PROBLEM   Herb Matthews, (who, whom) I sat next to, fell asleep during the last act of the play.

Step 1   The subordinate clause is *(who, whom) I sat next to.*

Step 2   In this clause, the subject is *I;* the verb is *sat.* The pronoun is the object of the preposition *next to: I sat next to (who, whom).*

Step 3   The object of a preposition is in the objective case.

Step 4   The objective form is *whom.*

SOLUTION   Herb Matthews, *whom* I sat next to, fell asleep during the last act of the play.

The sentence, of course, would be correct with the preposition before the pronoun: *Herb Matthews, next to whom I sat, fell asleep during the last act of the play.*

Remember that no words outside the clause affect the case of the pronoun. In the second problem, the entire clause was used as a direct object of the verb *do know,* but the pronoun was used as a predicate nominative (nominative case).

EXAMPLE   Do you know who she is?

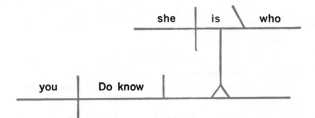

♦ USAGE NOTE   Frequently, *whom* in subordinate clauses is omitted (understood).

EXAMPLES   The man (whom) I just met is Mr. Nevins.
           The man (whom) I just waved at is Mr. Nevins.

● EXERCISE 11.   Copy on your paper each subordinate clause in the sentences that follow. Then tell how the pronoun (*who* or *whom*) is used in its own clause—as subject, predicate nominative, object of the verb, or object of a preposition.

EXAMPLE   1. Give the job to Stuart, whom you can trust.
          1. *whom you can trust, object of verb*

 1. Mr. Doyle is a man who likes young people.
 2. Mr. Doyle is a man whom young people like.
 3. The girl who spoke to me has just won a scholarship.
 4. The girl whom I spoke to has just won a scholarship.
 5. Can you tell me who that player is?
 6. She is a casual friend whom I seldom see.
 7. Students who attend the meetings will be excused from class.
 8. I wondered who it could be at the door.
 9. Whom Della finally married I do not know.
10. There is no one who really understands me.

● EXERCISE 12.   Number your paper 1–10. After the proper number, give the use of the pronoun in parentheses. Then write the correct pronoun.

EXAMPLE   1. I wondered (who, whom) it was.
          1. *predicate nominative, who*

 1. Ladies (who, whom) lived during the fifteenth century painted their teeth instead of their fingernails.
 2. Her older sister, to (who, whom) she sent the article, has moved to Santa Fe.
 3. It was Napoleon (who, whom) invaded Spain in 1808.
 4. Maureen finally guessed (who, whom) it was.
 5. I visited with Mr. Windlow, (who, whom) was trimming his rosebushes.
 6. Mr. Harvey, (who, whom) I work for on Saturdays, owns two poultry farms.
 7. Is there anyone (who, whom) plans to leave early?
 8. He is a teacher (who, whom) I respect.
 9. There is the man (who, whom) you were asking about.
10. Francis Drake, (who, whom) Queen Elizabeth I knighted, defeated the Spanish fleet.

● REVIEW EXERCISE C.   Number your paper 1–20. As you read the following sentences, notice carefully the case form of each pronoun. If all of the pronouns in a sentence are correct, write a *C* after the corresponding number on your paper. If a pronoun is wrong, write the correct case form of the pronoun.

1. Claire and me are the editors of the literary magazine that our school publishes. 2. A student who wishes to submit a manuscript for publication gives his material to either Claire or I. 3. After us two have gone over all the material submitted, a general staff meeting is called. 4. Then we students who make up the staff read the manuscripts together.

5. When the material for the month's publication has been selected by we staff members, it is sent to the printer. 6. Both Claire and I go periodically to the printer to make sure that he knows what we want done. 7. Sometimes he questions Claire and I about the makeup of a page.

8. Meanwhile, Lance and Dolores, who the art teacher recommended, are working on the illustrations and cover design for the magazine. 9. Claire checks the work done by them because she knows more about art than I do.

10. All of us who have worked hard on the magazine are relieved when it is finally ready for distribution.

11. Last month a prize was offered by we members of the staff to whomever should write the best short story. 12. The students who submitted stories selected pen names for themselves, so that even those of us on the staff did not know whom had written a particular story. 13. We did have an alphabetical list of all the students who had submitted stories, and we entertained ourselves by trying to match each story with an author on our list.

14. "Could 'The Last Journey' have been written by Carl or she?" Claire asked, pointing to names on the list.

15. "Neither he nor she wrote it," Dolores replied. 16. "This," Dolores continued, pointing to another name on the list, "is obviously the work of Jim or he."

17. "But the author could be she," Lance argued, "since this looks like the kind of story that only she could write."

18. And so the arguments went for each story that we read because each of us was sure that he could analyze the story and determine whom the writer was.

19. "The Last Journey" was chosen by the judges as the winner of the contest, and we staff members were surprised when the author was identified.

20. "It was not *he* or *she*, but *them!*" Claire exclaimed. Two students had collaborated on the mystery story.

The Pronoun in an Incomplete Construction

Notice the difference in meaning that the choice of pronouns can make in sentences with incomplete constructions.

EXAMPLES   You like Dean better than **I.**

You like Dean better than **me.**

In the first sentence, the choice of the pronoun *I* indicates that it is the subject of an understood verb: *You like Dean better than I like Dean.* In the second sentence, since the pronoun *me* is in the objective case, the meaning is: *You like Dean better than you like me.*

The case of the pronoun depends upon how the omitted part of the sentence would be completed.

7g. After *than* and *as* introducing an incomplete construction, use the form of the pronoun that you would use if the construction were completed.

The following sentences are correct because they clearly express the meaning intended by the writer. The words in the brackets show how each could be completed.

EXAMPLES   I lent you more money than **he** [lent you].

I lent you more money than [I lent] **him.**

Did he tell Alma as much as **I** [told Alma]?

Did he tell Alma as much as [he told] **me?**

● EXERCISE 13.   Beginning with the *than* or *as*, complete each sentence, using the correct form of the pronoun. After the sentence, write the use of the pronoun in its clause, telling whether it is a subject or an object.

EXAMPLE 1. Ron was as delighted as (I, me).
          1. *as I was—subject*

1. Lester can varnish floors better than (I, me).
2. The letter was odd; it baffled Sam as well as (we, us).
3. Is Eleanor younger or older than (he, him)?
4. Have they practiced as much as (we, us)?
5. We have known him longer than (she, her).
6. Perhaps you are more idealistic than (he, him).
7. Did you enjoy the movie as much as (I, me)?
8. The long trip exhausted them more than (we, us).
9. Were you as thoroughly uncomfortable as (she, her)?
10. Their children were even less fortunate than (they, them).

● REVIEW EXERCISE D. Number your paper 1–25. After each number, write the correct form of the pronoun in parentheses. Be able to give reasons for your answers.

1. Can you or (he, him) describe Pasteur's method of fighting germs?
2. (We, Us) boys gave reports on famous witch trials.
3. Each of (we, us) boys mentioned Joan of Arc.
4. In Egypt the nobles (who, whom) ruled were rich.
5. The laborers, (who, whom) the nobles ruled, were extremely poor.
6. Between you and (I, me), I think that Bob is deceiving himself.
7. Did the gift surprise Tim as much as (she, her)?
8. Is it really (they, them)?
9. Please give those pictures to Wanda and (I, me).
10. He can't swim as fast as (I, me).
11. Behind us stood Eric and (he, him).
12. My mother taught Winifred and (I, me) how to use a pressure cooker.
13. Do you need someone (who, whom) is dependable?
14. The winners, Carl and (I, me), got a free trip to New York.
15. Father told Cliff and (I, me) the answer.
16. Some of (we, us) girls preferred to skate.
17. Everyone except (she, her) has joined the club.
18. Surely you can do as well as (he, him).

7g

19. Her brother and (she, her) will help us.
20. Mary Ann, (who, whom) you have met, will be at the party.
21. At the end of the story, who married (who, whom)?
22. Please tell (we, us) boys what you know.
23. Doug and (we, us) fished far into the night.
24. The man stopped Steve and (we, us) at the gate.
25. Are you and (they, them) going to the banquet?

● REVIEW EXERCISE E.   Number your paper 1–25. If a sentence has no errors in usage of pronouns, write a *C* after the corresponding number on your paper. If a pronoun is incorrect, give the correct form.

1. Last Halloween, Herb and me prepared a little surprise for the children in our neighborhood.
2. When they came in their costumes to ask for treats, him and I put on a spook show of our own.
3. When the boys and girls came to the door, us spooks had some tricks all worked out.
4. We played the record "Night on Bald Mountain," a very eerie piece of music; and as the music grew louder, I, whom was standing near the lights, slowly opened the door.
5. Since I had turned out all the lights, the children could not see Herb or I.
6. They could only see the smoke pouring out the doorway from the dry ice that him and me had bought.
7. Then I focused a flashlight on Herb, who got up from his chair and moved slowly toward the children.
8. When he reached the doorway, he opened his mouth and, in a very scary voice, said, "I am him whom you fear—the Great Zombie."
9. "I am the one," Herb continued, "whom the priest of Allazand restored to life."
10. Outside the door, a little boy and his sister stood so still that I could almost hear he and she breathing.
11. Finally, after Herb was satisfied that he had frightened him and her enough, we gave them both special treats that we had prepared.
12. Him and her accepted the treats and ran away to tell the other children about the spook show which they had seen.

13. That Halloween our house swarmed with children who wanted to see the show.
14. Herb and me laughed at the children's reactions.
15. Some children, who Herb could not frighten, applauded and screamed for more.
16. Others, who had been stunned by the performance, stood like statues.
17. Many wanted to know whom the Great Zombie really was.
18. On a few occasions we were even more surprised than them.
19. Two sisters, for who Herb had put on an especially good show, stood for a long time without saying anything.
20. Then one said to the other, "Are you as scared as me?"
21. The other replied, "Naw, my friend and I ran into this same thing in California last year."
22. On another occasion, a child remarked, "Santa Claus is bigger than him."
23. So Herb and me and the children had a good time last Halloween.
24. Sometimes it was difficult to tell who was having the better time, them or us.
25. It is unlikely, though, that Herb and I can put on another show this Halloween; we're still exhausted from the last one.

● REVIEW EXERCISE F.   Number your paper 1–15. If a sentence is correct, write *C* after the proper number. If a pronoun is wrong, write the correct form of the pronoun after the appropriate number.

1. Keep this a secret between you and I.
2. Us boys will carry the baggage.
3. At camp Sam and me were tentmates.
4. If it is she who is supposed to be in charge, let me know.
5. Were you calling Jerry or me?
6. If you and her go, I'll go.
7. He kept Howard and I after school.
8. Please don't tell anyone but Mrs. Carter or her about our plan.
9. He thought it was us.
10. Please wait for Sid and him.
11. Are you and him related?

12. Frank and he are absent.
13. We girls were pretty angry.
14. Have you seen Helen or she?
15. It couldn't have been them.

● REVIEW EXERCISE G.   Write twenty sentences correctly using the following:

1. who
2. whom
3. we students
4. us students
5. you and I
6. you and me
7. her son and she
8. her son and her
9. Mr. Jordan and we
10. Mr. Jordan and us
11. as much as he
12. as well as him
13. Wesley and she
14. Wesley and her
15. he or she
16. him or her
17. my father and they
18. my father and them
19. more than I
20. more than me

The Correct Use of Modifiers

Comparison and Placement

A modifier describes or limits the meaning of another word. There are two kinds of modifiers, adjectives and adverbs. Besides one-word modifiers, you have studied several other kinds of modifiers—prepositional phrases, verbal phrases, and subordinate clauses, all of which may be used as adjectives or adverbs.

COMPARISON OF MODIFIERS

Adjectives state qualities of nouns or pronouns:

a **rough** road, **happy** children, a **friendly** dog

You can show the degree or extent to which one noun has a quality by comparing it with another noun which has the same quality. For instance:

This road is **rougher** than that road.

Similarly, you can show degree or extent by using adverbs to make comparisons:

Although I did my chores **quickly,** Dave did his work **more quickly.**

173

8a. The forms of modifiers change as they are used in comparison.

There are three degrees of comparison: *positive, comparative,* and *superlative.* Notice below how the forms of modifiers change to show comparison.

POSITIVE	COMPARATIVE	SUPERLATIVE
big	bigger	biggest
high	higher	highest
fearful	more fearful	most fearful
promptly	more promptly	most promptly
bad	worse	worst
good	better	best

Regular Comparison

(1) A modifier of one syllable regularly forms its comparative and superlative by adding *–er* and *–est*.

POSITIVE	COMPARATIVE	SUPERLATIVE
dark	darker	darkest
soon	sooner	soonest
kind	kinder	kindest

(2) Some modifiers of two syllables form their comparative and superlative degrees by adding *–er* and *–est*; other modifiers of two syllables form their comparative and superlative degrees by means of *more* and *most*.

In general, the *–er, –est* forms are used with two-syllable modifiers unless they make the word sound awkward. The *more, most* forms are used with adverbs ending in *–ly.*

POSITIVE	COMPARATIVE	SUPERLATIVE
simple	simpler	simplest
pretty	prettier	prettiest
foolish	more foolish	most foolish
gracious	more gracious	most gracious
slowly	more slowly	most slowly

♦ USAGE NOTE Some two-syllable modifiers may take either *–er, –est* or *more, most: handsome, handsomer, handsomest* or *handsome, more handsome, most handsome.*

When in doubt about which way a two-syllable modifier is compared, consult an unabridged dictionary.

● EXERCISE 1. Write the forms for the comparative and superlative degrees of these words:

1. loose
2. often
3. lazy
4. harmful
5. gentle
6. funny
7. wise
8. safely
9. eager
10. lovely

(3) Modifiers having more than two syllables form their comparative and superlative degrees by means of *more* and *most*.

POSITIVE	COMPARATIVE	SUPERLATIVE
intelligent	more intelligent	most intelligent
favorably	more favorably	most favorably

● EXERCISE 2. *Oral Drill.* Give comparative and superlative degrees of (1) *original*, (2) *reasonably*, (3) *significant*, (4) *appropriately*, and (5) *pessimistic*.

(4) Comparison to indicate less or least of a quality is accomplished by using the words *less* and *least* before the modifier.

POSITIVE	COMPARATIVE	SUPERLATIVE
useful	less useful	least useful
often	less often	least often

● EXERCISE 3. *Oral Drill.* Give comparison to indicate less and least of the five words listed above in Exercise 2.

Irregular Comparison

Adjectives and adverbs that do not follow the regular methods of forming their comparative and superlative degrees are said to be compared irregularly.

8 a

POSITIVE	COMPARATIVE	SUPERLATIVE
bad	worse	worst
good } well }	better	best
many } much }	more	most

Caution: Do not add the *–er, –est* or *more, most* forms to irregularly compared forms: *worse*, not *worser* or *more worse*.

● EXERCISE 4. Be prepared to give the correct forms of the comparative and superlative degrees when your teacher dictates the positive forms of the five adjectives and adverbs listed above.

● REVIEW EXERCISE A. Write the comparative and superlative forms of the following modifiers. If you are in doubt about the forms of two-syllable modifiers, look up the positive forms in an unabridged dictionary.

1. bad	6. witty	11. quiet	16. firmly
2. good	7. tough	12. widely	17. practical
3. neat	8. lonely	13. little	18. absorbent
4. late	9. weak	14. comic	19. precisely
5. many	10. well	15. trivial	20. desolate

Use of Comparative and Superlative Forms

8b. Use the comparative degree when comparing two things; use the superlative degree when comparing more than two.

The comparative form of a modifier is used for comparing two things, as these examples indicate.

EXAMPLES Of the two schools, Wilson is **bigger.**
Mount McKinley is **higher** than Pike's Peak.
Skywriting is **more spectacular** than billboard advertising.

The superlative form of a modifier is used for comparing three or more items.

EXAMPLES   Wilson is the **biggest** school in the county.

Mount McKinley is the **highest** peak in North America.

Skywriting is the **most spectacular** way to advertise.

◆ USAGE NOTE   In everyday conversation, it is acceptable in some cases to use the superlative degree in comparing two things: *May the best man* (of two) *win.*

● EXERCISE 5.   Using the correct forms of adjectives or adverbs, write five sentences comparing two things and five comparing more than two.

8c. Do not omit the words *other* or *else* when comparing one thing with a group of which it is a part.

It is illogical to say, "Mary Lou is more charming than any girl in her class." Obviously, Mary Lou is a member of class, and she cannot be more charming than herself. The word *other* should be supplied: "Mary Lou is more charming than any *other* girl in her class."

ILLOGICAL   My cat Grumpy is smarter than any cat.

RIGHT   My cat Grumpy is smarter than any **other** cat.

Similarly, "The left tackle weighs more than anyone on the football team" is incorrect, since the left tackle is a member of the team. Here *else* should be added: "The left tackle weighs more than anyone *else* on the team."

ILLOGICAL   Sidney jumped higher than anyone.

RIGHT   Sidney jumped higher than anyone **else.**

● EXERCISE 6.   *Oral Drill.* The comparisons in this exercise are illogical because of the omission of the words *other* or *else.* Supply the needed word as you read the sentences, so that the sentences will be logical.

8
b-c

1. Mr. Yardley is wiser than any person I know.
2. My sister makes more telephone calls than anyone in my family.
3. Your suggestion may be more sensible than any suggestion that has been made so far.
4. Russ can run faster than anybody on his team.
5. The picture he gave me is more valuable to me than anything I own.

8d. Avoid double comparisons.

A double comparison is one in which the degree is formed incorrectly by both adding *–er* or *–est* and using *more* or *most*.

WRONG   Leo is more friendlier than Morris.
RIGHT   Leo is **friendlier** than Morris.

WRONG   This coin is the most unusualest item in my collection.
RIGHT   This coin is the **most unusual** item in my collection.

● EXERCISE 7. Number your paper 1–10. Copy each incorrect modifier, crossing out the unnecessary part in order to eliminate the double comparison.

EXAMPLE   1. I am determined to study more harder this term than I did last.

    1. ~~more~~ harder

    2. That is the most elegantest tablecloth I have ever seen.

    2. *most elegantest*

1. Today is more colder than yesterday.
2. Mother is the most patientest person in our family.
3. Is Nita now working even more faster than before?
4. A pine tree grows more taller than a mesquite.
5. He is the most stubbornest child in the family.
6. About nine o'clock, the noise became more louder.
7. This is the most loveliest day!
8. Miss Adkins is the most finest teacher I've ever had.
9. The patient is more quieter than he was last night.
10. Then I made the most stupidest remark.

8e. Be sure your comparisons are clear.

Your sentences should state clearly what things are being compared; for example, in the sentence "The population of New York is greater than Chicago," the comparison is not clear. *The population of New York* is not being compared to *Chicago*, but rather to *the population* of Chicago. The sentence should read: *The population of New York is greater than the population* (or *that*) *of Chicago*.

WRONG   Statistics prove that traveling in airplanes is safer than automobiles.

RIGHT   Statistics prove that traveling in airplanes is safer than traveling in automobiles.

Often an incomplete construction will be used in a comparison: *I am happier than she.* Both parts of the comparison should be stated if there is danger of misunderstanding.

NOT CLEAR   I like her better than Isabel.

BETTER   I like her better than I like Isabel.

or   I like her better than Isabel likes her.

● REVIEW EXERCISE B.   Number your paper 1–20. If all the modifiers in a sentence are correct, write a *C* after the corresponding number on your paper. If a modifier is incorrect, rewrite the sentence, making whatever correction is needed.

1. When the tortoise and the hare raced, the hare proved to be faster, but the tortoise won the race because he was more persistent.
2. Of all the animals at the zoo, the monkeys were the noisier creatures.
3. She is the most happiest child I know.
4. My friend, who later became a star on Broadway, had more talent than any actor in his class.
5. Sarah has tried many recipes for fruitcake, and this is the best one that she has found.
6. Our guide explained that the next place we visited would be farther from the center of town.
7. The earth is more nearer the sun than Mars is.

8
d-e

8. She skied better than anyone in her group.
9. After the stranger had examined the two paths, he took the one that looked easiest to follow.
10. Tantalus was more cruelly punished than any legendary figure.
11. My aunt, who is a born pessimist, felt much more securer after she had inspected the plane.
12. Of the two pieces of cake, he politely chose the smallest one.
13. Which city is largest—Chicago or Los Angeles?
14. Sherlock Holmes is more famous than any detective in literature.
15. Donna thought that the masks worn in the ancient Greek plays were the most grotesque ones that she had ever seen.
16. After examining all three costumes, the director decided that this one was the most appropriate for our play.
17. For tomorrow's exhibition, Kevin worked longer on the bars than anyone on the gymnastic squad.
18. Which country is farthest from the United States—France or Japan?
19. Many people think that the black panther is the most fiercest animal in the world.
20. We were more interested in studying the history of the Egyptians than any other ancient people.

DANGLING MODIFIERS

8f. A modifying phrase or clause that does not clearly and sensibly modify a word in the sentence is a *dangling modifier*.

When a modifying phrase containing a verbal comes at the beginning of a sentence, the phrase is followed by a comma. Immediately after that comma should come the word that the word group modifies. Notice in the following two examples how the introductory expressions clearly and sensibly modify the words which follow the commas.

Sleeping during history class, I was marked absent. [*I* was sleeping.]

Nailed to the gate, a no-trespassing sign attracted Patty's attention. [The *sign* was nailed to the gate.]

Each of the following sentences contains a dangling modifier—that is, a modifier which either appears to modify a word other than the one it is meant to modify or doesn't modify any word at all.

Sleeping during history class, the teacher marked me absent. [The sentence implies that the teacher was sleeping.]

Nailed to the gate, Patty noticed a no-trespassing sign. [Obviously, Patty was not nailed to the gate.]

Walking down the street, his eyes showed constant surprise. [Did his eyes walk down the street?]

● EXERCISE 8.   Write complete sentences using the following introductory modifiers. Be sure that each modifier is followed by a word that it can *clearly* and *sensibly* modify.

EXAMPLE   1. Scampering down the stairs,
　　　　　1. *Scampering down the stairs, Ritchie tripped and fell.*

 1. Exploding unexpectedly,
 2. Shocked by Gerald's rudeness,
 3. Fluttering from limb to limb,
 4. Waddling along the beach,
 5. Scratching his head,
 6. Not expecting the interruption,
 7. Planning a birthday party for her,
 8. Paying close attention in class,
 9. To avoid being caught in the rain,
10. Trying to keep from laughing,

Correcting Dangling Modifiers

To correct a dangling modifier, you should either re-arrange the words in the sentence or add words to make the meaning logical and clear.

8f

WRONG   When shaving, Mother often tells Dad about her plans for the day.

RIGHT   When shaving, Dad often listens to Mother tell about her plans for the day. [sentence rearranged]

or   When Dad is shaving, Mother often tells him about her plans for the day. [words (*when* and *is*) added]

WRONG   To win and hold friends, petty quarrels and criticism should be avoided.

RIGHT   To win and hold friends, you should avoid petty quarrels and criticism.

or   If you wish to win and hold friends, you should avoid petty quarrels and criticism.

WRONG   Arranged on the mantelpiece. I used Christmas cards as colorful decorations.

RIGHT   I arranged Christmas cards on the mantelpiece as colorful decorations.

or   Arranged on the mantelpiece, Christmas cards made colorful decorations.

● EXERCISE 9.   Eliminate the dangling modifiers in the following sentences by rewriting each sentence so that each modifier clearly and sensibly modifies a word in the sentence. You will have to supply words.

1. Bumping along in the jeep, the moon looked beautiful.
2. Immediately after washing the car, the doorbell jingled.
3. To excuse our not doing homework over the weekend, the teacher was told we did not understand the assignment.
4. After having had a serious heart attack, the voters were concerned about the health of the mayor.
5. Strolling through the French Quarter, the cafés particularly impressed me.
6. Stepping on the brakes, the car skidded to the side of the road.
7. While flying over Vicksburg, the national military park came into view.
8. Being very hungry, this sandwich looks as good as fried chicken to me.

9. To go from Mexico to Texas, a vaccination certificate must be presented at the border.
10. Having died before I was born, I never knew my grandfather.

● Exercise 10. Many sentences below contain dangling modifiers; some do not. Number your paper 1–20. If a sentence is correct, write a *C* after the corresponding number. If it is incorrect, rewrite the sentence to eliminate the dangling modifier.

1. After saying grace, dinner was served.
2. To appreciate good music, you should learn to play an instrument.
3. While trimming the rosebushes this morning, a spider bit me.
4. Made of durable plastic, a child cannot easily break these toy trucks.
5. Glittering in the soft, silent moonlight, the water looked beautiful and seemed inviting to the boys.
6. Filled with high school students, the visitors could not find an empty seat in the auditorium.
7. While listening to the radio, I soon fell asleep.
8. While reading my assignment by the river, the wind kept blowing dust into my eyes.
9. Although ringing loudly, no one seemed to hear the bell.
10. Running across the meadow, my ankle was sprained.
11. To become a great athlete, physical endurance is necessary.
12. To become well informed, you should form the habit of reading newspapers and magazines.
13. To earn spending money, Mr. Lewis gave me a job as cashier in his store.
14. After mopping the kitchen, the baby woke up and began to cry.
15. After being in school all day, a long hike is refreshing.
16. Sitting up on its hind legs, the squirrel munched an acorn.
17. When learning to swim, everything that one tries seems ridiculous at first.
18. While walking alone in the woods, it is good to hear the birds singing.

19. While eating his dog food, Dad noticed that Spot seemed hungry.
20. When trying to understand the meaning of a sentence, look at the little words, the prepositions and conjunctions.

MISPLACED MODIFIERS

A dangling modifier, as the preceding exercises have shown, makes the meaning of a sentence absurd because the modifier either seems to modify a word which it cannot sensibly modify or is left without any word to modify at all. Just as damaging to the clear expression of ideas are misplaced modifiers.

8g. Modifying phrases and clauses should be placed as near as possible to the words they modify.

Misplaced Phrase Modifiers

The following examples of misplaced phrases show the importance of placing phrase modifiers as near as possible to the words they modify.

WRONG   Skipper enjoyed the chunks of steak slipped to him by the guests under the table. [Here *under the table* seems to indicate where the guests were.]

RIGHT   Under the table, Skipper enjoyed the chunks of steak slipped to him by the guests.

WRONG   At the age of four, my father taught me a lesson.

RIGHT   At the age of four, I learned a lesson from my father.

or   My father taught me a lesson when I was four years old.

WRONG   A lovely rose garden was planned by the President's committee behind the White House.

RIGHT   A lovely rose garden behind the White House was planned by the President's committee.

● EXERCISE 11. Rewrite the following sentences so that they make sense. Either place phrase modifiers as near as possible to the words they modify or turn a phrase into a clause. Be sure that you do not misplace another modifier in rewriting.

1. At five years of age, my grandmother bought me a pony.
2. On the bottom shelf of the refrigerator, I could not find the fruit juice.
3. There should be a letter written by Aunt Lizzy in your post office box.
4. I sent a sympathy card to the relatives of the dead man in a hurry.
5. The friendly policeman told the frightened children what they were doing wrong with a smile.
6. Homesick, Norma yearned to see the Rocky Mountains in Europe.
7. The job was selling boxes of candy to children with prizes in them.
8. In a tiny cage at the dog pound, we felt very sorry for the little bulldog.
9. I read about the kidnapers who were captured in this morning's paper.
10. The names of the men were called out by the announcer in the starting line-up.
11. I saw him make a thrilling touchdown on the forty-yard line.
12. He told us about roping steers in the school cafeteria.
13. Three freshmen were punished after the rules had been broken by the principal.
14. The governor agreed that the state should punish every driver who endangers the lives of others without delay.
15. A small group of boys were all watching a bright object in the sky on the school grounds.
16. On the way to the grocery store, the streets seemed slippery.
17. The fans jeered at the referee in the stands.
18. The thief was arrested soon after the grocery store had been robbed by the police.
19. Inside the oven I noticed that the turkey was burning.
20. We waved at the men repairing the highway from our car.

8g

Misplaced Clause Modifiers

Place an adjective or adverb clause as near as possible to the word it modifies. Notice how the meaning of the sentence below is distorted by a misplaced clause modifier.

WRONG   The car belongs to our neighbor that has long, sweeping tail fins.

Since the modifying clause *that has long, sweeping tail fins* seems to modify *neighbor*, the sentence is ridiculous. The clause should be close to the word it modifies, as follows:

RIGHT   The car that has long, sweeping tail fins belongs to our neighbor.

To correct misplaced clauses, place the modifying clause as close as possible to the word it modifies.

WRONG   The dress is hanging on the clothesline that I have sewed on for weeks.

RIGHT   The dress that I have sewed on for weeks is hanging on the clothesline.

WRONG   There was a flag on the stage which had only forty-eight stars.

RIGHT   On the stage there was a flag which had only forty-eight stars.

● EXERCISE 12.   Read each of the following sentences. Decide what word the misplaced clause should modify, and rewrite the sentence, placing the clause near this word.

1. A trunk stood on the step which was covered with labels.
2. A dog ran onto the football field that looked a lot like our club mascot.
3. We waved to the girl as we left the town that had given us directions.
4. There are several books on our shelves which were written by Arthur Conan Doyle.
5. The battered car now sits in the garage that went out of control on the expressway yesterday.
6. There was a rosebush behind the pile of trash which was very beautiful.

7. Birds were the main targets for our slingshots, which were eating chicken feed.

8. We crossed the Mississippi River on a long bridge which was almost a mile wide.

9. A large dog was trotting behind the little boy that was growling as if he were getting ready to attack me.

10. We played in two old shacks between the post office and the bank which weren't being lived in at the time.

● REVIEW EXERCISE C. The sentences below contain dangling modifiers, misplaced modifiers, and errors in comparison. Rewrite the sentences so that the meaning is clear.

1. He plays both baseball and football, but he likes baseball best.

2. She served sandwiches to Elmer and me, packed with pickles, garlic, tomatoes, and cheese.

3. Everyone was waiting for the teacher in English class.

4. Jack is certainly more taller than you.

5. We didn't see the tornado approaching in the storm cellar.

6. After boiling for exactly three minutes, Emma poured cold water over the eggs.

7. The dead snake was brought into camp by a cub scout six feet long.

8. Trying to remember my lines, my heart pounded against my ribs.

9. After eating ten watermelons, the hostess asked us to go inside and play games.

10. The height of these new buildings is not so great as the old buildings.

11. The motel was recommended to us by a tourist with hot and cold running water, television, and a swimming pool.

12. To avoid the hot sun, our plans were to travel at night.

13. Flying at half-mast, my heart grew sad when I saw the flag.

14. After completing my homework, the doorbell rang.

15. Before leaving school, my homework was all done.

16. We waited for you until the movie started at the theater entrance.

17. Stepping out into the blinding snowstorm, my teeth chattered, and my hands grew numb.
18. To hunt jack rabbits, my neighbor's oat field is a good place.
19. After knocking out the heavyweight champion, the referee announced the winner.
20. We found an old jack in the trunk which wouldn't work.

● REVIEW EXERCISE D. All of the following sentences contain errors in the use of modifiers or appositives: mistakes in comparisons or dangling or misplaced modifiers. After the proper number, rewrite each sentence so that it is clear and correct.

1. When traveling through the highlands in Scotland, I discovered that stories about monsters were more popular than any kind of story.
2. Having received a great deal of publicity, I heard especially about the so-called Loch Ness monster.
3. The first person to sight the monster, a veterinary student from Edinburgh, was Arthur Grant.
4. One day Grant came upon a strange creature cycling on a road near the shore of Loch Ness.
5. On cycling closer, the monster took two great leaps and plunged into the lake.
6. As you might expect, numerous theories were presented about the identity of the monster in the local newspaper.
7. Some people thought the monster must be a fresh-water species of sea serpent, and others believed the whole story was a hoax; of these two theories, the first is obviously the most fascinating.
8. Having found a huge, dead creature on the shore of the lake in 1942, the mystery of the monster was believed finally to be solved.
9. The scientists called it a large shark who examined the specimen.
10. Though having supposedly gone from the lake, many new sightings of the monster have been reported.

Glossary of Usage

This chapter contains a short glossary of English usage, supplementing the material in Chapters 5–8. The words and expressions in this glossary are listed for your reference. You may, if you wish, work straight through the chapter, studying the problems and using the exercises to test your knowledge of the various items. However, the glossary is included in the book mainly for you to refer to when you are uncertain about a question of usage.

Several kinds of usage problems are treated in this glossary. Some require the writer or speaker to choose between two words, according to the meaning intended. Others involve a choice between two words, in which one word is less acceptable than the other. A few of the words and expressions discussed here should be avoided altogether. (Spelling problems arising from the confusion of similar words are treated in Chapter 28.)

accept, except *Accept* is a verb; it means "to receive." *Except* may be either a verb or a preposition. As a verb, it means "to leave out" or "to omit"; it is usually used in the passive voice. (See pages 142–43.) As a preposition, *except* means "excluding."

EXAMPLES I **accept** your invitation.

Honor roll students will be **excepted** from this requirement.

I have done all my homework **except** my history assignment.

189

affect, effect   *Affect* is a verb meaning "to influence." *Effect* used as a verb means "to accomplish." Used as a noun, *effect* means "the result of some action."

EXAMPLES   The crisis may **affect** the outcome of the election.

The government is working to **effect** a solution to the crisis.

The **effect** of the crisis is being felt in government circles.

ain't   Avoid this word in speaking or writing; it is substandard English.

all the farther, all the faster   Used in some parts of the country to mean "as far as" or "as fast as."

DIALECT   This is **all the farther** we can go.
STANDARD   This is **as far as** we can go.

among   See between, among.

and etc.   *Etc.* is an abbreviation of the Latin phrase *et cetera*, meaning "and other things." Thus, *and etc.* means "and and other things." Do not use *and* with *etc.*

EXAMPLE   The school store sells pencils, paper, notebooks, ink, etc. [not *and etc.*]

anywheres, everywheres, nowheres, somewheres   Use these words without the final *s*.

EXAMPLE   My family didn't go **anywhere** [not *anywheres*] on the Fourth of July.

as   See like, as.

as if   See like, as if.

at   Do not use *at* after *where*.
WRONG   Where does he live at?
RIGHT   Where does he live?

beside, besides *Beside* means "by the side of" someone or something; it is always a preposition. *Besides* as a preposition means "in addition to." As an adverb, *besides* means "moreover."

EXAMPLES Come and sit **beside** me.

Besides cake and ice cream, we will have lemonade, sandwiches, and candy.

I cannot stay any longer. **Besides,** I am already late for my appointment.

between, among Use *between* when you are thinking of two things at a time, even though they may be part of a group consisting of more than two.

EXAMPLES In math, Carol sits **between** Geraldine and me.

The team has a short rest period **between** quarters. [Although there are more than two quarters, a rest period occurs only *between* any two of them.]

We are studying the War **Between** the States. [Although thirty-five states were involved, the war was *between* two sides.]

I could not decide which of the four candidates to vote for, as there was not much difference **between** them. [Although there are more than two candidates, each one is being thought of separately.]

Use *among* when you are thinking of a group rather than of separate individuals.

EXAMPLES There was considerable disagreement **among** the hunters as to the direction of the camp. [The hunters are thought of as a group.]

We had only four dollars **among** the six of us.

bring, take *Bring* means "to come carrying something." *Take* means "to go carrying something." Think of *bring* as related to *come*, *take* as related to *go*.

EXAMPLES **Bring** the book here.

Now **take** it over there.

bust, busted Avoid using these words as verbs. Use a form of either *burst* or *break*.

> EXAMPLES The beach ball **burst** [not *busted*] when George kicked it.
>
> The bat **broke** [not *busted*] when Swenson hit the ball.

● EXERCISE 1. This exercise covers the usage problems discussed on pages 189–92. Number your paper 1–20. After each number, write the correct word from the parentheses in the corresponding sentence.

1. Is page 216 (all the farther, as far as) you have read?
2. (Beside, Besides) the players themselves, their families and friends attended the dinner.
3. Will she (accept, except) the explanation for my absence?
4. He divided the work (between, among) the club members.
5. May I (bring, take) this book down to the library for you?
6. I (busted, broke) my leg skiing.
7. I could not find the answer to that question (anywhere, anywheres).
8. I saw no one I knew at the dance (beside, besides) Jane.
9. The audience seemed greatly (affected, effected) by his moving speech.
10. On the way to the pool, one of Nathan's bicycle tires (busted, burst).
11. I have to (bring, take) some books to the library before it closes.
12. The minutes of the last meeting were (accepted, excepted) as read by the secretary.
13. The dry farmlands clearly showed the (affect, effect) of the drought.
14. I'm not eager to see that film. (Beside, Besides), I have spent all my allowance.
15. (Bring, Take) the report downstairs to the principal's office.
16. Prize money is distributed equally (between, among) the six team members.
17. Experiments with the new serum showed surprising (affects, effects).

18. Basketball, volleyball, fencing, tennis, (etc., and etc.) are taught by the physical education staff.
19. He divided the candy (between, among) the three children.
20. I (brought, took) some flowers to my aunt, who is in the hospital in Jacksonville.

can't hardly, can't scarcely   See **The Double Negative** (page 202).

could of   *Could have* sounds like *could of* when spoken. Do not erroneously write *of* with the helping verb *could*. Use *could have*. Also avoid *ought to of, should of, would of, might of,* and *must of*.

EXAMPLE   Jamie could **have** [not *of*] telephoned us.

discover, invent   *Discover* means "to be the first to find, see, or learn about something that already exists." *Invent* means "to be the first to do or make something."

EXAMPLES   Archimedes **discovered** the scientific principle of displacement.

Edison **invented** the phonograph.

don't   *Don't* is the contraction of *do not; doesn't* is the contraction of *does not*. Use *doesn't*, not *don't*, after *he, she, it,* and singular nouns.

EXAMPLE   It **doesn't** [not *don't*] matter that Rick **doesn't** [not *don't*] know the rules.

effect   See **affect, effect**.

everywheres   See **anywheres, etc**.

fewer, less   *Fewer* is used with plural words, *less* with singular words; *fewer* tells "how many," *less* "how much."

EXAMPLES   **Fewer** guests were expected.
Less punch was needed.

good, well   *Good* is always an adjective. Never use *good* to modify a verb; use *well*, which is an adverb.

WRONG   The band marched good.
RIGHT   The band marched **well.**

Although it is usually an adverb, *well* is used as an adjective to mean "healthy."

EXAMPLE   He does not feel **well.** [predicate adjective meaning "healthy"]

♦ USAGE NOTE   *Feel good* and *feel well* mean different things. *Feel good* means "to feel happy or pleased." *Feel well* simply means "to feel healthy."

EXAMPLES   After his victory, he feels **good.**
The warm sun made me feel **good.**
She went to the nurse because she didn't feel **well.**

● The use of *good* as an adverb is increasing in conversational English, but it should not be so used in writing.

EXERCISE 2.   This exercise covers the usage problems discussed on pages 193–94. Number your paper 1–15. After each number, write the correct word in parentheses in the corresponding sentences.

1. He could (of, have) been seriously injured.
2. Who (discovered, invented) the internal combustion engine?
3. (Don't, Doesn't) Stanley know that Labor Day is a holiday?
4. I don't sing (good, well) enough to join the Glee Club.
5. Next time you bake a cake, use (fewer, less) eggs.
6. He (don't, doesn't) seem to know the meaning of *work*.
7. If you had called, I might (of, have) gone with you.
8. We have (fewer, less) school holidays this term.
9. The coach (don't, doesn't) want his players to stay up late.
10. Whoever it was that first (discovered, invented) the wheel was a great scientist.
11. Mother called the doctor because I wasn't feeling (good, well).
12. Unfortunately, there seem to be (fewer, less) volunteers for my committee.
13. You must (of, have) worked for weeks on that project.
14. Is John Fitch or Robert Fulton considered the (discoverer, inventor) of the steamboat?
15. Laura plays the piano so (good, well) that she has been invited to appear with the state symphony orchestra.

● REVIEW EXERCISE A.   This exercise covers the most important usage problems discussed in the glossary so far. If a sentence is correct, write *C* on your paper beside the number of the sentence. If a sentence contains an error in usage, write the correct form.

1. Beside the freshmen, a few sophomores were admitted.
2. The soap bubble floated upward and burst.
3. Are you planning to bring a house gift to your aunt when you go to Chicago?
4. Why does February have less days than any other month?
5. I wish I had excepted your assistance.
6. I am very sleepy, and it is effecting my concentration.
7. Little Bobby came home from the zoo, talking excitedly about lions, tigers, elephants, seals, and etc.
8. Could the accident of been prevented?
9. Don't anyone know who invented the steam engine?
10. I thought the rehearsal went rather well.
11. Is that all the faster you can type?
12. We can't decide between the red flowers and the blue ones.
13. Everywheres we looked there were people.
14. I was surprised that no one would except my suggestion.
15. Did Thomas Edison discover the phonograph?
16. What affect did the operation have on his speech?
17. We sat beside the pool and watched the diving exhibition.
18. Between the five of us we managed to raise a dollar.
19. The girl wearing the pearls don't look familiar.
20. Should I of consulted Mr. Madison before writing my essay?

had of   See **of.**

had ought, hadn't ought   Unlike other verbs, *ought* is not used with *had.*

   WRONG   Guy had ought to study harder; he hadn't ought to have gone to the movies last night.

   RIGHT   Guy **ought** to study harder; he **ought not** to have gone to the movies last night.

   or   Guy **should** study harder; he **shouldn't** have gone to the movies last night.

haven't but, haven't only　See **The Double Negative** (page 202).

he, she, they　In writing do not use an unnecessary pronoun after a noun. This error is called the *double subject*.

WRONG　Miss Page she is my algebra teacher.
RIGHT　　Miss Page is my algebra teacher.

kind, sort, type　In writing, the demonstrative words *this*, *that*, *these*, and *those* must agree in number with the words *kind*, *sort*, *type*: *this type*, *these types*.

EXAMPLE　I like **this kind** of candy better than any of **those** other **kinds**.

learn, teach　*Learn* means "to acquire knowledge." *Teach* means "to instruct" or "to show how."

EXAMPLE　Directors often **teach** classes in acting, and a young drama student can **learn** many valuable things from them.

leave, let　*Leave* means "to go away" or "to depart from." *Let* means "to allow" or "to permit."

WRONG　Leave him do what he wants to do.
RIGHT　　**Let** [allow] him do what he wants to do.
RIGHT　　**Leave** the house at nine.

less　See **fewer, less**.

lie, lay　See page 144.

like, as　*Like* is a preposition, introducing a prepositional phrase. In informal English, *like* is often used as a conjunction meaning "as"; but in formal English, *as* is always preferable.

EXAMPLES　She talks **like** her mother. [*Like* introduces the phrase *like her mother*.]

We should do **as** your parents suggest. [*Your parents suggest* is a clause and needs the conjunction *as* (not the preposition *like*) to introduce it.]

like, as if   In formal written English, *like* should not be used for the compound conjunctions *as if* or *as though*.

EXAMPLE   Scottie looks **as though** [not *like*] he has been in a fight.

might of, must of   See **could of.**

no, none, nothing   See **The Double Negative** (page 202).

nowheres   See **anywheres, etc.**

of   Do not use *of* with prepositions such as *inside, off, outside,* etc.

EXAMPLE   He jumped **off** [not *off of*] the diving board into the pool **outside** [not *outside of*] the hotel.

What was resting **inside** [not *inside of*] Pandora's box?

Of is also unnecessary with *had.*

EXAMPLE   If I **had** [not *had of*] seen you, I would have told you about it.

ought to of   See **could of.**

● EXERCISE 3.   This exercise covers the most important usage problems discussed on pages 195–97 of this glossary. Number your paper 1–20. Beside each number, write the correct word in parentheses in the corresponding sentence.

1. You (hadn't ought, ought not) to have missed class yesterday.
2. Mr. James (learned, taught) us the background of *Romeo and Juliet.*
3. (Shakespeare, Shakespeare he) wrote the play when he was a young man.
4. (Leave, Let) me tell you about the story.
5. I particularly like (these kind, these kinds) of plots.
6. The (Montagues they, Montagues) were rivals of the Capulets.

7. Perhaps Romeo, a Montague, (hadn't ought, ought not) to have gone to the Capulets' party.

8. However, if he (hadn't, hadn't of), he would not have met Juliet.

9. After the party, Romeo stood in the garden (outside, outside of) Juliet's room.

10. He (left, let) Juliet declare her love for him before he spoke to her.

11. Shakespeare writes (these kind, these kinds) of scenes very well.

12. Do you think Friar Laurence (ought, had ought) to have performed the marriage ceremony?

13. Perhaps the young couple (hadn't ought, ought not) to have been married at all.

14. Certainly Romeo (shouldn't have, shouldn't of) become involved in a fight so soon after his wedding.

15. Mr. James (learned, taught) us that in the fight Romeo killed Juliet's cousin Tybalt; because of this, Romeo was banished from Verona.

16. Juliet could hardly bear to (leave, let) Romeo go.

17. If Lord and Lady Capulet (had, had of) been more understanding, the tragedy might never have happened.

18. Nevertheless, Juliet (hadn't ought to, shouldn't) have taken the sleeping potion.

19. Believing Juliet dead, Romeo returned to Verona and killed Paris (outside of, outside) Juliet's tomb. Then he killed himself.

20. When (the Montagues and the Capulets, the Montagues and the Capulets they) learned of the death of Romeo and Juliet, they ended their feud.

rise, raise   See pages 147–49.

said, same, such   Avoid artificial uses like these:

AVOID   I entered P.S. 41 in the first grade and attended said school three years.

The policeman chased the bandit and finally caught same.

Mr. Nunez wanted an eight-room house with a yard, but such was not available in his price range.

shall, will   Some people prefer to use *shall* with first person pronouns and *will* with second and third person in the future and future perfect tenses. Nowadays, most educated Americans do not make this distinction. *Will* is acceptable in the first person as well as in the other two.

sit, set   See pages 146–47.

so   This word is usually overworked. Avoid using it in writing as a conjunction meaning *therefore*.

POOR   The baseball game lasted for twelve innings, so we did not interview the coach afterward.

BETTER   Because the baseball game lasted for twelve innings, we did not interview the coach afterward.

The baseball game lasted for twelve innings; therefore, we did not interview the coach afterward.

some, somewhat   In writing do not use *some* for *somewhat* as an adverb.

WRONG   My spelling has improved some.

RIGHT   My spelling has improved **somewhat**.

than, then   Do not confuse these words. *Than* is a conjunction; *then* is an adverb.

EXAMPLES   This pitcher of lemonade is sweeter **than** the first one was.

We finished drying the dishes. **Then** we watched television.

them   *Them* should not be used as an adjective. Use *these* or *those*.

EXAMPLE   Where did you find **those** [not *them*] pencils?

this here, that there   The *here* and the *there* are unnecessary.

EXAMPLE   I like **this** [not *this here*] dress better than **that** [not *that there*] one.

this kind, sort, type See **kind,** etc.

way, ways Use *way,* not *ways,* in referring to a distance.

EXAMPLE We still have a long way [not *ways*] to go.

when, where Do not use *when* or *where* incorrectly in writing a definition.

WRONG An aquarium is where fish are kept.

RIGHT An aquarium is a place in which fish are kept.

where Do not use *where* for *that.*

EXAMPLE I read in yesterday's paper **that** [not *where*] your sister is engaged.

which, that, who Remember that the relative pronoun *who* refers to people only; *which* refers to things only; *that* refers to either people or things.

EXAMPLES There is the man **who** telephoned us. [person]
Here is the car **which** he bought from my father. [thing]
It is the kind of car **that** I like. [thing]
He is a person **that** can be trusted. [person]

who, whom See pages 163–66.

without, unless Do not use the preposition *without* in place of the conjunction *unless.*

EXAMPLE I will not be able to go **unless** [not *without*] I finish my homework.

would of See **could of.**

● EXERCISE 4. The sentences in this exercise cover the most important usage problems presented on pages 198–200 of the glossary. Number your paper 1–20. Beside each number, write the correct one of the two expressions in parentheses in the corresponding sentence.

1. This jacket looks (some, somewhat) better than that one.
2. Do not make any more noise (than, then) you have to.

3. On the newscast I heard (that, where) the strike had been averted.
4. What did you do with (them, those) tennis balls?
5. (This, This here) watch belonged to my great-grandfather.
6. People came a long (way, ways) to attend the celebration.
7. (Them, Those) records should be stored upright in a cool place.
8. (Without, Unless) it stops raining, we shall have to cancel our picnic.
9. My father hopes to buy (that, that there) car.
10. Circe was the sorceress (who, which) advised Odysseus to beware of the Sirens.
11. She is feeling (some, somewhat) better today.
12. It is only a short (way, ways) from our farm to town.
13. The question was less complicated (than, then) it seemed at first.
14. At school today we learned (where, that) we will have a half-holiday on Friday.
15. Walt Whitman is the American poet (that, which) interests me most.
16. Frederick was (some somewhat) tired after his trip.
17. He would not have made that statement (without, unless) he had first checked his facts.
18. Please set (those, them) chairs around the table.
19. Is she the one (who, which) was elected head cheerleader?
20. (This, This here) tie and (that there, that) jacket need to be cleaned.

● REVIEW EXERCISE B.   This exercise covers the most important usage problems on pages 189–200. Rewrite each of the following sentences, correcting the errors in usage.

1. The girl which is visiting Barbara is some older than I.
2. Marion she is a more accomplished violinist than Rodney is.
3. Take this here cake and them jars of jam to Mrs. Mackintosh like Mother requested.
4. If I had of studied last night, I might of done some better on the exam this morning.
5. I saw in the paper where people may not vote without they have registered.

6. The apple fell off of the tree and rolled a long ways down the hill.
7. Mr. Crowell has promised to learn us about these kind of chemicals.
8. The man which saw the accident hadn't ought to have left.
9. My little brother he refused to leave me read in peace.
10. Them boys could of helped us.

THE DOUBLE NEGATIVE

A *double negative* is a construction in which two negative words are used when one is sufficient. Before the eighteenth century, the double negative—or triple negative or quadruple negative—was both useful and popular. The more negatives a person used in a sentence, the more emphatically he meant "No!" For example, look at the following sentence:

Barney does not never do no work.

This piling up of negatives is no longer good English usage. We now express the same idea with only one negative in the sentence:

EXAMPLE   Barney does **not** ever do **any** work.

    or   Barney **never** does any work.

    or   Barney does **no** work.

Keep your usage up to date by avoiding such double negatives as those listed below.

can't hardly, can't scarcely   The words *hardly* and *scarcely* convey a negative meaning. They should never be used with another negative word.

    EXAMPLES   I **can** [not *can't*] **hardly** lift this suitcase.

                We **had** [not *hadn't*] **scarcely** enough refreshments for everyone.

haven't but, haven't only   In certain uses, *but* and *only* convey a negative meaning and should not be used with *not*.

    EXAMPLE   We **have** [not *haven't*] **but** five dollars to spend.

no, nothing, none These words are, of course, negative. Do not use them with another negative word.

WRONG   It doesn't make no difference to me.
RIGHT   It **makes no** difference to me.
RIGHT   It **doesn't make any** difference to me.

WRONG   The searchers haven't found nothing.
RIGHT   The searchers **haven't found anything.**
RIGHT   The searchers **have found nothing.**

WRONG   We looked for gold, but there wasn't none.
RIGHT   We looked for gold, but there **wasn't any.**
RIGHT   We looked for gold, but there **was none.**

● EXERCISE 5. Rewrite each of the following sentences, correcting the usage errors.

1. Marvin hasn't done nothing to make him angry.
2. There isn't no ice cream left in the freezer.
3. I must go shopping, for I haven't only a few winter clothes.
4. Terry couldn't hardly move his arm yesterday.
5. This paragraph doesn't make no sense to me.
6. I went back to get another helping of potato salad, but there wasn't none.
7. We haven't but two more weeks of school before vacation.
8. Didn't you ever do nothing about that?
9. Nothing seems to make no difference to him any more.
10. I haven't ever seen no flamingos.

● REVIEW EXERCISE C. This exercise, which contains fifty usage errors, covers most of the problems discussed in this glossary. If a sentence is correct, write the number of the sentence and then write *C* after the number. If a sentence contains usage errors, write the number of the sentence and then rewrite the sentence, correcting the errors.

1. I heard where the committee must now choose between three different proposals.
2. I hadn't ought to go to the movies, for I haven't but two dollars to spend this week.
3. Unless the person who borrowed my book takes it back to me, I won't be able to do no more work on my essay.

4. Surely you could of done this some sooner then you did.
5. Mr. Newlan learned us about Samuel Morse, the man who discovered the telegraph.
6. My having slept less hours than usual last night may effect my performance on today's test.
7. The reward was divided equally among the three men.
8. That there debating team they spoke extremely good and must of done a great deal of research.
9. This semester I have accepted fewer invitations to parties and dances than I did last term.
10. Anthony doesn't never enjoy discussing those kind of subjects with people he don't trust.
11. I wish I had of told them children not to play inside of that old hut besides the quarry.
12. I can't hardly understand how you could of busted them dishes.
13. Hal don't plan to bring his tennis racket to camp next summer without he can find someone to learn him how to play.
14. Among my classmates, three students besides Mona and me have decided to learn more about that kind of architecture.
15. Leave me read you this here list of persons which have excepted our invitation.
16. I read where unemployment is having a serious affect everywheres on sales of food, clothing, automobiles, and etc.
17. We don't plan to go anywheres during our vacation except to visit my grandmother, who lives in Princeton.
18. If we leave early in the morning and walk as fast as possible, we had ought to be able to go a long ways before noon.
19. Eli Whitney had ought to be remembered because he was the man which discovered the cotton gin, the machine that affected great changes in the economy of the South.
20. Vince he rode his bicycle a long ways, but than one of the wheels busted.

PART THREE

Sentence
Structure

CHAPTER 10

Writing Complete Sentences

Sentence Fragments
and Run-on Sentences

In writing, the best way to communicate your ideas is to use effective, forceful sentences. To ensure that your meaning will be clearly understood, you should make certain that your sentences are punctuated correctly. Most important, you should know where they begin and where they end. That is, you must develop *sentence sense* in writing.

You already have sentence sense regarding spoken language. When you are speaking, your voice rises and falls naturally to indicate the beginning and the end of a sentence.

You can develop sentence sense in writing by "listening" to the sentences you write. If you practice "listening" to the exercise sentences in this chapter, you will learn to avoid the two common errors of writing discussed here: the *fragment* and the *run-on sentence*.

THE SENTENCE FRAGMENT

10a. A *fragment* is a separated sentence part that does not express a complete thought.

A fragment is usually an additional idea that has been incorrectly cut off from the sentence in which it belongs.

EXAMPLES   Scratching noises on the cabin porch indicated that I had a visitor. *Probably a raccoon or a wildcat.*

As we ran toward it, the bus drove off. *Leaving Ted and me standing helplessly on the corner.*

In the first example above, *Probably a raccoon or a wildcat* is a fragment cut off from the preceding sentence. It does not make sense by itself. In the second example, *Leaving Ted and me standing helplessly on the corner* is also a fragment; without a subject and verb, it does not express a complete thought. These fragments should be joined to the sentences preceding them.

EXAMPLES   Scratching noises on the cabin porch indicated that I had a visitor, **probably a raccoon or a wildcat.**

As we ran toward it, the bus drove off, **leaving Ted and me standing helplessly on the corner.**

Sometimes a fragment should be corrected by being placed at the beginning or within the sentence from which it was separated.

FRAGMENT   Hubert works slowly and deliberately on the mound. *Taking plenty of time between pitches.*

CORRECTED   **Taking plenty of time between pitches,** Hubert works slowly and deliberately on the mound.

FRAGMENT   We talked with Mr. Jackson in his office. *The principal of the school.*

CORRECTED   We talked with Mr. Jackson, **the principal of the school,** in his office.

● EXERCISE 1. How good is your "sentence sense"? Find out by deciding whether or not each group of words is a sentence. Number 1–10 on your paper. After the proper number, write *F* for *fragment* or *S* for *sentence*.

1. Thumbing through the first few pages of *Please Don't Eat the Daisies.*
2. To warn motorists of the ice forming on bridges.

10a

3. On the other side of the mountain is a beautiful valley.
4. Can you prove it?
5. After rehearsal we got together and memorized our lines.
6. Lawrence, playing as defensive linebacker for the Indians.
7. Playing the piano is her hobby.
8. An old two-story house with spacious rooms, designed to accommodate a large family of a dozen or more.
9. In the spring, when the warm sun shines upon the fresh green beauty of the earth and when red tulips wave in the March winds.
10. Even though he had to support his aged mother and six brothers and sisters with his earnings as a grocery clerk.

● EXERCISE 2. Each numbered group below contains a sentence and a fragment. Number your paper 1–10, and write the letter (A or B) of the fragment after the corresponding number.

1. (A) A few Eskimos live on the Barren Grounds. (B) In northern Canada.
2. (A) Having a forked tail almost a foot long. (B) The flycatcher in flight looks like something from outer space.
3. (A) When I offered to buy him a forty-cent sundae. (B) Frank said that he wanted four ten-cent limeades.
4. (A) The editor of the school paper interviewed Mr. Franklin. (B) The new history teacher who will also coach the debating team.
5. (A) Those rock formations were even older than Methuselah. (B) Because they had existed for more than 969 years.
6. (A) After I had thrown my chugger plug about twenty yards. (B) I waited for a long silver bass to strike the bait.
7. (A) Trying to earn a generous tip. (B) We did an especially good job of mowing and trimming the grass.
8. (A) In Wyoming we traveled through Cody. (B) A city named for W. F. Cody, better known as "Buffalo Bill."
9. (A) A showman who believed that a sucker is born every minute. (B) P.T. Barnum was a legendary American figure.
10. (A) At the drugstore I ordered a shipwreck. (B) A banana split without the banana.

Common Types of Sentence Fragments

10b. A subordinate clause must not be written as a sentence.

A subordinate clause always depends on an independent clause to complete its meaning. Notice that the subordinate clause fragment below does not express a complete thought.

Although Bert receives a large allowance

The clause has a verb, *receives*, and a subject, *Bert*. Because of the word *although*, however, the thought is not complete. Like all fragments, this one may be corrected by being placed in a sentence—that is, by being attached to an independent clause.

Although Bert receives a large allowance, he often seems miserly.

Bert often seems miserly although he receives a large allowance.

Remember that relative pronouns (*which, that, who, whom, whose*) and subordinating conjunctions (see the list on page 100) introduce subordinate clauses. These little words are very important; they can change a complete thought to a fragment.

SENTENCE   Claude told the truth.

FRAGMENTS   **Unless** Claude told the truth
            That Claude told the truth
            Claude, **who** told the truth

● EXERCISE 3.   Most of the items on the next page contain subordinate clauses which are punctuated as sentences. Correct these fragments by making them a part of the sentence in the item. You may have to leave out or add words. When you are rewriting, be particularly careful to avoid misplaced modifiers. If an item is correct, write a *C* after the appropriate number.

10b

1. Next week we are going to Williamsburg. Which is a historic city in Virginia.
2. Although it was nothing more than a small village in the seventeenth century. Williamsburg was the scene of several important events in the eighteenth century.
3. Though many of the buildings in Williamsburg today are not the original ones, they are exact likenesses. The town's only major industry is restoration.
4. What I want most to see is the Public Gaol. Which once housed fifteen of Blackbeard's pirates, thirteen of whom were hanged.
5. Completed in 1720, the Governor's Palace was later the official residence of the first two governors of the state. Who were Patrick Henry and Thomas Jefferson.
6. The Raleigh Tavern, which was the center of many heated political discussions. It was the inn in which both George Washington and Thomas Jefferson frequently dined.
7. The tools which were used for trade in the eighteenth century. These have been re-created in various craft shops.
8. While we were there, we visited my sister. She is a freshman at the College of William and Mary.
9. William and Mary is the second oldest college in the United States. Which has its original building still standing.
10. So that we can see where our President lives now. We may stop in Washington on the way home.

10c. A verbal phrase must not be written as a sentence.

As you learned in Chapter 3, present participles and gerunds are verbals ending in *–ing* (*coming, working, being*). Past participles usually end in *–d, –ed, –t, –n,* or *–en* (*looked, slept, broken*). Infinitives usually consist of *to* plus the verb (*to go, to play*).

A verbal phrase is a phrase containing a verbal. It is often mistaken for a sentence because the verbal is often mistaken for a main verb. However, a phrase does not have both a subject and a verb; it cannot express a complete thought. By itself, a verbal phrase is a fragment.

FRAGMENTS   Spilling clothespins from the basket
Poised on practiced toes
Saying good-by
To approve his son's marriage

Like subordinate clauses, verbals depend upon independent clauses to make their meaning complete.

SENTENCES   Spilling clothespins from the basket, I dashed for the porch steps.

Ballet dancers, poised on practiced toes, waited for the cue.

Carl and Sue parted quickly without even saying good-by.

Mr. Richardson refused to approve his son's marriage.

● EXERCISE 4.   Revise the ten fragments in the following paragraph by attaching them logically to independent clauses. Copy the paragraph, changing the punctuation so that there will be no verbal phrases standing by themselves.

Blown about like a reed in the wind. Bobby was never able to make a decision. His family and friends pointed out this fault. By criticizing him constantly. One day last week, however, Bobby did think, decide, and act quickly. Proving himself to everyone. One of his friends, Tim Ellis, was standing in the middle of the street. Flying a kite. Not seeing an approaching car. Tim didn't get out of its way. Having no time to warn Tim. Bobby dashed forward. He saved Tim's life. By pushing his friend out of the path of the speeding car. The car, however, did hit Bobby. Breaking his leg. And bruising his face. Bobby is now a hero. Praised and honored by all.

● EXERCISE 5.   Below are ten verbal phrases incorrectly written as sentences. Use each in a complete sentence.

1. Pushing his way forward.
2. Disturbed by a fidgety conscience.

10c

3. To mutter to himself and to the typewriter.
4. After sharpening four red pencils.
5. Before getting a short haircut.
6. Encouraged by my teacher's praise.
7. Patiently accepting the stern advice.
8. Completely swept off my feet by his blandishments.
9. To be not only wealthy but also healthy.
10. Not convinced by her logic but persuaded by her charm.

● REVIEW EXERCISE A.   Some of the following groups of words are sentences; others are subordinate clauses or verbal phrases incorrectly written as sentences. Number your paper 1–20. Place *S* after the corresponding number of each complete sentence. Write *F* after the corresponding number of each fragment. Be prepared to tell how you would correct each fragment by making it a part of a related sentence.

1. In 1628 William Harvey published his new theory.
2. Which explained the circulation of the blood by the motion of the heart.
3. Stated twelve years earlier.
4. This theory set forth the idea that the heart is a kind of pump.
5. To force the blood through the veins.
6. As medical men began studying the circulation of the blood.
7. They learned that the blood gives life to cells in the body.
8. Blood also helps to clean the cells.
9. By carrying away waste products.
10. In the blood stream are red blood cells.
11. Which are carriers of oxygen.
12. Provided by the lungs.
13. Every day new red blood cells are born.
14. As old ones wear out.
15. There are also white cells in the blood stream.
16. These white cells destroy harmful germs.
17. Some cells die as they fight the germs.
18. Too many white cells in the blood stream may indicate a serious infection.
19. When they are needed to fight hordes of germs.
20. The body manufactures a great number of white cells.

10d. An appositive phrase must not be written as a sentence.

An appositive is a word which means the same thing as the noun or pronoun it follows. (See Chapter 3.) An appositive phrase is made up of the appositive and its modifiers. Like other phrases, it does not contain the basic parts of a sentence. It is set off within a sentence by commas but cannot stand by itself as a complete thought. By itself it is a fragment.

FRAGMENT The reaper was invented by Cyrus McCormick. *A famous farmer of Virginia.*

SENTENCE The reaper was invented by Cyrus McCormick, **a famous farmer of Virginia.**

Occasionally an appositive fragment may be separated by other words from the noun or pronoun it refers to.

FRAGMENT Cyrus McCormick invented the reaper. *A famous farmer of Virginia.*

SENTENCE Cyrus McCormick, **a famous farmer of Virginia,** invented the reaper.

● REVIEW EXERCISE B. Number your paper 1–16. Each item in this exercise has two parts. If both parts are sentences, write after the corresponding number the last word in the first sentence, and follow it with a period. Then write the first word in the second sentence, using a capital letter. If one of the parts is a fragment requiring a comma, write the word preceding the comma, add the comma, and write the word that should follow the comma. Be sure you put the fragment in its proper place in the sentence. If no punctuation is required, write *C* for *correct*.

EXAMPLES 1. In English class we are studying types of humor my teacher is Miss Blevins.
1. *humor. My*
2. Miss Blevins defined two literary terms indirect satire and irony.
2. *terms, indirect*

10d

1. Miss Blevins gave us an interesting assignment   a composition dealing with an ironical situation.
2. In her paper Ann Welch described what recently happened to Mr. Myer   Ann's next-door neighbor.
3. A detective with wide experience   Mr. Myer gave a lecture to the Civic Club.
4. He is an interesting speaker   the stories he tells are fascinating.
5. In his lecture, he gave advice on one topic   methods of outwitting pickpockets.
6. The audience listened intently   because they had heard stories about citizens who had had their pockets picked.
7. An ironical thing happened the very next Saturday   the day of the big game.
8. Mr. Myer went to the game   expecting to meet at the ticket booth several invited friends.
9. In his wallet Mr. Myer had a great deal of money   approximately thirty dollars.
10. When he reached for his wallet to pay for the tickets   he discovered that his pocket had been picked by somebody in the crowd.
11. I wrote a composition on a similar situation   an incident involving my brother.
12. The city sponsored a poster contest   to promote Fire Prevention Week.
13. Being a good artist, Jack drew a poster   which he entered in the contest.
14. The contest judges gave first prize to his poster   the prize was a blue ribbon.
15. In his room I saw the ribbon   hanging on the wall above his desk.
16. The ribbon was scorched in a fire Jack accidently caused in his room   a few days after the presentation of the prize.

10e. Avoid other sentence fragments.

On page 215 is a list of other common types of fragments. Although you do not need to learn the names of these, you should be able to recognize them as incomplete ideas so that you can avoid writing them as sentence fragments in your compositions.

1. *Prepositional phrases:* The annual athletic awards were presented. After the last game of the season.

2. *Compound parts of a sentence:* On July 4 Donna picked up a sparkler by the wrong end. And of course burned her fingers.

3. *Parts of a comparison:* Her cooking tempts me. As much as a cage tempts a sparrow.

4. *Items in a series:* All his essays are written in the same fine style. Clear, concise, and interesting.

Each fragment should be attached to a complete sentence. Sentence 1, for example, may be rewritten as follows:

After the last game of the season, the annual athletic awards were presented.

The annual athletic awards were presented **after the last game of the season.**

● REVIEW EXERCISE C. Rewrite each item below so that the fragment is eliminated.

1. The old lady squeezed her hand into a narrow slit in her purse. Like a child playing "Who's got the button?"

2. When the cat sought refuge under the chair, Thelma gently broomed him out. And eventually cornered him.

3. The people of Grand Rapids, Michigan, manufacture many products. Such as chemicals, furniture, and tools.

4. Acorns are eaten not only by squirrels. But also by pigs.

5. Before going to sleep, I like to eat something. Especially ham sandwiches and chocolate bars.

6. This all-purpose cleanser brightens pots and pans. Including copper-bottomed skillets.

7. I don't know how to cook vegetables. To keep them from tasting flat.

8. On Saturdays I not only help Mom around the house. But also work with Dad in the yard.

9. Charles outgrew his childish temper tantrums. Having become a country preacher.

10. I learned many things at camp. Such as how to put up a tent.

10e

THE RUN–ON SENTENCE

Sentence fragments are usually the result of ending a sentence too soon—before a final idea has been included.

Sometimes writers don't recognize where a sentence ends, and they keep on going into the next sentence. They use a comma or no mark of punctuation at all instead of a period after a sentence. They permit the sentence to "run on" into the next.

10f. **A *run-on sentence* consists of two or more sentences separated only by a comma or by no mark of punctuation.**

Every sentence should begin with a capital letter and should be followed by an end mark: period, question mark, or exclamation point. Sentences should never be run together without punctuation.

WRONG   Where are Riff and Raff those cats won't come when I call them.

RIGHT   Where are Riff and Raff? Those cats won't come when I call them.

The comma should never take the place of an end mark.

WRONG   Last year we spent our vacation in Pennsylvania, this summer we plan to drive through the Southwest.

RIGHT   Last year we spent our vacation in Pennsylvania. This summer we plan to drive through the Southwest.

Correcting Run-on Sentences

In the example above, the run-on sentence was corrected by making two separate sentences. Notice, however, that the sentences are closely related. (Writers usually do not run unrelated sentences together.)

Instead of punctuating it as two sentences, you may prefer to correct a run-on sentence by making a compound sentence. If you do, use either a comma and a coordinating conjunction (*and*, *but*, *or*) or a semicolon and no conjunction between the two independent clauses.

EXAMPLES   Last year we spent our vacation in Pennsylvania**, but** this summer we plan to drive through the Southwest.

Last year we spent our vacation in Pennsylvania**;** this summer we plan to drive through the Southwest.

Occasionally a run-on sentence may be corrected by expressing one of the parts in a subordinate clause.

EXAMPLE   Although we spent our vacation in Pennsylvania last year, this summer we plan to drive through the Southwest.

● EXERCISE 6.   You will find the following passages hard to read because run-on sentences always interfere with the clear expression of ideas. Exercise your sentence sense to decide where each sentence should end. Then write the last word of each sentence on your paper after the corresponding number. Place the proper mark of punctuation after the word, and then write the first word of the next sentence, beginning it with a capital letter.

If you make the run-on sentence into a compound sentence, write the last word of the first clause, follow it with a comma and a coordinating conjunction or with a semicolon, and write the first word of the second clause.

If you decide to subordinate an element, write the first word of the clause or phrase, a dash, and the last word.

EXAMPLE   1. We were eating breakfast, Dad made a dramatic gesture and knocked over the sugar bowl, I choked a bit on my milk my grandmother chuckled so hard that the table quivered.

1. *While — breakfast, Dad*
bowl. I
milk, and my

10 f

1. The inventor of the typewriter probably thought that he was doing mankind a favor, it's too bad that he didn't consider the effect of his invention on me, in fact, typewriting lessons are making a nervous wreck out of me.

2. Why must all the letters of the alphabet be in such confusion on the keyboard why must typewriters in school have black tabs covering the jumbled letters why must my typewriter play hopscotch when I rest my thumb on the long bar?

3. It is fun to grow ornamental peppers, if you have one plant, you can start a forest of them because each pod has scores of seeds, each seed is a potential plant in the spring tiny white and purple blossoms appear.

4. These blossoms slowly transform themselves into green pods later the green turns to purple then it changes to yellow and orange finally it becomes a bright red, since each pod is at a different stage of growth, the plant looks like a Christmas tree.

5. At the age of nineteen, my mother taught arithmetic in a little town in Missouri since she loved her students and her work, Mother was happy as a single girl.

6. She had two boy friends—Frank, my father, and Percival, a neighbor neither one could win Mother's hand in marriage for five years Percival proposed to her in vain.

7. Finally Father won the contest for Mother's hand in marriage, Percival was an usher at the wedding, Mother's sister Rosemary was a bridesmaid, two months later Percival married Rosemary he is my favorite uncle.

8. Have you ever asked your grandmother for a recipe, she probably told you that the dish is extremely easy to prepare, "just fill the bowl and add a dash of this and a bit of that."

9. You decide to put the ingredients on the kitchen table, then you watch how she mixes everything together, however, this procedure fails to teach you the recipe because she cooks the ways she directs, she pours flour from the sack and scoops sugar out by the handful.

10. You should take my advice be content to eat her delicious concoctions be patient until fifty years from now then you can confuse your granddaughters with the same kind of "dash of this, bit of that" directions.

● REVIEW EXERCISE D.   Rewrite the following paragraphs, removing all fragments and run-ons.

I enjoyed history class this morning. Although I sometimes think that dates and historical events are dull. Today I learned many interesting facts about the history of medicine. Especially about the work of Harvey, Jenner, Pasteur, and Florence Nightingale.

For many centuries men knew very little about the blood, in the early seventeenth century William Harvey's theory of blood circulation started a kind of revolution in medicine. One hundred and fifty years later Edward Jenner found out that a person who had had cowpox was immune to smallpox, this discovery helped Jenner find a good way to fight smallpox, by vaccination. Thus preventing the disease rather than attempting to treat it. In the nineteenth century Louis Pasteur proved that germs cause disease, he also discovered several methods of killing germs. Including pasteurization, a process named after him. Though Florence Nightingale was not a scientist, she was dedicated to the nursing profession, after studying the latest nursing techniques, she traveled to the Crimea, there she helped wounded soldiers. Often working nineteen hours a day. Modern medicine is greatly indebted to these pioneers.

CHAPTER 11

Achieving Sentence Variety

Beginnings, Structure, and Length

You can add interest to your compositions by varying the way you construct sentences. As you study this chapter, remember that *how* you express your ideas will affect your reader's reaction to *what* you are saying. That is, the way you express your ideas will determine the amount of attention and interest given you by your reader. If too many of your sentences are short and choppy or long and stringy, your style becomes monotonous and makes the most interesting topic seem dull. Avoid monotony of style by learning to vary sentences effectively.

VARYING SENTENCE BEGINNINGS

Although sentences which have the subject first may be grammatically correct, too many of them in one paragraph are monotonous. To avoid a common cause of dullness in writing, then, you should learn to vary the beginnings of your sentences.

11a. Vary the beginnings of your sentences.

Read the following paragraph, in which every sentence begins with the subject.

I have now found a solution to my crying problems when I peel strong onions. I was at the dentist's office yesterday, and I read a magazine article entitled "Onions Without Tears." Seven persons, according to this article, once tested ways to peel onions without weeping. These guinea pigs, after making various experiments, discarded two popular but useless theories. Chewing buttered bread did not stop tears. Keeping an ice cube inside one's closed mouth did not help, either. The testers found three ways of helping to avoid watery eyes. The first one was keeping a bread slice between the teeth. The second one was biting on a sulfur-tipped match. The third way was using an electric fan to blow away onion fumes. All experimenters, however, agreed that there are only two really effective ways to peel an onion without crying. A person can shut his nose with a clip such as swimmers sometimes use. A person can talk or sing to keep his mouth open. I may try these ways, but not until I have tried my own method. I will get my sister a song book and a swimmer's nose clip. I will then ask her to peel the onions for me.

As you see, too many subject-first sentences in the paragraph lessen the effectiveness of the ideas presented. Notice the varied beginnings of sentences in a revision of the same paragraph.

Now I have found a solution to my crying problems when I peel strong onions. At the dentist's office yesterday, I read a magazine article entitled "Onions Without Tears." *According to this article*, seven persons once tested ways to slice onions without weeping. *After making various experiments*, these guinea pigs discarded two popular but useless theories. Chewing buttered bread did not stop tears, *nor did* keeping an ice cube inside one's closed mouth. Some of the testers found these three ways of helping to avoid watery eyes: by keeping a bread slice between the teeth, by biting on a sulfur-tipped match, or by using an electric fan to blow away onion fumes. *Finally*, however, all the experimenters agreed that there are only two really effective ways to peel an onion without crying. *First*, to shut his nose, a person can use a swimmer's clip. *Second*, to keep his mouth open, he can talk or sing. *Al-*

11a

though I may try these ways, I will first try my own method. I will get my sister a song book and a swimmer's nose clip and ask her to peel the onions for me.

As this paragraph shows, there are many ways to begin sentences. Instead of putting the subject first in every sentence, you can vary your style by starting with a modifying word, phrase, or clause.

(1) You may begin sentences with single-word modifiers.

Learn to use adjectives, adverbs, and participles at the beginnings of sentences.

ADJECTIVES **Angry,** the umpire turned his back.

Dark and **empty,** the house looked very different from the way I remembered it.

Informal and **friendly,** she put everyone at his ease.

ADVERBS **Soon** her cold glances reached the freezing point.

Unfortunately, Aunt Eloise did not stifle her yawns.

PARTICIPLES **Sighing,** Adam shoved the spinach aside.

Delighted, the squirrel grabbed the nut and bounded away to bury it.

● EXERCISE 1. The following sentences, all of which begin with the subject, contain a modifier that can be placed at the beginning of the sentence. Find this modifier, and write it on your paper.

1. Theresa babysits occasionally.
2. The ball, spinning, whirled past.
3. Monty and Earl, exhausted, pitched camp.
4. Charles often reads himself to sleep.
5. We approached the icy bridge cautiously.
6. The league leaders, unbeaten and untied, expected little trouble from our team.
7. My dog Rags, wet and dirty, tracked across Mom's clean floor.

8. Mr. Johnson's fingers impatiently drummed on the desk.
9. The ghost appeared to Hamlet again.
10. Wilbur, stumbling, fell into the gully.

● EXERCISE 2.   Use the following modifiers to begin sentences of your own.

1. often	6. surely
2. hurriedly	7. courageously
3. whispering	8. suddenly
4. bewildered	9. daydreaming
5. hungry and cold	10. alone and afraid

(2) You may begin sentences with phrases.

Another good way to achieve sentence variety is to place prepositional, participial, or infinitive phrases at the beginning of sentences.

PREPOSITIONAL PHRASES   **On the other side of the island,** there is a fine, natural harbor.

Behind Edward and me stood Mr. Soames, the night watchman.

PARTICIPIAL PHRASES   **Chugging down Main Street,** our jalopy began to fall apart.

Turned to stone by Zeus, Niobe continued to shed tears.

INFINITIVE PHRASES   **To be polite,** I chuckled at all of Grandpa's jokes.

To determine the age of the mummy, the scientists tried various chemical tests.

● EXERCISE 3.   The sentences on the following page, all of which begin with the subject, contain phrase modifiers that can be placed at the beginning of the sentence. Rewrite each sentence, placing the modifying phrase at the beginning. (Remember that a modifying phrase used as an adjective should be placed as close as possible to the word it modifies.)

1. We should eat each year approximately sixteen pounds of salt, for the sake of our health.
2. The kitten, frightened by the thunder, cowered under the sofa.
3. The men bored holes through the cement and poured poison beneath the porch to kill the termites.
4. The whole episode, to tell the truth, was a hoax.
5. The wispy fog along the highway looks like gray ghosts prowling in the darkness, in the Smoky Mountains about midnight.
6. Flood waters no longer cause soil erosion in the Tennessee River basin.
7. The hides of bears, stitched with the hair turned inward, provide warmth for Eskimos.
8. Little Tippy, having nipped the carpenter, spent ten unhappy days in a veterinarian's cage.
9. We never thought of looking there, to be truthful.
10. The natives speak Tagalog in Luzon.

● EXERCISE 4.   Write ten sentences that begin with modifying phrases. Include at least two prepositional, two participial, and two infinitive phrases. After each sentence, name the kind of phrase with which it begins.

(3) You may begin sentences with subordinate clauses.

EXAMPLES   **After Dad had crushed out a half-smoked cigarette,** he said solemnly, "Never again."

While the clerk waited patiently, Sheila emptied her purse on the counter in a final effort to find two pennies.

If the cloud cover remains, temperatures over the state will be higher than predicted.

● EXERCISE 5.   The ten simple sentences in this exercise begin with the subject. Using the examples above as a guide, add an introductory subordinate clause that is related to the main idea. Place a comma after each one of your introductory clauses. (You may find the list of subordinating conjunctions on page 100 helpful.)

1. Milton always tried to do the right thing.
2. He began to sense that something was amiss.
3. She obviously did not remember my name.
4. We could not answer the riddle.
5. The motor clanked more loudly than before.
6. The mouse raced toward the pantry.
7. I saw that the bed had not been slept in.
8. They decided to cancel the game.
9. She was determined to attract more attention.
10. We tried a different way to avoid working.

● REVIEW EXERCISE A. Rewrite each of the following sentences, changing the beginning as directed.

Begin these sentences with single-word modifiers:

1. We finally reached the Tennessee River basin.
2. The large lakes, man-made, there have dams that control the flow of the Tennessee River.
3. There is less soil erosion in this region nowadays.
4. The Tennessee Valley Authority has certainly made many improvements since 1933.
5. Our family, vacationing, saw many other points of interest in the South.

Begin these sentences with modifying phrases:

6. Eskimos live in igloos during the winter.
7. They hunt wild game to provide food for themselves.
8. Eskimos need warm clothing for the cold climate.
9. Eskimos use the hide of a walrus for making shoes.
10. The people in Arabia, unlike the Eskimos, have no difficulty keeping warm.
11. The Arabs wear flowing garments to protect themselves from the hot wind and sun.
12. They move about from place to place, seeking water and grass for their sheep and camels.
13. They use light, movable tents for shelter.

Begin each of the following sentences with a subordinate clause:

14. There are many coffee plantations in Brazil, because the mild climate is ideal for growing coffee.
15. The coffee thrives when heavy rains fall during the winter months.
16. Men begin working when the golden berries fall from the trees in May.
17. The harvest will be a good one if heavy rains have not damaged the blossoms in September.
18. A long process of washing and drying is necessary before the coffee beans are ready to sell.
19. Trains haul tons of coffee to market after the workers have dried the beans for two months.
20. These crops bring prosperity to Brazil because the plantation owners seldom produce more coffee than they can sell.

● REVIEW EXERCISE B.   In the following paragraphs, every sentence begins with the subject. Rewrite the paragraphs to demonstrate what you have learned about varying the beginnings of sentences. Use single-word modifiers, phrases, and clauses. If you wish, you may also join sentences with one another.

1. We have been studying table manners in our home economics class. Miss Melton is our teacher. She gave us five rules to study today after telling us never to be greedy or make noise at the table. One of the most important rules concerned handling a napkin. You should not tuck a napkin under your chin. You should leave it on your lap instead. You should lay the napkin to the right of your plate after the meal. Miss Melton gave us several other pointers. A teaspoon should not be left in a cup from which you are drinking. You should not butter a whole slice of bread at once. You should break the bread, and you should butter only one part at a time. Crackers should not be crumbled into soup. You should not dunk doughnuts into coffee. Miss Melton is going to tell us tomorrow about correct ways to use silverware at a formal dinner.

2. Frank and I always celebrate the Fourth of July together. We usually either go to the lake for a swim or go on a picnic. We decided this year, however, to take a boat ride up the river. An outboard motor was out of the question, because we didn't have much money. We rented a light boat with two battered oars. We started upstream, attacking the swift water like a couple of woodchoppers clearing out underbrush. The river, growing narrow, suddenly became shallow and made rowing a problem. Frank decided that he would jump onto the bank in order to pull me with a rope. He missed his footing when he tried to leap from the boat. The expression on his face, as he sat in the river, showed that only his feelings were hurt. His clothes were soaked, and his shoes were full of mud. He gradually fretted his way toward dry land, mumbling under his breath. "We are going to the lake next year," he informed me.

VARYING SENTENCE STRUCTURE

Another common cause of sentence dullness is lack of variety in the kinds of sentences in a paragraph. Too many simple or compound sentences can make your style just as monotonous as too many subject-first sentences.

11b. Vary the kinds of sentences you write.

Study the following pairs of sentences. The first sentence in each pair is compound. The second sentence is complex. (See pages 106–08.) Notice that in the second sentence the relationship between ideas is clearer than in the first sentence. (The subordinate clauses are in bold-faced type.)

We visited the Old North Church in Boston, and we went to see the Bunker Hill Monument.

After we had visited the Old North Church in Boston, we went to see the Bunker Hill Monument. [The introductory subordinate clause tells *when* the visit to Bunker Hill was made.]

11b

Samuel apologized to Donna; his conscience had been troubling him.

Samuel apologized to Donna **because his conscience had been troubling him.** [The subordinate clause tells *why* he apologized.]

I saw a man running across the field, and he later proved to be an escaped prisoner.

The man **whom I saw running across the field** later proved to be an escaped prisoner. [The subordinate clause tells *which* man.]

● EXERCISE 6.   Change each compound sentence below to a complex sentence. Relate the ideas in each part of the sentence by using the subordinating conjunction or relative pronoun given in parentheses.

EXAMPLES   1. The frightened best man had unexpectedly run out of the church; an altar boy was asked to take his place. (after)

1. *After the frightened best man had unexpectedly run out of the church, an altar boy was asked to take his place.*

1. Louise plays the piano beautifully, and so we will ask her to entertain at our party. (who)
2. The school bus suddenly slowed down, and we saw the road-block. (when)
3. My cut hand was not healing properly, and so I finally saw a doctor. (because)
4. Charlene had studied the spelling list for thirty minutes, but she did not pass the test. (although)
5. We harbor ill will, and it usually grows and becomes a troublesome grudge. (if)
6. The boys play soccer at my house, but they are careful about the lawn and the flowers. (who)
7. We put antifreeze into the radiator of our car, and the first cold wave struck. (before)
8. In the library, Kathryn was reliving joyous events of the summer; she sat with her elbows propped on her open history book. (as)

9. We saw the teacher approaching; we stopped talking and started studying. (as soon as)
10. I enjoy having a room of my own, and I try hard to take care of it. (since)

● EXERCISE 7. Rewrite the following paragraph, which consists wholly of simple and compound sentences. To vary the style, change or combine some of the sentences into complex sentences using both adjective and adverb clauses. Do not, however, make all of the sentences complex, since your purpose is to achieve variety.

The music and thump of the drums grew louder, and the people lined up along the streets. In another minute, the high school band would come around the corner. Finally, with a blast of brass, the band emerged from behind the buildings. The majorettes raised their feet high and proudly like prancing horses. The girls were followed by the musicians. They were wearing red jackets. The band led the parade of colorful floats. Cheers and applause came from the crowd. Every child stood watching with shining eyes. Each one dreamed of being in the high school band someday.

● REVIEW EXERCISE C. Write a paragraph of about 100 words, describing a habit or attitude of yours or of a friend or relative. You may wish to write on one of these topics:

The inability to remember names correctly
The knack of saying or doing the wrong thing at the worst time
A tendency to spill or break things
The ability to make others feel at ease or important
A talent for seeing beauty in ordinary objects
A habit of asking pointless questions or giving absurd advice

As you write, avoid monotony of style by varying the kinds of sentences you use.

● REVIEW EXERCISE D. Write a composition of about 200 words, sharing a funny story, true or imaginary, with your classmates. You may want to tell two or three short anecdotes that are among your favorite conversation pieces. As you write, pay close attention to your style. Underline all beginning phrases and clauses and all subordinate clauses.

VARYING SENTENCE LENGTH

Since sentences of the same length are monotonous, you should strive to write some short sentences, some middle-sized ones, and some long ones.

11c. **Vary the length of your sentences.**

A series of short sentences often makes for a babyish style. Long, stringy sentences are also a common cause of dullness.

(1) Avoid too many short sentences.

Although short sentences are useful for describing exciting action, a composition consisting entirely of short sentences gives the effect of being chopped up. There are too many choppy sentences in the following paragraph.

> My cat's name is Bitsy. Bitsy is extremely affectionate. I think she genuinely loves me. It was Christmas Eve. Dad and I were decorating the tree. Mother was wrapping presents. Bitsy was nowhere to be seen. Suddenly we heard scratching at the front door. We heard Bitsy meowing. Dad opened the door. There was Bitsy. She had a mouse in her mouth. She walked into the house. She laid the mouse at my feet. Thus she delivered her Christmas present to me.

Notice how these short, choppy sentences can be combined into longer, smoother sentences.

> My cat Bitsy is so extremely affectionate that I think she genuinely loves me. On Christmas Eve, Dad and I were decorating the tree while Mother wrapped presents. Bitsy was nowhere to be seen. Suddenly we heard scratching at the door and Bitsy's meowing. When Dad opened the door, there

was Bitsy with a mouse in her mouth. Walking into the house, Bitsy laid the mouse at my feet. Thus she delivered her Christmas present to me.

There are still two short sentences in the paragraph. However, they contribute to effective variety. With the longer sentences, they do not create a choppy effect.

● EXERCISE 8. The following groups of sentences are unnecessarily short or monotonous. Combine the ideas in each passage into one or two varied, smooth, effective sentences. Use any means you wish—compound verbs, introductory phrases, appositives, verbals, subordinate clauses, and so on.

EXAMPLE 1. Hugh climbed up the hillside. He edged forward quietly and stealthily. He moved toward the spot. He had seen the mountain lion there.

1. *Climbing up the hillside, Hugh quietly and stealthily edged toward the spot where he had seen the mountain lion.*

1. The door swung open. We wheeled around. We saw Mr. Cates. He lumbered into the room.

2. Pinky grew impatient. He yowled at me. He wanted to go rabbit hunting. I could not get my gun fast enough. Pinky then lifted both front paws. He danced around in excitement on his hind legs.

3. You can build up self-confidence. Read books and magazines. Become interested in other people.

4. A doctor uses a stethoscope. With it he listens to the heart beat. He also listens to the lungs.

5. Hazel put out the cat. She locked the door. Then she fell into bed for a long night's sleep.

6. Joe is a handy man about the house. He can repair a broken window. He can also repair any electrical gadget. He can stop leaks in the roof.

7. I soaked the stamps in water. Then I placed them in my album. I used gummed hinges.

8. Betsy likes loud music. She likes jazz. She is particularly fond of recordings that grown-ups don't like.

11c

● EXERCISE 9.   Follow the directions for Exercise 8 as you revise the following groups of sentences.

1. My hobby is photography. I have here an unusual picture. It is a picture of the stars. In this picture, the stars are long white streaks.
2. I worked hours to get this effect. I propped up the camera in my backyard. Then I set the time exposure. Hours later, I closed the shutter.
3. The picture shows the movement of the earth. The movement of stars is very slow. We cannot see it happen. This picture made me curious about the stars.
4. Stars do not really rise and set. They apparently do so in my picture. The earth is turning. We cannot see the real motion of the stars. They are too far off.
5. We have, of course, seen streaks of light. We call these streaks shooting stars. They are not stars at all. They are meteors.

● EXERCISE 10.   Use each group of facts below in one sentence.

EXAMPLE   1. Englewood: a city in Hackensack Valley, fourteen miles from Jersey City, near the George Washington Bridge.

1. *Located in the Hackensack Valley, fourteen miles from Jersey City, Englewood is not far from the George Washington Bridge.*

1. My brother: graduated from high school last year, went to college, is now taking science courses, wants to enter medical school.
2. The car: air-conditioned, power steering, automatic transmission, power-adjustable seats, beautiful design.
3. Boxing match: September 21, at Yankee Stadium, Killer Wales downed Hurricane Jones, ninth round, remained champion.
4. Disorderly room: scattered papers, empty pop bottles, dusty furniture, cigarette ashes, an overturned chair.
5. Midnight movie: Halloween, the Palace, a double feature, terrifying scenes, screams from the audience.

(2) Avoid long, stringy sentences.

When you strive to eliminate short, choppy sentences, you may make the mistake of writing long, stringy sentences. An occasional long sentence is good; it characterizes a mature style, and it adds both smoothness and variety to your compositions. Stringy sentences, however, in which main clauses are monotonously strung together with *and, but, for, or, nor,* are bad. To correct the stringy sentences in your compositions, use subordinating conjunctions (see page 100), compound verbs, and verbals.

STRINGY   Cleveland caught the pass, and he ran twenty-two yards, and so he made a first down.

BETTER   **After** he had caught the pass, Cleveland ran twenty-two yards, **making** a first down.

STRINGY   Janet went to the board, and she drew a map, but her directions were still not clear to the class.

BETTER   **Although** Janet went to the board and drew a map, her directions were still not clear to the class.

Sometimes it is better to break a long, stringy sentence into two or more sentences.

STRINGY   I read the assignment, and then I began making notes on cards, for I wanted to memorize the main points in the lesson, but the bell rang, and I was not through, and so I had to carry my heavy book home.

BETTER   **After reading the assignment,** I began making notes on cards **so that** I could memorize the main points in the lesson. **Since I was not through when the bell rang,** I had to carry my heavy book home.

● EXERCISE 11.   Revise the following stringy sentences by using subordinating conjunctions, compound verbs, and verbals. Some of the very long sentences should be made into two or more sentences.

1. An accident occurred at the busy intersection, and several persons were injured, and then the police decided to put up a traffic light.

2. A small child may swallow a dozen aspirins, or he may wander out into the street, for he is not old enough to think for himself, and adults must make decisions for him.

3. Fever is usually the first sign of measles, and the eyes soon grow red, or the eyelids swell, and later the sneezing and coughing make a person think that he has a cold.

4. The trouble with New Year's resolutions is that they are always broken, for people make too many of them, or they hope for impossible reform, and they often try to become perfect all at once.

5. We are all creatures of habit, and bad habits are hard to break, but a person can make one resolution a year, and he can concentrate on that one aim, and then he can keep it.

● REVIEW EXERCISE E.   After you have reviewed the rules in this chapter, write a composition about 300 words in length. After you have written the first draft of your composition, revise it, keeping in mind the need for a lively style to keep your reader interested. As you write the final draft of your paper, demonstrate your ability to use varied, emphatic sentence structure. Be sure that you vary the beginnings, kinds, and length of your sentences.

PART FOUR

Composition

CHAPTER 12

Writing Paragraphs

Structure and Development of Paragraphs

The paragraph as a part of a longer composition functions in two ways. First, it is a division that the reader can see. As his eye travels down the page, each paragraph, set off by spacing or indention, appears as a distinct part of the whole, like a brick in a wall. Second, and more important, a paragraph is a stage in the writer's thinking. Compositions are built with ideas, and each idea is developed or explained in a separate paragraph. The paragraph may be long or short, depending upon the idea it develops; but it must make a single point that the reader can grasp. It must stick to that point.

When you are learning to write, you can learn a great many skills by writing one-paragraph compositions. This chapter will show you the characteristics of a good paragraph, and the exercises will provide practice in writing one-paragraph themes.

THE STRUCTURE OF A PARAGRAPH

12a. A *paragraph* is a series of sentences developing one topic.

As a unit of thought, a paragraph contains a group of related sentences developing one central idea. This topic is usually stated in a *topic sentence* somewhere in the paragraph.

As you read the following paragraph, notice that every detail is related to the raging fire or "inferno" mentioned in the first sentence.

> The main tent was an inferno. Fed by the furnace of the crackling seats below, the flames shot into the sky. Burning ropes writhed through the air like incandescent snakes, and the roaring of the blaze drowned out the shouts of the performers running about to save their possessions and drag the animals' cages to safety.[1]

● EXERCISE 1. Before going on with this chapter, try your hand at writing a well-unified paragraph. Write from 50 to 75 words describing a hobby, an interesting place, or an exciting event, such as a fire, an accident, a storm. As you write, keep your controlling idea firmly in mind, and make sure that every sentence in your paragraph is closely related to it.

The Topic Sentence

12b. The topic sentence states the one topic of a paragraph.

In the paragraph by Paul Gallico on this page, the topic sentence is the first sentence. This sentence contains the controlling idea of the whole paragraph; it tells the reader what the paragraph is about. The other sentences develop the idea expressed by the topic sentence.

As in this paragraph, the topic sentence ordinarily comes at the beginning. It may appear elsewhere in the paragraph —in the middle or at the end. Until you have had more experience with writing paragraphs, however, you will be wise to begin with your topic sentence.

[1] From "The Hungry Ones" by Paul Gallico in the January 5–January 12, 1963 issue of *Saturday Evening Post*. Reprinted by permission of Harold Ober Associates.

12
a-b

● EXERCISE 2. Find the topic sentence in each of the paragraphs below. Be ready to explain how the other sentences develop the topic sentence.

1

It is a sad thing that as soon as the hands of the clock have turned ten, the shadow of going to bed begins to creep over the evening. We have never heard bedtime spoken of with any enthusiasm. One after another we have seen a gathering disperse, each person saying (with an air of solemn resignation): "Well, I guess I'll go to bed." But there was no hilarity about it. It is really rather touching how they cling to the departing skirts of the day that is vanishing under the spinning shadow of night.[1]

2

Emerson is right in saying that friendship can't be hurried. It takes time to ripen. It needs a background of humorous, wearisome, or even tragic events shared together, a certain tract of memories shared in common, so that you know that your own life and your companion's have really moved for some time in the same channel. It needs interchange of books, meals together, discussion of one another's whims with mutual friends, to gain a proper perspective. It is set in a rich haze of half-remembered occasions, sudden glimpses, ludicrous pranks, unsuspected observations, midnight confidences when heart spoke to candid heart.[1]

12c. Every sentence in a paragraph should be closely related to the topic.

A paragraph is a unit. Any sentence in a paragraph which does not relate to the topic of that paragraph spoils the unity and should be taken out.

The paragraph on the next page contains a sentence that is not related to the topic sentence. As you read the paragraph, notice how this sentence, printed in bold-faced type, distracts the reader from the problem of awkward hands.

[1] From *Pipefuls* by Christopher Morley. Copyright 1920, 1948 by Christopher Morley. Published by J. B. Lippincott Company.

I never know what to do with my hands when I am in an awkward situation. For instance, when I am making an oral report in history class, I have trouble with my hands. Sometimes I self-consciously clasp them behind me so that they won't show. At other times, I hide them in my pockets and start jingling coins noisily. **A good speaker does not have disconcerting mannerisms—such as saying "uh" at every pause, pacing back and forth, or looking out the window instead of at his audience.** I can understand why Napoleon went through life as a one-armed man, why he always kept his other hand safely buried beneath his coat.

The topic of the following paragraph is the beauty of a perfect day. Every detail should relate to this central idea. Which sentence in the paragraph is not related to the topic?

All of the elements of nature must have contrived to produce such a perfect day. It was a day that made everything seem possible and anything wonderful. The sun didn't shine down— it drew one up to it. Every blade of grass was saturated with light. The wind whipped the leaves in the trees and then parted the wildflowers as it ran through them. In the wintertime I have to stay indoors so much that I like to be outdoors in the spring and summer. It was a day when every living cell seemed to vibrate with the joy of life as the sun and wind had a glorious frolic with the earth.

● EXERCISE 3.   In each of the following paragraphs, there is one sentence that is not closely related to the topic. Find this sentence, and copy it on your paper.

1

Like the singer of the song "Mañana," Robert is a procrastinator. When the roof leaks, he says, "I'll fix it, after the rain stops." If the yard needs mowing, Robert uses the morning dew as an excuse for delay; in the afternoon, he complains of the hot sun and murmurs, "I'll get at that mowing later, maybe tomorrow." Worst of all, however, was his procrastination last spring, when armies of fleas invaded his block. Everyone else in the neighborhood quickly got rid of the invading fleas, but not Robert! Robert's guests, swatting at the nipping fleas,

12c

begged him to spray the house immediately, not "later." After a lazy yawn, Robert responded, "Oh, there's no hurry. Sure, the fleas hop on you, but in a little while they hop off. What's the rush about spraying?" Of course, as everyone knows, Robert has many admirable qualities; for instance, he is unusually charming and generous.

2

There is hardly a more exciting way to travel than by ship. Perhaps it is the complete isolation from land or the feeling of living in another world inhabited only by the passengers on board which makes one so ready for adventure. Of course, sometimes I get bored because every day is alike; it is as monotonous as riding a train across barren wastelands. What a thrill it is to wake early in the morning and go up on deck to see nothing but water sparkling in the morning air! It's fun to sight an occasional gray hump of land away in the distance. All day the ship breaks through the water with a burst of foam, and although her journey seems endless, there are no tracks in front of or behind her. At night the ocean around becomes a dark world with only one moonlit path to nowhere.

3

Yesterday Ann, Jean, and I went to the beach. Arriving about two o'clock, we parked the car, flung open the door, and leaped out, running over the sand with our bare feet. Then we spread out a large blanket and sprawled out side by side to let the hot rays of the sun turn our white skins to golden red. In a little while, Jean, by far the smallest girl in the group, jumped up and bellowed, "Let's take a dip! Last one in is a rotten egg!" Of course, Jean was the rotten egg. Lately Jean has been dieting; she eats very few sweets and starches. In the water, we dived for shells and pretended that we were graceful ballet dancers. At five o'clock, when we were exhausted, it was moved and seconded that we leave the beach and go eat.

4

Even though they know that speed is a major cause of traffic accidents, many Americans persist in racing toward death on the highway. Rather than be late for a round of golf or a week's visit with relatives, drivers speed around sharp curves, pass other cars on steep hills, and squeeze in and out of a line of cars. Frequently the oncoming drivers, taken by surprise, must swerve to the shoulder of the road or crash headlong into a speeding automobile on the wrong side of the road. Newspapers are filled with the gory details of mangled bodies found in car wrecks that occur because of slick highways, faulty brakes, or drivers falling asleep at the wheel. The speeder is a daredevil who gambles that he will not become a statistic in the files of the state highway department. A menace to society, he must "make good time," even though he risks his own life and endangers the lives of others who must share the highway with him.

THE DEVELOPMENT OF A PARAGRAPH

To develop a paragraph, you usually supply additional specific information to make clear the meaning of the topic sentence. As you read the following paragraph, taken from an article entitled "Mysteries of the Sea," notice the way the author explains key words in his topic sentence.

Waves are described in terms of their height, wave-length, and period. "Height" is the vertical distance between the high point of a wave crest and the low point of the adjacent trough. "Wave-length" is the distance from one crest to the next, and "period" is the time it takes two adjacent crests to pass a fixed point, such as the end of a pier. The mathematics of wave theories are usually concerned with relationships between these and related characteristics.[1]

The first sentence sets forth the topic: the description of waves in terms of their height, wave-length, and period. Every other sentence in the paragraph develops this idea. The second sentence defines the term *height*, and the third explains both *wave-length* and *period*. The last sentence emphasizes the importance and the relationship of these terms.

[1] From *Frontiers of the Sea: The Story of Oceanographic Research*, by Robert C. Cowen. Garden City: Doubleday & Company, Inc., 1960.

12d. Make a working plan for developing the topic sentence into a paragraph.

As you have now learned, a paragraph is a unit containing a series of closely related sentences developing one central idea. To organize your thoughts effectively, you should learn to make a working plan, a kind of outline for the paragraph.

Paul Gallico's paragraph on page 237 reveals this plan:

Topic   The main tent was an inferno.

Specific information

        crackling seats—like a furnace
        shooting flames
        burning ropes—like snakes
        roaring blaze
        performers—running about

As you write your plan of a paragraph, keep your topic sentence firmly in mind so that every bit of additional information will be closely related to your central idea.

Suppose, for example, that you are to write a paragraph on this topic: "Everyone in my family likes to read different kinds of books." You should give the names of the members of your family and should tell exactly what each one likes to read. By holding strictly to the topic sentence, you are not likely to include any discussion of the reading taste of a friend or a teacher or someone else, nor will you ramble off to favorite radio or television programs. Notice how the additional information below sticks closely to the topic sentence.

Topic   Everyone in my family likes to read different kinds of books.

Specific information

        Brother—comics
        Sister—novels
        Mother—magazines about housekeeping
        Father—how-to-do-it books
        I like science fiction.

● EXERCISE 4.   Choose two of the following topic sentences, and for each write a plan for a paragraph. First, copy the topic sentence, and then list four points to support it. Save your plans for use later in Review Exercise B.

1. There are several reasons why I like Sundays.
2. My little brother is always pretending.
3. Teen-agers have their own ideas about going steady.
4. It's fun to take a walk in the snow.
5. Some television programs are really funny.
6. When riding in a jet, I never become bored.
7. Some remedies are worse than the disease.
8. No one seems interested in my troubles.
9. Every time I look at the stars, I am a philosopher.
10. Some promises are easy to make and hard to keep.

12e. A paragraph may be developed by giving details or examples.

The topic sentence is a general statement. It should be supported by specific details and examples that make its meaning clear. Well-chosen details make for effective paragraphs. Compare the general statements that follow with the detailed ones.

1. People who are noisy or angry may inspire fear or even hatred, but they are neither clear nor persuasive.

1. A wife screaming at her husband, a sergeant roaring at a platoon, a father bellowing at his son, create fear, and even hatred, but they do not manage to explain what they want done and persuade their hearers to do it.[1]   —GILBERT HIGHET

2. As a reader, she had a poor memory.

2. She read the same novels over and over again without knowing it.   —GRAHAM GREENE

[1] From *The Art of Teaching* by Gilbert Highet, published by Alfred A. Knopf, Inc.

12
d-e

3. I love old china, even more than I love fine paintings. I don't know why.

3. I have an almost feminine partiality for old china. When I go to see any great house, I inquire for the china-closet, and next for the picture gallery. I cannot defend the order of preference, but by saying that we have all some taste or other, of too ancient a date to admit of our remembering distinctly that it was an acquired one. I can call to mind the first play, and the first exhibition, that I was taken to; but I am not conscious of a time when china jars and saucers were introduced into my imagination.

—CHARLES LAMB

As you compare the following two paragraphs, which develop the same topic sentence, notice the importance of numerous, concrete details which give vitality to description.

GENERAL (skimpy development)

It is little wonder that wind-driven waves have been a powerful factor in carving the shore lines. These waves have an influence upon the various and sundry shapes of rocks on or near the shore. They are also the cause of caves and other types of holes in the ground.

SPECIFIC DETAILS (well developed)

It is little wonder that wind-driven waves have been a powerful factor in carving the shore lines. They can attack and remove even solid rock cliffs, often creating curious shapes such as rock pinnacles standing a little from shore or joined to it by a natural bridge. Similarly, waves can hollow out caves in the rock. Then, having eroded a cave, they may pound upward until they break through the roof. One sometimes sees spray shooting up out of apparently solid ground behind the main shore line.[1]

Sometimes you may wish merely to list details to explain or emphasize an important word in the topic sentence. By listing the items on the breakfast menu, Thomas Wolfe used this method of development in the following paragraph.

We could see the circus performers eating tremendous breakfasts, with all the savage relish of their power and strength. They ate big fried steaks, pork chops, rashers of bacon, a half-dozen eggs, great slabs of fried ham and great stacks of wheat cakes which a cook kept flipping in the air with the skill of a juggler, and which a husky-looking waitress kept rushing to their tables on loaded trays held high and balanced marvelously on the fingers of a brawny hand. And above all the maddening odors of the wholesome and suc-culent food, there brooded forever the sultry and delicious fragrance—that somehow seemed to add a zest and sharp-ness to all the powerful and thrilling life of morning—of strong boiling coffee, which we could see sending off clouds of steam from an enormous polished urn, and which the circus performers gulped down, cup after cup.[2]

Some topic sentences, like the one in the following para-graph, clearly call for supporting examples.

Whenever you buy a gift, you should always consider the interests of the receiver. For example, if you are buying a birthday present for a friend who likes to read detective stories, you might select *The Adventures of Sherlock Holmes* or *The Case of the Red Rooster*. If, on the other hand, you are choosing a gift for your little cousin who likes to play "cow-boys and Indians," you might decide upon a cap pistol, a toy sheriff's badge, or an Indian suit. Similarly, if you must choose a gift for your mother on Mother's Day, you should remember

[1] From *Frontiers of the Sea: The Story of Oceanographic Research*, by Robert C. Cowen. Garden City: Doubleday & Company, Inc., 1960.
[2] Quotation from "Circus at Dawn" by Thomas Wolfe (Copyright 1935, Charles Scribner's Sons) is used by permission of Charles Scribner's Sons.

that she especially likes new things for her kitchen. You can
please her by buying a novelty cooky jar or a new gadget for
slicing potatoes.

● EXERCISE 5. Choose one of the following topic sentences, and develop it into a paragraph. By answering the
questions in brackets, you can make your paragraph interesting with specific details. Use the topic sentence as the
first sentence of your paragraph.

1. I took a good, long look into the mirror. [What exactly did
   you see there? What was the condition of your hair? The
   expression of your eyes? What movements did you make?]
2. Almost everyone is a teacher. [Can you list several persons
   you know and point out specifically what they teach and to
   whom?]
3. Walking down the hall today, I heard many interesting sounds.
   [When did you notice the sounds—between classes, during
   the noon hour? Can you give specific details about each
   sound? How do these noises reflect the personalities and
   activities of the teachers and pupils?]
4. Ninety-five percent of the things we worry about never happen. [Can you apply this common saying to your own experiences? Are you a chronic worrier? Can you point out
   two or three things that once caused you needless anxiety?
   Can you convince your reader, by your specific details, that
   worry is senseless?]
5. Money cannot buy the best things in life. [What exactly are
   the "best things" in life? Who can possess or enjoy these
   things? How?]
6. When I criticize others, I usually complain loudest about
   those weaknesses that I dislike about myself. [Can you make
   a list of traits that you wish you didn't have, the very traits
   that you dislike and criticize most in others?]
7. Without actually saying so, she seemed glad that we had
   dropped by. [How did she greet you? Exactly what did she
   do? How did her actions indicate her pleasure?]

● EXERCISE 6. Choose one of the topic sentences on the
next page, and develop it into a paragraph by using specific

examples. If you prefer, you may write on a topic of your own choosing.

1. The customer isn't always right.
2. When called upon to speak, a person should consider the interests of his audience.
3. My friends have a strange assortment of pets.
4. Emerson is right in saying that good manners are made up of petty sacrifices.
5. As Lincoln said, "Truth is generally the best vindication against slander."

12f. A paragraph may be developed by telling a story or relating an incident.

Another way to develop a paragraph is to select a story or incident from your own experience that will support and explain your topic sentence. The incident described in the paragraph below shows Einstein's "incapability of behavior that was not genuine."

Typical of Einstein is the story of the popular lecture he was finally prevailed upon to give, for it shows his incapability of behavior that was not genuine. He had been asked many times to speak to a certain audience, but had always begged off on the basis that he had nothing to say. Finally, however, the pressure became so great that he was forced to accede. Came the evening of the lecture, and amidst applause Dr. Einstein was led to the front of the stage and introduced. For a few moments he looked out at the audience, tongue-tied and silent. Finally he could stand it no longer and, smiling sheepishly, said, "I find that I have nothing to say," and returned to his seat.[1]

● EXERCISE 7. Develop a paragraph by using a story or incidents from your experience to support your topic sentence. You may select one story to illustrate the truth or

[1] From "Albert Einstein: Appraisal of an Intellect" by George R. Harrison from the June, 1955 issue of *The Atlantic Monthly*. Reprinted by permission of the author and The Atlantic Monthly.

12f

untruth of a well-known saying such as "Love is blind" or "Ignorance is no excuse." Or you may first state in a topic sentence a lesson that you have learned—for example, "I have learned what responsibility means" or "Now I know the value of silence"—and then develop your topic by giving one or more incidents from your experience.

12g. A paragraph may be developed by giving reasons.

Especially when dealing with a controversial topic, you can develop a paragraph effectively by giving reasons. As you read the following paragraph, notice that the author states his topic first and then gives reasons why high school graduates now wish they had been made to work harder in school.

> It is not uncommon today to find young men and women who, when they have graduated from high school, wish they had been made to work harder. Why? Suddenly adults have been spurred into believing that only education will save us from lagging behind the Russians; suddenly bright students have a new status which a few years ago they sadly lacked— often to the point of being ostracized by their contemporaries. The "grind" and the "brain" were formerly looked down upon, a reflection of the intellectual distrust on the part of parents. Now the winds blow in a different direction.[1]

12h. A paragraph may be developed by making comparisons or contrasts.

When developing a paragraph by making comparisons, you emphasize similarities; by making contrasts, you emphasize differences. The first paragraph on the next page is developed by comparison; it stresses the similarities of the Pacific Ocean and a highway. The second paragraph em-

---

[1] From "Teen-Agers Mirror Their Parents" by Russell Lynes. © by The New York Times Company. Reprinted by permission.

ploys contrast to show the differences in the behavior of a woman and a man.

1

There is only one sensible way to think of the Pacific Ocean today. It is the highway between Asia and America, and whether we wish it or not, from now on there will be immense traffic along that highway. If we know what we want, if we have patience and determination, if above all we have understanding, we may insure that the traffic will be peaceful, consisting of tractors and students and medical missionaries and bolts of cloth. But if we are not intelligent, or if we cannot cultivate understanding in Asia, then the traffic will be armed planes, battleships, submarines, and death. In either alternative we may be absolutely certain that from now on the Pacific traffic will be a two-way affair.[1]

2

Now, no woman minds at all walking the length of a room and sitting in the front row, even when the room is full of people. In fact, she rather likes it. If she sees a seat in the front row, she goes for it; and her ears do not get red, either. For her, walking to that seat is a purely practical matter. Why should her ears get red? Watch her as she sails down the aisle at a lecture or in church, cool as a cucumber; and then watch her husband as he slinks after her. He has clearly been trying to slide into the back row, and has made several little bolts in that direction; but she properly ignores him. She never gives in to his manly timidity, for she hopes, sooner or later, to train him to overcome it.[2]

● EXERCISE 8. The following topics can be developed by drawing a comparison or making a contrast. Select one of the topics; write a topic sentence stating the point of your paragraph; then develop the topic sentence into a paragraph of about 100 words by making a comparison or contrast. If you prefer, write on a topic of your own choosing.

[1] From *Return to Paradise*, by James Michener. Copyright, 1951, by James A. Michener. Reprinted by permission of Random House, Inc.
[2] Reprinted from the essay, "The Timid Sex," by Robert M. Gay by permission of The Atlantic Monthly.

12
g-h

1. Dogs and cats as pets
2. Football and soccer (or baseball)
3. My aunt and my uncle
4. Elementary school and junior high (or ninth grade)
5. English and mathematics
6. This community and the one I formerly lived in
7. Types of parents
8. Two jobs I have held
9. Hairdos
10. Two TV programs

● REVIEW EXERCISE A.   Choose any one of the following words (or any other word that your teacher may suggest) and use it as a key word in a topic sentence that clearly expresses an idea or opinion. Then develop the topic sentence by giving additional information—specific details, examples, a story, incidents, reasons, comparisons, or contrasts. As you go over your paragraph, be sure to remove any sentence that is not closely related to the topic sentence.

1. noses	6. surprise
2. brave	7. glamour
3. watching	8. pigheaded
4. nightmare	9. water
5. spectacular	10. bargains

● REVIEW EXERCISE B.   Using one of the plans that you prepared for Exercise 4, write a paragraph developed by one of the means listed in rules 12e–h.

COHERENCE

The sentences in a paragraph should all be closely related to the main point. In addition, they should flow smoothly and naturally from one to another. When they do, the paragraph is said to have *coherence*.

Arrangement of Ideas

One of the best ways to achieve coherence is to present a clear arrangement of ideas.

12i. To achieve coherence in a paragraph, arrange details in a logical order: chronologically, spatially, or in order of importance.

(1) Details in a paragraph may be arranged *chronologically*.

The natural way of telling how to do or make something is to arrange the steps of the process in the order in which they must be carried out. The natural way of relating a story or incident is to give the events in the order in which they happened. This method of organizing information is called *chronological*—the order of time.

Let us make the simplest kind of photograph—a shadow picture. — topic sentence

If you have dark shades, pull them down and put out the lights in the room. Now, even if it is daylight outside, it is dark enough inside the room to take a piece of photographic "contact" paper out of its package for a moment without spoiling it. . . . In the darkened room, put on a table top the piece of paper you are going to use, with the smooth, coated side up. Lay two or three keys on top of the paper. Be sure they are separate and lying flat. Make sure the rest of the paper in the package is covered. Turn on the room lights for a minute. When

steps in process arranged chrono-logically

12i

the paper is developed, you will find it bears a white shadow picture, or photographic image, of the keys.[1]

(2) Details in a paragraph may be arranged *spatially*.

Just as it is natural to take up events in the order they happen and to describe steps in doing or making something in order, it is natural to describe objects by their position in relation to each other. This arrangement of sentences is *spatial*. In the following paragraph from Mark Twain's *Autobiography*, the various details are arranged spatially, or by position.

The [1] farmhouse stood <u>in the middle</u> of a very large [2] yard, and the yard was fenced on three sides with rails and on the <u>rear side</u> with high [3] palings. <u>Against these</u> stood the [4] smoke house; <u>beyond the palings</u> was the [5] orchard; <u>beyond the orchard</u> were the [6] tobacco fields. The front yard was entered over a stile made of sawed-off logs of graduated heights; I do not remember any gate. <u>In a corner</u> of the front yard were a dozen lofty hickory [7] trees and a dozen black walnuts, and in the nutting season riches were to be gathered there.[2]

objects 1–7 described in relation to each other (Underscored words indicate spatial arrangement.)

[1] From *Exploring the Sciences* by Paul Brandwein *et al.* Reprinted by permission of Harcourt Brace Jovanovich, Inc.

[2] From *The Autobiography of Mark Twain*, edited by Charles Neider (Harper & Brothers, 1959). Reprinted by permission of Harper & Row, Publishers.

(3) Details in a paragraph may be arranged in order of importance.

In a paragraph that deals with ideas that do not involve time or position, details or examples may be organized in order of their importance. Such a paragraph may be developed by facts, some of which are more striking or important than others. If it is an argumentative paragraph developed by listing reasons, undoubtedly some reasons will be more convincing than others. The order may be from least to most important, or vice versa. Either method, if followed consistently, should result in understandable arrangement.

In the following paragraphs, ideas are arranged in order of importance. In the first, the order is from least to most important; in the second, the order is reversed, with the most important idea stated first.

Americans came to regard the spoils system as a stumbling block in the way of good government. — topic sentence

1 Rapid, large-scale changes of public officials made it difficult for the government to carry out plans efficiently. (1) first idea

2 Men of ability hesitated to take jobs that might last only for a few years. The jobs themselves changed as the nation developed. (2) more important idea

3 Most important, public positions came to require more and more skill. City, state, and national governments needed doctors, chemists, engineers, and other trained people. Such public officials must be hired for their ability, not for their loyalty to a political party.[1] (3) "most important" idea

[1] From *Story of the American Nation* by Mabel B. Casner, *et al.* Reprinted by permission of Harcourt Brace Jovanovich, Inc.

During the postwar period the interest in traditional spectator sports rose markedly. [1]Baseball remained the most popular professional game, with an average yearly attendance of between 9 and 10 million at major-league games. Babe Ruth replaced Ty Cobb as the idol of fans and in 1927 astounded the baseball world by hitting a record number of sixty home runs. [2]College football drew some 30,000,000 spectators in the same year. Red Grange, a halfback for the University of Illinois, became a national hero and won a movie contract. [3]Prizefighting continued to enjoy tremendous popularity, and in 1927 ardent boxing fans spent $2,658,660 to see the famous Dempsey-Tunney match. [4]Professional golf and tennis matches also increased their audiences during the 1920's.[1]

— topic sentence

(1) baseball, most important (most popular) supporting details

(2) football, next in importance

(3) prizefighting

(4) golf and tennis—least popular

● EXERCISE 9. For each of the following topics, indicate the kind of order—chronological, spatial, or order of importance—you would use in writing a paragraph on the subject. Number your paper 1–20, and write *C* (for *chronological*), *S* (for *spatial*), or *I* (for *importance*) beside the corresponding number. Be prepared to explain the reasons for your choice of each.

1. The double play in baseball
2. My newly decorated room

[1] From *Rise of the American Nation* by Lewis Paul Todd and Merle Curti. Reprinted by permission of Harcourt Brace Jovanovich, Inc.

3. The honor system in junior high school
4. Drawing a map
5. Why homework (should, should not) be abolished
6. My plans for the future
7. A pleasant picnic site
8. Washing my dog
9. The duties of the class secretary
10. Locating a book in the library
11. Why I frequently visit the library
12. The reference room in the library
13. How to make fudge
14. Ordering decorations for a dance
15. Decorating the gym for a dance
16. The reasons for organizing a dramatic club
17. My favorite picture
18. The stage setting for our class play
19. Learning to drive
20. Why driver education should be required in high school

● EXERCISE 10. Choose ten of the topics from Exercise 9, and write a topic sentence for each. Choose at least three that you would treat chronologically, three that you would treat spatially, and three that should be treated in order of importance.

● EXERCISE 11. Using three of the topic sentences that you prepared for Exercise 10, write one chronologically arranged paragraph, one that is spatially arranged, and one arranged in order of importance.

Connecting Sentences in the Paragraph

In writing paragraphs, you need to connect the sentences, to bridge the gaps between them so that your paragraphs will read smoothly. There are two different ways in which this may be done: by *transitional devices* and by *direct references*.

12j. To make a paragraph read smoothly, use *transitional devices* and *direct references*.

Transitional devices are connecting words or phrases that show the relationship between ideas, details, examples, etc., in the paragraph. The following are examples of transitional expressions:

accordingly	finally	nevertheless
after	first (second, third, etc.)	next
after that	for example	one
afterward	for instance	once . . . now
also	for this reason	on the contrary
and	furthermore	on the other hand
another	hence	or
as a result	however	other
as soon as	in addition	otherwise
at first	in spite of	similarly
at last	instead	soon
at the same time	in the first (second, etc.)	that is
before long	place	then
besides	in the meantime	therefore
but	later	to begin with
consequently	likewise	thus
even if	meanwhile	when
even so	moreover	yet

Of course, a paragraph in which all the sentences were linked by means of transitional devices would be dull. A transitional device is not required in every sentence and should not be used if it is not needed. Sentences may also be linked by *direct references*.

(1) Use pronouns that refer to nouns in a preceding sentence or to the idea in a preceding sentence.

EXAMPLE   Larry spent Saturday cleaning out the garage. **This** did not seem to **him** to be a proper use of the holiday; but **it** had to be done. [*This* refers to "cleaning out the garage," as does *it*. *Him*, of course, refers to "Larry."]

(2) You may repeat a word from the preceding sentence.

EXAMPLE My personal library includes several rather valuable books. These **books** were a gift from my grandmother.

(3) Use a word or phrase that means the same thing as a word or phrase in a preceding sentence.

EXAMPLE The runaway engine sped down the inclined track. On and on the **mighty monster** raced, as we watched in horror, overcome by the unharnessed power of the **giant machine**. [Both refer to *engine*.]

As you read the following paragraph, refer to the marginal key. It shows you how the numbered words link ideas.

People who use different languages do not necessarily use all the same sounds. [1] For instance, the French do not use either of the [2] sounds which English-speaking people represent by *th;* the Icelanders use [3] both, and have two different signs for them, þ for the sound in *th*in and ð for the sound in *th*en. [4] Thus an alphabet tailored to the needs of one language may provide no signs for certain sounds in [5] another. [6] It may also provide signs for which another language has no need.[1]

topic sentence

(1) transition

(2) repetition of key word

(3) pronoun reference to sounds

(4) transition

(5) pronoun reference to language

(6) pronoun reference to alphabet

● EXERCISE 12. Carefully study the following paragraphs, observing the bold-faced words which connect the ideas of sentences. Be prepared to point out in class discussion the ideas which these transitional devices and direct references

[1] From *The Wonderful World of Communication* by Lancelot Hogben. Reproduced by permission of Rathbone Books.

12j

link. The lines of the paragraphs have been numbered for your convenience.

1.   Suppose you go into a fruiterer's shop, wanting an apple.
2.   **First,** you take up **one,** and on biting it, you find it is sour;
3.   **then** you look at it and see that it is hard and green. You
4.   take up **another one,** and **that** too is hard, green, and sour.
5.   The shopman offers you **a third.** Before biting it, **however,**
6.   you examine it and find that it is hard and green. **There-**
7.   **fore,** you immediately say that you will not have it, as it
8.   must be sour, like those that you have already tried.
9.   Nothing can be more simple than **that,** you think. If
10.   you will take the trouble to analyze and trace out into its
11.   logical elements what has been done by the mind, **however,**
12.   you will be greatly surprised. **In the first place,** you have
13.   performed the operation of induction. You have found
14.   that, in two experiences, hardness and greenness in apples
15.   went together with sourness. It was so in the **first** case, and
16.   it was confirmed by the **second. True,** it is a very small
17.   basis, but still it is enough to find sourness in apples where
18.   you get hardness and greenness. You found upon **that** a
19.   general law that all hard and green apples are sour; and
20.   **that,** as far as it goes, is a perfect induction.[1]

● EXERCISE 13.   Write a paragraph explaining how to do something. Give each step clearly, and use transitional devices and direct references for bridging gaps between ideas. You may write on a serious topic, such as how to play a game or how to make good soup or build a bird feeder. Or you may write on a humorous topic, such as how to make others think that you are a genius or how to eat popcorn in a theater. Underline each transitional device or direct reference that you have used.

● REVIEW EXERCISE C.   Write a paragraph beginning with one of the topic sentences on page 259. Put into practice what you have learned in this chapter. After you have

[1] Adapted from *Collected Essays* (1893) by Thomas Henry Huxley.

written your paragraph, ask yourself these questions about it:

Does the topic sentence clearly state the central idea of the paragraph?

Have I given enough additional information to develop the topic fully?

Is this information interesting and specific?

Does every sentence in the paragraph relate closely to the topic sentence?

Do connective words help to clarify the explanation as they bridge the gap between ideas?

1. My friends have various attitudes toward money.
2. I do not believe everything I read in newspapers.
3. The three most popular magazines in my home are . . .
4. My bicycle and I are no longer friends.
5. Western movies are healthful entertainment for young people.
6. Only a few snakes are poisonous.
7. A hurricane can do great damage.
8. There is a right way to put on makeup.
9. Educational TV programs vary in quality.
10. Anyone can learn to play volleyball.
11. I have trouble making decisions.
12. There are many ways to use leftovers.
13. I know three good "icebreakers" for a party.
14. If you know how, you can build a fire without using a match.
15. The way that a thermometer works is interesting.
16. Uranium is an important element.
17. The greatest hazard in going to the moon is . . .
18. I notice other people's eyes.
19. Limestone has many uses.
20. There is an art to taking good colored snapshots.

● REVIEW EXERCISE D. Study the following paragraphs so that you can discuss them in class. Be prepared to give the topic sentence or the central idea of each paragraph and to tell what method (or combination of methods) is used to develop it: many details, examples, a story, incidents, reasons, comparisons, or contrasts. Point out transitional expressions.

1

The whole place seemed designed for midgets. We scraped our knuckles against the ceiling when we dressed. Sinks, tables, and the purple plush armchairs were much too low. Mirrors reflected our chests. Worst of all, from Joe's point of view, were the low lintels. He seriously considered wearing a crash helmet around the house.[1]

2

The word *gold* has a glamorous sound! It has power, too, enough to lure thousands of hopefuls to Alaska around the turn of this century, and it meant different things to different people. Some who came wanted a fortune, overnight, if possible. Some were fleeing the crowded, dirty cities and wanted only untainted air to breathe and lots of space. Many were running from trouble, real or imagined—family, work, or money trouble. For some older men it was the last, lone hope of making a "success." A few women, considered very daring, came too. Idealists, cynics, workers, loafers, adventurers, and writers—they all poured into the territory. There was plenty of room for them in Alaska.[2]

3

We went to a country school, which was on our own ranch, where the children of five or six other families attended. Most of them rode to school horseback. One of our games was "cats and dogs." This, we boys—for girls did not join in it—played at noon recess. The "cats" would set out in the brush afoot. About three minutes later the "dogs," mounted on horses and yelling like Apache Indians, would take after them. The brush had thorns and the idea of the "cat" was to get into brush so thick that the "dog" could not follow him, or to crawl into a thicket where he could not be seen. Sometimes the chase would last

[1] From "Lucky American Women" by Maya Pines from the January, 1963 issue of *Harper's* Magazine. Reprinted by permission of Harper's Magazine.

[2] From *Here Is Alaska* by Evelyn Steffansson. Reprinted by permission of Charles Scribner's Sons.

until long after the bell had sounded. I remember one great chase that kept us out until three o'clock. An hour later eight or nine boys were alone with the teacher and a pile of switches.[1]

4

Pinch hitters fall into categories. Philley, for example, is a slap hitter who can be counted on to meet the ball. Men of this type are summoned for singles, and seldom for power. Others, such as Smoky Burgess of the Pirates, Charley Maxwell of the Tigers, Carl Sawatski of the Cardinals and Chuck Essegian of the Indians, are called on when the situation demands a long ball.[2]

5

To a philosopher all *news*, as it is called, is gossip, and they who edit and read it are old women over their tea. Yet not a few are greedy after this gossip. There was such a rush, as I hear, the other day at one of the offices to learn the foreign news by the last arrival, that several large squares of plate glass belonging to the establishment were broken by the pressure— news which I seriously think a ready wit might write a twelve-month, or twelve years, beforehand with sufficient accuracy. . . .

—HENRY DAVID THOREAU

6

Suppose that you were going to paint a picture of a hillside on a windy day. There are two ways you might go about it. One would be to paint a blade of grass and then another blade of grass and then another, until you had put down all the blades of grass you could see, sketched in the rest of the hillside, and were ready to start on the trees, limb by limb, and then the clouds — with a stray butterfly thrown in for good measure. If you could do all of this accurately, reproducing exactly the perspective and color, you would have produced something known as "photographic realism." The other way of going at this picture would be to paint *what you really see* when you look at that hillside;

---

[1] From "When I Was a Boy on the Ranch" by J. Frank Dobie.

[2] From "Baseball's Hitters in Waiting" by Jerome Holtzman in the July 28–August 4, 1962 issue of *Saturday Evening Post*. Reprinted by permission of the author.

that is, not when you dissect the scene to do a realistic painting of it, but when you look at it for the pure pleasure of seeing that hillside on a windy day. You don't see the grass blade by blade.[1]

7

The weather that winter was cold and sunny. We had one five-inch snow that lingered on the ground in patches for about a week, but little rain or sleet. The schools were bitterly cold, and there were many absences among the children. Three boys in the class dropped out with tuberculosis. Milk that winter was available only from the drugstore and on a doctor's prescription, for sick babies, but I was able to get powdered milk for them. Transportation was hideous. Trains and streetcars were cold, dirty, and often windowless as well as jammed to the roof. People climbed in through the windows after the aisles and steps were filled. Cloth of all kinds was so scarce that even the worn green plush upholstery had been cut off by passengers and taken home to patch clothes. It was not unusual for people to have their ribs broken in the crush, and I myself saw a pencil that had been splintered in a man's breast pocket.[2]

8

The hurricane charged into Connecticut coast lands, gutting seaside resorts, fishing fleets, summer homes, and industrial areas. Flying limbs and chimney bricks were spat like machine-gun fire through the air. As far inland as twenty miles, salt spray destroyed vegetation, and salt traces were later discovered nearly fifty miles from the sea. Winds far over a hundred miles an hour raked the peaceful New England countryside, uprooting some 275 million trees, destroying or damaging thousands of buildings, and chopping up thousands of miles of telephone lines.[3]

[1] Adapted from "Caval-Comment," *Literary Cavalcade* Magazine, by permission. Copyright, 1956, by Scholastic Magazines, Inc.

[2] From *Windows for the Crown Prince* by Elizabeth Gray Vining. Copyright 1952 by Elizabeth Gray Vining. Published by J. B. Lippincott Company.

[3] From *Nature on the Rampage* by Ann and Myron Sutton. Copyright © 1962 by Ann and Myron Sutton. Published by J. B. Lippincott Company.

9

Men are all advocates of togetherness, up to a point. They will agree that it is "our house," "our mortgage," and, of course, "our song." It is interesting, however, to observe the circumstances under which items that once were "our" joint concern suddenly become your exclusive possession. For instance, a man will return from a stroll through "our backyard" to tell you, "Honey, I think your daffodils are getting clump-bound" or, on another occasion, "I see that the hinge is off your medicine chest." In my opinion, this policy of dissociating from anything that is temporarily out of order reaches its ultimate confusion with statements like "Hey, your man is here to fix the chimney." My man? I never saw him before in my life.[1]

● REVIEW EXERCISE E. Using a paragraph in Review Exercise D as a model (the numbered items correspond to the paragraph numbers in Review Exercise D), choose one of the following topic sentences and develop it into a paragraph. Put into practice what you have learned in this chapter using any method of development that you feel is suitable for the topic.

1. The whole place seemed designed for robots.
2. The word *success* has a glamorous sound as well as power.
3. I went to P.S. 83, a school with almost two hundred in the first grade.
4. Popular musicians fall into categories.
5. To my parents, all television-watching is a waste of time.
6. Suppose that you were going to give a party on April Fool's Day.
7. The weather this summer was hot and wet.
8. The arctic blast charged across our state.
9. Freshmen are all advocates of "school spirit," up to a point.

[1] From *The Snake Has All the Lines* by Jean Kerr. Copyright © 1958, 1959, 1960 by Jean Kerr. Reprinted by permission of Doubleday & Company, Inc.

CHAPTER 13

Writing Compositions

Some of the writing you do is purely personal, intended for you alone. This kind of writing includes your diary, the notes you take on your reading and in your classes, and the things you may occasionally write—or perhaps only outline—to clarify your thinking.

Most of your writing, however, is done to communicate your ideas and your experiences. Writing has been called a kind of shared living. It is a way of saying, "I want someone to know what I know, to see what I have seen, to feel what I have felt, to discover what I have discovered, to think what I think."

You learn to write by writing, just as a baseball player learns the game by playing it. This is why it is important for you to do a great deal of writing when you are in school. The only way your teachers can be sure that you are getting enough writing practice is by assigning many compositions.

You will help yourself best if you look upon your composition assignments as chances to communicate your thoughts in the most effective way possible. Do not consider them as tasks you do just because you have to, just to carry out an assignment. This may result in compositions that are lifeless, dull, and worth very little. Empty writing is bad writing.

THE MATERIALS OF WRITING

13a. Choose a subject that you know something about.

Your Own Experiences

Taking a good look at yourself and your life is an excellent way to begin to find materials for writing. You are unique, special. You are special in the things that have happened to you, in the people you know best, in the way you see things. Begin to share your uniqueness by writing about your special experiences.

What it takes, first of all, is a new way of looking at your experiences. The person who says, "I haven't had any experiences worth writing about," just means that he hasn't learned how to look at his experiences. Here are some general topics that are part of everyone's experience but which may seem unique and special if they are described effectively in writing.

1. *People you've known.* The odd and the eccentric or the wonderfully "average person" both have uniqueness. In the first, the uniqueness comes from the surface nature of the person; people who act, dress, or talk differently fascinate us. In the second, the uniqueness comes from the way we look at a person who *seems* average or ordinary. If we explore deeply enough, even the ordinary becomes exciting.

Look at your grandfather with a "new eye," as if you had never seen him before. What would you say about him so that on reading it over twenty years from now you will remember him vividly? How would you describe him to a classmate who has never seen him, so that your classmate would not only be able to picture him but also to understand what kind of person he is?

2. *Trips and vacations.* Don't write the usual account of "first we did this, then we did that." Try instead to remem-

13a

ber someone special whom you met, some little incident that you remember, some ordinary place that somehow impressed you. Focus on one person, one town, one motel, one little part of the trip. Enlarge its interest or its importance by the manner in which you write about it and remember it.

3. *Hobbies and special skills.* There would be little that is unique in a composition by you on the history of stamp collecting. This information can be obtained from any good encyclopedia. But you perhaps can tell something special about what stamp collecting means to you, what you have learned from it, what you know about your own special collection, what suggestions you would give to a person about to start the hobby.

What special skill do you have? What can you do that most young people cannot do so well? Put together a stereo set? Knit a sweater? Rope a steer? Repair a car?

4. *Ideas and information.* The two go together. What do you believe, and what facts do you know to support your belief? What about the topic, "The United States should withdraw from the UN," for example? It sounds imposing. But what facts do you have that would convince your reader? Do you have enough knowledge of your topic to discuss it effectively?

"High school students don't need a curfew." That's different. You have some special knowledge—about your habits and reactions to rules, your experiences with curfews, and your friends' attempts to avoid them. Tell what you think about curfews, and support what you say with your special experiences and special knowledge.

5. *Something you have owned.* Do you particularly remember a certain pet, a hat, a book, a picture, a toy, or something seemingly useless? Why do you remember it? What was special about it? How can you convince someone else of its specialness?

Places, events, skills, ideas, people, things—these make up some important materials of writing. You take a look at your own experience; you see it with a fresh eye; you "zero in" on one aspect of it; you share your uniqueness.

● EXERCISE 1. Titles don't tell everything, but sometimes a title can give a clue to what follows. On the basis of what you have read about the use of experience in finding material, decide whether each of the following titles suggests a good topic for a composition based on someone's personal experience. Number your paper 1–10, and copy the titles. After each, write either "probably good" or "probably not good." Compare your answers with those of your classmates.

1. An Exhausting Vacation
2. A Visit to the Stock Exchange
3. Fashions Through the Ages
4. Shoes I Have Known
5. Suburban Housing
6. I'm Sick of Our Split-Level
7. Juvenile Delinquency
8. Will an Honor System Work at Our School?
9. Famous Coin Collections
10. Why I Collect Pennies

● EXERCISE 2. "There's something I have to tell you." That's the basis of all writing. What is it that you have to tell? Find five things in your own experience that you think are important and unique. Write them down in complete sentences (for example, "I have developed the world's speediest method of washing a car") and submit them to your teacher. Then select one that your teacher likes and write a composition of 100–150 words based on it. Begin the composition with the sentence you wrote.

The Experience of Others

Most composition books, including this one, tell you, "Write about the things you know." This doesn't mean, however, that you always have to write about things you know from *firsthand* experience, or that writing is always based on the world you know now. A good writing assignment can enable you to enlarge your world, to dig up information, facts, discoveries.

How can you enlarge your world, expand your horizons?

1. *Talk to people.*   Ask them questions, and solicit their views.

2. *Look around.*   Investigate out-of-the-ordinary places in your school, in your community, in your home, in a nearby city. Take along a pencil, a notebook, a sharp eye, and an inquisitive mind.

3. *Read.*   Not all great writers have been great scholars or great travelers. They have all been great readers, however. Expand your world through reading. Read with pencil in hand to note interesting expressions, points you disagree with, quotations you wish to remember.

● EXERCISE 3.   Do any one of the following activities that seems most interesting to you. Then share your experience with the rest of the class by writing about it.

1. Visit the oldest building in your town or neighborhood.
2. Talk with the oldest resident in your town or neighborhood.
3. Find out when and how your church or synagogue was organized.
4. Interview a shoemaker, a tailor, a baker—any skilled craftsman who may feel that he is being threatened by big business.
5. Interview a veteran of World War I or World War II. Ask him about his recollections and about his impressions of the changes that have taken place.
6. Visit a local florist. What is his rarest flower? his favorite? the local bestseller?
7. What is the unemployment rate in your town? Is anybody taking steps to find jobs for the unemployed?
8. Which teacher has served longest in your school? What was the school like when he began teaching there?
9. What compact car is rated by consumer testing organizations as the best buy? Why is it so rated?
10. How did your town get its name?

11. Which football team does your coach consider the best he has ever coached?
12. Review the voting record of your local ward or precinct for the last twelve years. What pattern does it show?
13. Talk with the local fire chief. What is the chief cause of fires in your community?
14. When was your school paper first issued? What was it like in its early days?
15. Talk to the local police chief. Which case does he consider his most interesting?
16. What was happening in your town twenty years ago? fifty years ago?
17. What are the five most popular songs of the current year? Which five songs were most popular ten years ago? Do these two lists suggest any change in taste?
18. Read any five consecutive issues of *Life* or another picture news magazine published the year you were born. What picture do they give of American life in those days?
19. Find someone in your community who has achieved the kind of success you would like to achieve. What does he consider the secret of his success?
20. Take a close look at a current issue of any young people's magazine. Examine the format, contents, illustrations, advertising. What picture does it give of the American high school student? Would it be a good magazine to send to a pen pal overseas, or would it give a distorted view?

Two Looks at Dogdom: An Illustrative Example

Perhaps all that has been said here about the materials of writing can best be illustrated by two examples. The first is a student composition. The second is from a best-selling book by a skilled writer of humorous essays based on experience.

DOGS

Dogs were probably the first domestic animals. They are descended from the wolf. They date back at least to the Paleolithic period, and two breeds were known in early Egypt.

From earliest times dogs have been bred for special purposes. Sporting dogs include the griffon, pointer, retriever, setter, spaniel, and hound, and many breeds of terrier. Working dogs include the collie, Eskimo, German shepherd, and St. Bernard. Nonsporting dogs include the bulldog, chow, Dalmatian, and poodle. Toy dogs are small dogs bred as pets; among them are the toy spaniel, Mexican hairless, Pekingese, pug, and toy poodle.

Mongrels are mixtures of several breeds. They may look a little like the breed of the father or mother. Mongrels may be very clever and make fine companions; they can be trained to perform in circuses and they make good watchdogs.

Purebred dogs can be registered with the American Kennel Club, which will give them numbers to show that they are listed with the pedigreed dogs of their own breed. The American Kennel Club is the official club that regulates all matters that have to do with the dog breeds in America. It also makes the rules for the big dog shows that are given all over the country.

Dogs That Have Known Me

I never meant to say anything about this, but the fact is that I have never met a dog that didn't have it in for me. You take Kelly, for example. He's a wire-haired fox terrier and he's had us for three years now. I wouldn't say that he was terribly handsome, but he does have a very nice smile. What he doesn't have is any sense of fitness. All the other dogs in the neighborhood spend their afternoons yapping at each other's heels or chasing cats. Kelly spends his whole day, every day, chasing swans on the millpond. I don't actually worry because he will never catch one. For one thing he can't swim. Instead of settling for a simple dog paddle like everybody else, he has to show off and try some complicated overhand stroke, with the result that he always sinks and has to be fished out. Naturally, people talk and I never take him for a walk that somebody doesn't point him out and say, "There's that crazy dog that chases swans."

Another thing about the dog is that he absolutely refuses to put himself in the other person's position. We have a pencil sharpener in the kitchen and Kelly used to enjoy having an occasional munch on the plastic cover. As long as it was just a nip now and then, I didn't mind. But one day he simply lost his head and ate the whole thing. Then I had to buy a new one and, of course, I put it high out of Kelly's reach. Well, the scenes we were treated to—and the sulking! In fact, ever since, he has been eating things that I know he doesn't like just to get even. I don't mean things like socks and mittens and paper napkins, which of course are delicious. Lately he's been eating plastic airplanes, suede brushes, and light bulbs. Well, if he wants to sit under the piano and make low and loving growls over a suede brush just to show me, OK. But frankly I think he's lowering himself.[1]

The second example is infinitely better for many reasons. Two of the most important are the uniqueness of the material and the sharpness of the focus. The student composition gives generalizations available from any encyclopedia. There is nothing special here, nothing known only to the writer. He has accomplished nothing by writing this composition except mechanically to fulfill an assignment.

This is not to say that writing should not give information. Much good writing is done mainly for this purpose. However, it is not worthwhile simply to serve up information that someone else has already collected and organized. The difference between writing and copying is what the writer adds of his own.

Sharpness of focus counts, too. Let us examine this important aspect of good writing.

BRINGING MATERIAL INTO FOCUS

Good writing has sharpness, vividness, clarity. It also has substance, body, "muscle." All these qualities come about when you write about a manageable subject, focus upon it,

[1] From "Dogs That Have Known Me" by Jean Kerr. Copyright © 1957 by Condé Nast Publications. From the book *Please Don't Eat the Daisies* by Jean Kerr. Reprinted by permission of Doubleday & Company, Inc.

and portray its concrete details—when you look closely at something special. There are several ways of looking closely, of focusing material for writing.

13b. Limit your subject.

You could write a full-length book about a single dog, or you could write one paragraph about dogs in general. Ordinarily, neither attempt would be successful. In general, the scope of the subject determines the length of the treatment. The bigger the subject, the longer the writing.

In practical terms, this means that your shorter compositions will be successful only if they deal with very limited subjects. How do you limit a subject? Here are some possibilities and examples of each:

a. *Deal with a limited time period* (The Most Popular Breeds of Dogs Today)
b. *Deal with a limited place.* (Popular Breeds of Dogs in America)
c. *Deal with a limited type.* (Cocker Spaniels)
d. *Deal with a limited use.* (Dogs in Hunting)

Each topic will, of course, suggest its own limitations. The important thing is to carry on the limiting process until you have a subject to which you can add your own special point of view or knowledge within the length of your paper. The following examples may show the relationship between subject and length.

SUBJECT	LENGTH
1. Dogs	Book
2. History of Dogs	Encyclopedia article
3. Cocker Spaniel in America	Long magazine article
4. How to Judge a Cocker Spaniel	750 word article
5. Training My Cocker Spaniel	500 word article
6. One Trick My Dog Can Do	100 word paragraph

● EXERCISE 4. On a separate sheet of paper, list for each of the five subjects on the next page a topic which would be appropriate for these lengths: a book, a long article, 750 words, and a 100-word paragraph. Use the form shown in the following example.

EXAMPLE 1. Cars
        1. *Cars*
          Book: Cars
          Long article: American-made Cars
          750 words: The Compact
          100-word paragraph: The Advantages of a Two-seater

1. Politics
2. Cooking
3. Football
4. Horses
5. Inventions

13c. Adapt your subject to your readers.

Even if you have a manageable topic, in terms of length, about which you are fully informed, you still need to make another adjustment. You must adjust the topic and the content to the audience for which you write. For example, suppose you were writing an article on "Training My Cocker Spaniel" for a magazine read by dog fanciers who know quite a bit about basic obedience training. The article would certainly have a focus and content different from an essay on the same subject written for fellow students who know little about training dogs. The topic for the magazine article might be better stated, "Some Special Techniques I Have Learned in Training My Spaniel." The essay topic might be, "Basic Procedures for the Beginner in Training the Spaniel."

Just as important as knowing your subject, then, is knowing your audience: their interests, reading level, prior knowledge, and attitudes. This knowledge of your audience influences more than just your focusing of the topic and the content of your essay. It should affect also the way you begin, the number of illustrative examples you use, and the words you select.

13
b-c

● Exercise 5.   Choose two of the topics below and write a brief composition on each. Choose one *a* and one *b*.

1. How We Elect Our Class Officers
   a. for a friend in a nearby school
   b. for a student in Germany
2. How to Find My House
   a. for a friend in a neighboring community
   b. for a visitor from a distant state
3. What It's Like to Be a High School Student
   a. for a fifth-grade pupil
   b. for an elderly person who never went to high school
4. How to Watch a Football Game
   a. for a girl who has seen many games but knows little about the rules
   b. for a foreign visitor who has never seen a game
5. Why the Right to Vote Is Important
   a. for a fellow student
   b. for a student living under a dictatorship

13d. Determine the purpose of your composition.

Assuming that you have a workable topic and a good idea of your audience, there is still one more basic decision you must make about the special direction or focus of your paper: the *effect* you wish to have on your audience. Do you want your paper to amuse them, inform them, anger them, persuade them, establish a certain mood, or make them visualize a scene or person?

Suppose that you have chosen the topic "Buying a Cocker Spaniel," and you intend it for an audience of high school students who know little or nothing about the subject. Do you wish to inform them so that they can make better choices? Do you wish to persuade them that they should buy a dog? Or do you wish to amuse them by describing humorously some of the difficulties involved in buying a dog? Your decision about purpose will have an important effect on your composition.

A good topic then is not selected by accident. You should decide upon it only after you have settled three important matters:

1. the way in which the subject will be limited
2. the audience for whom it is intended
3. the effect you desire to produce

● EXERCISE 6. Below is a list of limited topics. Number your paper 1–10. After the appropriate number, write what your purpose would be in writing about each topic: (1) to amuse, (2) to inform, (3) to persuade, (4) to establish a mood, (5) to make the reader visualize someone or something.

1. Why I Am a Conformist (or Nonconformist)
2. Three Legends in Our Family
3. Amusing Events Inside a Classroom
4. Characteristics of an Ideal Friend
5. Types of Car Salesmen
6. Whose Side Is the Law On?
7. Facts About the Attitudes of Teen-agers
8. Traffic Laws Should Be More Strictly Enforced
9. Three Gifts I Like to Receive
10. How to Get Along with Eccentric Relatives

PLANNING YOUR COMPOSITION

13e. Plan your composition before writing it.

Some people like to take aimless trips, making no plans at all but rambling over the countryside, exploring side roads, stopping when they wish, and not much caring when or where they arrive. When people want to reach a definite destination at a specific time, however, they generally make detailed plans of their route and schedule their time.

Writing is much the same. Some writing—letters to friends, for example—is unplanned. It rambles on aimlessly and spontaneously, making digressions and having no

13 d-e

fixed objective. For most formal writing, however, you need a plan which shows you where you are headed and how you expect to get there.

(1) List your specific ideas.

As soon as you have chosen and limited your subject and have decided upon your purpose, make a list of your ideas. Write them down rapidly as they come to you, without worrying too much at this time about their value or where you would include them in your composition. Later, when you are organizing, you can omit those that you decide not to use. The important thing is to see what material you have to work with. In a composition on "My Pet Peeves," for example, the first list of ideas might look something like this:

FIRST LIST OF IDEAS

Title of Composition: My Pet Peeves
Purpose: To define and give examples of my pet peeves

long assignments, especially on Friday	arguing about TV channels
women's hats	riding with a back-seat driver
homework in general	interruptions when I am talking
hate to play bingo	a show-off at a party
any dull game	nagging hostesses
also games like musical chairs	boring talks in assembly
my brother's "I told you so"	preparing oral reports
having to go to bed early	stage fright

(2) Group related ideas under headings.

After you have made a list of your ideas, you are ready to group them so that your plan will gradually develop into a few larger divisions. How you group them will depend upon the subject. Some topics, especially those dealing with a process, are easily arranged in chronological (time) order. Other topics also fall into a chronological pattern; for example, *morning, noon, night,* or *childhood, youth, maturity, old age.* For all subjects, however, you should group your ideas according to the phase of the subject they deal with.

IDEAS FOR THE COMPOSITION ON "MY PET PEEVES"
GROUPED UNDER HEADINGS

I. At home
   arguing about TV channels
   hearing "I told you so"
   having to go to bed early

II. At school
   homework
   assignments on Friday
   preparing oral reports
   boring assembly programs

III. At parties
   dull games
   bingo
   musical chairs
   nagging hostesses
   a show-off

Notice that four of the items on the first list have already been omitted. "Women's hats," "riding with a back-seat driver," "interruptions when I am talking," and "stage fright" do not specifically fall under any of the three main headings, *home*, *school*, and *parties*. With the choice of these main headings and the omission of some of the ideas on the first list, the topic has been further limited.

(3) Arrange your ideas in order.

Your next job is to arrange the ideas in the order in which you will discuss them in your composition. Some subjects will require a certain order. For example, if your composition gives instructions on how to assemble the parts of a model airplane, you will need to follow a chronological order. If, on the other hand, you are writing about your reasons for joining the Scouts, you may arrange your ideas with the most important coming last.

Sometimes the material under one heading is necessary for understanding the material under one of the other headings. For instance, if you are explaining how to process a roll of film, you will first need to point out the differences between panchromatic and orthochromatic film (one heading) because the kind of film determines whether or not a person should develop the negatives in complete darkness (another heading). You would have to put the first heading before the one which depends upon it.

If the ideas themselves do not determine the order in which they should come, you must decide yourself upon the clearest and most interesting arrangement.

● EXERCISE 7.   Without listing minor points of development, list the main headings you would use in planning a composition on the following topics. List at least three headings for each topic.

1. How to find a book in the library
2. Juvenile vandalism
3. A good club
4. The honor system in our school should be (abolished, retained)
5. Characteristics of a good teacher
6. My advice to eighth-graders
7. The trouble with (boys, girls)
8. The drawbacks of adolescence
9. Types of relatives we could do without
10. The value of intramural sports

Making an Outline

Your next step is to write down your plan in orderly fashion. This will enable you—and your teacher—to see exactly how your composition should grow. The easiest and best way to do this is by means of an outline.

The first step in making an outline is to arrange your ideas in a definite order. Besides indicating the order of ideas, an outline often shows the relative importance of the ideas.

The outline consists of main headings with subheadings under them. For most of the compositions you write, a *topic* outline is satisfactory. A topic outline is one in which the various items are topics, not complete sentences.

Remember that an outline is a working plan, the first step in writing the composition. Do not try to be literary or to crowd in too many details here. The language of the outline should be simple and clear. Use as few words as possible for each topic to make your meaning clear and to show the organization of your ideas.

On page 277, ideas for a composition on "My Pet Peeves" were arranged under main headings. Here is a topic outline resulting from that arrangement of ideas. Refer to this outline as you study the rules that follow.

TOPIC OUTLINE

MY PET PEEVES — *title*

Purpose: To define and give examples of my pet peeves — *purpose*

I. At home — *main topic*
   A. Hearing "I told you so"
   B. Arguing about TV channels — *subtopics*
   C. Going to bed early

II. At school
   A. Boring assembly programs
   B. Homework
      1. Assignments on Friday
      2. Preparation of oral reports — *further subdivisions of subtopics*

III. At parties
   A. Dull games
      1. Bingo
      2. Musical chairs
   B. A show-off — *note use of words or phrases, not sentences, throughout outline*
   C. Nagging hostesses

Outline Form

13f. Observe rules for form in making an outline.

As you study these rules, refer to the example given on
page 279. It will help you to remember the purpose and
form of a topic outline.

**(1) Place the title (and the purpose) above the out-
line. It is not one of the numbered or lettered parts
of the outline.**

**(2) Use Roman numerals for the main topics. Sub-
topics are given capital letters, then Arabic numerals,
then small letters, then Arabic numerals in parentheses, and then small letters in parentheses. Study
this outline form:**

CORRECT OUTLINE FORM

I.
   A.
   B.
      1.
      2.
         a.
         b.
            (1)
            (2)
               (a)
               (b)
II. etc.

**(3) For each number or letter in an outline, there
must be a topic.**

Each number or letter must stand on a line by itself.
Never, in an outline, write IA or A1.

**(4) There must always be, under any topic, more
than one subtopic.**

Subtopics are divisions of the topic above them, and you
cannot divide anything into fewer than two parts. If you

find yourself wanting to use a single subtopic, rewrite the topic above it so that this "sub idea" is included in the main topic.

WRONG   C. Hostesses
            1. Those who nag
RIGHT   C. Nagging hostesses

(5) A subtopic must belong under the main topic beneath which it is placed. It must be closely related to the topic above it.

WRONG   A. Dull games
            1. Bingo
            2. Not enough refreshments [not related to topic]

(6) Indent subtopics. Indentions should be made so that all letters or numbers of the same kind will come directly under one another in a vertical line.

(7) Begin each topic with a capital letter.

Since a topic is not a sentence, you need not place a period after it.

(8) The terms *Introduction*, *Body*, and *Conclusion* should not be included in the outline.

Of course, you should have an introduction and a conclusion in your composition, but the terms are not topics that you intend to discuss. Therefore, they should not be listed as topics in the outline.

● EXERCISE 8.   The items in the unsorted list of ideas below can be grouped under the four main headings given before the list. On your paper, write these main headings, leaving several blank lines beneath each; then under each, list the topics which properly belong there. Number, letter, and arrange them in a correct outline.

TITLE   What I Like About My Hometown
MAIN HEADINGS   location
                  school
                  entertainment facilities
                  people

13f

UNSORTED LIST	friendly	well-trained teachers
	near a large city	in the mountains
	charitable	modern classrooms
	superior library	recreation center
	parks	well-balanced curriculum
	on a river	theaters

● EXERCISE 9.   Decide on answers to the questions in one of the following numbered items. Then write a topic outline based upon your answers. Group your subtopics properly under the main headings, and follow the correct form of an outline.

1. Do "good fences make good neighbors"? Why or why not?
2. What is the best book you have ever read? What are three reasons for its excellence? What specific references to the book will support your opinion?
3. Do you find cooking fun? What are three or four joys of cooking?
4. What exactly are the advantages or disadvantages of being the youngest (oldest) in the family?
5. Before joining a club, what three or four things should a person consider? Why?
6. Do high school athletics encourage sportsmanship, school spirit, and teamwork? How?
7. What are the main characteristics of a good speaker? Of what importance are preparation, voice, and delivery?
8. What are the necessary steps in getting ready for school, for church, or for a camping trip?
9. In your opinion, what are the most interesting attractions of a state or county fair—the midway, acrobats, motorcycle or automobile races, exhibits? Why?
10. How have your friends influenced your thinking? Which three or four friends have influenced you most? In what ways?

● EXERCISE 10.   Write a topic outline for any one of the subjects listed in Exercise 6, page 275.

● EXERCISE 11.   Write a composition of about 300 words based upon the outline you wrote for Exercise 10.

WRITING THE COMPOSITION

13g. Every composition has an introduction, a body, and a conclusion.

When you begin to write a composition, you should re-member that you will need a good beginning (introduction), a main discussion of the topics in your outline (body), and an effective ending (conclusion).

(1) The introduction should arouse the reader's in-terest and state the main idea of the composition.

The beginning of every composition must do two things:

    a. It must catch the reader's interest.
    b. It must inform him about the main point of the com-position.

How much space you devote to each will depend on your audience and on the length of the composition. If your readers already have a strong interest in your subject, you won't have to worry too much about arousing interest at the beginning. If they are likely to be uninformed, however, you must begin by arousing their interest and stimulating their curiosity.

In a very short composition, the introduction may be only the first one or two sentences of the first paragraph. In a composition of medium length, the introduction will prob-ably be a 50–75 word paragraph. In a long composition, the introduction may run to 100–150 words. Generally one paragraph is sufficient for the introduction. A good practice for you to follow is to state the subject of the composition at the end of the first paragraph.

There are several specific ways of arousing audience in-terest and stating your subject.

    1. *Begin with an interesting anecdote or example.* This is a useful device when you are writing for an uninformed audience. It should probably not be used in a very short

13g

composition, since the anecdote will take up too much of the total length.

For example, in a longer composition on "The Joys of Mowing the Lawn," you might begin:

> Marching behind a power mower was a teen-aged boy with a blissful smile on his face. To passing friends who taunted him about his chore, he called out the same answer, "Best fun I ever had!" Far from being a lunatic or an idiot, this young man was another member of the growing group of people who have discovered the joys of mowing the lawn.

2. *Begin with a question.*   The question again stimulates interest because it seems to push the reader on to find an answer. For example:

> What is there about mowing the lawn that compels otherwise lazy individuals to do this weekly chore? My own experience as a practiced lawn mower indicates that it's the physical exercise, the routine nature of the job, and the sense of accomplishment involved that keep us mowers moving.

Be careful not to overuse this device; it may seem quite artificial if used too often.

3. *Begin with a direct statement of the topic.*   In a short composition, and especially in one where reader interest is already strong, you may begin with a simple statement of your main idea. This device must be well handled, however; otherwise such beginnings can seem too abrupt and rather childish. Contrast these two examples:

INFERIOR   I would like to write about the joys of lawn mowing. It can be fun if you have the right lawn, the right tools, and the right attitude.

SATISFACTORY   Lawn mowing can be fun if you have the right lawn, the right tools, and the right attitude.

4. *Begin with a negative statement of your topic, followed by a positive or direct statement.*   This technique is useful when you are taking a position that contradicts prevailing

opinion. It catches the reader off-guard by stating a widely held notion and then refuting it.

> Most people think of lawn mowing as an arduous chore to be done only under threat of bodily injury. They couldn't be further from the truth. Given the right lawn, the right tools, and the right attitude, mowing can actually be a joy.

5. *Begin by providing general background information.* Although this method can make for a very slow start, it can be useful when dealing with a topic about which the average reader knows very little.

> In recent years, lawn mowing has become big business. Each spring and summer, millions of dollars are spent by Americans on gadgets and devices designed to make the task easier and the results more attractive. All the gadgetry and all the advertising ballyhoo about lawn mowers, however, tend to obscure the fact that cutting the grass remains one of the simple joys of life.

● EXERCISE 12.   Rewrite the introduction to the composition you wrote for Exercise 3 (page 268) in any *two* of the five ways you have just studied.

(2) The body should state and develop the main points in the outline.

In stating and developing your main points, you should pay special attention to the paragraphs comprising the body of your composition—the *developmental paragraphs*. In Chapter 12, you learned how to write a paragraph and how to develop paragraph ideas. As part of a longer composition, the paragraph still needs to be fully developed, unified, and coherent. Also it should still have a topic sentence. In addition, it must now fit into and become a natural part of the longer composition. Your task at this stage, then, is to move from the outline to a rough draft of the whole composition.

Decide on the number of paragraphs for each main topic of your outline. For the most part, your outline can be a guide to paragraphing. Ordinarily you will devote one paragraph to each of your main topics. However, there may be a topic which is so important that you will want to devote two or more paragraphs to it. The important thing to remember is that each paragraph must be the full development of a single idea.

You might find it useful at this stage to go back over your outline and indicate the number of paragraphs you intend to devote to each main heading.

(3) The conclusion should clinch the main points made in the body of the composition.

The conclusion of a composition may be an entire paragraph, or it may be only a sentence or two. No matter what its length, it has two important functions: to provide a graceful ending for your composition and to provide a final chance to stress the main points.

There are no rules for ending a composition; however, some specific types of conclusions do seem to fit certain types of compositions.

1. Very short compositions should conclude merely with a restatement of the most important main topic.

EXAMPLE   I maintain, then, that lawn mowing, rather than being a tiresome chore, is actually fun.

2. Explanations of how to do, or make, something should conclude with a statement of the final product.

EXAMPLE   If you have followed my suggestions carefully, you should have a lawn that is attractive, easily cared for, and hardy under all conditions.

3. A persuasive composition should end with a final call to action or a warning of the consequences if no action is taken.

EXAMPLE   Mowers of the world, the challenge is clear. Grab that rotary, whistle a happy tune, and make your lawn a work of art.

4. Longer compositions may end with a summary, a re-statement of the main idea—but not a mere listing of the main points.

EXAMPLE   With a bad lawn, inferior tools, and a negative atti-tude, mowing the lawn can be depressing, tedious work. Given the right conditions, however, it can be sheer pleasure.

5. Descriptive compositions should end with a general impression of the object, person, or place.

EXAMPLE   The whole lawn seems to be one large green velvet mat. The separate blades are indistinct. One is aware only of where the grass begins and where it ends.

6. Compositions of criticism or evaluation should end with a general judgment of the work you are writing about. You will find this technique extremely useful when you are writing book reports. For example, you might end a report on a relatively uninteresting book as follows:

All things considered, this book is merely a routine adven-ture story, with no glaring weaknesses but no special claims to our attention.

● EXERCISE 13.   In a magazine that you may cut up, find an effective introduction and a strong conclusion to an article. Paste these onto a sheet of paper, and in two or three sentences, tell why the introduction and conclusion are in-teresting or effective and how each is related to the body of the article.

● REVIEW EXERCISE A.   Choose a topic from the list of suggestions at the end of this chapter (pages 295-97), or se-lect one of your own. Prepare a topic outline, and then write a composition based on it. Applying what you have learned in this chapter, make sure that you write an effec-tive introduction, a well-developed body, and a smooth conclusion.

Connecting Paragraphs

13h. **Use linking expressions to bridge the gaps between paragraphs.**

You have already learned that bridging the gaps between ideas within a paragraph is essential for good writing (see page 257). The very same words that connect ideas within a paragraph can help you bridge the gaps between paragraphs.

Become familiar with the following list of linking words so that you can use them to make your thoughts flow along smoothly. If you will make it a habit to use one of them in the first sentence of a new paragraph, you can clearly show the reader the relationship between the paragraph he is starting and the one that he has just read.

LINKING EXPRESSIONS

To indicate another point

finally	in addition	to begin with
at last	another	at the outset
then	after that	to sum up
too	first	in conclusion
moreover	second, etc.	also
besides	in the next place	furthermore

To indicate another time

next	not long after	meanwhile	later
soon	at length	then	finally

To indicate results

therefore	thus	consequently	as a result	hence

To show contrast

nevertheless	on the contrary	instead
however	on the other hand	in spite of this

To show relationships

accordingly	similarly	likewise	such

To introduce examples

for instance	an example of this	for example

When you write an explanatory composition, in which ideas are often arranged in chronological (time) order, you will find transitional expressions like *first* (*second, third,* etc.), *next, meanwhile, soon, later, then, finally* especially useful. (Avoid the overuse of *then.*)

As you read the following paragraphs, notice how the author uses linking words that express time in order to bridge the gap between the ideas of one paragraph and those in the next.

Eight years ago, when Enid Larson came to Carmel High, biology was virtually a dead subject. Only one year of it was offered, and only 30 out of 300 students took that. The "laboratory" boasted a single display: a pretty arrangement of sea shells purchased from a gift shop.

At first the students didn't know what to make of their new teacher. They kept asking, "When do we study animals?" She kept replying, "When you bring them in." Months passed without the class's studying a single animal.

Finally a boy brought in a strange, hard object shaped like a cocoon. He found from the reference shelves that it was a pellet regurgitated by a barn owl to dispose of indigestible wastes. Opening it before his awed classmates, the boy sorted out a collection of tiny bones that started the whole class doing detective work. It took them two weeks to identify the skull of a gopher and the bones of meadow mice and shrews.

The boy later went back to the reference shelves to prepare a painstaking paper on the food of predatory birds. His report on the great extent to which the barn owl aids man in checking our destructive rodent population was the first lesson Miss Larson's students ever had on the balance of nature. They were fascinated, and they reacted by swamping the laboratory with specimens of plant and animal life, whose behavior and interrelationships they proceeded to study.

Within two years more and more students were electing the course, and a second year had to be offered. Word got around: "She's fabulous." Students finally petitioned the Board of Trustees for a third year, and until recently Carmel High School was offering the state's only three-year se-

13 h

quence in biology. Miss Larson **now** teaches six crowded classes a day.[1]

● EXERCISE 14. In a magazine that you may cut up, find three paragraphs that contain linking expressions which help to bridge the gap between paragraphs. Paste these paragraphs neatly on a sheet of paper. Underline the linking expressions.

13i. In the first sentence of a new paragraph, you may refer to the thought in the preceding paragraph.

You can bridge the gap between paragraphs by using words such as *this, that, those, these, such, other, another.* Suppose, for example, you are writing a composition about the traits of a person you admire. You have just finished a paragraph about his consideration for other people, and now you are ready to begin a discussion of his ability to hold his temper. You may bridge the gap between these ideas by starting the second paragraph with: "*Another* praiseworthy characteristic is his ability to hold his temper."

A second method of making the change to another idea in a new paragraph is to refer directly to the preceding paragraph by mentioning again the principal idea in the preceding paragraph. For instance: "Tom is not only considerate of other people but also even-tempered in dealing with his associates." Another way to do this is: "Just as important as his consideration for others is his ability to hold his temper."

Every time that you go from one paragraph to a new one, you should use either a linking expression or a linking reference in order to make a skillful and clear connection between the ideas of the paragraphs.

---

[1] From "The Teacher Who Won't Answer Questions" by Frances V. Rummell in the April, 1957 issue of *Reader's Digest.* Reprinted by permission of The Reader's Digest.

● EXERCISE 15. Assume that the first sentence in each pair below is the last sentence of one paragraph and that the second is the first sentence of the next paragraph. Your job is to rewrite the first sentence of the second paragraph so that it will include a linking expression or some other device to bridge the gap between the ideas.

EXAMPLES
1. a. I found that visiting the Grand Canyon was an unforgettable experience.
   b. The Yellowstone National Park is filled with nature's wonders.
1. *Although the Grand Canyon impressed me with its beauties, the Yellowstone National Park has an even greater variety of the wonders of nature.*
2. a. Clean hands and fingernails, then, are essential to good grooming.
   b. A person should pay attention to the appearance of his clothes.
2. *A well-groomed person also pays attention to the appearance of his clothes.*

1. a. Of course, this kind of stamp collecting can be a very expensive hobby.
   b. Building model airplanes does not require much money.
2. a. Certainly boats built for racing should be made of sturdy material.
   b. The engines of the racing boat should be capable of seven thousand revolutions a minute.
3. a. Perhaps I shall someday realize this secret ambition by riding in the caboose of a freight train.
   b. I have always wanted to wear a pair of blue jeans to a formal party.
4. a. In other words, a calf roper must have proper equipment.
   b. He should use "horse sense" as he practices roping a calf.
5. a. As this incident illustrates, my parents usually understand my personal problems.
   b. My friends sometimes do not care about what troubles me.
6. a. A person who can sew can also design her own clothes.
   b. She can make pretty things for her home.

13i

7. a. As these figures show, a boy can earn a great deal of spending money by delivering newspapers.
   b. A girl can make several dollars a week by baby-sitting.
8. a. The band finished its performance with the "wagon wheel" stunt.
   b. Two high school girls began to twirl flaming batons.
9. a. You can see that my mother has a wonderful sense of humor.
   b. My father takes pride in telling the truth at all times.
10. a. It was certainly a lot of fun playing these games outdoors.
    b. We enjoyed the entertainment indoors.

Achieving Emphasis in the Composition

All the parts of your composition will not be of equal importance. The introduction and the conclusion are less important to the development of your ideas than is the middle section of your composition. This middle section, the main body of the composition, should reflect the proper emphasis. Even within this main section, however, you should indicate to the reader which parts should receive the strongest emphasis.

Emphasis in a composition is ordinarily achieved in three ways:

1. *Direct statement.* Phrases like "the most important reason," "the major step in preparation," and "the most significant result" are ways of stating directly which ideas you think are most important and should receive the greatest emphasis.

2. *Emphasis by position.* Ordinarily the strongest positions in the body of your composition are the first and last parts. In argumentation or persuasion, it is usually wise to begin and end strongly, putting your weakest arguments in the middle. Another type of emphatic organization frequently used is the *order of climax*, which moves from weakest to strongest.

3. *Emphasis by proportion.* The most important kind of emphasis is this type, in which the amount of space you de-

vote to a phase of your subject reflects its importance. In other words, the more important the topic, the more space it gets. If you tell a reader that a given topic is most important, he will expect that topic to be given the most extensive treatment.

Remember, however, that the number of subtopics a topic has in the outline does not necessarily determine the amount of emphasis that the topic should receive in the final composition.

Summary of the Steps in Writing a Composition

1. Choose an interesting subject that you have experienced or investigated.
2. Focus your material by limiting the subject, determining its purpose, and adapting it to your readers.
3. Plan your composition through specific ideas.
4. Organize your ideas by making an outline.
5. Write your composition, keeping in mind the following:
   a. Create interest and state your main idea in the introduction.
   b. State and develop the main points in the body.
      (1) Decide on the number of paragraphs for each main topic and on the method of development you will use for each paragraph.
      (2) Achieve emphasis through position, statement, and proportion.
      (3) Connect your paragraphs with linking expressions or by referring to the thought in the preceding paragraph.
   c. Write a concluding sentence or paragraph that clinches the main points made in the body of the composition.

● REVIEW EXERCISE B. Write a composition of about 300 words based upon the outline that you prepared for Exercise 9. Write a brief and interesting introduction that states your purpose; carefully develop each paragraph in the body of your composition; and write a short concluding paragraph. When you hand in your paper, be sure to include your outline.

● REVIEW EXERCISE C.   Write about 300 words on any one of the following subjects. Word your own title as you decide upon your purpose. After making an outline, write the composition, carefully developing each paragraph.

1. How we lost (or won) the game
2. My fight with a wasp's nest
3. TV commercials
4. Chivalry is not quite dead
5. Why I always trust people
6. Human beings can be parasites
7. When I get the fidgets
8. Definition of a sportsman
9. An athlete I admire
10. How not to pack a suitcase
11. I think of clever remarks too late
12. Memories of my first days in school
13. My artistic efforts
14. It pays to be courteous
15. The value of basketball (or any other sport)
16. Mother and father as disciplinarians
17. How important to success is good luck?
18. Tricks of memory
19. The promises of advertisers
20. The language of dogs (cats, flowers, birds)

● REVIEW EXERCISE D.   Following the "Summary of the Steps in Writing a Composition" on page 293, write a composition about one of your discoveries, describing your search and leading up to your finding. You may wish to use one of these titles: "Finding a Loyal Friend," "Searching for a Notebook," "Solving a Mystery," or "Discovering a Treasure in My Own Backyard." If, however, you wish to describe an accidental discovery, you could use the title "Serendipity." *Serendipity* refers to the experience of happening onto a lucky discovery when you are not expecting it.

A Checklist for Writing Compositions

The checklist below is for use **before** and **after** you write; use it to remind yourself of the techniques of good writing and to help you detect weaknesses in your writing.

1. Does my outline clearly and logically develop my subject?
2. Does every idea stick to the subject and carry out my purpose?
3. Is my composition properly divided into well-constructed paragraphs?
4. In developing each paragraph, have I been generous with interesting, specific details?
5. Are my paragraphs properly tied together with linking expressions?
6. Are all of my sentences clear, grammatically correct, and varied?
7. Are my punctuation and spelling accurate?
8. Can I improve the choice of words?

SUGGESTED TOPICS FOR COMPOSITIONS

Places
1. Exploring a Cave
2. Curiosities in a Museum
3. Drive-in Movies
4. A Modern Turkey Farm
5. In the Corridor of a Hospital
6. The Lights of Broadway
7. My First Glimpse of Niagara Falls
8. These Amazing Motels
9. Legends About My State
10. The Golden Gate Bridge
11. Sights Along the Seashore
12. Sailing Down the Hudson River
13. A National Park
14. The Plan of Our Library
15. Visiting a Zoo
16. My Favorite View
17. A Crowded Beach
18. A Day in the Mountains
19. The Comforts of a Station Wagon
20. The School Grounds at Night

School

1. Students Need a Code of Conduct
2. The Problem of Copying Homework
3. Stagehands Are Artists
4. Controlling Hall Traffic
5. A Teacher I Will Always Remember
6. Going Out for Track
7. What My Science Book Doesn't Tell Me
8. In Study Hall
9. Getting on Good Terms with a Typewriter
10. I Like Foreign Languages
11. Student Types
12. Rummaging Through the Lost and Found Department
13. Subjects I'd Like to Study
14. Planning an Amateur Show
15. Our High School Orchestra
16. The Latest Fad at School
17. Presenting a One-Act Play
18. Learning About Nature's Laws
19. The Value of Mathematics
20. My School's Policies
21. An Important Class Meeting
22. Burning the Midnight Oil
23. We Learn Good Manners
24. Parents' Day
25. An Experiment in Shop
26. Mass Vaccinations
27. We Put Out a School Paper
28. Raising Money for Group Projects
29. What I Admire About Teachers
30. What Sports Teach You

Personal

1. My Declaration of Independence
2. The Importance of Self-Discipline
3. My Reading Tastes
4. I Didn't Believe It!
5. I Had Twenty-five Cents
6. Idleness Is My Imagination's Workshop
7. A Fragment from My Diary
8. Gangs I Have Known
9. Among My Souvenirs
10. Why I Gave Up Short Cuts
11. Adventures of a Would-be Hero
12. Why I Can't Save Money
13. Neighbors
14. A Struggle with My Conscience
15. Why I Like Folk Songs
16. My Impressions of the Ocean
17. Three of My Secret Ambitions
18. The Life and Death of a Daydream
19. My Luck Often Runs Out
20. Self-Examination

21. Am I Gullible!
22. Controlling My Temper
23. Three Things I Cherish
24. I Learned How to Say No
25. Traditions in My Family
26. My Good Intentions
27. What I've Learned from Watching Television
28. I Always Do Things the Hard Way
29. If I Were a Newspaper Editor
30. Why I Hate Alarm Clocks
31. A Stroke of Luck

Occasions

1. A Family Reunion
2. Exploring the Attic
3. Winning a Prize at the Fair
4. Wrapping Gifts
5. When to Be Silent
6. Effects of TV Sports on Family Life
7. On Making a Tape Recording
8. An Hour in a Bargain Basement
9. Christmas at Our House
10. Prizefights
11. Parents' Parties
12. Sleeping Outdoors
13. An Unlucky Winner
14. My First Ride in an Airplane
15. An Addition to Our Family
16. A Birthday to Remember
17. The Day Unexpected Relatives Moved In
18. The Night the Lights Went Out
19. Celebrating the Fourth of July
20. A Decision That Changed My Life
21. It Finally Happened

People

1. Characteristics of a Popular Teacher
2. The Way to a Girl's Heart
3. Two Heads Are Not Better than One
4. The Wisdom of Little Children
5. The People on Our Block
6. Bores I Have Known
7. Two's a Crowd
8. A Stranger I'll Never Forget
9. My Admirable Aunt
10. Memories of My Grandfather
11. Four of a Kind
12. My Curious Kid Sister
13. The Voices in My Family
14. A Practical Joker
15. A Man of Action

Hobbies

1. A Bird's-Eye View of My Scrapbook
2. Saving Coupons
3. How to Care for a Pet Alligator
4. Photography Is My Hobby
5. Making Home Movies

6. The Art of Sailing
7. Model Building
8. I'm a Bird Watcher
9. My Glass Menagerie
10. How to Handle a Bow and Arrow
11. My Parents' Hobbies
12. Water-Skiing
13. I Work with Wood
14. I Learned to Play the Harmonica
15. Weather Watching

CHAPTER 14

Writing Letters

Friendly Letters, Social Notes, Business Letters

In school or out, almost everyone writes one kind of composition—the letter. Whether you write to a pen pal in Europe, a friend on vacation, a relative in the hospital, a mail-order clerk in a faraway city, or a businessman in your hometown, you should put into practice the suggestions in this chapter. If you take time to make your letters clear, correct, and interesting, you should not only enjoy writing them but also receive interesting answers to them.

FIVE TIPS ON WRITING LETTERS

No matter what kind of letter you write, you should remember to do these things:

1. *Use the proper form for your letter.* The choice of the form of your letter depends upon the type of letter you are writing. Later in this chapter, you will learn the differences in form between the friendly letter and the business letter. As you write a letter, keep in mind its type, and choose the proper form for each part of it.

2. *Make your letter clear.* Remember that when your letter is read, you will not be there to explain what you mean. In order not to leave out important details in a business

letter, plan what you are going to say and how you are going to say it. Furthermore, if you will think about what you are going to say *before* you write a friendly letter, you can avoid many careless errors that often interfere with clarity.

3. *Make your letter attractive.* A letter represents *you;* you should therefore take pride in its appearance. Whether your letter is neat and clearly written or messy and illegible will affect your reader's opinion of you. For example, businessmen frequently receive letters from people they have never met and probably will never meet. A businessman must judge the writer entirely by the letter. If he receives a messy, illegible letter, he naturally assumes that the writer either doesn't know any better or doesn't care enough to take time to make the letter readable and attractive.

4. *Use correct grammar, punctuation, and spelling.* A letter filled with grammatical errors will not only lead the reader to assume that you are uneducated but also mar the clear expression of your ideas. Run-on sentences or fragments, mistakes in usage, and misspelled words will not make a good impression.

5. *Be yourself.* Above all, make your letters natural. Don't try slavishly to imitate model letters in textbooks. Originality is always better than imitation. There are few better ways of reflecting your personality than a letter written by you, in your own style, saying what you want to say in your own words.

THE FRIENDLY LETTER

The friendly letter is informal, casual, and personal. It is the kind of letter you write to your family and friends. There are no rigid, inflexible rules for writing friendly letters; but you should learn to follow a few widely accepted practices.

14a. Choose stationery and ink that are appropriate for a friendly letter.

Use letter paper, unlined and preferably white or lightly tinted. (Boys should always use white or light-gray paper.) Monogrammed stationery or paper printed with your name and address is appropriate. Girls' stationery may have a small, simple design or a border. It is considered poor taste even for girls to use paper that is gaudy or perfumed.

Use a pen, not a pencil; ink is much easier to read and is more attractive on the page. Use blue, black, or blue-black ink generally; green, purple, or red ink should be used only for letters to your closest friends, not for writing to a new acquaintance or someone else that you do not know very well. It is all right to type friendly letters, but be sure to sign your name in ink. If you do use the typewriter, do not strike over letters or make messy erasures on the paper. Whether you write in longhand or type, always be neat.

14b. Observe standard practices regarding the arrangement of the pages of a friendly letter.

You should arrange your letter so that your reader can easily follow your train of thought. Pay special attention to the margins, page order, and spacing.

Margins

Be sure to have even margins on both sides of the page. Don't run lines or afterthoughts up and down the margins. If you must add something you forgot to include, use a postscript (P.S.). Also remember that margins at the top and bottom of the page are just as important as those at the sides.

Page Order

You may use stationery consisting either of single or double sheets; boys generally use only the single sheets. If

14
a-b

you use folded stationery and if your letter is more than two pages long, use the page order of a book. Write the second page on the back of the first page. If the letter is only two pages in length, write the second page on the third page of your stationery.

Spacing

Always have *at least* two lines of your last paragraph on the last page of your letter. Never finish your last paragraph on one page and then put the closing and signature on the next.

14c. **Learn the proper form for the five parts of a friendly letter.**

The parts of the friendly letter are the *heading, salutation, body, closing,* and *signature.* The parts labeled in the illustration below are discussed on the following pages.

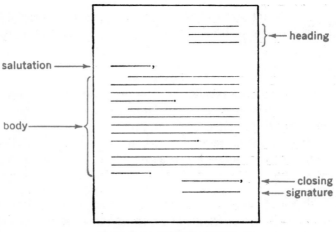

Form for a Friendly Letter

1. The Heading

The heading gives your address and the date. It usually consists of three lines placed at the top right-hand corner of the page, at least a half inch from the top. (Start the first word of the first line slightly to the right of the center of the page.)

The first line of the heading contains your street address, the number of your rural route, or your post office box number.

The second line has the name of your town, the name of your state, and the ZIP code number. Place a comma between the town and the state. Do not use a comma between the state and the ZIP code number.

The third line includes the month, day, and year in which the letter is written, with a comma after the day of the month.

The heading may be written in either *block* or *indented* style.

EXAMPLES

Block Style	*Indented Style*
2108 Ferdinand Street	P.O. Box 1426
Seattle, Washington 98108	Albuquerque, New Mexico 87106
November 29, 1972	January 15, 1972

The rules for the heading are especially flexible, depending on the person to whom you are writing. For instance, if you are writing to your father, who is out of town on business, you certainly do not need to give your home address; and "Wednesday morning" or "Friday, 4:30 P.M." might be enough for the date. You give your complete address when you are not sure that the receiver will know this information.

If you prefer, you may put your address and the date at the end of the letter, in the lower left-hand corner of the page.

14c

2. The Salutation

The salutation is your greeting to your reader. In a friendly letter, the usual form is the word *Dear* (capitalized), followed by the name of the person to whom you are writing. Begin the salutation well below the heading (four spaces if you are typing the letter) at the left margin. Follow it with a comma.

EXAMPLES   Dear Herbert,   Dear Dr. Fleming,
             Dear Aunt Sue,   Dear Miss White,
             Dear Mrs. Matthews,

Note that the abbreviations of titles before a person's name are followed by a period. (*Miss* is not an abbreviation, but *Mrs.* is.)

3. The Body

The body is the letter itself. Be sure to divide your letter into fairly short paragraphs, making clear indentions of the first line of each paragraph. If you type your letter, double-space below the salutation, between paragraphs, and before the closing.

4. The Closing

Among the many appropriate closings for a friendly letter are: *Sincerely yours*, *Sincerely*, *Love*, *With love*, *Affectionately*. Do not use formal phrases such as *Very truly yours* or *Respectfully yours*, which are used in business letters. Begin the closing just to the right of the middle of the page. Notice that only the first word of the closing is capitalized and that the closing is followed by a comma.

Do not try to be clever in your closing; avoid trite phrases like "Hoping to hear from you soon." The conventional closings are always appropriate.

5. The Signature

Whether you type your letter or use longhand, always sign your name *legibly* below the closing. If you use the block style, place the first letter of your name under the first letter of the closing. In the indented style, the signature begins a little to the right of (and below) the first letter of the closing. Do not trail your signature into the space reserved for the right margin.

You may sign only your first name or nickname when writing to relatives and close friends. If there is a chance that the person to whom you are writing might not know which Bob or which Anne the letter is from, you should sign your full name.

● **EXERCISE 1.** After studying the proper form for the five parts of a friendly letter, close your book and write these parts in their proper places on a sheet of paper. Use your own address in the heading. Draw six lines to represent the body. Be especially careful about spacing and about correct punctuation of the heading, salutation, and closing. In the margins of your paper, label each part of the letter. You may use either block or indented style, but be consistent in whichever you use.

14d. Make the content of your friendly letters lively and interesting.

The most important things for you to remember when writing friendly letters are *to be yourself* and *to say what you mean.* Certainly this book cannot tell you what to say in your letters. After all, a friendly letter is like a conversation, and your letters should be filled with lively, original comments that reflect your interests and personality.

There are, however, several "do's" and "don't's" that you should keep in mind as you write friendly letters.

1. *Write about those things that will interest your reader.* Just as a good speaker considers his audience, a good letter writer remembers the interests of the person to whom he is writing. Your friend Bill may enjoy hearing about your

14d

recent hunting trip; Aunt Martha may be more interested in canning strawberries. Your relatives will probably want to know news about your family and about your progress at school. When you are corresponding with friends of your own age, write about what you and they usually talk about when you are together. In short, make the content of your letter appropriate to the receiver.

2. *Be specific.* Generalizations are always dull. A sentence like "School is about the same" is never so interesting as one with specific details, such as "At school, Miss Nelson is still trying to make us think for ourselves as we read editorials and advertisements," or "Our good friend Jerry Cates still maintains that he can't see anything through a microscope." Telling in detail about a definite incident at home is always more interesting than commenting lazily, "The family is fine."

3. *Don't gossip.* Talking about mutual friends is always interesting and appropriate. Do not, however, make sarcastic remarks or repeat malicious gossip. Instead, think of your friends' good characteristics as you speak of what they say, where they go, and what they do.

4. *Don't ask too many questions.* Don't start your letter with a series of questions like "How goes it with you? Are you still going out with Larry? Has your father started teaching you to drive yet? Are you and he still arguing about money? What have you been doing lately? Why don't you write to me more often?" The person to whom you write wants a letter from you, not a questionnaire.

5. *Answer questions.* If you are replying to a letter, you might keep that letter at hand so that you can answer any questions raised by your correspondent. Be sure that you refer to the question asked so that the person who receives your letter will understand your reply. You might answer, "Jackie appreciated your asking about his progress with trombone lessons. He says to tell you that he thinks he

is doing very well—even though his teacher says it's lucky he intends to be a doctor, not a musician."

6. *Write a strong last paragraph.* When you plan a composition, you often save the most important point until the last; and when you write a letter, you should make the last paragraph especially interesting. Don't suddenly stop with "I've got to go eat now," "No more news," or "I'll see you in my dreams." Instead, you might suggest that you will have other news to report in your next letter, after the ball game on Friday or the dance on Saturday. Or you may refer to something you would like to hear about when your friend answers your letter.

● EXERCISE 2. Number 1–10 on your paper. Seven of the following sections of a friendly letter are incorrect; three are correct. If a part is correct, write a *C* after its proper number. If a part is incorrect, either revise it or supply a correct example of your own.

1. *Heading:*   May 22, 1972
    261 Main Street
    Reading, Massachusetts· 01867
2. *Closing:*   With love,
3. *Salutation:*   Dear John:
4. *Closing:*   Very truly yours,
5. *Heading:*   P.O. Box 692
    Los Angeles, California   90069
    August 23, 1972
6. *Salutation:*   Harry—
7. *Salutation:*   Dear Mr. Blake,
8. *Last sentence in the body:*   "Time to eat—no more news anyway."
9. *Closing:*   Sincerely Yours,
10. *Closing:*   Yours till the Milky Way rains milk,

● EXERCISE 3. You probably either owe someone a letter or know someone who might like to hear from you—a friend who moved from your town, a shut-in relative, or perhaps a pen pal abroad whom you know only through correspondence. Write that letter. Follow the rules of form you have studied in this chapter. Make the letter lively as you write specifically about your experiences. Write in ink on regular letter stationery. Then hand in the letter as your assignment. After your teacher has returned it to you with comments, copy and mail it if you wish.

THE SOCIAL NOTE

The social note is a short letter usually written for one of the following purposes: (1) to extend an informal invitation; (2) to accept or decline an informal invitation; (3) to thank someone for a gift or for entertaining you.

The form of the social note is very much like that of a friendly letter. The address and the date are either in the top right-hand corner or the lower left-hand corner of the page. The salutation is simply *Dear* ——, and the closing is usually *Sincerely yours* or *Sincerely.*

The social note may be written on regular note paper, on correspondence cards, or on personal note paper.

The Informal Invitation

14e. Include all necessary information when you extend an informal invitation.

The telephone has greatly reduced the need for written invitations; still there are circumstances under which you may find it necessary to write rather than phone. Be careful to include the following information: (1) your full address, (2) the date, time, and place to which the invitation refers, (3) any necessary explanation regarding the kind of affair it is to be. Give your correspondent ample notice, two weeks if possible.

46 Deal Road
Island Park, Long Island
New York 11558
June 17, 1972

Dear Ellen,

Once again, Mom and Dad are having a barbecue to celebrate the Fourth of July. This year they're letting me have my friends, too. I thought this would be a good time for you to pay your old hometown a visit. We all miss you. Everyone keeps asking when you're going to come back to see the old crowd.

If you can make it, we hope you'll be able to arrive Saturday morning, July 3, and stay until Monday afternoon. Be sure to bring your bathing suit, since we'll probably be going to the beach on Saturday.

Mom said she would write your mother about the train schedule.

Love,
Susan

An Informal Invitation

14f. Answer an invitation by accepting gracefully or declining courteously.

You may reply by telephone to an informal written invitation, but if this is not practical, write your reply. Whether you accept or refuse, you should always show that you are glad you were invited. If you accept, show your

14
e-f

pleasure. If you must decline, do so graciously, with regret and with courtesy. In every letter that you write, politeness is important, and especially so when you accept or decline an invitation.

When you refuse an invitation, you should give a good reason for not accepting. Do not be offensively vague with

---

27 Broadview Avenue
West Orange, New Jersey 07050
June 20, 1972

Dear Susan,

I wouldn't miss the chance to see you and the old gang for anything. Mom got the schedule. I'll be arriving at Island Park at 10:42 Saturday, with bathing suit, and will take the 3:10 back on Monday afternoon.

The barbecue sounds terrific, and it's been so hot here I can hardly wait to go swimming.

Love,
Ellen

A Note of Acceptance

sentences such as "Sorry I can't make it because I'll be busy."

As you read the following note, notice its courteous tone.

27 Broadview Avenue
West Orange, New Jersey 07050
June 20, 1972

Dear Susan,

Everything seems to happen at once. My aunt and uncle are coming to see us from Ohio the weekend of the Fourth on their way to New York. Mom says that since we hardly ever see them, I should, of course, be here.

I really hate to miss seeing you and the old gang, and I know the barbecue will be great. Thanks for asking me. I hope I can have a raincheck!

Love,
Ellen

A Note of Refusal

● EXERCISE 4. Write an informal invitation inviting someone to spend a weekend with you and your family during the spring vacation. You may suggest a convenient bus or train that he or she might take.

● EXERCISE 5.   Write a note accepting an invitation to a party—for example, a going-away party or a birthday party.

● EXERCISE 6.   Write a letter refusing an invitation to spend Thanksgiving with a friend who lives in a neighboring town. Express your regret courteously, and give a definite reason for being unable to accept. Be sure to express your appreciation of the invitation.

● EXERCISE 7.   Your best friend has invited you to a party welcoming his cousin to your town. You are going away with your parents the weekend of the party and will not be able to attend. Write a gracious refusal.

The Thank-You Note

14g. Write thank-you notes promptly.

Never fail to acknowledge a gift. When someone thoughtfully remembers you with a present, let him know that you appreciate it. Write a thank-you note within a week after you receive the present, and be sure to mention what it is. If you say merely "Thanks for the gift," the sender may think that you have forgotten what he sent or that you have no use for the gift.

After you have been entertained at someone's home, you should write a prompt thank-you letter; this note, often called a "bread-and-butter" letter, is addressed to your hostess. You should thank her for her hospitality and say what a good time you had. If you write a hasty note vaguely referring to "kindnesses too numerous to mention," your hostess may think that you do not appreciate or remember her kindnesses. Show your appreciation by mentioning the things you especially liked during your visit.

P. O. Box 542
Cedar Falls, Iowa 50613
December 30, 1972

Dear Aunt Margaret,

How in the world did you ever find time in your busy life to cook up a batch of miniature fruitcakes and send them off to your starving niece in the snow-covered Midwest?

Since I couldn't wait until Christmas morning to find out what was in the package, I immediately opened it and "sampled" the contents by eating <u>three</u> cakes. When I finally shared the others with the family, you should have heard the "oh's" and "ah's."

Thank you ever so much for this delicious Christmas gift. Mom thanks you, too, and says she will write after she recovers from the holidays.

Love,
Jo

A Thank-You Note

● EXERCISE 8. Write a thank-you note to a friend who has sent you a birthday gift. Be sure to mention the gift by name; don't just refer to it as "your gift" or "the present." Or, if you prefer, write a thank-you note to an uncle thanking him for an unusual Christmas gift that he sent you. Be sure to say why you are pleased to have this particular present.

14g

943 Pike Street
Pine Bluff, Arkansas 71604
April 21, 1972

Dear Aunt Jen,

Mom and Dad must be getting bored, I think, because I still haven't stopped talking about what a wonderful time I had in Tulsa with you and Bob. The trip to the Claremore Museum was especially fun. I liked seeing Will Rogers' old cowboy costumes and lariats and the scenes of Oklahoma when it was still Indian territory.

Your meals were great, and I'm sure you could tell I thought so. Thank you for having me there for my spring vacation.

Sincerely,
Phil

A Bread-and-Butter Note

● EXERCISE 9.   Write a bread-and-butter note that would be appropriate in one of the following situations. Be specific about details of the visit that you particularly enjoyed.

1. You have just spent the weekend at a friend's house in a nearby city. Your hostess (your friend's mother) cooked your favorite dishes and provided you with tickets to a show you wanted to see.

2. You have been entertained at the cottage of your best friend's family. On the first day there the weather was bad, but your friend's father entertained you by teaching you new card games. The next day the weather was perfect, and you spent most of it on the beach.

3. You have accompanied your friend's family on a trip to Gettysburg, where you toured the battlefield. (Substitute another historical site, if you wish.) Be sure to mention the details of the trip that you found particularly memorable.

THE BUSINESS LETTER

The letters that you write to a place of business or to a person in a firm are business letters. Whether you are ordering merchandise or making a request, you should make your business letters short and to the point and state your purpose clearly and courteously.

Stationery and Appearance

14h. Choose appropriate stationery for business letters.

When you write a business letter, never use the folded or tinted stationery that you use for friendly letters or social notes. Businessmen much prefer that you write on an $8\frac{1}{2}$ × 11 inch plain white sheet.

14i. Make your business letters attractive and easy to read.

A neatly typed letter is more legible and therefore more quickly read than a handwritten one. If you write the letter by hand, however, use your very best penmanship. Do not expect a businessman to try to decipher or decode your letter; he doesn't have the time. Also be sure to space your letter attractively, leaving wide margins as you do for friendly letters.

14
h-i

Letter Form

14j. Learn the proper form for the six parts of a business letter.

In addition to the five parts of a friendly letter, the business letter has an *inside address*, which is identical with the outside address on the envelope.

The semiblock form is a popular type of business letter. As the following model shows, the first line of each paragraph is indented; and the heading, closing, and signature are begun just to the right of the middle of the page. (The pure block form, which has no indentations of the first lines of paragraphs, is also acceptable for business letters.)

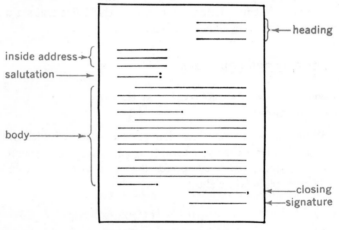

Form of a Business Letter

Carefully notice the spacing of the parts of the business letter above. It is centered on the page, with approximately the same margin at the top as at the bottom and with the same margin on each side of the page. If you type your business letters, double-space after the inside address, after the salutation, between paragraphs, and after the last line of the last paragraph.

1. The Heading

Beginning no less than one inch from the top of the page, put your *complete* address and the *full* date in the upper right-hand corner of the page. It is better to write this heading without abbreviations.

EXAMPLE   685 Lawton Street
              Dayton, Ohio   45411
              October 9, 1972

2. The Inside Address

The inside address is placed several spaces (at least four if you are typing) below the heading, flush with the left-hand margin. It should include the full name and address of the company you are writing to. If you are writing to a person in the firm, use his full name and title, with a comma between the two if they are on the same line. If the name and title are too long to look attractive on the same line, put the title on the next line.

EXAMPLES

Ajax Auto Supply	Editor
6890 Clifton Road	*Field and Stream*
Dayton, Ohio 45412	383 Madison Avenue
	New York, New York 10017
Miss Ann King, President	Dr. William N. Kirkpatrick
American Humane Society	Assistant Director
P.O. Box 1266	Defense Research Labora- tory
Denver, Colorado 80201	The University of Texas
	Austin, Texas 78712

3. The Salutation

The salutation is placed two spaces below the last line of the inside address and flush with the left-hand margin. The proper salutation for a letter written to a firm is *Gentlemen* followed by a colon. *Dear Sirs* is also used. When

14j

you are writing to an individual within the firm, the correct salutation is *Dear Mr.* —— (or *Mrs.* or *Miss*). If you are writing to a professional man or woman, use his title (*Dr.*, *Professor*, etc.) instead of *Mr.* A colon always follows the salutation.

EXAMPLES   Gentlemen: Dear Miss King:
             Dear Sir: Dear Dr. Kirkpatrick:

If you know the name, use it in both the inside address and the salutation. If you don't, then use *Dear Sir* (for one individual), *Dear Sirs* or *Gentlemen* (for a firm).

4. The Body

The form of the body of a business letter is the same as that of any letter. If your letter is very short (7 lines or less), you may double-space the entire body of the letter. When you are typing a longer letter, however, you normally single-space the paragraphs and double-space between them.

5. The Closing

The closing comes between the body of the letter and the signature. The closings that you use for friendly letters are *not* appropriate for business letters. In business letters, appropriate closings are limited.

Very truly yours, *Yours truly*, and *Yours very truly* are the ones most frequently used. *Sincerely yours* and *Yours sincerely* are also correct. The closing is placed just to the right of the center of the page, two spaces below the last line of the body of your letter. It is followed by a comma.

EXAMPLES   Very truly yours,
             Yours sincerely,

Do not end your letter with old-fashioned phrases such as "I beg to remain," "Hoping to hear from you soon, I am," or "Thanking you in advance, I am." End the body of your letter with a *period*, not a comma. Then begin your closing.

303 Clayton Street
Huntington, West Virginia 25703
February 10, 1972

Executive Secretary
Chamber of Commerce
Mystic, Connecticut 06355

Dear Sir:

    I am writing a report on whaling in old New
England and would appreciate your sending me any
pamphlets and pictures you have about Mystic Seaport.

    I would especially like pictures of the town itself,
as well as information on early whaling ships and
equipment. Any maps you have of Mystic Seaport and
of early sailing routes would be useful, too.

                 Very truly yours,

                 Theodore Jonas

                 Theodore Jonas

A Business Letter

6. The Signature

Sign your full name to your letter. Do *not* put *Miss* or
Mr. before your name. If an unmarried woman is writing to
a stranger, however, she may place *Miss* in parentheses
before her signature so that the receiver of the letter will
know how to address his reply.

EXAMPLE   (*Miss*) *Mary Jane Fiske*

A signature should always be handwritten. If your letter is typewritten, type your name flush with the first letter of the closing and far enough (usually four spaces) below to allow room for your signature above it.

● EXERCISE 10.   Copy in the proper form and arrangement on the page the business letter given below.

1. *Heading:*   2420 Nicholson Drive, Portland, Oregon 97221, November 12, 1972
2. *Inside Address:*   Mr. James E. Clark, Business Manager, Allison's Greeting Card Company, P.O. Box 3452, Los Angeles, California 90035
3. *Salutation:*   Dear Mr. Clark
4. *Body:*   As the secretary of the freshman class at my high school, I am writing to you to find out more about the offer you are advertising in local newspapers. Since my class is working to raise money for the "Toys for Tots" campaign, we are interested in selling your Christmas cards. Will you please send me more information about the kinds of cards you have, the price range, and the percentage of profit made on each box sold.
5. *Closing:*   Very truly yours
6. *Signature:*   Charles Evans

Request Letters

14k. Make your letters of request simple and clear.

A letter of request asks for information from the company or businessman to whom you are writing. It is a good idea to state your request in your first sentence. The other sentences can give further details. The business letter on page 319 and the letter in Exercise 10 are examples of the request letter.

● EXERCISE 11. Write to any place of business (a department store, a publishing firm, a motor company, a rental-equipment house, a sporting-goods store) requesting information about a particular product. Ask for circulars describing the merchandise and listing the prices. (This is an exercise in letter-writing. Do not mail the letter unless you are seriously interested.)

● EXERCISE 12. Thumb through one of your favorite magazines, noticing the advertisements. Choose a firm that interests you, and write a letter of request. A steel company, for example, may send you circulars about the uses of steel. A manufacturer of flour may give away a recipe book. A travel bureau may have interesting, free pamphlets available. Some companies may have information that will help you in making reports in your classes at school. (Don't mail the letter unless you are really in need of the information and unless the information cannot be found in the library.)

Order Letters

141. Write order letters that contain complete and accurate information.

Although printed order blanks and "clip-it-out-and-mail" coupons are growing in popularity, there are still times when you need to write a letter ordering merchandise.

When writing an order letter, you should list the items you wish, one below the other, with complete information (style, size, price, catalogue number, or trade name) about each item. The price should be put at the right-hand side (flush with the right-hand margin). Each price should be placed directly under the one above so that the column of figures will be easy to add. List the cost of shipping, if you know it, and include it in the total, unless you know that the firm pays for shipping. Also be sure to say how you are paying for the order—by check, money order, or C.O.D.

14
k-l

R.F.D. 2
Cedar Falls, Iowa 50613
April 30, 1972

Ajax Auto Supply
6890 Clifton Road
Dayton, Ohio 45410

Gentlemen:

        Will you please send me the following merchandise as advertised in your spring catalogue:

1 pr. swimming fins, Cat. No. S20, adjustable
  straps, heavy duty $6.00

2 skull caps, Cat. No. B261, one blue (size 7)
  and one red (size 6 1/2), at 60¢ each   1.20

1 bicycle mirror, Cat. No. M45, small (4 by
  2), chrome trimmed   1.75
                                                        ‾‾‾‾‾
                                                       $8.95

        I enclose a money order for $9.40 to cover the cost of the order and the postal charge of $.45.

                        Yours very truly,

                        Byron Moore

                        Byron Moore

An Order Letter

● EXERCISE 13.   Write an order letter to Academy Novelty Company, P.O. Box 3975, Los Angeles, California   90064, for the following merchandise: 2 green Wizard shirts, one size 14 and the other size 15½, at $5.98 each; one OO–GA whistle, at $.49; 6 yellow Bond pencils, with the name "Skippy" printed in gold, at $.07 each; and 1 set of Canton carving knives, with white handles, at $7.50. You are enclosing a money order to cover the total cost as well as an extra $.40 for postage.

Adjustment Letters

14m. Write courteous adjustment letters.

When filling an order, businessmen sometimes make mistakes; and sometimes you make errors or leave out im-

R.F.D. 2
Cedar Falls, Iowa 50613
May 5, 1972

Ajax Auto Supply
6890 Clifton Road
Dayton, Ohio 45410

Gentlemen:

    In my letter of April 30, I ordered a pair of heavy-duty swimming fins with adjustable straps. Advertised on page 26 of your spring catalogue, these fins are numbered S20. This morning, however, I received a deep-sea diving helmet, which I am returning to you by parcel post. I'll appreciate your exchanging the helmet for the fins.

        Yours truly,

        Byron Moore

        Byron Moore

An Adjustment Letter

14m

portant information in your order letter. An adjustment letter is one that you write after an error has been made.

When you are trying to straighten out a mistake, by all means be courteous. Your adjustment letter should not include curt remarks like "Can't you read? Why didn't you send me what I ordered?" or "I'll never buy another thing from your store." Always be polite as you explain what happened and as you ask for an adjustment.

Also be very prompt about correcting a mistake. Don't wait two or three weeks before you exchange an article or complain about not receiving something that you ordered.

● EXERCISE 14.   Let's suppose that the Academy Novelty Company (see Exercise 13, page 322) failed to send you the six pencils that you ordered; moreover, you received blue shirts instead of green ones. It has been four days now since you received the package, and you still have had no word from the company about the missing pencils or a refund of your money. Write an adjustment letter.

THE ENVELOPE

14n.   Fold your letter to fit your envelope.

There are specific procedures for folding stationery before putting it into the envelope. Stationery used for friendly letters generally has matching envelopes. A double sheet is usually folded in half and placed in the envelope with the fold at the bottom. According to the size of the envelope, single sheets may also be folded in half, or they may be folded twice. If they must be folded twice, you should first fold the bottom third of the page up. Second, fold the top of the letter down to about a half inch from the bottom, so that it will be easy to open. Place the letter in the envelope with the open end up.

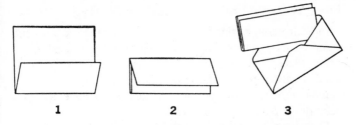

1 2 3

There are two kinds of standard business envelopes, for either regular mail or air mail: $6\frac{1}{2} \times 3\frac{1}{2}$ inches and $9\frac{1}{2} \times 4\frac{1}{2}$ inches. You should fold your business letter (on the standard $8\frac{1}{2} \times 11$ inch sheet) to fit the size of the envelope you are using.

For the large-size envelope, the letter is folded twice and inserted into the envelope. Use the same procedure as for the friendly letter on single sheets. (See the diagram above.)

If your envelope is small, fold your letter up from the bottom to within a quarter of an inch of the top; then fold the right side over a third of the way; finally, fold the left side over, leaving about a fourth of an inch so that it can be opened easily.

If your letter is more than one page long, it is better to use the large envelope.

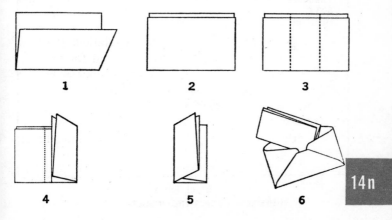

1 2 3

4 5 6

14n

14o. Address your envelope correctly.

In addressing a friendly letter, use either the block or the indented style, depending upon which form you used in the letter. Place your own name and address in the upper left-hand corner of the envelope. If you use stationery with your name and address printed on the back of the envelope, you need not repeat the information.

Do not give yourself a title such as "Miss" or "Mr." You do, however, always use a title before the name of the person to whom you are writing. Except for titles, do not use abbreviations on the envelope.

Place the name and address of the person to whom you are writing on the lower half of the envelope, about midway between the ends. In general, the first line contains the name; the second, the street address; and the third, the city, state, and ZIP code number. If you wish, you may write the name of the state with the ZIP code on a separate line.

The envelope for a business letter is addressed in block form. Again, your name and address appear in the upper left-hand corner. The lower half of the envelope should

---

Theodore Jonas
303 Clayton Street
Huntington, West Virginia 25703

                    Executive Secretary
                    Chamber of Commerce
                    Mystic, Connecticut 06355

Block Form
(Business Letters and Friendly Letters)

have the same address on it as the inside address on your
letter.

Anthony C. White
  8 Hillvale Circle
    Knoxville, Tennessee 37911

          Mr. William McMurray
            55 Potomac Street
              Ogden, Utah 84401

Indented Form
(Friendly Letters only)

● EXERCISE 15.   After drawing two envelopes on your
paper, use the following information as you correctly
address them. (You will not use every word given below.)

1. *Block Style*
   Sender: Miss Jane Black, Boulder, Colorado   80302,
              P.O. Box 297
   Receiver: Mr. Robert Cleveland, 1112 Rose Boulevard,
              Utah   84112, Salt Lake City

2. *Indented Style*
   Sender: Mr. Thomas Flanders, New York City, 81 Wa-
              verly Place, New York State, ZIP code 10013
   Receiver: Miss Florence White, Grand Rapids, Michigan,
              ZIP code 49506, 336 East High Street

● EXERCISE 16.   Using appropriate envelopes, properly
address the letters that you wrote for Exercise 3 (page 307)
and Exercise 11 (page 321). Be sure that the return address
is accurate. Also be sure that the address on the envelope
for the business letter is identical with the inside address

in your letter. Fold your letters and place them in the envelopes; do not seal the envelopes.

Checklist for Writing Letters

1. Is my letter attractive? Is the form correct, with each of the parts correctly placed?
2. Does the heading give my complete address and the full date, if this is needed? Have I used commas to separate the city from the state and the day of the month from the year?
3. In a business letter, is the inside address accurate, complete, and properly spaced?
4. Is the salutation appropriate? Is it followed by a comma for a friendly letter or a colon for a business letter?
5. In the body of my letter, are my sentences grammatically correct and accurately punctuated? Are all words correctly spelled? Have I used paragraphing properly?
6. Is the closing appropriate? Is the first word capitalized; do other words begin with a small letter? Does a comma follow the closing?
7. Have I been consistent in the use of block or indented style both in the letter and on the envelope? For a business letter, is the address on the envelope identical with the inside address in the letter?
8. Is the address on the envelope accurate, complete, and attractively placed?
9. Have I folded the letter to fit the envelope?
10. Have I remembered to put my return address on the envelope?

● REVIEW EXERCISE. Choose one of the following assignments. Use the checklist both *before* and *after* you write the letter. Properly address an envelope, and fold your letter to fit it. Do not seal the envelope or mail the letter.

1. Write to the Commissioner of Patents, Department of Commerce, Washington, D.C.   20025, asking for information regarding recent patents of interest to hunters. Request a copy of Patent 3,065,821 and mention that you are enclosing twenty-five cents to cover the cost.
2. Write to the Service Bureau, Popular Mechanics, 525 Lexington Avenue, New York, New York   10022. Ask for the free "Where-to-Find-It List."
3. Write to the Forest Service, U.S. Department of Agriculture, Washington, D.C. 20025. Ask for information about America's national forests.
4. Read an editorial in a newspaper or an article in a magazine, and then write a letter to the editor clearly and courteously expressing your opinion about it.

CHAPTER 15

Writing Stories

Essential Elements in Narratives

As soon as man developed language, he began to tell *narratives*, or stories. He told what happened to him or to someone else, what he dreamed had happened, or what he wished would happen. He told his stories, and people listened. A good storyteller always has an audience.

When spoken language developed into written language, the stories that had been told from generation to generation were written down. These stories compose the vast literature of folklore, mythology, and legend. As civilization developed and life became less simple, more and more happened; people's imaginations broadened. Thus more and more stories were told and written. Those that were factual accounts of happenings to large groups of people became history. Those that were personal happenings to individuals and were told with some truth and more imagination, as well as those that were completely imaginative, became literature.

Essentially, all narrative writing is concerned with *what happened.* In telling what happened, a storyteller concerns himself—though perhaps he does not always think of it in this way—with setting, characterization, action, climax, and outcome. These are the essential elements in narrative writing, and you will become a better storyteller and storywriter if you learn something about how to handle them.

The Setting

Every story happens *somewhere at some time*. The place and time of a story form the *setting* of the story. In newspaper writing and historical writing, the *when* and *where* are clearly stated, but this is not necessarily so in story writing. An American writer of today, writing about his own time, generally takes his setting for granted; so does the reader. However, if the author is writing about the past —for example, about the 1930's—he will be more explicit.

If a story of today is good enough and is still read twenty-five years from now, the reader will be able to figure out from certain details that the story takes place in the 1970's. Thus we know when we read the works of O. Henry that the setting of most of his stories is New York in the early 1900's—O. Henry's "own time."

The Characters

Every story usually has at least one leading character. This hero or heroine of the story is called the *protagonist*. Often there will be another character, called the *antagonist*, who opposes the plans or wishes of the hero or heroine. There may also be other characters, of major or minor importance.

In our story, let us assume that the protagonist is a high school boy. (The other characters will appear later.)

The Situation or Conflict

A writer can set his characters somewhere at some time and still not have a story. Something has to happen; the story has to have a *plot*. Nothing usually happens in the course of the plot, however, unless the leading character has a *problem*. He must find himself in *conflict* with someone or something; he must be in a *situation* which must be resolved. The situation of our story might be this: the boy is doing poorly in his work; he wants to drop out of school.

The Action

Now *action* begins to take place; things begin to happen. The situation sets events in motion. This is where "the plot thickens." For example, the boy's father objects to his dropping out of school. (Now, along with action, we have an antagonist, the father.) The boy decides to run away. He draws his savings from the bank and takes a bus to New York.

The Climax

The action arising out of the situation continues until it reaches the point of highest interest. This high point is called the *climax*. For example, in our story, perhaps the boy gets to New York, wanders around the streets, becomes lost, is stopped by a policeman, and taken into custody. The policeman notifies the boy's father. The father drives to New York and enters the station house. The boy sees his father again, hesitates, then rushes toward him. The father smiles and holds out his arms to his son.

The Outcome

After the climax has been reached, the situation or conflict is resolved. This *resolution* is the outcome of the story. It winds up the plot (which, as you now know, consists of the situation, action, climax, and outcome). For example, the boy returns home with his father. On the drive back, they have a long talk. The boy decides to go on with school; the father agrees to be more understanding and to spend more time with his son.

Setting, characters, plot (situation, action, climax, outcome): you will find these essential elements in anything that tells what happened—in short stories, novels, plays, television shows, movies. The story may be simple or complicated, light or serious, sad or comic, dramatic or undramatic; but the elements of narrative are present.

PLANNING A SHORT STORY

A short story is usually limited to *one* incident. It happens once, at one time, in one place, to one set of persons. One thing happens (though several events may be involved in the one particular incident).

Because of these limitations, a short story must be carefully planned in order to be effective. By now you must have realized this. You can see that a writer doesn't just sit down and write a story; he first plans it. You, who are not a professional writer, must certainly plan your stories.

At this point, you may feel like saying, "That's right; I'm not a professional writer! What have I got to write about?" The answer is—*yourself*. Things have been happening to you since the day you were born. Some of them you remember dimly, some not at all; but you've heard your parents talk about them. Some were important; some may have been trivial; but *many of them were and still are interesting*. Everybody has similar experiences, but everybody also goes through the same experiences in different ways.

Where does a writer get his story material? He makes it up, of course; but *from what* does he make it up? The answer is from his own experience, the world he knows. He can do that much better than make up a world he doesn't know.

"What about science-fiction writers?" you may ask. Of course, a writer does not have to stick to the facts as they are. He changes names, places, characters; he may use only one little part of what happened; he may leave things out or add things. This is where his imagination comes in—not in creating something out of nothing, but in creating something out of something else. A science-fiction writer is the extreme example of this. He uses his imagination primarily, but he does start with basic facts, with some part of the world he knows. For example, his characters talk or communicate with each other. They are living beings. They may look different or act differently, but basically they are like people the author knows, and their feelings may be similar to those of the author. They may have six arms, purple hair, and three heads, but, again, they are living beings— like the author.

Your own experience means more than just what happened to you alone. It includes what you have seen and heard and thought and believed. It includes what has happened to your family, friends, and neighbors. Your experience is you and your world—at home, in school, away from both. This is what you have to write about.

15a. Plan a story before you write it, basing your plan on the elements of narrative writing.

The easiest kind of story for you to write is one based on a personal experience, something that happened to you. You have been writing compositions of this kind for a long time. Your letters to friends contain narratives—accounts of experiences.

Now, however, for purposes of planning, you should think of an incident in your life. Forget, however, that it happened to you. Think of the incident in terms of material for a story.

You may write your story in first person—from your own point of view, using first-person pronouns (*I, me*) to refer to yourself—or in third person—as if you were someone else, using *he, she*—whichever you find easier. Writing in the third person has distinct advantages. You can be the hero or heroine, just by giving yourself a name. You can have blond hair or brown eyes, be taller or shorter, fatter or slimmer, better-looking or plainer. You can make yourself be popular, brilliant, lucky. You can make your dreams and daydreams come true. And when you finish, the incident you have related will no longer be a simple event in your life—it will be a story.

When you begin to think about your story material, you should make a story plan. Jot down the following:

1. *Setting*—when and where the events take place. You may note the time and place specifically. This does not mean, however, that when you write the story, you must begin by describing the setting.

2. *Characters*—the persons involved. Name the characters, and next to each name, write something of importance about his role in the story.

3. *Situation*—the problem. Write down the problem facing your main character, the situation in which he finds himself when the story opens.

4. *Action*—what happens. Write a brief summary.

5. *Climax*—the culminating point. Indicate the point to which the action leads.

6. *Outcome*, or *resolution*—the ending. Indicate what this will be.

● EXERCISE 1.   Select a personal experience or incident which you wish to use as the basis for a story. Describe the incident in a brief essay. Do not attempt to write a story at this time; just give a straight description of what happened.

● EXERCISE 2.   For the incident you have chosen in Exercise 1, write a story plan. Include the steps given above, and also indicate under *Characters* whether you plan to tell the story yourself. (See point of view, page 336.)

WRITING THE STORY

Planning a story is relatively simple compared with writing it. There are certain ways of handling the elements of narrative that will help you bring your story to life and keep your reader interested. These include establishing and maintaining a point of view, arousing interest from the beginning, using dialogue to carry the action forward and to reveal character, using description to present characters and setting, and bringing the story to a satisfactory close.

15a

15b. Decide upon the point of view from which you will tell your story.

A story can be told from two points of view: *first person* and *third person*. A story that begins "*I* think the most remarkable day of *my* life occurred the summer *I* was ten when *I* was visiting *my* grandparents" is an example of first-person narration. The first-person point of view is sometimes called the "I" point of view because the first personal pronoun *I* is used so frequently. It is the point of view of a person called the narrator, who has been involved in the story and is telling it from his own point of view. The narrator is usually a central character in the story, but not always. He may be an observer who has witnessed the important events and tells about them. In either case he can only describe things that have happened to him directly or things that he has seen happen to others.

A story that begins "The most remarkable day in *John Anderson's* life occurred the summer *he* was ten when *he* was visiting *his* grandparents" and then goes on to describe John's actions and thoughts as though the writer had some way of knowing everything important about them is an example of the third-person point of view. You may think of this as the "he" point of view.

One of the first decisions a writer must make is which point of view he is going to use. You may find the first person easier, especially if the story is actually something that happened to you. On the other hand, third person gives you more freedom because it allows you to tell everything the characters do and think, things you could not know as a first-person writer.

● EXERCISE 3.   Describe the incident you chose in Exercise 1 as someone else who participated in it or heard about it might write it. In other words, tell the incident from a different point of view.

15c. Try to arouse the reader's interest from the very beginning of the story.

Some people won't read beyond the beginning of a story if they don't find it interesting. In writing a story, you should try to capture the reader's interest immediately. This may mean starting somewhere in the middle of the plot and then working back, or opening with a startling statement, or beginning with dialogue even before the characters have been introduced.

Here are some examples of story openings that arouse interest. Notice how the authors use elements of surprise, curiosity, or suspense to persuade the reader to read on.

1

"But, my dear," said Mrs. Culverin, with a tiny gasp, "you can't actually mean—*a tail!*"

Mrs. Dingle nodded impressively. "Exactly. I've seen him. Twice. Paris, of course, and then, a command appearance at Rome—we were in the royal box. He conducted—my dear, you've never heard such effects from an orchestra—and, my dear," she hesitated slightly, "he conducted *with it*."[1]

2

Wed. Apr. 12

I am sixteen of age and am a caddy at the Pleasant View Golf Club but only temporary as I expect to soon land a job some wheres as asst pro as my game is good enough now to be a pro but to young looking. My pal Joe Bean also says I have not got enough swell head to make a good pro but suppose that will come in time, Joe is a wise cracker.[2]

3

When the front door had shut them out and the butler Baines had turned back into the dark heavy hall, Philip began to live. He stood in front of the nursery door, listening until he heard the engine of the taxi die out along the street. His parents were gone for a fortnight's holiday; he was "between nurses," one dismissed and the other not arrived; he was alone in the great Belgravia house with Baines and Mrs. Baines.[1]

Narratives may start with a description of a person, a place, a situation, or an event. The writer tries to give the setting, or to introduce one or more of the characters, or to create a mood or atmosphere. But while achieving this, he must above all create enough interest so that the reader will keep on reading.

Planning your story will help you with the opening, because you know what is going to happen. If you have difficulty getting started, just start. Once you get going, you may have an idea for a better beginning. When you reread the story and revise it, you may get still another idea.

15d. Use dialogue to tell part of the story and to reveal character.

When people talk, they reveal a great deal about themselves: their education, their intelligence, their personality, their social group, where they come from, their experiences. To seem real, the characters that you write about in a narrative must talk, also.

It is sometimes said of a particular writer that he has an "ear" for dialogue. That is, the speech of his characters is very true to life. If you are writing about high school students, for example, your characters will use colloquial language and slang, and perhaps even make grammatical

---

[1] From "The Basement Room" by Graham Greene. Reprinted in *Stories from Six Authors*, New York, McGraw-Hill, 1960. Used by permission.

errors. The conversation of a teacher or other educated adult, on the other hand, will be somewhat different. If the character lives in or comes from a foreign country, he may from time to time use expressions, usually short phrases or interjections, in his native language.

Before you attempt to write natural dialogue, spend some time listening to people in real life as they carry on conversations. Notice how they say things and what they do while they are talking. Observe their expressions and habits of speech. As you start writing conversations, keep in mind the following requirements of natural dialogue that will make your characters "come alive" and reveal themselves.

(1) *The words should fit the character.* Let each character sound like himself. Should you quote your six-year-old brother, do not give him the vocabulary and the attitudes of a high school sophomore. If a messenger boy is talking, let him sound like a messenger boy, not like a taxicab driver, a cowhand, or an English teacher.

(2) *Long speeches are unnatural.* Orations are for political conventions or for conversational bores. In real life, most persons make brief comments; they say what they have to say in a few sentences or pieces of sentences. Even then, they are often interrupted by an impatient listener. To write natural conversation, be as brief as you can.

If you attempt to report all of the conversation of a character, your story will lose its focus and become boring. Always remember to edit the conversation so that it will (1) advance the action of your story and (2) reveal the personality of the speaker. For instance, if you are writing about an athlete trying to become a good blocker, do not waste space by having him talk about his girl friends or his desire to get a summer job. Instead, let him talk enthusiastically about football plays involving skillful blocking, the excitement of a big game, and so forth.

In their conversation, your characters can help you get your story going and keep it moving. The characters can

15d

reveal what happened before the story began. Sometimes they even foreshadow what will happen. More important, the characters can tell things about themselves or other characters. By what they say and how they say it, we get to know what kind of people they are.

● EXERCISE 4.   Listed below are groups of characters in specific situations. After choosing one out of the seven, write a conversation (about 150 words) that reveals the personality of each speaker. For this exercise, use dialogue only.

1. Two girls have been shopping. One describes a new dress she has bought on sale; the other girl discovers that she has one just like it.
2. Two football fans talk about an exciting game.
3. A policeman has difficulty trying to tell a woman driver how to make turns in heavy traffic.
4. Two strangers discuss the weather. One is a Missourian and the other a Texan.
5. A boy argues with his girl friend on the telephone.
6. Two sophomores talk about the fish they have caught.
7. A sophisticated junior tries to get a date with a shy freshman.

15e.   Use description to present characters and setting.

A story with no description at all would be flat and colorless. Although lengthy descriptive passages like those in nineteenth-century stories and novels are rarely found in contemporary writing, every good writer uses bits of description throughout a story. Vivid description helps the reader visualize the people and places in the story.

When you write narratives, use words which appeal to the senses; make comparisons; select descriptive words carefully; include sharp, interest-arousing details. Notice how the writer Joseph Conrad does all these things in the following passage from his story "Youth," as he describes the skipper of a sailing ship.

He was sixty if a day; a little man, with a broad, not very straight back, with bowed shoulders and one leg more bandy than the other, he had that queer twisted-about appearance you see so often in men who work in the fields. He had a nut-cracker face—chin and nose trying to come together over a sunken mouth—and it was framed in iron-gray fluffy hair, that looked like a chin-strap of cotton-wool sprinkled with coal-dust. And he had blue eyes in that old face of his, which were amazingly like a boy's, with that candid expression some quite common men preserve to the end of their days by a rare internal gift of simplicity of heart and rectitude of soul.[1]

Descriptions of setting should create an atmosphere or mood for the development of the action. You know that you feel different on a bright, sunny day from the way you feel on a cold, windy, rainy day. Weather is often used in a story to prepare the reader for something to match the mood created by the weather.

In today's writing, description of the setting does not always begin the story. Often it is included as an integral part of the action. But wherever he does it, a writer must tell enough to provide a convincing background.

● EXERCISE 5.   Write a short, but complete, description of one of the characters in your story plan.

● EXERCISE 6.   Write a description of the setting of the story you have planned. It is best, remember, to have a setting with which you are familiar.

● EXERCISE 7.   The following story involves a personal experience told in the third person and in the past tense. Note that there is only one character and that the situation is simple. There is enough action to maintain interest with a minimum of dialogue, and the ending is satisfying. Read and discuss it with your classmates.

[1] Reprinted from *Youth* by Joseph Conrad by permission of J. M. Dent & Sons Ltd.

15e

THE WINNER

As the day for the big swimming carnival approached, Jim Morris found each class period getting longer. He felt responsible for the success of Splash Day this year, because he was in charge of most of the arrangements. Up until the last minute, Jim worked at selling tickets, supervising banana-tree decorations, and practicing for the 100-yard free-style. He knew he could win it. In fact, just the other day, Mr. Phillips, the coach, had stopped him in the hall and said, "We're counting on you to win the free-style next Saturday, Jim." All he'd been able to do was grin, but inside he felt good.

He had that same "good feeling inside" on the day of the carnival, as he stood on the edge of the open-air pool. Waiting for the starting gun, Jim noticed the colors in the water as it crinkled in the sunlight. There was the signal! Sp-p-p-lash! Bodies hurled themselves into the water. Then came the hurting whack of a confused dive, for one of Jim's feet slipped as he pressed to make a fast start. Many people stood up to see what had happened. Others called out. Mr. Phillips knew that Jim would finish the race, although he was hopelessly behind.

Jim was the last one to get out of the water, and he wished there were some way for him to go through the bottom of the pool to the dressing room. But he knew that he had to face the spectators and that they would see the violent red of his face, although they would not be able to see the burning tears in his eyes. His embarrassment was almost more than he could bear as he called himself the biggest fool in the world.

Standing up, he heard cheering and noisy clapping. Voices shouted, "Hard luck, Jim!" "Wonderful carnival, Jim!" "Don't worry, Jim!" He saw that everyone was clapping for *him*, Jim Morris, fool swimmer who had messed up everything. He couldn't believe it, and his face grew a deeper red. Then, Mr. Phillips was walking toward him. He put his arm around Jim's shoulder and said, "You didn't win, boy, but this whole afternoon is your big win. It's a great success, and we're all grateful to you."

All Jim could do was grin. The "good feeling inside" was coming back again, and as he looked down into the water he saw that the ripples were made up of smiles.

— CARMEL FLEMING COLEMAN

● EXERCISE 8. Having planned your story and worked on certain parts of it, you are now ready to write it. You have already made a story plan. You have chosen the incident, have possibly written some dialogue for it, and have prepared descriptions of a character and the setting. Using all these (adapting them if necessary), and applying the rules for good writing that you have studied in this chapter, write your story.

CHAPTER 16

Writing Summaries and Reports

Most of the compositions you write are based on your personal experiences and opinions. Two important kinds of compositions, however, are based on your reading. These are (1) the *summary* of an article and (2) the *report* giving information taken from several sources.

Since the exercises in this chapter will require you to use the library, you should study Chapter 17 before you study this chapter.

WRITING A SUMMARY

In almost any of your classes, you may be asked to read an article in a magazine, an encyclopedia, or a book, and write a summary of it. Your problem is to give in a brief composition the main points in the article. To do this, you must read carefully and write a summary in your own words, being careful not to omit important information or to add any ideas of your own.

In preparing a summary, you should proceed in four steps, some of which overlap.

16a. Read the article carefully.

It is wise to read the article at least twice. The first time, you may skim it quickly to note the overall organization and to identify the major ideas. Pay special attention to any subtitles, because they indicate the important points made in the article.

The second time, you should read the article more carefully. Read the introductory paragraph slowly and thoughtfully, since the whole idea of the article is usually expressed there in a general way. As you read the body of the article, noting subtitles, pay special attention to the first and last sentences in each paragraph; the topic sentences and "clincher" sentences are usually found in these positions. Also, watch for signaling words and phrases (like *another factor, a major reason*) that indicate key supporting points. Finally, read the last paragraph carefully; it often sums up the major points of the article.

16b. Take notes in your own words, using your own abbreviations.

At the top of the page or card on which you are taking notes, record the facts about the article as follows: author (last name first); title in quotation marks; name of magazine or encyclopedia, underlined; date of magazine (volume of encyclopedia); page numbers. If the article is anonymous, begin with the title.

Magazine Krutch, Joseph Wood, "Men, Apes, and Termites," *Saturday Review*, Sept. 21, 1963, p. 22.

Encyclopedia Grey, Francis Temple, "Capital Punishment," *Encyclopædia Britannica*, vol. 4, p. 809.

Book Hamilton, Edith, "The Quest of the Golden Fleece," *Mythology*, p. 117.

Having recorded the facts about the article, you proceed to read and take notes on its contents. You will find it to your advantage to force yourself to use your own words in taking notes. You should do very little copying. If you find phrases or lines that will be useful as a direct quotation in your summary, copy the exact words accurately and en-

16 a-b

close them in quotation marks. *Remember, however, that the summary is to be in your own words, not a series of sentences copied from the article.*

You will find it useful to use abbreviations in your note-taking. Be sure, however, that the abbreviations you use are clear so that you will understand them later.

The notes you take should consist of only the main ideas or the most important pieces of information in the article. You should omit examples, anecdotes, minor details, and digressions. Stick to the essentials. You are not rewriting the article; you are summarizing it.

16c. Write the summary, making it one fourth to one third the length of the article.

Put aside the article, and use your notes in writing the summary. If you have jotted down the principal ideas in the order in which the article presented them, you need only write out these ideas in sentence form, following your notes. In writing the summary, pretend that you are the author of the article, summarizing what your article said. Don't begin with "This article is about. . ." or "In this article, Mr. White says. . . ." Begin directly, "Capital punishment, which is the death penalty for crime, has existed as long as there have been laws and courts. . . ." It is very important that you do not leave out any important ideas and that you do not add any that are not in the article.

16d. Compare your summary with the article.

If the article is still available, skim it rapidly, comparing your summary with it. Is the summary complete and accurate? Is it written in your own words, not those of the original? Does it follow the order of the original? Finally, is your summary free of grammatical and mechanical errors?

You will find on page 350 two summaries of the following article on meteors. Read the article and the summaries.

METEORS AND METEORITES

On September 1, 1962, above Covington, West Virginia, and then again on September 5, over Clarksburg, West Virginia, great fireballs struck down through the atmosphere. The sky was ablaze with their bursting fragments, and sonic booms rattled dishes, furniture, and windows. Newspaper advertisements asked for eye-witness accounts to help plot the paths of these fireballs so they might be traced to the spots where they fell.

An amazing number of meteors hit the earth—at which time they become meteorites—in a 24-hour period, yet no one has ever been killed by one as far as is known. Only one human injury has been definitely recorded when, on November 30, 1954, "stars fell on Alabama." A small, stony meteoritic fragment weighing about 9 pounds crashed through the roof of a house in Sylacauga, Alabama, where Mrs. E. H. Hodges was resting on a sofa after lunch. The fragment ricocheted off a radio and struck her on the upper thigh, causing a slight bruise.

Called meteoroids in space, meteors as they penetrate the earth's atmosphere, and meteorites if they strike, very few of these stony, stony-iron, or iron bodies are ever recovered. For the most part, they land in the oceans, at the poles, or in such sparsely inhabited regions as forests and deserts. The bright but transitory streaks they make in the sky, which give them the name shooting stars, are due to friction with the atmosphere. The streaks are usually described as white, and sometimes as greenish, reddish, or yellowish. Very large and brilliant meteors are called fireballs, and when, rarely, these fireballs explode, they may be known as bolides. The term meteoroid, or meteoric body, is reserved for any small object in space, smaller than an asteroid and considerably larger than an atom or molecule, before it enters the earth's atmosphere, which only a very small proportion of them ever do. Meteoroids in space are nonluminous and thus not detectable by optical telescopes, but eventually some may be picked up by radar telescopes. Because of the threat to space probes and ships, meteoroid-detection satellites with 50-foot wings are being launched to measure the probable extent of

16
c-d

meteoroid penetration to which spacecraft on long flights may be exposed.

Here is the history of one meteorite that fell in Alberta, Canada, just a few years ago and was observed in some detail. It entered the earth's atmosphere at 1:06 A.M., Mountain Standard Time, on March 4, 1960. It was an evening meteor, entered the atmosphere at a velocity close to 8 miles a second (29,000 miles an hour), and detonated when about 20 miles above the surface. Fragments from the explosion were discovered across an ellipse-shaped area about 3.3 miles long by 2 miles wide, near Bruderheim, 30 miles northwest of Edmonton, Alberta. The flash of the detonation was visible for some 200 miles, and the noise audible over an area of 2,000 square miles (the equivalent of a square 450 miles on a side). Many fragments were subsequently recovered. Some were picked up on the snow over which they had bounded and rebounded, and farmers plowed up others that spring. The fragments had not had time to disintegrate, as many do. Some 188 sizable chunks were collected, weighing a total of 670 pounds. The Bruderheim meteorite was a chondrite, one type of stony meteorite, gray in color, with a low iron content.

It has been estimated that about 24 million visible meteors pass through the atmosphere of the entire earth in 24 hours. Observations with telescopes up to the 10th visual magnitude indicate that 8 billion meteors must plunge into the earth's atmosphere a day. Added to this are the much more numerous micrometeorites, objects with a diameter of less than a millimeter, and the cosmic debris or dust.

Among the over 1,500 meteorites actually recovered, the stony type predominates, with over 900; then come the irons with about 550; and, finally, the very scarce stony-irons, of which only 67 are known. Of the total number of meteorites recovered, 680 were picked up or located after actually being observed falling. A greater number, 860, were discovered and identified merely by their characteristics.

Meteoroids are traveling at many miles a second when they dash into the earth's atmosphere, but meeting the resistance of the gases high in the atmosphere begins to slow them down. Their great energy of motion must be dissipated, and by the time they have reached a height of 75 to 50 miles they are glowing in the sky because of the heat that has been produced. They become white-hot and their surfaces molten, streaming back from the direction of their travel, with drops flaming off and sometimes exploding or fragmenting and forming a number of wakes or trains in the sky. They lose fluid and vapors to the atmosphere in the process known as ablation, by which heat is rapidly carried away. The same ablation effects have been used to advantage in the design of spacecraft or missile cones, which must re-enter the atmosphere with as little destruction as possible. The intense heat produced by the friction of their passage through the air must run off or be shucked off, as it were, with the molten nose-cone material.

As they pass through the atmosphere the larger meteors produce loud booms, the result of shock waves formed by their supersonic speed of entry. Few meteors are large enough to survive the atmosphere. Those that reach the earth's surface have been so slowed down that they have lost most of their surface heat, have formed what is called a fusion crust on their surfaces, and are barely warm, or may even be cold. They cannot possibly start fires, as one might assume. The Hoba iron meteorite of southwest Africa probably weighed 100 tons when it fell, and a number of others weighing from 10 to 30 tons are known. Meteorites of over 100 tons will probably never be found, since their impact would be so explosive that they would be entirely vaporized or fragmented. Meteor craters constitute the sole evidence that such massive bodies have fallen from the sky.

The place of origin of meteorites, particularly the stones, and the paths and times taken to reach the earth, are up in the air, both literally and figuratively. The theories now current hold that the meteorites came from the breakup of an original planet-sized body, occupying the space between Mars and Jupiter, from a number of bodies the size of the moon, from comets, or perhaps from a variety of smaller asteroidal or planetesimal bodies.[1]

[1] From *Pictorial Guide to the Planets* by Joseph H. Jackson. Copyright © 1965 by Joseph H. Jackson. Reprinted by permission of Thomas Y. Crowell Co., Inc.

AN ACCEPTABLE SUMMARY

Meteors are pieces of stone and iron from space that enter the earth's atmosphere. Those that land on the earth are called meteorites. Although a great many meteors do strike the earth, they are only a small proportion of those that enter the atmosphere. As far as is known, no one has ever been killed by a meteor, and there is only one known instance of anyone's being struck by one.

About 24 million visible meteors go through the atmosphere every 24 hours. From telescope observations, however, astronomers estimate that 8 billion actually enter the atmosphere daily.

Stone meteorites are the most common kind; iron are about half as common as stone; meteorites that are a combination of stone and iron are very rare.

Entering the atmosphere at a speed of many miles a second, meteors are slowed down and, at a height of 75 to 50 miles, become white hot from the heat generated by friction with the atmosphere. Pieces of their molten surface fly off, carrying away heat and forming a tail. Those meteorites large enough to get through the atmosphere are so cooled by the time they reach the earth that there is no danger of their starting fires. The largest known meteorite probably weighed 100 tons; others are known that weighed from 10 to 30 tons. A meteorite larger than 100 tons would be so vaporized or fragmented on landing that nothing would be left of it.

Although no one really knows the origin of meteors, astronomers think they come from the breakup of a planet or some smaller bodies in space.

A POOR SUMMARY

This article says that an amazing number of meteors hit the earth—at which time they become meteorites—in a 24-hour period, yet no one has ever been killed by one as far as is known. An Alabama woman, Mrs. E. H. Hodges of Sylacauga, was struck on the thigh by a 9-pound meteor that came through the roof of her house after lunch one day.

Called meteoroids in space, meteors as they penetrate the atmosphere, and meteorites if they strike, very few of these stony, stony-iron, or iron bodies are ever recovered. Because of their appearance, they are called shooting stars.

A meteorite exploded over Alberta, Canada, in 1960 about 20 miles above the ground. The flash was visible from 200 miles away. Some 188 sizable chunks of meteorite were collected, weighing 670 pounds.

While about 24 million visible meteors pass through the atmosphere in 24 hours, astronomers with telescopes estimate that 8 billion must plunge into the earth's atmosphere a day.

Meteors glow in the sky because they are white hot as a result of friction produced when they hit the earth's atmosphere. They travel eight miles a second. By the time a meteor reaches the earth, it is so cooled off it can't start a fire.

This paper violates much of what is essential to a good summary. It begins incorrectly with, "This article says . . .." Half of the summary consists of sentences copied word-for-word. The writer was so much interested in the examples in the original article—Mrs. Hodges and the Alberta incident—that he had little space for the main ideas the article expresses. The summary omits mention of the size of meteors and ignores the probable origin of meteors.

● EXERCISE 1.   Read the following article, carefully taking notes on the most important ideas. Then write a summary based upon your notes. After you have written it, check your work by answering the questions in the first paragraph under rule 16d.

A professor who's spent thirty years gathering tall tornado tales says tornadoes are "pretty much like people."

"They have their likes and dislikes, whims and ambitions, their impulses good and bad," says Dr. Howard C. Key, North Texas State University English professor.

From folklore he has gathered, Dr. Key made this analysis of tornadoes' personalities:

1. Tornadoes are partial to infants. Dr. Key has collected thirty-two stories about miraculous preservation of infants. One tornado in southeastern Kansas about fifty years ago gathered a six-week-old baby out of its cradle and deposited

him unscathed but plastered with mud in a haystack a mile away.

2. They like flowers. Houses and furniture have been scattered over many acres, but a vase of roses will be left undisturbed on the living room table. Dr. Key has this story from Arkansas, Oklahoma, Texas, and Louisiana.

3. Twisters don't care for chickens. One storm picked thirty chickens absolutely clean and left them bolt upright, but dead, on their perches. Another popped a rooster into a jug, leaving only its head sticking out.

4. Tornadoes are musically inclined. Dr. Key gave this account of Colonel William Porter, who was carried away in an 1893 twister at Cisco.

"He found that instead of running toward the back room as he intended, he was waving his arms and legs somewhere in mid-air. Seconds later he slammed into some object that felt like a wire fence. Then he heard music and decided he was either dead or dying.

"It was their new player piano, the kind that had to be pumped with foot pedals. The suction of the storm had somehow started it going and it was appropriately playing 'Nearer My God to Thee.' Both Mr. Porter and the piano were lodged in a pecan tree 50 yards away. Neither was much damaged."

5. Tornadoes can be accommodating. One lady in a farm town had written her sister in Ponca City, Oklahoma, 35 miles away. The letter was lying stamped and addressed on the dining room table and disappeared when the storm struck. The letter fell uncanceled in Ponca City in the yard of a neighbor only a block away from its intended address.

6. Tornadoes like to show off. An east-bound Northern Pacific locomotive was uncoupled from its freight cars by a twister, which set it down full steam ahead on a parallel track headed west. Tornadoes in East Texas and Arkansas have turned cast-iron washpots inside out. One in Central Kansas forty years ago whipped together the branches of a 60-foot cottonwood tree and dropped a cast-iron wagon wheel over it the way you would put a ring on your finger.

"The worst mistake tornadoes have ever made was to venture into New England in 1954," Dr. Key said. "Up until that time tornadoes had been running wild all over the rest of the United States and people had been accepting them—like measles.

"But not New Englanders. They immediately set up a public howl and demanded that Congress do something. So now, through special appropriations to the U.S. Weather Bureau, the awful eye of science has been turned upon these murderous intruders. And justice is about to be done."

Dr. Key is apparently optimistic about the results. He doesn't own a storm cellar.[1]

A REPORT BASED ON SEVERAL SOURCES

The second type of reading-based writing is the *report*, which might also be called the *library paper*, since it requires the use of library sources. The report, or library paper, is likely to be 500 words or more in length, factual in nature, and based on information derived from three or more sources.

Writing a report can be a challenging assignment. As with the summary, however, the task will be easier if you follow certain definite steps.

Choosing Your Subject and Sources

16e. Choose and limit the subject.

Frequently, you will be assigned a specific topic to investigate and write on. If you are given a choice of topic, however, much depends on how you choose. The wrong topic can result in additional work for you and an inferior report. Two considerations are important in choosing a topic:

(1) Choose a subject for which sufficient material is readily available.

Don't make trouble for yourself by selecting a subject not discussed in the books and periodicals in your school library.

[1] From "Tornado Record Shows Humanlike Ambitions" by Dr. Howard C. Key. Reprinted by permission of Wide World Photos, Inc.

16e

Subjects on which you are likely to find little or no information in your library include the following:

a. Subjects too recent in development (a new kind of camera invented just last month)
b. Subjects too limited in scope (automobile production during the past few months)
c. Subjects too technical in content (the use of iambic meter in the poetry of Robert Frost)

After you have made a tentative choice of subject, check the card catalogue (books) and the *Readers' Guide* (magazines) in your library to make sure that there are enough references at hand.

(2) Choose a subject sufficiently limited in scope.

Good writing of any sort gains depth from full detail. Shallow writing, which just skims the surface, lacks conviction and interest. A 50-word report will be effective only if it deals with a topic sufficiently limited to permit you to discuss it in detail. (See p. 272 in Chapter 13.)

Suppose, for example, you have become interested in exploration, after reading a book of short biographies of explorers. Would "Explorers" be a good subject for a short report? Probably not, for you would have space for only a very short account of many explorers. You decide to limit the subject. Note the successive stages of this limitation:

Explorers
Antarctic Explorers
Twentieth-Century Antarctic Explorers
Roald Amundsen

You could, of course, write a 500-word report on the life of Roald Amundsen, the heroic explorer who won the race with Robert Scott to the South Pole. Again, however, such a report would necessarily be rather sketchy. You decide to focus on one of the major expeditions: "Amundsen's Defeat of Scott in the Race to the Pole."

Perhaps it would be wise to limit this still further: "The Last Day of Amundsen's Race to the Pole." Your decision, again, would depend on the library resources available and on the amount of detail you wish to include in your report. Probably you would choose the broader subject. However, the title is a little long. You decide to revise it to "Amundsen's Discovery of the South Pole."

● EXERCISE 2.   For each of the following broad subjects, write a limited subject that can be handled in a 500-word paper. Since you will want a limited topic for use in succeeding exercises, pick the one that interests you most. If you prefer, choose another broad subject and limit it, after you finish limiting the ten subjects below. At the bottom of your paper, write: I have chosen as the topic of my report ——.

1. Missiles	6. Young People's Fashions
2. Venezuela	7. Sports Cars
3. Robert Louis Stevenson	8. The Common Cold
4. The United Nations	9. Cancer
5. Professional Football	10. Space Exploration

16f. Locate source materials.

Suppose that you have decided upon the topic "Amundsen's Discovery of the South Pole." You are ready to begin your own exploration—for information. Since encyclopedias give a general description or history of a subject broader than the one you have chosen, you will need to use other sources, though you may use encyclopedias at first to familiarize yourself with general information about your topic. You should try to locate magazine articles, reference books, and nonfiction works that will give you the kind of factual detail you need. If in your preliminary check you do not find at least three good references, it would be wise (with your teacher's permission) to change your topic. Even in a short paper you should not rely on a single source, no matter how good it may be. Using three or more sources will enable you to include more detail, obtain a balanced view of your subject, and do a better job in your final paper.

You should list these sources, called your *bibliography*, on a separate sheet of paper so that you have them available for future reference. Or you may enter each source on a separate note card (3 × 5 inches or 4 × 6 inches). Give the author's name (last name first) if this is given, the title of the article (in quotation marks), the name of the book or magazine (underlined), the date for a magazine or newspaper, and page numbers. For a book, record also the place of publication (New York, Chicago, etc.), the name of the publisher, the year of publication, and page numbers.

EXAMPLES   Fox, Lorene K., *Antarctic Icebreakers*, New York, Doubleday, 1937, pages 126–36.

                Vaeth, J. Gordon, *To the Ends of the Earth: The Explorations of Roald Amundsen*, New York, Harper & Row, 1962, pages 114–34.

● EXERCISE 3.   For the limited topic which you chose in Exercise 2, locate at least three books or magazine articles that would be of use. List these on a page headed "Bibliography," or record them on separate note cards, one source to a card. Give all the required information.

Reading and Taking Notes for the Report

With a limited topic and a preliminary outline, you are ready to begin reading and taking notes. In general, you follow the same procedure described for making the summary notes. Since, however, you are using several articles and are going to rewrite your notes into one long paper, you should use note cards.

16g. Develop a preliminary outline.

In Chapter 13 (pages 275–81), you learned how to make an outline. You can do a better job of reading and taking notes for your report if you first develop a rough outline for it. At this stage, the outline does not have to be too detailed; its chief purpose is to guide you in your reading. Of course, you will revise your outline when you are ready to write the report so that the outline will reflect the research you have done.

In making your preliminary outline, you may find it helpful to read one of your sources first, especially if you know little about your topic. The outline below shows the form the preliminary outline should take:

AMUNDSEN'S DISCOVERY OF THE SOUTH POLE

I. Significance and importance of the discovery
II. The decision and the preparations
    A. The decision to try for the South Pole
    B. Setting up the base at Framheim
    C. Winter preparations
    D. The false start
III. The journey to the pole
    A. The first stage
    B. The second stage
    C. The third stage
    D. The last miles
IV. The journey back

● EXERCISE 4.   Submit a preliminary outline on the topic you chose in Exercise 2 and used for your bibliography in Exercise 3. Check Chapter 13 (pages 280–81) for proper outline form.

16h. Use a separate card for each topic and for each source.

To make it easy to gather together information on the same topic from several different articles, all notes on a card should relate to a single topic and be from the same source. Thus, notes for a single magazine article covering several of your outline topics might use up several cards.

16
g-h

1 — | *Preparation* | | *Kearns, pp. 83-84* | — 2

Food: canned pemmican, choc., dried milk powder, trail bisc. (oatmeal, sugar, dr. milk). Planned to eat dogs as they became surplus.

3 — | *First Stage* | | *Kearns p. 84* | — 2

Oct. 20. 4 sleds, 52 dogs. Hansen, Wistling, Bjaaland, Hassel, Amundsen.
"... according to Amundsen, a beauti- — 4
ful day of clear mild weather...."
Made better than 24 m. per day, one day just under 30 m.

The numbers at the side indicate the various entries which will appear on your note cards:

1. Outline topic
2. Source (author's name and page number)
3. Outline subtopic
4. Direct quotation

In the upper left-hand corner of each card, you should write the topic from your preliminary outline with which the note card deals. Since you have made a bibliography sheet or bibliography cards, you may identify the sources on your note cards with just the author's name and the page number. A good place for this information is in the upper right-hand corner of the card.

Suppose that in preparing the report on Amundsen, you have found the following selection. It deals with some of the topics in your preliminary outline; therefore, you want to take notes on it. Read the article and study the sample note cards on the opposite page.

RACE FOR THE SOUTH POLE

For food the Norwegians had canned pemmican, chocolate, dried milk powders in meal-sized packages, plus trail biscuits made of oatmeal, sugar, and dried milk. This was all, but Amundsen also counted on eating dog meat. He calculated that there was about fifty pounds of edible meat in a husky, and included that in his planning for both dogs and men.

This was another reason Amundsen had selected dogs to pull his sled. He calculated the day-to-day weight requirements on the sledges from Framheim to the Pole and back. The daily loss of weight in food and equipment, either eaten or stored, would finally result in the surplus pulling power of one dog at a time. At that point, the extra dog would be converted from pulling power into food.

On September 8, 1911, Amundsen was ready to head for the Pole. His entire party was to make the trip—seven sledges, eight men, and ninety dogs. But two days out from Framheim, Amundsen gave the order to turn back. Severe cold, with temperatures as low as 108 degrees below zero, hit the dogs and the strain was too great. He would have to wait.

When seals and skua birds appeared near Framheim, Amundsen set out again. This time he took five men, four sledges, and fifty-two dogs, plus provisions for four months. The party was made up of Hansen, Wistling, Bjaaland, Hassel, and Amundsen. The date was October 20—and according to Amundsen, a beautiful day of clear, mild weather, with temperature just above freezing. Across the barrier, the men moved on skis and the dogs pulled heavily loaded sledges.

Amundsen planned to hold the teams to a maximum of about twenty-four miles a day. But the fresh dogs made better than that on good territory. One exceptional day's run was just under thirty miles.[1]

Writing the Report

16i. Revise the preliminary outline.

As explained previously, it usually is wise to revise your preliminary outline after you have finished reading and taking notes. You now have a better grasp of your subject; you can be more careful about form. For example, you may have decided that you have so much material on Amundsen's actual journey that you should not deal with his decision to try for the Pole or with his setting up the base at Framheim. The final outline might look like this:

AMUNDSEN'S DISCOVERY OF THE SOUTH POLE

I. Significance and importance of the discovery

II. The preparations
    A. Supplies for the journey
        1. Transportation and housing
        2. Clothing and other small articles
        3. Food
            a. Prepared food
            b. Decision to eat dogs
    B. The false start
        1. Concern about Scott
        2. Severe weather

III. The journey to the Pole
    A. The first stage: the shelf ice
    B. The second stage: Axel Heiberg
    C. The third stage: the polar plateau

[1] From *The Silent Continent* by William H. Kearns, Jr. and Beverley Britton (Harper & Brothers, 1955). Reprinted by permission of Harper & Row, Publishers.

    D. The last miles: the South Pole
       1. Good weather
       2. Planting of the flag
       3. Defeat of Scott in race
  IV. The journey back

16j. Write the rough draft.

With your final outline at hand, go through your note cards, discarding those that are no longer needed and re-arranging the remaining ones so that they conform to your final outline. In other words, all cards dealing with the same outline topic, regardless of the article from which they come, should be placed together.

Referring to your cards only for facts and information, begin to write your rough draft. You will use all those skills you learned in Chapter 13. In addition, here are two special reminders:

(1) Use your own words.

Again, be sure not to use exact words from your sources without giving credit. If you do so, you are committing *plagiarism*. This not only is dishonest but also diminishes the value of your paper as an original work. If you take notes in your own words, you will not be likely to plagiarize.

(2) Acknowledge sources when you do quote.

If you decide to use a word-for-word quotation from one of your sources, enclose it in quotation marks as you did in the summary. Also, you must identify the source by giving at least the author, title, and page number of the quotation.

There are three places where this information can be given: (1) in parentheses right after the quotation, (2) in a footnote at the bottom of the page, or (3) in a list with all the other sources on a page at the end of your paper. Your teacher will tell you how much identifying information is required and where it should be given.

16
i-j

16k. Write the final draft.

Read your rough draft carefully with the following points in mind:

Checklist

1. Is there an effective introductory paragraph which states the main idea of the paper?
2. Are transitions used to show how paragraphs are related?
3. Is there a good concluding paragraph which effectively draws the paper to a close?
4. Is the paper written in your own words, with proper acknowledgment given when you have quoted directly?
5. Does your paper follow the order of your final outline and avoid digressions?
6. Have you used three or more sources of information?
7. Is the paper free from errors in spelling, punctuation, sentence structure, and usage?
8. Have you used the proper heading and form required by your teacher?

With these points all checked, type or write in ink your final draft. Include a footnote page if your teacher specifies this. Also list on a separate page entitled "Bibliography" the sources you have used, arranged alphabetically by the author's last name. Give all the information which was suggested for a bibliography list and note cards.

Here is an example of a final report. Notice how the writer smoothly transforms his information into a coherent paper by the various means you have learned in this chapter as well as in Chapter 13.

AMUNDSEN'S RACE TO THE SOUTH POLE

Some men blunder into success, achieving victory only through sheer luck. Even some great explorers of the — begins with a contrary, provocative statement

past have made discoveries in this way. The discovery of the South Pole by the Norwegian explorer Roald Amundsen, however, was a masterpiece of <u>planning.</u> ingenuity, and dogged persistence.

leads into topic of explorers

The crucial <u>planning</u> actually began in February and March of 1911 at Framheim, Amundsen's base at the Bay of Whales in the Ross Sea. Sledges were rebuilt and shaved to a forty-eight-pound weight; trail tents were painted a dark color to absorb the sun's rays. No detail was left to chance: boots and underwear were redesigned; tent pegs, skis, and ski bindings were carefully checked; special dog whips were fashioned. Prepared food included canned pemmican, chocolate, dried milk powders, and trail biscuits made of oatmeal, sugar, and dried milk. Crucial weight was saved by Amundsen's ingenious plan to eat the huskies as they became surplus on the trip. Though <u>impatient</u> to get started, Amundsen did not slight the most minute detail.

repetition to link paragraphs; beginning of time sequence

(Note that paper reflects revised outline.)

(Compare these sentences with note cards on page 359.)

Events proved, <u>however,</u> that he was too <u>impatient.</u> Worried about the progress made by the British Captain Robert F. Scott, who was also planning to set out for the Pole, Amundsen began his

transitions

16 k

push on September 8, 1911, in the dead of winter. Two days later, he realized that he had made a mistake. Temperatures as low as 108 degrees below zero drove him back to Framheim.

The next try was successful. Four sledges, five men, and fifty-two dogs set out on October 20, a day that Kearns and Britton tell us was described by Amundsen as "a beautiful day of clear, mild weather."[1] Before them—according to Shackleton, the explorer who had made a previous, unsuccessful attempt to reach the Pole—was a trek consisting of three stages. plus the final push to the Pole.

The first stage of the trek. the trip across the shelf ice, was uneventful. On very good days, the dogs made almost thirty miles across the ice. The second stage involved a climb of ten thousand feet up a glacier called Axel Heiberg; at one point in this climb, the expedition was pinned down by blizzards for four days. The men were all anxious to reach the polar plateau, which Shackleton had called the third stage of the journey.

This third stage was marked by two climactic events. Halfway up the pla-

[1] William H. Kearns, Jr., and Beverley Britton, *The Silent Continent*, p. 84.

[margin notes]
source briefly identified in body; actual words quoted

transitions

chronological sequence

chronological sequence

footnote identifies source more fully

teau, twenty-four of the dogs had to be killed, at a spot Amundsen called "The Slaughterhouse." Although the men were reluctant to kill the dogs, they knew they had no choice if they were to survive. Then, on December 6, they reached the farthest point south that Shackleton had reached before them. After this, everything was virgin territory!

The final push into this unexplored land covered only sixty miles. Amundsen reported that the weather was surprisingly good; as Fox wrote. "All of nature seemed to be smiling on Amundsen's little party as they moved across the great unknown like ants in vast acres of sand."[1] On December 13, the men realized they were within a day's journey to the South Pole; there was little sleep that night. Finally, at three o'clock in the afternoon of December 14, 1911, all five members of the expedition together planted the Norwegian flag at the South Pole. They had beaten Captain Scott—by more than a month, as was proved later.

The return journey was begun on December 17. Since favorable weather

chronological sequence

source for quotation identified briefly in body

---

[1] Lorene K. Fox, *Antarctic Icebreakers*, p. 134.

source identified more fully in footnote

continued and their luck held, Amundsen and his men were able to complete the return journey without mishap in thirty-nine days, arriving at Framheim on January 25. Thus, there was a small element of luck in that the expedition was blessed with good weather. The real triumph, however, came about only because of the wisdom and courage of Roald Amundsen and his four teammates.

— final sentence ties in with first paragraph of report

Bibliography

"Amundsen, Roald," *Encyclopædia Britannica*, 1960, Volume 1, page 854.

Fox, Lorene K., *Antarctic Icebreakers*, New York, Doubleday, 1937, pages 126–36.

Icenhower, Joseph B., *Man Against the Unknown*, Philadelphia, John C. Winston Company, 1957, pages 96–98.

Kearns, William H., Jr., and Beverley Britton, *The Silent Continent*, New York, Harper & Row, 1955, pages 74–93.

Vaeth, J. Gordon, *To the Ends of the Earth: The Explorations of Roald Amundsen*, New York, Harper & Row, 1962, pages 114–34.

● EXERCISE 5. You should now be ready to write a good library paper based on three or more sources. Either take the topic for which you have submitted outlines and bibliography, or start from scratch, using one of the topics listed below.

1. Origin of jazz
2. Life on Mars
3. Types of clouds
4. Care of house plants
5. Jet propulsion
6. Hurricanes
7. Recent oil discoveries
8. Soap sculpture
9. Optical illusions
10. Tarantulas
11. Ventriloquism
12. Asian flu

13. Artificial respiration
14. Outdated state laws
15. Strip mining
16. Flying saucers
17. The America's Cup Races
18. Armadillos
19. Science fiction
20. Tattooing customs
21. Uses of atomic power
22. Language of dolphins
23. Emotional maturity
24. Heart surgery
25. Fads for reducing
26. Effects of tobacco
27. Hypnotism
28. Florence Nightingale
29. Automation
30. Space stations
31. Ice hockey
32. Alaska
33. Insecticides
34. Artificial snow
35. Soapbox derbies
36. St. Lawrence Seaway
37. Waterspouts
38. Sleepwalking
39. Teaching machines
40. Tranquilizing drugs

PART FIVE

Aids
to Good
English

CHAPTER 17

The Library

Location and Arrangement of Facilities

Anyone who can read and who has a desire to learn can educate himself in a library. Books on every subject known to man are found in the library. One of the greatest values of a library is that it puts all its resources at your disposal in such a way that you can find information quickly.

KNOW YOUR LIBRARY

17a. Know your library so that you can make effective use of it.

No doubt there is a library in your school, and there is probably a library in your community. You should be familiar with both, so that you don't wander around aimlessly or have to ask the librarian for help each time you go there. Learn the location of the reading room, the fiction and nonfiction books, the card catalogue, the reference books, the newspapers and magazines, and the circulation desk.

17b. Observe the rules of your library.

Remember, first of all, that the library is a quiet place, a place where people read or study or sometimes just relax. You may be able to think clearly with the radio blaring, your phonograph playing, or even a television program going, but many people cannot. Study requires concentration, and concentration demands quiet. There is little talk in libraries; all necessary conversation should be in whispers. There is little movement in libraries, for people are sitting and reading or writing. Remember these things when you are in the library, and be considerate of others who are there.

The librarian is there to help you, but not you alone. Be courteous when you ask her for assistance, appreciative when you receive it, and thoughtful enough not to demand unnecessary time from her.

Take care of the books you use. You may mark passages in books you own but not in those belonging to the library. When you take a book home, be sure that it does not fall into the hands of your baby brother or into the teeth of the dog. Return books when they are due. If they are overdue, pay your fine; and if by some misfortune you have damaged a book, pay for it willingly.

The library deserves your cooperation in return for the services it offers you. Chief among these services is its simple, practical arrangement of books for your convenience.

ARRANGEMENT OF BOOKS

Library books are arranged in two ways, depending on whether the book is fiction or nonfiction. You probably know that the two kinds of books are kept in different parts of the library.

Fiction

17c. **A separate section of the library is set aside for books of fiction.**

Books of fiction are placed together in one section and are arranged in alphabetical order according to the last

17
a-c

name of the author. If there are several books by the same author, these are further arranged alphabetically by the first word of the title (not counting *A*, *An*, or *The*).

For example, suppose you want to find Robert Louis Stevenson's *The Master of Ballantrae*. Having located the fiction section, you move to the *S*'s, to find authors whose last name begins with *S*. You need not be concerned with titles just yet. You may see books by Sabatini, Savage, Scott, Shippen, Slaughter, Steinbeck, and Stevens before you come to Stevenson. You may then find books by Dorothy Stevenson and Janet Stevenson before you come to Robert Louis Stevenson. When you find his books, you then begin to look at titles. Perhaps you will see *The Black Arrow* and *Kidnapped* before you find *The Master of Ballantrae; Treasure Island* may follow your book.

◆ NOTE   Books by authors whose names begin with *Mc* are arranged as though the name were spelled *Mac; St.* is arranged as though spelled out (*Saint*).

● EXERCISE 1.   Arrange the following fiction books in the order that you would find them on the library bookshelf. Remember, the alphabetical order is first for authors' names, and then for titles by the same author.

1. *Trap-Lines North*, Stephen W. Meader
2. *Behind the Ranges*, Stephen W. Meader
3. *Casuals of the Sea*, William McFee
4. *Neither 5 nor 3*, Helen MacInnes
5. *Aunt Bel*, Guy McCrone
6. *The Late George Apley*, John P. Marquand
7. *The Good Earth*, Pearl Buck
8. *The Call of the Wild*, Jack London
9. *Show Boat*, Edna Ferber
10. *So Big*, Edna Ferber
11. *The Incredible Journey*, Shelia Burnford
12. *The Sea Wolf*, Jack London
13. *Laughing Boy*, Oliver La Farge
14. *The Bridge of San Luis Rey*, Thornton Wilder

Nonfiction

17d. **Nonfiction books are arranged according to the Dewey decimal system.**

The Dewey decimal system was developed by Melvil Dewey, an American librarian. Under this system, all books are numbered and grouped according to ten subject classes. The classifications with the numbers that stand for them are as follows:

000–099   General Works (encyclopedias, periodicals, book lists, books about the library). Since many of these are reference books, some libraries use the letter *R* before the number.

100–199   Philosophy (psychology, conduct, personality)

200–299   Religion (bibles, theology, mythology)

300–399   Social Sciences (economics, education, etiquette, fairy tales, folklore, government, law, legends)

400–499   Philology or Language (grammars, dictionaries, foreign languages)

500–599   Science (animals, astronomy, biology, botany, chemistry, geology, general science, mathematics, physics)

600–699   Technology (agriculture, astronautics, aviation, business, engineering, health, home economics, manual training, television)

700–799   The Arts (motion pictures, music, painting, photography, sculpture, recreation, sports)

800–899   Literature (poetry, drama, essays, criticism, history of literature)

900–999   History (geography, travel, collective biography)

Biographical works dealing with the lives of several persons (collective biography) are marked 920. However, individual biographies (the life of one person) are handled somewhat differently. Like fiction, they are generally kept in a separate section. In most libraries they are marked **B**, but in some they are given the number 92. Under the **B** (or the 92) comes the initial of the last name of the subject of the biography, since you are more likely to be thinking of the

17d

name of the person whose life interests you than the name of the person who wrote about him. Thus, a life of Franklin D. Roosevelt would be marked $\frac{B}{R}$—Biography, Roosevelt. All the books about Roosevelt are then arranged alphabetically by author on the same shelf. You can then find a *particular* biography of Roosevelt.

Nonfiction books other than individual biographies are marked on the spine of the book with their proper number. Each of the main subject groups is divided into ten more subgroups, and each of the subgroups is further divided. Still more specific subdivisions are made by using decimals. For example, if you are looking for a play by Shakespeare, the general subject is Literature, which is numbered 800–899. The exact number for English drama is 822, and the number for Shakespeare is 822.3. Though at first glance this may appear quite complicated, in practice it makes it simple for you as a library user to find any book you are looking for—once you know its number.

This does not mean that you have to memorize the Dewey decimal system; it simply means that you should understand how it works.

● EXERCISE 2.   In which Dewey number range will you find each of the following?

1. a book on manners
2. lives of sports figures
3. the Encyclopædia Britannica
4. a play
5. a French-English dictionary
6. a collection of humorous essays
7. myths of ancient Greece
8. a book on child psychology
9. a book on the War of 1812
10. a book about North American flowers
11. a civics text
12. a cookbook
13. a book on chess
14. a book about Victorian literature
15. a book on crop rotation
16. a history of the movies
17. a book on the care of dogs
18. a book on handicrafts
19. a history of religious art
20. a book about Buddhism

THE CARD CATALOGUE

Every book in the library has a Dewey decimal system number of its own. It is not necessary, however, to search through the shelves to find the number and the book. The number appears on any one of several cards arranged in a cabinet of small drawers. This cabinet, called the *card catalogue*, is usually conveniently located in the front of the library near the circulation desk. On cards in the card catalogue you will find the number that leads you to the shelf where books in that number category are kept. This number is called the *call number*.

17e. **Every nonfiction book has a call number which appears on its catalogue card.**

The call number appears in the upper left-hand corner of the catalogue card. For example, a nonfiction travel book on Germany may have the number 941.3. Fiction books may be marked **F** or may have no number at all.

In a very large library, books are kept in "stacks," and you cannot look for a book yourself. Instead, you give the call number to the librarian, and he sends for the book.

For each book in the library's collection, the card catalogue contains a *title card*, an *author card*, and, if the book is nonfiction, a *subject card*.

17f. **The card catalogue lists books by title, author, and subject.**

The cards in the card catalogue are filed in alphabetical order in drawers. The drawers are labeled like the volumes of an encyclopedia, for example A–AMY, AN–AZ, B–BIO, BIP–BUL, and so on.

The Title Card

The simplest way to find a particular book is to look for the title card. At the top of the title card is the title of the

17
e-f

book. Its position in the alphabetical order is determined by the first word of the title, unless the first word is *A, An,* or *The,* in which case the book will be listed under the second word of the title. For example, *The Last of the Mohicans* will be listed under **L**.

The Author Card

Occasionally you may know the name of the author but not the title of the particular book you want. Or perhaps you have read one of the author's books and would like to read another. On the author card, the author's name appears at the top. All books by the same author will then be arranged in alphabetical order according to the title. For example, the author card for *The Master of Ballantrae* will precede the card for *Treasure Island,* also by Stevenson, in the card catalogue, with "Stevenson, Robert Louis" printed at the top of the card. As with the arrangement of books on the shelves, names beginning with *Mc* are listed as if they were spelled *Mac; St. George* would be filed as if it were spelled *Saint George.*

The Subject Card

Sometimes you are not looking for a particular book by a particular author but are merely interested in a book on a certain subject. Nonfiction books are also catalogued according to the subject with which they deal. If, for example, you're a "shutterbug" and want to learn how prints are developed, you look for cards under "Photography." Under this large subject classification there may be further divisions, such as "Photography—Print Developing."

Often books may be listed under more than one subject heading. A book about baseball may be listed under "Sports," "Athletics," "Baseball," and even "Games."

"See" and "See Also" Cards

A "see" or "see also" card refers you to another section of the catalogue; they are cross-reference cards. Suppose you want to find some books by Mark Twain. You might look for the author card under **T**. Instead of finding cards for his books there, you possibly would find under "Mark Twain" a card saying, "See Clemens, Samuel Langhorne" (Twain's real name). The "see" card, then, directs you to a different part of the catalogue, in this case the **C** file.

"See also" cards refer you to other subjects closely related to the one in which you are interested. If you are looking under "Newspapers," you may find a card saying "See also Journalism." Looking up "Journalism," you will find more books on your subject.

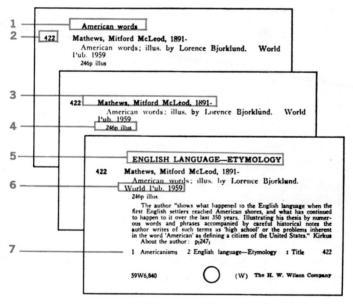

Top to bottom: title, author, and subject cards

1. Title
2. Call number
3. Author and date of birth
4. Number of pages and indication that book is illustrated

5. Subject
6. Publisher and date of publication
7. Other headings under which the book is listed (In some libraries this book is shelved with books on etymology.)

In addition to the title, author, and subject, the catalogue card also tells you the publisher of the book, the place and date of publication, the number of pages, whether the book has illustrations or maps, and occasionally it gives a brief statement about the contents of the book. There is a general trend toward simplifying these cards, and many libraries use cards like those on page 377, which omit place of publication.

Summary of Information in the Card Catalogue

1. The **call number,** showing the location of the book on the library shelves
2. The **author,** his full name, date of birth, and—if no longer alive—date of death (Many libraries omit the dates.)
3. The **title**
4. The **subject**
5. **Cross references** to other books or subjects, where appropriate
6. **Publisher,** place and date of publication, number of pages, illustrations

● EXERCISE 3.   Number from 1–15 on your paper. Using the card catalogue in your library, find the following information:

A. Find the author cards for each writer, and write the title of one of his books. If there is no card, put "not in our library" after the proper number.
   1. Robert Frost
   2. James Thurber
   3. Willa Cather

B. Look up these title cards to see if these books are in your library. If they are, list the author and biographical dates; if not, write "not in our library."
 4. *The Diary of Anne Frank*
 5. *I Knock at the Door*
 6. *To Kill a Mockingbird*

C. Find a book in your library on each of these subjects:
 7. nuclear energy
 8. exploration of space
 9. adolescents or teen-agers

D. List the title, author, call number, and date of publication for the following:
 10. a book of essays or articles
 11. a book on careers
 12. a book of poetry

E. List the title and author of a book *about* the following:
 13. William Shakespeare
 14. Walt Whitman
 15. John F. Kennedy

REFERENCE BOOKS

Your library may have a special reference room where reference books are kept and where people using these books may work. In any case, all reference books will be kept in one section of the library. Some may be on closed shelves, and you must ask the librarian for them. Others are usually on open shelves or on tables. Since reference books are in such constant demand, they must be used only in the library; they may not be checked out.

Every library has several main types of reference books: (1) dictionaries, (2) encyclopedias, (3) biographical dictionaries, (4) atlases, (5) almanacs, (6) books on specific subjects such as literature, authors, etc., and (7) reference guides showing where information may be found. You should familiarize yourself with the kinds of information they offer you.

The Readers' Guide

17g. To find a magazine article, use the *Readers'
Guide.*

The *Readers' Guide to Periodical Literature* may be regarded as the card catalogue for magazines. It indexes all
the articles, poems, and stories in more than a hundred
magazines; the magazines are listed in the front of each
volume.

The *Readers' Guide* appears in a paperback edition twice
a month (except for July and August, when it appears once
a month). Each issue lists articles that were published two
to four weeks previously. From time to time these issues
are combined into single volumes covering periods of
several months. Clothbound cumulations appear at two-
year intervals.

As you can see from the sample entries on page 381,
magazine articles are listed by subjects (BAHAMA IS-
LANDS) and by authors (BAILEY, J. W.). Except for
stories, magazine articles are not listed by title in the
Readers' Guide. The subject and author entries appear in a
single alphabetical list; the subject BAKERS and bakeries
is followed by the author entry BAL, Arya K. The first
word of the subject entry and the author's last name in
the author entry are printed in capital letters. Each entry
lists the title of the article, the name of the magazine, and
the publication date. The subject entry also lists the author
of the article. The *Readers' Guide* employs in its entries a
system of abbreviations; a key to these abbreviations appears in the front of the *Readers' Guide.* Most names of
magazines are also abbreviated (*Bsns W* for *Business Week*);
these are noted in the list of magazines which also appears
at the front.

You will observe that "see" and "see also" references are
also given in the *Readers' Guide;* for example BAHAMA
ISLANDS, *see also* Fishing—Bahama Islands.

Of course, finding out what articles have been published on a certain topic or by a certain author will be of little help to you unless you can obtain the magazines in which the articles appear. Usually you will find near the *Readers' Guide* a list of the magazines to which your library subscribes and a notation on which back issues are available. If there is no list, the librarian can supply the information.

BAHAMA ISLANDS ——————————————— subject entry
    See also
Fishing—Bahama Islands
    Description and travel ————————— division
Camera guide. L. Barry. il Pop Phot 52: of main subject
  76-7+ Mr '63
BAILEY, J. W. ——————————————————— author entry
Veterinary helps (title varies) See issues of
  Successful farming
BAILEY, Mildred ———————————————————— title of article
  Sad story of Mildred Bailey. R. De Tole-
  dano. Nat R 14:204-6 Mr 12 '63
BAIRD, R. E.
  Single sideband simplified. Electr World 69:
  52-4+ F '63
BAKER, Dorothy
  No visitors till noon; story. Sat Eve Post ——— magazine
  236:46-53 Mr 9 '63
BAKERS and bakeries ——————————————— subject entry
      Wages and hours
Four days on, four off: Bridgford packing
  co. Bsns W p 120 F 23 '63 ——————————— date
BAL, Arya K. and Gross, P. R. of magazine
Mitosis and differentiation in roots treated
  with actinomycin. bibliog Science 139 584-
  6 F 15 '63 ———————————————————— volume number
BALANCE of payments
Economic report of the President; excerpts.
  J F. Kennedy. Dept State Bul 48:228-9
  F 11 '63 ———————————————————— author's name
Increasing US exports. New Repub 148:5 Mr
  9 '63
Our international financial position; address,
  January 21, 1963. M. M. Kimbrel. Vital
  Speeches 29 303-5 Mr 1 '63
United States as a world trader and banker, —— page reference
  by H. B. Lary. Review
  Bsns W p 156+ Mr 9 '63

Reproduced by permission of The H. W. Wilson Company.

● EXERCISE 4. Referring to the "Key to Abbreviation" and to the "List of Periodicals Indexed" at the front of the *Readers' Guide*, give the meaning of each of the following:

1. Sci N L   5. v   8. abr
2. cond   6. Je   9. +
3. 54:320–56   7. Sch & Soc   10. por
4. Atlan

17g

● EXERCISE 5.   Find in the *Readers' Guide* one article listed under any five of the following subjects. For each article, give the title, author (if given), magazine, date, and page numbers.

EXAMPLE   1. High school graduates

> Entry: *Employment of June '60 high school graduates. S. Cooper. il Mo Labor R 84:463–70 My '61*
>
> *Employment of June '60 High School Graduates by S. Cooper, illustrated, Monthly Labor Review, Volume 84, pages 463–70, May 1961*

1. Cars
2. Television
3. National parks
4. Comics

5. United Nations
6. Football
7. Boating

8. Jet travel
9. Leisure
10. Music

● EXERCISE 6.   Select someone you want to know more about—a personality in the entertainment world, a great pilot or explorer, a government official—*or* something that interests you—a hobby, cooking, outer space, stars. Then look through several volumes of the *Readers' Guide* and find five magazine articles about the topic you chose. List these articles, giving complete information about each one, as in Exercise 5.

The Vertical File

17h. To find a pamphlet, use the vertical file.

Much valuable information is published in pamphlet form. The Division of Public Documents of the U.S. Government Printing Office alone publishes hundreds of pamphlets each year; many industrial concerns and educational organizations also issue pamphlets regularly. Your librarian files these materials in a vertical file. Sometimes newspaper clippings of special interest will also be included.

Each pamphlet or clipping is placed in a folder and filed away in a cabinet. For up-to-the-minute material, you will find the vertical file very useful. Consult your librarian to see whether a file folder is available on a topic you are studying.

Dictionaries of Synonyms

There is a different kind of dictionary with which you may not be acquainted and which can be of great help to you in your writing: the dictionary of synonyms. The most famous of these is *Roget's Thesaurus of the English Language*. *Thesaurus* means "treasury," in this instance a treasury of words. If, for example, you have overused the adjective "good" in the first draft of a composition, you can find in the *Thesaurus* over a hundred synonyms for "good," as well as many antonyms and cross-references to related words.

Originally the arrangement of the *Thesaurus* was rather complicated, but now it is in dictionary form. All entries are arranged in alphabetical order, with synonyms grouped according to meaning. If you know how to use the dictionary, you can use the *Thesaurus*.

Similar to the *Thesaurus* is *Webster's Dictionary of Synonyms*. Either of these books will help you to avoid needless repetition and, incidentally, to enlarge your vocabulary.

Encyclopedias

While you may own a dictionary, you may not have an encyclopedia, which generally appears in many volumes and is therefore more costly. Encyclopedias are made up of a collection of articles, alphabetically arranged, on almost all subjects within the scope of man's knowledge. There are also many valuable illustrations. As you proceed with your education, you will find that the encyclopedia is more and more valuable to you. It is usually the first source you use in obtaining information on a subject. If you are writing a

17h

long paper or giving a report, you will turn to the encyclopedia for general information and an overall view of your subject before proceeding to books and periodicals.

To find information on a particular subject in the encyclopedia, you may use first the guide letters on the spine of each volume and then the guide words at the top of the pages. If you depend wholly upon this method of finding material, however, you may overlook other important information. It is better to look in the index, usually the last volume of the set. Here you may find that your subject is discussed in several different articles which may appear in several different volumes. By using the index you can find *all* the material on your topic that the encyclopedia contains.

Although encyclopedias are rewritten and revised continuously, you may find (by looking on the title page) that the encyclopedias in your library were published several years ago. For up-to-date information, you should check the annual or yearbook which many encyclopedia companies publish every year. These yearbooks will give the most recent events and latest developments in your subject field.

The following well-known encyclopedias are usually available in most libraries:

Collier's Encyclopedia
  24 volumes
  Index in Volume 24
  Publishes *Collier's Yearbook*

Compton's Pictured Encyclopedia
  15 volumes
  One third of space is pictures
  Fact index (which itself gives information) at end of each volume
  Publishes a yearbook and an annual supplement

Encyclopedia Americana
  30 volumes
  Index in Volume 30
  Publishes *Americana Annual*

Encyclopædia Britannica
  24 volumes
  Index and atlas in Volume 24
  Publishes *Britannica Book of the Year*

World Book Encyclopedia
  20 volumes
  Index in Volume 20
  Publishes an annual

Compton's Pictured Encyclopedia and *World Book Encyclopedia* are written especially for younger readers:

One-volume encyclopedias include *The Columbia Encyclopedia, The Columbia-Viking Concise Encyclopedia*, and the *Lincoln Library of Essential Information*.

Biographical Reference Books

Although encylopedias include biographical articles, there are several special books devoted entirely to accounts of the lives of famous people.

The *Dictionary of American Biography* contains articles about famous Americans who are no longer living. The set includes twenty volumes. Similar to the *D.A.B.* is the *Dictionary of National Biography*, which presents the lives of distinguished Englishmen who are no longer living.

Current Biography is the best source of information about currently prominent persons. It is published monthly in pamphlet form and bound in an annual volume. By using the cumulative index in each issue, you can locate biographies of persons in the news in previous months. Frequently photographs of the persons discussed are included in *Current Biography*.

Another important reference book is *Who's Who*, which contains essential facts—parentage, important biographical dates, positions held, achievements and awards, publications, present address—about distinguished international figures. This book is published annually. Since biographies of Englishmen predominate in *Who's Who*, you may find that *Who's Who in America* is more useful to you. Similar to *Who's Who*, although published only every two years, this work contains data about famous Americans only. Remember that both *Who's Who* and *Who's Who in America* deal only with living persons and give only essential biographical information.

A valuable series of reference works by Stanley Kunitz is composed of biographies of authors. Unlike the two *Who's Who* books, Kunitz' works give much "human-interest" information and also include photographs.

Stanley J. Kunitz:
  Authors Today and Yesterday
Stanley J. Kunitz and Howard Haycraft:
  The Junior Book of Authors (about writers of juvenile literature)
  British Authors of the Nineteenth Century
  American Authors 1600–1900
  Twentieth Century Authors
  Twentieth Century Authors: First Supplement
Stanley J. Kunitz and Vineta Colby:
  European Authors 1000–1900

Other biographical reference books which you may use from time to time are *Webster's Biographical Dictionary*, *World Biography*, and *American Men of Science*.

Atlases

An atlas is much more than just a book of maps. It contains a vast amount of information about the cities and countries of the world—facts about population, resources, industries, natural wonders, climate, exports and imports, history. You should know where the atlases are located in your library and should familiarize yourself with some of them. Especially useful are the following:

  The Encyclopædia Britannica Atlas
  Goode's World Atlas
  Hammond's Ambassador World Atlas

Life World Atlas
National Geographic Atlas of the World
Rand McNally Cosmopolitan World Atlas

Almanacs

Almanacs are full of information on current events. They also contain much of historical interest: facts, dates, statistics, sports records, etc. The three most useful almanacs are *The World Almanac and Book of Facts*, the *Information Please Almanac*, and the *New York Times Encyclopedic Almanac*. All are published annually. Remember to use the index to find information quickly; it is found in the front of the *World Almanac* and in the back of the others.

Reference Books About Literature

There are several collections of quotations, the most famous of which is Bartlett's *Familiar Quotations*. Bartlett's is useful when you want to know the following:

(1) The author of a quotation

(2) The literary work in which the quotation appeared

(3) The complete quotation when you know only a part

(4) A few famous lines by any author

(5) Quotations by various authors on a particular subject

Familiar Quotations is arranged chronologically by author. Under each author's name, the quotations are further arranged chronologically according to the date on which they were said or written. An index in the front of the book lists the authors alphabetically; the index in the back is an alphabetical listing of subjects or key words of the quotations. You can use the author index to find the number of the page that contains quotations from a particular author's works. If you know the quotation or a part of it, you can use the index to find its author or the full quotation. Suppose, for instance, that you want to find out who wrote

Ring out the thousand wars of old,
Ring in the thousand years of peace.

If you look under either *ring* or *peace*, both key words in the quotation, you will find the page given where the quotation appears, along with references to other quotations containing the same key words.

In addition to Bartlett's, Stevenson's *Home Book of Quotations* is especially useful if you want a quotation on a certain subject. The quotations in Stevenson's book are arranged alphabetically by subject. There are also many cross-references. If, for example, you are looking under *Freedom*, you will find several entries there and also a note, *see also Liberty*, with five subheads.

Other good indexes of quotations include the following:

Flesch's *Book of Unusual Quotations*
Mencken's *A New Dictionary of Quotations*
Oxford Dictionary of Quotations
Stevenson's *Home Book of Proverbs, Maxims, and Familiar Phrases*

Granger's *Index to Poetry and Recitations* tells you *where* to find a poem or popular prose passage, but it does not *quote* these. Granger's book lists poems and recitations according to subject, title, and author. You can use it to learn where you can find a certain literary work, who wrote a certain work, and what poems and recitations have been written on a particular subject. Again, you will not find the poem or recitation itself in Granger's *Index*.

If you are looking for a poem, however, you will probably find it in Stevenson's *Home Book of Verse* or *Home Book of Modern Verse*. These large collections contain many well-known poems, classified under general headings such as "Love Poems" or "Familiar Verse." Three additional excellent poetry anthologies are Van Doren's *An Anthology of World Poetry* (arranged by countries) and Untermeyer's *Modern American Poetry* and *Modern British Poetry* (arranged in chronological order; also available in a single volume). All five books have indexes by title, author, and first line.

Other useful reference books on literature are:

Oxford Companion to American Literature
Cambridge History of American Literature (4 volumes)
Burke & Howe's *American Authors and Books*
Oxford Companion to English Literature
Cambridge History of English Literature (14 volumes)
Harper's Dictionary of Classical Literature
Brewer's *A Dictionary of Phrase and Fable*
Benét's *The Reader's Encyclopedia*
Book Review Digest
Short Story Index
Essay and General Literature Index
Oxford Companion to the Theatre
Logasa's *Index to One-Act Plays*

Other Special Reference Books

Among other reference books, you might find the following of interest, according to the subject which you are researching:

Dictionary of American History (companion to the *Dictionary of American Biography*)
Carruth's *Encyclopedia of American Facts and Dates*
Encyclopedia of the Social Sciences
Encyclopedia of Sports
Encyclopedia of Religion
Encyclopedia of Music
Grove's *Dictionary of Music and Musicians*
McGraw-Hill *Encyclopedia of Science*
Murphy's How and Where to Look It Up
Webster's Geographical Dictionary (companion to *Webster's Biographical Dictionary*)

● EXERCISE 7.   Go to the library and locate the encyclopedias, atlases, and almanacs. After you have looked up each of the following items, write after the appropriate number on your paper the name of the reference work you used. Do not use the same book twice.

1. a list of national parks
2. a picture of Michelangelo and reproductions or photographs of his works
3. a chart of Archimedes' principle of specific gravity
4. a list of points of interest in Kansas
5. types of cosmetic makeup used for motion pictures
6. the origin and development of polo
7. a discussion and illustrations of three kinds of mosquitoes
8. last year's major-league baseball statistics
9. the population of Vermont
10. a map of Sweden

● EXERCISE 8.   Disregarding unabridged and abridged dictionaries, as well as encyclopedias, decide what reference book would be best to use for looking up each of the following. Number your paper 1–10. After the corresponding number, write the title of the reference book.

1. a picture and biography of Mickey Mantle, a baseball player for the New York Yankees
2. the names of the five states that border on Nevada
3. a list of quotations about science and beauty
4. a quotation from the works of Rudyard Kipling
5. a biography of the American author Sinclair Lewis
6. a book listing synonyms for *creative*
7. a brief list of facts about John Mills, the English actor
8. a list of facts about Edward Stone, the American architect
9. the complete poem "Song of the Open Road"
10. a book containing the limerick by Edward Lear beginning "There was an Old Man in a boat"

● EXERCISE 9.   Suppose that you have been assigned reports on the following subjects. Give for each subject the names of at least two reference books that you might use.

1. DNA, the genetic code
2. fluoridation of water
3. Robert Frost
4. the climate of Africa
5. John Glenn, astronaut

● EXERCISE 10.   Referring to the proper reference book, answer the following questions. Give your sources.

1. What is the Pulitzer prize? Name the most recent Pulitzer prizewinning (a) novelist, (b) poet, (c) playwright. Cite the work for which each won the award.
2. What is the Nobel prize? Who was the first American to win the Nobel prize for literature? What other Americans have won it?
3. Identify each of the following and give the most recent winner of each: Walker Cup, Stanley Cup, Davis Cup.
4. Who won the Academy Awards for best actor and best actress last year?
5. What television show won the Emmy award for Program of the Year last year?

● EXERCISE 11.   Find the author of the following quotations. Remember to look under a key word. A short quotation like "leave no stone unturned" (Euripides), for example, may be cited under *leave*, *stone*, and *unturned*.

1. I'll tell the world.
2. As good as gold.
3. What fools these mortals be!
4. All mankind love a lover.
5. All that glisters is not gold.
6. Early to bed and early to rise
   Makes a man healthy, wealthy, and wise.
7. Uneasy lies the head that wears a crown.
8. The almighty dollar.
9. To thine own self be true.
10. To strive, to seek, to find, and not to yield.
11. The fault . . . is not in our stars, but in ourselves. . . .
12. They also serve who only stand and wait.
13. A little learning is a dangerous thing.
14. With malice toward none, with charity for all.
15. The only thing we have to fear is fear itself.

● REVIEW EXERCISE.   Write a report or prepare a talk on what your library means to you personally and what it offers you and your community.

CHAPTER 18

The Dictionary

Arrangement and Content of Dictionaries

The reference book that you will use most often from now on is the dictionary. In addition to giving the spelling and meaning of words, a good dictionary tells you how a word is pronounced, what its part of speech is, how it is used by educated speakers, and many other things as well.

If all of the information contained in a dictionary is to be of any use to you, you must know that it is there and know how to find it. You should also know that, even though it is customary to speak generally of "the dictionary," there are in fact many different kinds of dictionaries, each with its special uses. A skillful user of dictionaries knows enough about each major type to enable him to go to the one that best suits his purposes. This chapter is intended to show you the differences between kinds of dictionaries and to suggest in a general way what you may expect to find in each of them.

KINDS OF DICTIONARIES

There are so many special kinds of dictionaries—crossword puzzle dictionaries, scientific dictionaries, rhyming dictionaries, and so on—that it would take a much longer chapter than this to describe all of them. Here we will consider the three kinds of dictionaries that you will be making most use of right now: the unabridged dictionary, the abridged or "college-size" dictionary, and the school dictionary.

The Unabridged Dictionary

The unabridged dictionary is probably a familiar sight to you from your visits to the reference section of your library. It usually has a stand of its own and looks big enough to contain all of the words there are. Although an unabridged dictionary may contain upwards of 450,000 words, it does not list all the English words in daily use, but it does list most of them. Because new words come into the language every day, no dictionary can be completely up to date. The word "unabridged" merely means that a dictionary is not based on some still larger dictionary.

There are several unabridged dictionaries in print. Undoubtedly the best known is Webster's New International Dictionary, which has been kept up to date through succeeding editions. The word "international" means that this dictionary contains information about words as they are used throughout the English-speaking world. That is, it has some entries and spellings that are mainly used in Scotland, Australia, Canada, and so on. It is, however, mainly an American dictionary, and the great majority of its entries deal with meanings, pronunciations, and usages that are current in the United States. The newest unabridged dictionary is the *Random House Dictionary of the English Language: Unabridged Edition*.

You will be hearing more about unabridged dictionaries and how to use them as you go on in high school. For now, it is enough that you have an idea of the kind of information included in this kind of dictionary. On the next page you will find three entries for the word *funnel* reproduced from the *New International Dictionary*.

SAMPLE ENTRIES FROM
AN UNABRIDGED DICTIONARY

¹fun·nel \'fənᵊl\ *n* -s *often attrib* [ME *fonel, funel,* fr. OProv. *fonilh,* fr. ML *fundibulum,* short for L *infundibulum,* fr. *infundere* to pour in, fr. *in* + *fundere* to pour — more at IN, FOUND] **1 a** : a utensil that has typically the shape of a hollow cone with a tube extending from the point, is designed to catch and direct a downward flow of liquid or some other substance, and is sometimes fitted or combined with a strainer or filter — see SEPARATORY FUNNEL **b** : something shaped like a funnel (as a conical part, passage, or hole); *specif* : the swimming funnel of a cephalopod **c** : one that serves as a constricted channel or central agent or organization through which some-

funnel 1a

thing passes or is transmitted **2** : a stack or flue for the escape of smoke or for ventilation; *specif* : the stack of a ship **3** : a cylindrical band of metal; *esp* : one around the top of an upper mast around which the rigging fits **4** : RUNNING GATE **5** : FUNNEL CLOUD **6** : a black usu. cylindrical metal hood attached to a spotlight to prevent the spill of light outside the illuminated area of a stage

²funnel \"\ *vb* funneled *also* funnelled; funneled *also* funnelled; funneling *also* funnelling; funnels *vi* **1** : to have or take the shape of a funnel : NARROW, WIDEN ⟨a shallow, rounded valley bottom ∼s into a miniature gorge with steep bluffs —*Jour. of Geol.*⟩ **2** : to move to or from a focal point or into a central channel ⟨the gang . . . ∼ed onto the end of the jetty off the slope —R.O.Bowen⟩ ⟨orders were ∼ing out to the ships from the flagship —Alexander Griffin⟩ **3** : to pass through or as if through a funnel; *specif* : to move through a constricted passage or central medium ⟨the fierce winds which ∼ed up the valley center —John Steinbeck⟩ ⟨through the great port ∼s much of the overseas commerce —*Newsweek*⟩ ⟨thousands of pictures . . . ∼ed back to the press and public through the public-relations division —*Newsweek*⟩ ⟨thousands of pictures . . . ∼ed back to the press and public through the public-relations division —Robert Moora⟩ ∼ *vt* **1** : to cause to funnel: **a** : to form into the shape of a funnel ⟨∼s his hands and shouts through them⟩ **b** : to cause to move to or from a focal point or into a central channel ⟨traffic is ∼ed into consolidation stations . . . and fanned out to destinations —*Distribution Age*⟩ ⟨airlift's traffic pattern ∼s planes from widely separated . . . bases into two 20-mile-wide corridors —*Nat'l Geographic*⟩ **c** : to direct to a single recipient or distribute from a single source ⟨impurities ∼ed into the air by automobiles, backyard bonfires, and factory chimneys —*N.Y. Times*⟩ ⟨∼ the kerosine into the tank⟩ **d** : to send or direct through a narrow passage or central medium ⟨pass . . . through which were ∼ed troops and supplies —F.T.Chapman⟩ ⟨cupped her hands over the lens of the flashlight, ∼ing the light through a small opening —E.S. Gardner⟩ ⟨if a bank ∼s its news through a public-relations firm —*Banking*⟩ **2** : to serve as a means for the transmission or direction of ⟨accused the press of ∼ing secret military information to Soviet Russia —*Newsweek*⟩ ⟨∼ . . . high-caliber young people to the agency business —*Printers' Ink*⟩

³fun·nel \'fùnᵊl, 'fən-\ *n* -s [origin unknown] *dial Eng* : HINNY

SAMPLE ENTRIES FROM A COLLEGE DICTIONARY

fun house ──────────────── guide word

──────────────── entry word

fun house *n* : a building in an amusement park that contains various devices designed to startle or amuse

word derivation

¹fun·nel \'fən-²l\ *n* [ME *fonel*, fr. OProv *fonilh*, fr. ML *fundibulum*, short for L *infundibulum*, fr. *infundere* to pour in, fr. *in-* + *fundere* to pour — more at FOUND] **1 a** : a utensil that is usu. a hollow cone with a tube extending from the point and is designed to catch and direct a downward flow   **b** : something shaped like a funnel   **2** : a stack or flue for the escape of smoke or for ventilation

alternate spelling

²funnel *vb* **fun·neled** *also* **fun·nelled; fun·nel·ing** *also* **fun·nel·ling** *vi* **1** : to have or take the shape of a funnel   **2** : to pass through or as if through a funnel   ~ *vt* : to cause to funnel; *esp* : to move to a focal point or into a central channel

fun·nel·form \'fən-²l-,form\ *adj* : INFUNDIBULIFORM

fun·ni·ly \'fən-²l-ē\ *adv* : in a funny manner : ODDLY

fun·ni·ness \'fən-ē-nəs\ *n* : the quality or state of being funny

pronunciation

¹fun·ny \'fən-e\ *adj* **1 a** : affording light mirth and laughter : AMUSING   **b** : seeking or intended to amuse : FACETIOUS   **2** : differing from the ordinary in a suspicious way : QUEER   **3** : involving trickery or deception   **syn** see LAUGHABLE

synonym entry

²funny *n* : a comic strip or a comic section of a periodical

funny bone *n* [fr. the tingling felt when it is struck] **1** : the place at the back of the elbow where the ulnar nerve rests against a prominence of the humerus   **2** : a sense of humor

spelling of verb form

¹fur \'fər\ *vb* **furred; fur·ring** [ME *furren*, fr. MF *fourrer*, fr. OF *forrer*, fr. *fuerre* sheath, of Gmc origin; akin to OHG *fuotar* sheath; akin to Gk *pōy* herd, Skt *pāti* he protects] *vt* **1** : to cover, line, trim, or clothe with fur   **2** : to coat or clog as if with fur   **3** : to apply furring to   ~ *vi* : to become coated or clogged as if with fur

²fur *n, often attrib* **1** : a piece of the dressed pelt of an animal used to make, trim, or line wearing apparel   **2** : an article of clothing made of or with fur   **3** : the hairy coat of a mammal esp. when fine, soft, and thick; *also* : such a coat with the skin   **4** : a coating resembling fur: as **a** : a coat of epithelial debris on the tongue   **b** : the thick pile of a fabric (as chenille) — **fur·less** \'fər-ləs\ *adj*

numbered definitions

fu·ran \'fyū̇(ə)r-,an, fyù-'ran\ *also* **fu·rane** \'fyù̇(ə)r-,ān, fyù-'rān\ *n* [ISV, fr. *furfural*] : a flammable liquid C_4H_4O that is obtained from wood oils of pines or made synthetically and is used esp. in the manufacture of nylon

fur·be·low \'fər-bə-,lō\ *n* [by folk etymology fr. F dial. *farbella*] **1** : a pleated or gathered piece of material : RUFFLE; *specif* : a flounce on women's clothing   **2** : something that suggests a furbelow esp. in being showy or superfluous — **furbelow** *vt*

primary and secondary accents

part of speech

fur·bish \'fər-bish\ *vt* [ME *furbisshen*, fr. MF *fourbiss-*, stem of *fourbir*, of Gmc origin; akin to OHG *furbir* to polish] **1** : to make lustrous : POLISH   **2** : RENOVATE, REVIVE — **fur·bish·er** *n, archaic*

¹fur·cate \'fər-,kāt\ *adj* [LL *furcatus*, fr. L *furca* fork] : branching like a fork : FORKED — **fur·cate·ly** *adv*

²furcate *vi* : to branch like a fork — **fur·ca·tion** \,fər-'kā-shən\ *n*

fur·cu·la \'fər-kyə-lə\ *n, pl* **fur·cu·lae** \-,lē, -,lī\ [NL, fr. L, forked prop, dim. of *furca*] : a forked process or part; *esp* : WISHBONE — **fur·cu·lar** \-lər\ *adj*

fur·cu·lum \-ləm\ *n, pl* **fur·cu·la** \-lə\ [NL, fr. L *furca*] : FURCULA

fur·fu·ra·ceous \,fər-f(y)ə-'rā-shəs\ *adj* [LL *furfuraceus*, fr. L *furfur* bran] : consisting of or covered with flaky particles

By comparing this page with the entry for the same word in the sample column on page 395, you will be able to see how the treatment of a common word differs in an unabridged dictionary from that in a smaller dictionary. Notice the many examples of actual uses included in the entry in the unabridged dictionary. These illustrative quotations are set off in angle brackets ($<\ >$).

The College Dictionary

A "college-size" dictionary is shorter and less detailed than an unabridged dictionary. It may contain from 125,000 to 150,000 words, but less is likely to be said about each of these words than in an unabridged dictionary. College dictionaries are designed for the convenience of students, secretaries, letter writers, and everyone else who has occasion to look up a spelling, meaning, pronunciation, or point of usage. The sample column on page 395 reproduces a number of entries more or less typical of college dictionaries.

One college dictionary differs from another in its methods of presenting information. You will be hearing more about such differences later. However, if you use such a dictionary in school or at home, it is essential that you find out for yourself the arrangement and method of presentation used in that book. All dictionaries have introductory notes that explain such matters. Read them. You would not try to use a new camera or phonograph without reading the instructions; or, if you did, the results would almost certainly be unfortunate. To use your dictionary well, you have to know how it is meant to be used.

The School Dictionary

The dictionary that you probably know best is the *school dictionary*—one designed with students of your age and background specifically in mind. Such dictionaries, particularly the one you are likely to be using this year, are much

SAMPLE ENTRIES FROM
A HIGH SCHOOL DICTIONARY

ju di cial (jü dish′əl), *adj.* **1.** of or having to do with courts, judges, or the administration of justice. **2.** ordered, permitted, or enforced by a judge or a court. **3.** of or suitable for a judge; impartial; fair: *A judicial mind considers both sides of a dispute fairly before making a decision.* [< L *judicialis* < *judicium* judgment < *judex* judge] —**ju di′-cial ly,** *adv.*

ju di ci ar y (jü dish′ē er′ē), *n., pl.* **-ar ies,** *adj.* —*n.* **1.** branch of government that administers justice; system of courts of justice of a country. **2.** judges of a country, State, or city. —*adj.* of or having to do with courts, judges, or the administration of justice.

ju di cious ₍(jü dish′əs), *adj.* having, using, or showing good judgment; wise; sensible: *A judicious historian selects and considers facts carefully and critically.* [< F *judicieux* < L *judicium* judgment < *judex* judge] —**ju di′cious ly,** *adv.* —**Syn.** prudent, astute.

Ju dith (jü′dith), *n.* **1.** a Hebrew woman who saved her countrymen by killing an Assyrian general. **2.** book of the Apocrypha and of the Douay Version of the Bible that relates her story.

ju do (jü′dō), *n.* jujitsu.

Ju dy (jü′dē), *n.* wife of Punch in the puppet show of *Punch and Judy.*

jug (jug), *n., v.,* **jugged, jug ging.** —*n.* **1.** container for liquids. A jug usually has a spout or a narrow neck and a handle. **2.** *Slang.* jail. —*v. Slang.* jail. [probably originally proper name, alteration of *Joan,* fem. of *John*]

Jug ger naut (jug′ər nôt), *n.* **1.** idol of the Hindu god Krishna, pulled around on a huge car. Devotees of the god are said to have thrown themselves under the wheels to be crushed to death. **2.** something to which a person blindly devotes himself or is cruelly sacrificed. [< Hindu. *Jagannāth* < Skt. *Jagannātha* lord of the world]

jug gle (jug′l), *v.,* **-gled, -gling,** *n.* —*v.* **1.** do tricks that require skill of hand or eye. **2.** do such tricks with: *He can juggle three balls, keeping them in the air at one time.* **3.** change by trickery: *The bookkeeper juggled the company's accounts to hide his thefts.* —*n.* **1.** a juggling. **2.** trick; deception; fraud. [< OF *jogler* < L *joculari* joke < *joculus,* dim. of *jocus* jest]

jug gler (jug′lər), *n.* **1.** person who can do juggling tricks. **2.** person who uses tricks, deception, or fraud. [< OF *jogleor* < L *joculator* joker, ult. < *jocus* jest. Doublet of JONGLEUR.]

jug gler y (jug′lər ē), *n., pl.* **-gler ies. 1.** skill or tricks of a juggler; sleight of hand. **2.** trickery; deception; fraud.

like college dictionaries. The difference is that the school dictionary contains fewer words, and these are defined with a younger student's experience in mind.

School dictionaries also differ one from the other. The method of each one is carefully explained in its introductory section, and again, it is essential that you study this material carefully. This part of a school dictionary usually gives a simpler and more detailed account of dictionary features than the introduction in a college dictionary. In addition, exercises are often included. The sample column on page 397 will give you an idea of the treatment of words in a school dictionary.

● EXERCISE 1.   Study the table of contents at the front of your dictionary. Notice where the introductory notes are to be found, where the definitions start, and where special tables, charts, or other features may be found. Then write on your paper the part of your dictionary in which you think each of the following items of information can be found. Use *front* for anything that comes before the actual definitions, *main part* for the alphabetical listing of entries, and *back* for anything that comes later. If you think an item might be in two places, give both.

EXAMPLE   1. The pronunciation of the word *naïve*.
        1. *main part*

1. An explanation of the way syllables are divided in the dictionary entries.
2. The meaning of the abbreviation *F.O.B.*
3. The population of Tokyo.
4. The capital of Alaska.
5. The life dates (birth and death) of George Washington.
6. The number of square yards in an acre.
7. The meaning of the abbreviations *n.*, *adj.*, and *v.t.*
8. The meaning of *prism.*
9. An explanation of the meaning of *vowel* and *consonant.*
10. An explanation of the treatment of prefixes in the dictionary.

● EXERCISE 2. Now find each of the items of information in Exercise 1, giving the number of the page on which it appears. Check your answers in Exercise 1, correcting those that turn out to be wrong.

● EXERCISE 3. Judging from your study of the sample columns (394, 395, and 397) and from descriptions of the different kinds of dictionaries, indicate in which kind of dictionary you would expect to find the following items. (Use *unabridged, college,* or *school* in your answers. If two or more of the kinds would be likely to have it, give two or more answers. Use a question mark for a doubtful case.)

EXAMPLE   1. The meaning of the British word *windscreen.*
            1. *unabridged, college* (*?*)

1. The meaning of the abbreviation *etc.*
2. The pronunciation of a word used mainly in Scotland.
3. A pronunciation key.
4. Five different ways of pronouncing the word *Algonquin.*
5. A detailed explanation of the way alphabetical order is used in a dictionary.
6. A list of major colleges and universities in the United States.
7. Two dozen definitions for the word *get.*
8. A chart showing the Indo-European languages.
9. An extended list of words using the *non-*suffix.
10. The date on which Guy Fawkes Day is celebrated in Great Britain.

KINDS OF INFORMATION IN DICTIONARIES

18a. Learn what your dictionary tells you about words.

Refer often to the sample entries from the unabridged and abridged dictionaries (pages 394, 395, and 397) as you study the following.

18a

Spelling

When you don't know how to spell a word, you can look it up in the dictionary, which is the authority on correct spelling. If a word may be spelled two ways—like *acknowledgment* or *acknowledgement*—the dictionary usually gives the more common spelling first.

If there is a spelling problem connected with forming the plural of a word or with adding a suffix (like *-ed, -ing, -ness*), the dictionary shows you how to spell these words. Examples are *fur, furred* and *judiciary, judiciaries*.

● EXERCISE 4.   Number your paper 1–10. Find the answers to the following questions in your dictionary.

A. Which is the more common spelling for the following?

    1. neighbor, neighbour
    2. flunkey, flunky
    3. lodestar, loadstar
    4. draught, draft
    5. catalogue, catalog

B. Correctly add the suffix listed on the right to the word on the left:

    6. funny   est
    7. refer   ed
    8. usual   ly
    9. happy   ness
    10. travel   ing

Capital Letters

If you are not sure about capitalizing a word, the dictionary will help you. Notice on page 397 the capitalized words like *Judith* and *Juggernaut*. Some words, like *democratic*, may or may not have a capital, depending upon how you use the word. Usually *democratic* is listed as an uncapitalized common adjective; however, when the *particular* party is designated in the list of definitions, then a capital is used—"*Democratic party*." Sometimes, however, when a word is commonly used as a proper name, it is listed with a capital—for example, *Victrola.* When the word is applied generally *not cap.* appears.

● EXERCISE 5.   Check your dictionary to find out whether (or when) the following words are capitalized. If the words may be used both ways, write sentences illustrating both uses.

1. arab   5. mercury   8. republican
2. bible   6. mumbo jumbo   9. scot
3. escalator   7. president   10. state
4. god

Syllables

Whenever you need to divide a word at the end of the line, you should split it between syllables only. The dictionary divides all words into syllables: for instance, *ac cu rate* is divided into three syllables.

If your dictionary should use a small dot or dash to show the breaks between syllables, *do not confuse this dash or dot with the hyphen.* Be sure that you know what the hyphen looks like in your dictionary by looking up such words as *mother-in-law* or *ack-ack.*

● EXERCISE 6.   Divide the following words into syllables. Check your work in the dictionary.

1. forevermore   4. preliminary
2. impractical   5. recognize
3. old-fashioned

Pronunciation

To show how a word is pronounced, the dictionary uses *diacritical marks*, which indicate the sounds of vowels, and it respells the word using certain consonants to mean certain sounds. Dictionaries differ somewhat in the marking system they use. As you learn to master your dictionary's method of showing the correct pronunciation of a word, you will need to refer to the pronunciation key (usually given at the bottom, or the top, of each page).

Your teacher may wish to have you learn the common pronunciation markings now so that in your dictionary practice you will be able to understand how to pronounce any word you look up. If so, you should turn to pages 407–13, where you will find further explanation and exercises.

Part of Speech

A part of speech label is given for every word listed in your dictionary. The label is likely to be one of the following abbreviations:

n.	noun	*pron.*	pronoun
v.	verb	*prep.*	preposition
adv.	adverb	*conj.*	conjunction
adj.	adjective	*interj.*	interjection

In addition, most dictionaries label those verbs that take objects *v.t.* (for *transitive verb*) and those that do not *v.i.* (for *intransitive verb*). Many verbs that can be used with or without an object have some of their meanings labeled *v.i.* and some labeled *v.t.* The distinction between transitive and intransitive verbs is discussed on pages 14–15 of this book.

Dictionary practices differ in the placing of the part of speech label. The label may appear immediately after the pronunciation respelling (as in the samples in this chapter) or it may appear at the end of the entry.

● EXERCISE 7.   Look up these words in your dictionary, and classify each one according to its part of speech. (If a word may be used as three or four parts of speech, write each use after the proper number on your paper.)

1. base	5. jerk	8. play
2. beside	6. not	9. regular
3. court	7. out	10. row
4. forward		

Derivation

Your dictionary also tells you the derivation or the origin of a word. To indicate the languages from which a word has come, abbreviations like *L.* (Latin) and *F.* (French) are used. The meanings of these and other abbreviations are given in the key to the abbreviations at the front of the dictionary. Look on page 395, and notice the origin of *funnel*, and on page 397 for the derivation of *juggle*. Knowing the derivation of a word can sometimes help you remember its meaning.

● **EXERCISE 8.** Write after the proper number on your paper the origin of each word listed below. If your student dictionary does not give the derivations, go to an unabridged or college dictionary. If a word is unfamiliar to you, learn its meaning when you look up its origin.

1. chlorophyll
2. exorbitant
3. kaleidoscope
4. phosphorus
5. pince-nez
6. procrastinate
7. quixotic
8. sponsor
9. sporadic
10. sympathy

Meaning

Of course, you know that a dictionary defines words. But do you make full use of its definitions? When a word has many different meanings, do you seek out the particular definition that you are looking for? Notice on page 394 the different meanings for *funnel* as a noun. There is a difference between a *funnel* for liquid and a stage *funnel*. Again, as you can see on page 397, there are three meanings for the adjective *judicial*. These are indicated by numbers.

Some dictionaries place the oldest meaning first; others list the meanings in the order of their use, the most common meaning being given first. Either way, you will need to look over the many definitions until you find the one that fits the sentence in which you have found the word.

● EXERCISE 9. Number your paper 1–10. Look up the exact meaning of each italicized word in these sentences, and write the meaning after the corresponding number.

1. Now I will *pose* for a snapshot.
2. His attitude seems to be a *pose*.
3. On the counter was a novelty key *ring*.
4. The *rings* indicated that the tree was twenty years old.
5. The *kite* lives on snails.
6. When the breezes are not too strong, sailors use *kites*.
7. The third *volume* in the series is the most useful.
8. The *volume* control on my radio is broken.
9. Government employees must pass a *civil* service test.
10. He wasn't even *civil*.

Labels Showing Usage Levels

All dictionaries give some indication as to levels of usage. Words or meanings may be labeled *Slang, Colloq.* (colloquial) *Obs.* (obsolete, no longer in common use), etc. Not all dictionaries use the same labels, and even when they do, the labels may not mean the same thing. It is therefore essential that you read the introductory section of your dictionary to find out what the usage labels mean. Words and meanings that are not labeled are understood to be *standard:* in general use by educated speakers of English.

● EXERCISE 10. Look up the following words in your dictionary to see whether or not they are standard English. If you find no label anywhere in the definitions of a word, write "standard" on your paper after the proper number. If you find a label indicating a special classification, write the label on your paper, using the abbreviations found in your dictionary.

1. blob	5. egghead	9. pep
2. bug	6. fink	10. smithereens
3. case	7. hydrogen	11. snooze
4. cosmos	8. note	12. stratum

Synonyms and Antonyms

A synonym is a word having almost the same meaning as the word being defined: *calm, serene.* An antonym is a word having the opposite meaning: *hot, cold.* Frequently, you will find a small paragraph set aside not only listing synonyms but also showing the distinctions of meanings. Look, for instance, at the entry *funny* on page 395. Notice the "Syn. See LAUGHABLE." If you then look up *laughable* in this dictionary, you will find a paragraph of synonyms, each with its special meaning. When you want to choose the exact word for your meaning, your dictionary, with its listings of synonyms and its cross references, will help you find the word.

● EXERCISE 11. Look up the following words in your dictionary, and make a list of the synonyms given for each word.

1. freedom
2. laughable
3. shrewd
4. rough

Illustrations

If the meaning of a word can best be shown by a picture, the dictionary may give an illustration. If, for example, you are studying gauges or the ancient Pyramids, the chances are that you can find these illustrated in your dictionary.

18b. Find out what your dictionary tells you about people and places.

In your dictionary the names of people and places are either listed in a special biographical, geographical, or "proper names" section, or listed in the main body along with all other words. You can easily discover which method your dictionary uses.

To learn what your dictionary can tell you about a person, look up *David Livingstone* under *L.* First of all,

18b

you find his name correctly spelled, and you can see how to pronounce it. In parentheses you find 1813–1873, the dates of his birth and death. Next is information about his nationality, which is Scottish. Finally, you learn why he became famous, that he was an explorer in Africa. Should you look up the name of a President, you would find the dates of his term of office. Your dictionary also has interesting information about people in the Bible (Moses, Lazarus) as well as about mythological and literary characters (Hercules, Robin Hood).

Now look up the name of a place—say *Hwang Ho, Patmos*, or *Richmond*—in your dictionary. Notice that you can find out (1) how to spell and pronounce the word; (2) what it is (city, river, island); (3) where it is; (4) how big it is; (5) why it is important. Very frequently information about history and government is given.

● EXERCISE 12. When your teacher gives the signal, look up the answers to the following questions in the dictionary you have. Write the answers on your paper. Accuracy is more important than speed, but speed *is* important. Your speed shows to some extent your knowledge of the dictionary.

1. Where is Madagascar?
2. In what year did Christopher Columbus die?
3. How high is Mount Everest?
4. When was Charles Dickens born?
5. What is the Hydra?
6. How large is Lake Huron?
7. What was the nationality of John Drinkwater?
8. How long is the Rio Grande?
9. Who was Merlin?
10. Where is Gatun Dam?

● REVIEW EXERCISE. Number your paper 1–10. By using your dictionary, correctly answer each of the following questions.

1. What is the correct syllable division of *hypochondriac*?
2. Which is the more usual spelling—*pretence* or *pretense*?

3. When, if ever, is the word *army* capitalized?
4. What part of speech is *please?*
5. Is *nincompoop* slang?
6. What is the origin of the word *jujitsu?*
7. What is the meaning of the word *ossify?*
8. What is the meaning of *NCO?*
9. Who was Alfred Bernhard Nobel?
10. Is it correct to use the word *swell* as an adjective in formal writing?

PRONUNCIATION

18c. Use your dictionary for pronunciation.

The regular way of learning to pronounce a word is to listen to the pronunciation of your parents, teachers, and friends. The dictionary gives pronunciations for all of its entry words, but you will use it mainly for the pronunciation of words that you have never heard or do not hear often. Dictionary makers try to give the pronunciation of educated people, but since words are pronounced differently in different places, it is not always possible to give a single pronunciation that is suitable for Boston, Chicago, Houston, and Atlanta. For this reason, you may sometimes find that your dictionary tells you one thing about the sound of a word and that you hear it spoken quite differently in your part of the country. When this happens, you may wish to ask your teacher about the acceptable pronunciation of that word in your area. You should not, however, assume that a pronunciation you hear is wrong just because the dictionary does not give it.

Because the actual spelling of many English words does not clearly indicate how they are pronounced, dictionaries use simplified respellings to indicate the sound of a word. Moreover, since there are more sounds in English than there are letters to represent them, special symbols called *dia-*

18c

critical marks must be used to show different speech sounds represented by the same letter. The following pair of words illustrates both respelling and the use of diacritical marks:

bit (bit)   bite (bīt)

Notice that *bite* is respelled without the silent *e* and that the different sounds of *i* are distinguished, the *i* in *bit* being unmarked and the one in *bite* being written with a straight line above it.

Indicating pronunciation is one of the dictionary maker's most difficult tasks, and it is not surprising that there is some disagreement as to how it should be done. The systems used in various dictionaries differ in a number of details. You will see some of these differences in this chapter. However, when you have need of a pronunciation, you will not need to know all the different ways of indicating it. What you will need to know is how to interpret the pronunciation given in your own dictionary. To do this you must familiarize yourself with the explanatory notes dealing with pronunciation and with the pronunciation key. Most dictionaries explain the system they use in the introductory pages. A full key is usually given inside the front cover. Many dictionaries print a shorter key on each page or each set of facing pages. The key illustrates the use of each letter and symbol used by means of simple examples that everyone knows how to pronounce.

Consonant Sounds

The sounds that a speaker makes by squeezing or cutting off his stream of breath are called *consonants*. The last sounds in *with*, *this*, and *itch* are made by forcing the breath through a narrowed passage at one point or another between the throat and the lips. The last sounds in *first*, *wasp*, and *break* are made by cutting off the breath momentarily.

Consonants present few problems in representing pronunciation because most of them are pronounced in essentially the same way in all words. In a few cases, ordinary English spelling uses one letter for two different consonant sounds. For example, the letter *c* stands for two quite different sounds in *cake* and *cell*. In giving the pronunciation of these words, the dictionary would spell the first with a *k* and the second with an *s*.

Two closely related sounds, the first one in *thin* and the first one in *then*, are distinguished in different ways in different dictionaries. For example:

	WSSD [1]	NCD	T-B	SCD
thin	/thin/	/thin/	(thin)	(thin)
then	/t̲h̲en/	/t̲h̲en/	(ᴛʜen)	(t̶h̶en)

Notice that all of these dictionaries use plain "th" for the sound of the consonant in *thin* and that they differ only in the symbol they use for the related sound in *then*. Whichever dictionary you use, the sound represented by the plain letters will be the one in *thin*, *thimble*, and *thank*.

Vowel Sounds

The sounds that a speaker makes when he does not squeeze or stop his flow of breath are called *vowels*. Although we use five letters (*a, e, i, o, u*) and sometimes a sixth (*y*) in representing vowel sounds in writing, there are actually nine different vowels that are used by most speakers of English in America. To indicate these sounds, dictionary makers use the letters above in combination with diacritical marks.

Long Vowels

The long straight mark over a vowel is called the *macron*. When the macron appears over a vowel, the vowel is said to have the sound of its own name. Such vowels are called *long vowels*.

[1] The abbreviations stand for *Webster's Secondary School Dictionary*, *New Collegiate Dictionary*, *Thorndike-Barnhart High School Dictionary*, and *Standard College Dictionary* respectively.

EXAMPLES   **fate** (fāt)
             sleep (slēp)
             side (sīd)
             lone (lōn)
             fuse (fūz)

Short Vowels

The vowels in the words *cat*, *beg*, *dig*, *odd*, and *up* are called *short vowels*. Dictionaries differ in their methods of showing the sound of short vowels.

One method uses this symbol (ˇ), called a breve (brēv) over the vowel. Another method is to leave short vowels unmarked.

EXAMPLES   **add**   (ăd) or (ad)
             bed   (bĕd) or (bed)
             big   (bĭg) or (big)

Sometimes, when all that we say in an unaccented syllable is the sound of the consonant, the pronunciation respelling in certain dictionaries may omit the short vowel altogether.

EXAMPLES   **localize** (lōk′ l īz)
             pagan (pāg′ n)

The Schwa

If your dictionary is a recent one, you are probably already familiar with the symbol (ə), called the *schwa* (shwä). This upside-down *e* is used to represent the blurred, unclear sound of "uh" in such words as

                    alone   (ə·lōn′)
                    nickel   (nik′ əl)
                    Hannibal (han′ ə·bəl)
                    collect   (kə·lect′)
                    support   (sə·pôrt′)

Most modern dictionaries use the schwa, but some use it more than others. Dictionaries prepared by the G. & C. Merriam Company (*Webster's Secondary School Dictionary*, the *New Collegiate Dictionary*, and others) use this symbol in respelling one-syllable words and other words in which the schwa appears in an accented syllable. Most other dictionaries use the schwa only for unaccented syllables. The examples that follow illustrate this difference:

	WSSD [1]	NCD	T-B	SCD
bun	'bən	'bən	bun	bun
color	'kəl-r	'kəl-ər	kul′ər	kul′ər
supper	'səp-r	'səp-ər	sup′ər	sup′ər

● EXERCISE 13.   Look up the pronunciation of each of the following words in your dictionary and copy it after the appropriate number on your paper. Follow the practice of your dictionary in using parentheses or slant lines to enclose the pronunciation.

1. acknowledge
2. aghast
3. athletic
4. choir
5. generous

6. phonograph
7. pressure
8. suppose
9. these
10. thought

Accent Marks

In words of more than one syllable, one syllable is always spoken louder than the others. The syllable stressed in this way is said to be accented, and it is marked in the pronunciation in one of several ways, depending again upon the dictionary you are looking at.

	WSSD [1]	NCD	T-B	SCD
battery	'bat-r-ē	'bat er-ē	bat′ər i	bat′ər ē

In some words, the placing of the accent makes a great deal of difference. For example, if we accent the first syllable of *rebel*, we have a noun meaning "a rebellious

412   *The Dictionary*

person," while if we accent the second, we have a verb meaning "to rise up or battle against authority."

For certain words of three or more syllables, the dictionary gives two accents. The first, as on page 411, is called the *primary accent;* the second is called the *secondary accent.* Dictionaries handle accent marks in different ways. Some put accent marks before the syllable being stressed; some after. Some use a light mark for the secondary accent; some place the secondary accent to the left and below the stressed syllable. Notice how it is done in four dictionaries for the word *elevator.*

	WSSD [1]	NCD	T-B	SCD
elevator	'el-ə₁vāt-r	'el-ə-₁vāt-ər	el′ə vāt′ər	el′ə·vāt′ər

● EXERCISE 14.   Look up the pronunciation of the following words in your dictionary and copy it after the appropriate number. Be sure to include accent marks and diacritical marks. Indicate syllable division in whatever way your dictionary does.

1. appropriate (adjective)
2. appropriate (verb)
3. establish
4. foreground
5. fraternity
6. instrumental
7. lighthouse
8. promote
9. serpent
10. wheelbarrow

● EXERCISE 15.   Rewrite each italicized word, showing the accented syllable and the part of speech as in your dictionary.

EXAMPLE   1. What can his *object* be?
 I don't know, but I *object* to his method.
 1. (*ob′ject*), *n.*
  (*ob·ject′*), *v.*

1. What is your favorite *subject?*
 You should not *subject* him to ridicule.

[1] The abbreviations stand for *Webster's Secondary School Dictionary, New Collegiate Dictionary, Thorndike-Barnhart High School Dictionary,* and *Standard College Dictionary* respectively.

2. Many people *protest* against a nuclear war.
   Their *protest* is objected to by others.
3. No one is *perfect*, but people do try to *perfect* themselves.
4. I do not *suspect* him of malice, but his attitude is *suspect*.
5. All young people *rebel*, but he remained a *rebel* all his life.
6. 'I *reject* your hypothesis.
   This one is a *reject* because it is defective.
7. We cannot *refuse* to help those in need.
   All *refuse* should be thrown into the proper receptacle.
8. Do you like this *console* table?
   No one could *console* her in her grief.

WORDS COMMONLY MISPRONOUNCED

Using the key below, practice saying the following commonly mispronounced words correctly.

accept (ak·sept′)
alias (ā′lē·as)
almond (ä′mənd, am′ənd)
architect (är′kə·tekt)
athlete (ath′lēt)
attacked (ə·takt′)
auxiliary (ôg·zil′yər·ē, ôg·zil′ ər·ē)

bade (bad)
because (bi·kôz′)
bicycle (bī′sik·əl)
blackguard (blag′ərd, blag′ ärd)

café (ka·fā′, kə·fā′)
candidate (kan′də·dāt, kan′ də·dit)
cello (chel′ō)
cement (si·ment′)

champion (cham′pē·ən)
chasm (kaz′əm)
children (chil′drən)
column (kol′əm)
comparable (kom′pər·ə·bəl)
contrary (kon′trer·ē)
curiosity (kyŏor′ē·os′ə·tē)

demonstrative (di·mon′strə· tiv)
discretion (dis·kresh′ən)
docile (dos′əl)
drowned (dround)

elm (elm)
everybody (ev′rē·bod′ē, ev′rē· bud′ē)

faucet (fô′sit)
film (film)

PRONUNCIATION KEY: add, āce, câre, pälm; end, ēven; it, īce; odd, ōpen, ôrder, tŏŏk, pōōl; up, bûrn; ə = a in *above*, e in *sicken*, i in *flexible*, o in *melon*, u in *focus*; yŏŏ = u in *fuse*; oil; pout; check; go; ring; thin; this; zh, vision.

From Funk & Wagnalls *Standard College Dictionary*. Used by permission.

finale (fi·nä′lē, fi·nal′ē)
forbade (fər·bad′, fôr·bad′)
further (fûr′thər)
futile (fyōō′təl)

genuine (jen′yōō·in)
geography (jē·og′rə·fē)
geometry (jē·om′ə·trē)
gesture (jes′chər)
gigantic (jī·gan′tik)
grimy (grī′mē)

handkerchief (hang′kər·chif)
height (hīt)
hundred (hun′drid)

impious (im′pē·əs)
indicted (in·dīt′id)
infamous (in′fə·məs)
influence (in′flōō·əns)
introduce (in′trə·dōōs′)
irreparable (i·rep′ər·ə·bəl)
Italian (i·tal′yən)
italics (i·tal′iks)

just (just)

length (lengkth, length)
library (lī′brer·ē, lī′brə·rē)

mischievous (mis′chi·vəs)
municipal (myōō·nis′ə·pəl)
museum (myōō·zē′əm)

perform (pər·fôrm′)
perhaps (pər·haps′)
perspiration (pûr′spə·rā′shən)
piano (pē·a′nō)
poem pō′əm)
preferable (pref′ər·ə·bəl)
prescription (pri·skrip′shən)
probably (prob′ə·blē)

quantity (kwon′tə·tē)

recognize (rek′əg·nīz)
remonstrate (ri·mon′strāt)
reputable (rep′yə·tə·bəl)
rinse (rihs)

strength (strengkth, strength)
suite (swēt)
superfluous (sōō·pûr′flōō·əs)

telegraphy (tə·leg′rə·fē)
theater (thē′ə·tər)

vehicle (vē′ə·kəl)
victual (vit′l)

wrestle (res′əl)

CHAPTER 19

Vocabulary

Context Clues, Synonyms, Word Analysis

The best way to increase your vocabulary is to read widely and to remember a good deal of what you have read. This may seem like an old-fashioned method, but there are really no shortcuts. There are, however, ways of improving your efficiency in learning the new words that you encounter. Knowing how to find clues to the meaning of a word elsewhere in the sentence and knowing something about the ways words are formed will help.

This chapter is intended to help you develop skills that will be useful in building a better vocabulary. But before you begin, take the following test on the meanings of words that appear in books commonly read by students of your age. What percentage of these words do you know now?

Diagnostic Test

Number your paper 1–25. After the proper number, write the letter of the word which is nearest in meaning to the italicized word at the left.

1. *absolve*   a. forget   c. pardon
                   b. accuse   d. figure out

2. *allusion*   a. reference   c. mistaken idea
                   b. criticism   d. disappointment

415

3. *anarchy*
   a. dictatorship
   b. lawlessness
   c. entryway
   d. country ruled by a queen

4. *benevolence*
   a. laziness
   b. mysteriousness
   c. rudeness
   d. kindliness

5. *bizarre*
   a. childish
   b. poorly chosen
   c. strange
   d. common

6. *candid*
   a. small
   b. straightforward
   c. hidden
   d. unjust

7. *competent*
   a. capable
   b. aggressive
   c. incapable
   d. sane

8. *discrepancy*
   a. difference
   b. dishonesty
   c. dislike
   d. noise

9. *docile*
   a. stupid
   b. easily tired
   c. easily misled
   d. easily managed

10. *exasperated*
    a. irritated
    b. undecided
    c. puzzled
    d. overjoyed

11. *flaunt*
    a. betray
    b. point out
    c. show off
    d. give in

12. *grueling*
    a. questioning
    b. frightening
    c. exhausting
    d. stubborn

13. *haven*
    a. paradise
    b. town
    c. shelter
    d. small river

14. *immune*
    a. in bad health
    b. alone
    c. healthy
    d. protected

15. *incomprehensible*
    a. startling
    b. too expensive
    c. not understandable
    d. not flammable

16. *ingenious*
    a. dishonest
    b. clever
    c. simpleminded
    d. frank

17. *jaunty*
    a. light-hearted
    b. strolling
    c. nervous
    d. yellowish

18. *lethal*
    a. deadly
    b. explosive
    c. criminal
    d. warlike

19. *meander*
    a. walk rapidly
    b. untie
    c. examine
    d. wander

20. *mediocre*	a. ignorant	c. ill-tempered
	b. ordinary	d. boring
21. *ominous*	a. altogether	c. threatening
	b. disappearing	d. hungry
22. *retrieve*	a. recover	c. make up
	b. hunt	d. overlook
23. *skeptical*	a. doubting	c. cruel
	b. unfriendly	d. untrustworthy
24. *tawdry*	a. gay and charming	c. tattered and worn
	b. showy and tasteless	d. ill-fitting
25. *wary*	a. trusting	c. tired
	b. cowardly	d. cautious

19a. List new words with their meanings in your notebook, and use them in speech and writing.

When you learn a new word, list it in your notebook with its meaning. Use it in speech and writing as often as you can in order to make it a permanent part of your vocabulary. Begin now by listing any words that were new to you in the diagnostic test. Keep a special section of your notebook for this purpose; after each exercise in this chapter, add to the list all words you did not know. Add any other words you learn from day to day.

WAYS TO LEARN NEW WORDS

Context

The total situation in which a word is used is called its *context*.

19b. Learn new words from their contexts.

The words that surround a particular word are one part of the context; the circumstances in which it is used are another part.

19
a-b

Verbal Context

The other words in the sentence are the *verbal context* of a word. They often supply clues to meaning. For example, if you did not know the meaning of the word *pedestrians*, you would probably be able to guess it from the surrounding words in the following sentence:

> Because there were no sidewalks, **pedestrians** had to be careful to avoid cars.

Sidewalks are intended for people to walk on. Since the absence of sidewalks makes this street or road dangerous for *pedestrians*, the word probably has something to do with "walking people" or "people who are on foot." Of course, guesses based on context turn out to be wrong sometimes, but they are well worth making. In fact, you have learned most of the words you know by making guesses of this kind.

Physical Context

The actual situation being discussed is the *physical context*. Suppose that you happen to hear someone say "At last he's got a strike." This time the other words in the sentence are not much help if you do not know what *strike* means. What does help is knowing what the speaker is talking about. If he is watching a baseball game, *strike* means one thing; it means quite another if he is talking about fishing or bowling. We call this *physical context* because the surroundings—in this case, a baseball park, a boat, or a bowling alley—usually give us the clue we need.

Since the two kinds of context work together to help you discover the meaning of unfamiliar words, it is not important that you be able to distinguish one kind from the other. What is important is that you remain alert to all possible clues that a situation may provide to the meaning of a new word.

● EXERCISE 1. Number your paper 1–10. For the italicized word in each of the sentences, select the definition from the list below that is closest in meaning. Write its letter beside the proper number. When you have finished, check the meaning of any words you are not sure of in your dictionary. You will not need all of the definitions in the list.

a. warn gently
b. youthful
c. able to float
d. having little resistance to
e. trace
f. one who is too enthusiastic
g. expert
h. frighten
i. good-natured
j. burdensome
k. proverbial saying
l. repeat
m. showing good judgment
n. injury to repay injury

1. The people threatened to revolt unless the king repealed the *oppressive* new tax.
2. Not a *vestige* of the old path remained to guide the explorers.
3. Life jackets are necessarily made from *buoyant* materials.
4. The State Police will *reiterate* their earlier warnings to motorists about to set out on holiday trips.
5. People in public life are expected to be *discreet* in both their private and public affairs.
6. Some people seem to be more *susceptible* to colds than others.
7. Jack is so *amiable* that people sometimes take advantage of him.
8. Mr. Collins, who never could remember an *adage* exactly, was fond of saying, "The early worm gets eaten."
9. The master of ceremonies occasionally had to *admonish* the children to stop eating the prizes.
10. The general of the occupying army threatened to make *reprisals* unless the townspeople cooperated with his men.

● EXERCISE 2. Number your paper 1–10. Copy each italicized word in the following passage, and write next to it what you think it means. Write either a definition or a *synonym*. When you have completed the exercise, check with dictionary meanings, rewrite those you had wrong, and restudy the context which you missed. Add new words to your notebook list.

Although our team had played a good game, the second half of the ninth inning found our (1) *adversaries* holding a three-run lead, and this seemed too big for us to (2) *surmount*. Our hope (3) *diminished* further when our first batter flied out to center, but it revived a little when Frank, our pitcher, hit a double. Our opponents decided to use (4) *strategy*, and they gave an (5) *intentional* base on balls to George, our third batter. Excitement reached a (6) *climax* when Eddie, the fourth man up, hit a sharp grounder which the second baseman was unable to (7) *intercept*. (8) *Subsequent* events were almost too quick to follow. With the bases full, Joe, our catcher, hit a home run, and the (9) *frenzied* spectators rushed out on the field and carried him with wild (10) *acclaim* to the clubhouse.

19c. Learn to find the meaning you want in the dictionary.

Although there are some words in English, like *carbon dioxide*, that have only one meaning or only a few very closely related meanings, most common words have many. The word *point*, for example, may mean "a place," "the tip of a pencil," "a unit of scoring in a game," "the main idea that someone is trying to express," and many other things as well. Since dictionaries define all of the important uses of a word, it is important not to settle for the very first definition that is listed for an entry word.

The best way of testing definitions in context is to keep in mind the context in which you read or heard the word. You can then try the various meanings until you find the one that fits. Take this sentence, for example:

The general **dispatched** his captives quickly and painlessly.

The meaning of the sentence depends upon the meaning of *dispatched*. Keeping the whole sentence in mind will help you to choose the right meaning for *dispatched* in this sentence. Of the three definitions your dictionary is certain to give—(1) to send away; (2) to put to death; (3) to dispose of quickly, as business—only the second really fits. The sentence means that the general put his captives to death in a quick and painless way.

To make the differences between a word's various meanings clear, dictionary makers often provide sample contexts as part of the definition. The same context for meaning (1) of *dispatch* might be "to dispatch a messenger." When such illustrative examples are given, you can easily compare your context with this one to make sure you have found the meaning you want.

● EXERCISE 3.   The italicized words in the following sentences all have a number of different meanings. Using your dictionary, find the meaning that fits best and write it after the proper number on your paper. Be sure to test each meaning given in the context of the sentence before making your choice.

1. Both of the candidates appeared to tire in the last *hectic* days of the campaign.
2. The modest hero of "The Great Stone Face" *ascribes* to others all of the excellent qualities he does not recognize in himself.
3. The courts of the dictator made a *farce* of justice.
4. Occasionally one of his friends would *impose* on George's generosity.
5. Many of Poe's most famous short stories have distinctly *morbid* themes.
6. It was like Harry never to think of the *orthodox* solution to a problem.
7. Having been wiped out by his partner's treachery, Mr. Marple merely shrugged and set about *retrieving* his fortune.
8. The lost party of explorers found only muddy water to *slake* their thirst.
9. Only the pilot's coolness in the face of danger prevented a *tragedy*.
10. It was soon evident to the white hunter that the cannibal chief's civilized manners were only a *veneer*.

19c

Determining the Part of Speech

Many words in English can be used as different parts of speech. Since these words do different jobs in sentences, the meanings have to be stated differently if they are to fit into the proper kinds of context. For example, a dictionary would list all of the meanings for *seal* illustrated by the following sentences:

That is the **seal** of the State of New York.
Christmas **seals** raise money to fight tuberculosis.
The sailors desperately **sealed** the leak.
The notary **sealed** the document to make it official.

In the first two sentences, *seal* is used as a noun; in the second two, it is used as a verb. Most dictionaries indicate in some way the part of speech of each meaning they define. Some group the noun meanings, the verb meanings, etc., together, and others show the part of speech of each meaning at the end of the entry. However your dictionary does it, it will save you time to know the part of speech of the meaning you are looking up. (If you are not clear how dictionaries indicate the part of speech, review page 402.)

● EXERCISE 4.   Look up *root* and *iron* in your dictionary. List as many parts of speech as you can find for each entry and indicate the number of meanings given for each.

● EXERCISE 5.   Use each of the following words in a sentence of your own as the part of speech indicated.

EXAMPLE   1. seal [as a noun]
1. *The archbishop signed the paper and affixed his seal.*

1. affront [as a noun]
2. alien [as an adjective]
3. epic [as a noun]
4. intrigue [as a verb]
5. moor [as a verb]
6. plot [as a noun]
7. tutor [as a verb]

8. solvent [as an adjective]
9. testimonial [as a noun]
10. wrangle [as a verb]

● EXERCISE 6. Follow these instructions for each of the ten sentences below. (1) Write the italicized word after the proper number. (2) After the word, write its part of speech in this sentence. (3) Then write a synonym or a short definition. Be sure that you give the appropriate meaning for words that have more than one definition.

EXAMPLE   1. Cross-country racing demands great *stamina*.
           1. *stamina, noun, endurance*

1. Comedians who imitate well-known people have to be excellent *mimics*.
2. The barons *wrested* power from the tyrannical King John at Runnymede.
3. Many movie stars attended the *premiere*.
4. Despite the evidence against him, the defendant continued to *aver* his innocence.
5. There was a *perceptible* improvement in assembly attendance after the principal's short speech.
6. A winter of terrible hardship and constant rumors of the enemy's strength had *demoralized* the troops.
7. Although the general never rode horses when he could help it, he is the subject of many *equestrian* statues.
8. No one ever thought of offering him any but the most *menial* jobs.
9. A duel between the two warriors *climaxed* the action in the third scene.
10. There is little room for *dissent* under a dictatorship.

● REVIEW EXERCISE A. The words in this exercise have been chosen from those you have studied so far in this chapter. Number your paper 1–20. After the proper number, write the letter of the word which is nearest in meaning to the italicized word at the left.

1. *admonish*   a. warn gently   c. prohibit
                    b. punish   d. applaud

2. *adversary*
   - a. reversal
   - b. bearer of bad news
   - c. opponent
   - d. spy

3. *ascribe*
   - a. tell about
   - b. give as a cause
   - c. envy
   - d. speak ill of

4. *dispatch*
   - a. receive
   - b. command
   - c. send away
   - d. punish

5. *hectic*
   - a. calm
   - b. feverishly excited
   - c. noisily cheerful
   - d. angry

6. *impose*
   - a. take advantage
   - b. show off
   - c. pretend
   - d. reveal

7. *intrigue*
   - a. plot
   - b. entertain
   - c. slander
   - d. imitate

8. *menial*
   - a. cruel
   - b. servantlike
   - c. ordinary
   - d. by hand

9. *mimic*
   - a. show
   - b. imitate
   - c. envy
   - d. perform

10. *morbid*
    - a. gloomy
    - b. fatal
    - c. imaginative
    - d. ordinary

11. *oppressive*
    - a. respected
    - b. burdensome
    - c. unfair
    - d. unfriendly

12. *orthodox*
    - a. religious
    - b. public
    - c. conventional
    - d. unusual

13. *perceptible*
    - a. slight
    - b. proverbial
    - c. noticeable
    - d. frightening

14. *retrieve*
    - a. search for
    - b. locate
    - c. follow
    - d. bring back

15. *stamina*
    - a. ability to reason
    - b. speed
    - c. endurance
    - d. part of a flower

16. *strategy*
    - a. planning
    - b. warfare
    - c. sport
    - d. rules

17. *subsequent*
    - a. less important
    - b. hidden
    - c. coming before
    - d. something that follows

18. *surmount*	a. climb on	c. give up
	b. overcome	d. tower
19. *veneer*	a. thin coating	c. fault
	b. locality	d. decoy
20. *vestige*	a. trace	c. ceremony
	b. honor	d. secret

Using the Right Word

19d. Select the word that conveys the precise meaning and impression you want to give.

There is little point in knowing a large number of words unless you make some use of them. While many of the new words you learn from now on will be more useful to you in your reading than in your own writing and speaking, you will certainly find that some of them will help you to express your thoughts with greater clarity and precision.

The English language is rich in synonyms—words that have the same general meaning but that have subtle shades of difference between them. Choosing the right synonym can mean a great deal when you are trying to write clearly and effectively.

● EXERCISE 7. Number your paper 1–10. For each sentence below, select the most appropriate synonym for the word *walk* from the following list. Use a different word in each sentence. You may use any tense needed to fit the structure of the sentence. Write that word next to the number, and be prepared to explain in class why each word is most appropriate. If you are in doubt, use your dictionary.

amble	stride
march	stroll
pace	tramp
plod	tread
promenade	wander

19d

1. The referee picked up the ball, —— back five yards, and put it on our thirty-yard line.
2. Over a thousand veterans —— in the Memorial Day parade.
3. —— the deck of a large ocean liner is an exhilarating experience.
4. In his haste he —— ahead of his companions through the crowded street.
5. The horse —— slowly along the path as his rider enjoyed the scenery.
6. Unaware of the surroundings, the blissful couple —— slowly, arm in arm.
7. The cows had —— a path to the stream.
8. The happy boy on his vacation —— idly along beside the brook.
9. Hoping to make up the lost time, the hikers —— resolutely through the woods.
10. The weary workman, lifting each foot with obvious effort, —— up the hill.

● EXERCISE 8. Number your paper 1–10. Refer to the dictionary for the exact meaning of each adverb. Then answer each of the questions below by writing the most appropriate adverb next to the number of the question which the adverb answers.

barbarously	grotesquely
comprehensively	nocturnally
defiantly	reluctantly
ferociously	reverently
genially	ungraciously

1. How did the tiger bare his teeth at the visitors in the zoo?
2. How did the tourists stand at the tomb of the unknown soldier?
3. How did the Goths and Vandals act when they sacked and burned the city of Rome?
4. How did the nervous patient approach the dentist's chair?
5. How did the captured hero stare at his enemy?
6. How did the master of ceremonies smile as he greeted the contestant in the quiz contest?
7. How was the unnatural-looking clown dressed?

8. How did the weary housewife greet the unexpected guests at dinnertime?
9. How did the well-prepared student answer the examination questions?
10. When do owls hunt for prey?

● EXERCISE 9. Number your paper 1–18. Next to each number, write the letter of the correct synonym for the italicized word. Refer to your dictionary whenever necessary.

1. *abate*	a. help	b. lessen	c. return
2. *aloof*	a. awkward	b. scared	c. standoffish
3. *defile*	a. sharpen	b. line up	c. make dirty
4. *durable*	a. lasting	b. tired	c. hard
5. *encounter*	a. meet	b. reach	c. reckon
6. *falter*	a. need	b. hesitate	c. misplay
7. *futile*	a. old	b. frail	c. useless
8. *gaudy*	a. general	b. useful	c. showy
9. *intricate*	a. complicated	b. interior	c. pretty
10. *laconic*	a. slow	b. funny	c. terse
11. *manifest*	a. strengthen	b. reveal	c. displace
12. *poise*	a. composure	b. beauty	c. pride
13. *potency*	a. pretense	b. strength	c. view
14. *realm*	a. bone	b. kingdom	c. coin
15. *repel*	a. drive back	b. bring forward	c. hide
16. *requisite*	a. necessary	b. late	c. early
17. *turbulent*	a. ancient	b. young	c. violent
18. *ultimate*	a. final	b. aged	c. reliable

19e. Learn to understand and use literary terms.

High school students are frequently asked to discuss books or plays. The words in the following exercise will help you to carry on a literary discussion with intelligence and clarity.

● EXERCISE 10. Number your paper 1–10. If necessary, look up in the dictionary the numbered words in column A.

19e

Write the letter from column B which is appropriate for the numbered word in column A.

A	B
1. atmosphere	a. the main story
2. comedy	b. the main character
3. foreshadowing	c. an unchanging conventional character
4. plot	d. the main subject or idea of a literary work
5. protagonist	
6. setting	e. a hint of something to come
7. soliloquy	f. speech by an actor to himself
8. stereotype	g. the color or feeling pervading a literary work
9. theme	
10. tragedy	h. a play making fun of something
	i. a serious play having an unhappy ending
	j. a historical literary work
	k. a play with a happy ending
	l. the place and time of a literary work

● EXERCISE 11. Number your paper 1–10. If necessary, look up in the dictionary the numbered words in column A. Write the letter from column B which is appropriate for the numbered word in column A.

A	B
1. biographical	a. painfully moving or touching
2. didactic	b. freely imaginative and fanciful
3. farcical	c. appealing to the emotions by sensationalism and exaggeration
4. fictitious	
5. hackneyed	d. marked by broad or boisterous humor
6. melodramatic	e. ornate in style
7. poignant	f. attacking or ridiculing a custom, habit, or idea
8. realistic	
9. romantic	g. of a person's life
10. satirical	h. overused, commonplace, stale
	i. clear and simple
	j. representing in literature life as it actually is
	k. intended to instruct, teacherlike
	l. not real, imaginary, made-up

PREFIXES AND ROOTS

When you look up a word in the dictionary, you often find older words listed as the origin. English has borrowed words from almost all languages, but particularly from Latin and Greek. Sometimes one Latin or Greek word element is found in many English words. Knowing the meaning of a Greek or Latin word element gives you an understanding of a great many English words.

These word elements may be the part of a word that comes first, called the *prefix;* they may be the main part, called the *root;* they may be the part added at the end, called the *suffix.* Many words have only one or two of these parts, but some have three. Consider the word *semiannual.* This word is composed of the prefix *semi–,* meaning "half" in Latin; the root *–annu–* meaning "year" in Latin; and the suffix *–al* from a Latin word meaning "pertaining to." The word *semiannual* means "pertaining to an event that occurs every half year." (The same root may show a vowel change in different words. In *biennial,* for example, *–enni–* is the same root as *–annu–* although two of its letters are changed.)

19f. Learn some of the common Latin prefixes and roots.

The following word parts from Latin are commonly used in English words. If you learn the meaning of these prefixes and roots, you will be able to figure out the meaning of a great many words in which they occur.

LATIN PREFIX	MEANING	LATIN ROOT	MEANING
ad–	to, toward	–cis–	cut
con–	two	–fid–	faith
con–	with	–ped–	foot
in–	into	–spec–	look
intro–	within	–voc–	call

● EXERCISE 12.   Number your paper 1–5. Write the prefix and its meaning and the root and its meaning for each word

19f

in the numbered list below. Then write the meaning of the whole word. Use your dictionary if necessary.

EXAMPLE 1. submarine
  1. *sub (under)* + *mare (sea)* = *underwater boat*

1. biped
2. incise
3. confide

4. advocate
5. introspect

Here are some other commonly used Latin prefixes and roots. Before you do the exercise below them, try to think of words in which these parts appear. Can you see a relationship between the meaning of the part and the meaning of the whole word?

LATIN PREFIX	MEANING	LATIN ROOT	MEANING
ab–, abs–	off	–cogn–	know
re–	back, again	–cid–	kill
sub–	below, under	–dic–, –dict–	say, speak
		–hom–	man
		–pond–	a weight
		–prob–	prove
		–sed–	seat
		–ten–, –tens–	hold
		–tract–	draw
		–vert–, –vers–	turn

● EXERCISE 13. Number your paper 1–10. For each italicized word, write the part or parts derived from Latin and their meanings. Then write the meaning of the word as it is used in the phrase. Use your dictionary if necessary. Ignore the suffixes in this exercise.

EXAMPLES 1. *dictate* letters
  1. *dict (speak)* = *speak a message for someone to write down*
  2. *subtract* the balance
  2. *sub (below)* + *tract (draw)* = *withdraw or take away the balance*

1. to *recognize* a friend
2. a detective from the *homicide* division
3. faultless *diction*
4. act of *subversion*
5. a *ponderous* elephant

6. on *probation*
7. *retract* the statement
8. *abstention* from food
9. a *versatile* musician
10. a *sedentary* job

19g. Learn some of the common Greek prefixes and roots.

There are many words in English which are derived from Greek words. Study the following list of common prefixes and roots.

GREEK PREFIX	MEANING	GREEK ROOT	MEANING
auto–	self	–astr–, –aster–	star
eu–	good	–chir–	hand
hydr–	water	–dox–	opinion
micro–	small	–geo–	earth
ortho–	right, straight	–graph–	write
sym–	together	–log–	speech, science of (something)
tri–	three		
		–nomy–	law
		–phobia–	dread of
		–phon–	sound
		–pod–	foot

● EXERCISE 14.   Number your paper 1–10, skipping a line after each number. Copy the italicized words that follow. After referring to your dictionary, write the part or parts derived from Greek and their meaning. Then write the meaning of the word as it is used in the phrase. Ignore the suffixes in this exercise.

EXAMPLE   1. a case of *hydrophobia*
1. *hydro (water) + phobia (dread) = a case involving a dread of water*

19g

1. marked by an *asterisk*
2. an *autograph* collector
3. granted *autonomy*
4. treated by a *chiropodist*
5. a flattering *eulogy*
6. studying *geology*
7. examining a *microphone*
8. an *orthodox* believer
9. a flutist in the *symphony*
10. standing on a *tripod*

● EXERCISE 15. As your teacher dictates them, write the meaning of each of the following Latin and Greek prefixes. Then write a word in which the prefix appears. Be prepared to explain the relationship between the meaning of the prefix and the meaning of the word.

1. ab–
2. ad–
3. auto–
4. bi–
5. con–
6. di–, dia–
7. hydr–
8. in–
9. intro–
10. micro–
11. ortho–
12. re–
13. sub–
14. sym–
15. tri–

● EXERCISE 16. As your teacher dictates them, write the meaning of each of the following Latin and Greek roots. Then write a word in which the root appears. Be prepared to explain the relationship between the meaning of the root and the meaning of the word.

1. –astr–
2. –cogn–
3. –chir–
4. –cid–
5. –cis–
6. –dict–
7. –dox–
8. –fid–
9. –geo–
10. –graph–
11. –hom–
12. –log–
13. –nomy–
14. –ped–
15. –phobia–
16. –phon–
17. –pod–
18. –pond–
19. –prob–
20. –sed–
21. –tend–, –tens–
22. –tract–
23. –vers–
24. –vert–
25. –voc–

19h. Learn the origins of words as an aid to remembering meaning.

(1) Words with interesting histories

Study the origin of each word when you look it up in the dictionary. For example, in the entry for the word *candidate* you will find the following: [L. *candidatus*, clothed in white]. *L.* means "Latin," and *candidatus* is the Latin word from which *candidate* comes. The explanation of this word origin is that in ancient Rome candidates wore white robes. Many other words, like the ones in the following exercise, have interesting stories connected with them.

● EXERCISE 17. Number your paper 1–10. Next to the appropriate number, write the italicized word. By referring to the dictionary, write the definition of each word and the language of its origin. Be prepared to explain the origin orally in class.

1. The *assassination* of the Austrian Archduke touched off the explosion of World War I.
2. Electronic machines now do in a few seconds *calculations* which would take mathematicians months or years to complete.
3. Exhibits of armor in museums remind us of the days of *chivalry*.
4. Diogenes, a famous *cynic*, used a lantern in daylight as he searched for an honest man.
5. The workman *detonated* the explosive, and the rock split.
6. Yellow fever has been *eradicated* through the work of Walter Reed.
7. The disloyal citizen was *ostracized* by his fellow townsmen.
8. The *supercilious* senior ignored the freshmen.
9. *Tantalizing* odors from the kitchen made the hungry boys' mouths water.
10. The gypsy fortuneteller was decked out in heavy, *tawdry* jewelry.

(2) Foreign words in English

You have seen that many English words have a foreign origin. In addition to these, many foreign expressions have become part of the English language. Sometimes their pronunciation becomes "anglicized," while their spelling remains as it was in the original language. Examples of such expressions are *en masse*, meaning "in a group," *joie de*

19 h

vivre, meaning "joy in living," *tête à tête* meaning "a private conversation between two people." If you are alert to such expressions in your reading and listening, you will find that your vocabulary is growing in this direction.

● EXERCISE 18. Ten familiar foreign expressions are given below in column A. Number your paper 1–10. Refer to the dictionary and copy next to each number the letter of the appropriate meaning from column B. Write the name of the language from which the expression comes.

A	B
1. cliché	a. the best people
2. deluxe	b. the masses
3. elite	c. witty replies
4. hoi polloi	d. a midday rest
5. incognito	e. a meal at a fixed price
6. patio	f. a marble floor
7. repartee	g. with name concealed
8. siesta	h. timeworn expression
9. table d'hôte	i. never satisfied
10. terra firma	j. a terrace
	k. solid earth
	l. elegant

● REVIEW EXERCISE B. The words in this exercise have been chosen from all those you have studied in this chapter. Number your paper 1–33 and write the correct synonym next to each number.

1. *acclaim*
    a. acquisition   c. desire
    b. applause   d. land

2. *aver*
    a. assert   c. compare
    b. evade   d. approach

3. *benevolence*
    a. kindliness   c. health
    b. sensation of   d. wealth
       flying

4. *biped*
    a. animal with   c. pedigree
       two feet
    b. bison   d. three-footed stand

5. *cynic*
   a. criminal
   b. sneerer
   c. picturesque
   d. tourist

6. *didactic*
   a. tightened
   b. knocking
   c. teacherlike
   d. flowerlike

7. *discreet*
   a. sly
   b. having good judgment
   c. hypocritical
   d. secretive

8. *exasperated*
   a. arranged
   b. annoyed
   c. decorated
   d. enervated

9. *falter*
   a. fail
   b. hesitate
   c. rise
   d. transport

10. *frenzied*
    a. wearied
    b. carried
    c. excited
    d. with carved edges

11. *gaudy*
    a. strange
    b. gay and showy
    c. elegant
    d. wicked

12. *hectic*
    a. feverish
    b. colorful
    c. stout
    d. emphatic

13. *incise*
    a. look into
    b. cut into
    c. sharpen
    d. intend

14. *intricate*
    a. complicated
    b. clever
    c. ingenious
    d. interesting

15. *intrigue*
    a. entertain
    b. plot
    c. gossip
    d. give alms

16. *meander*
    a. walk rapidly
    b. examine
    c. wander
    d. untie

17. *mimic*
    a. argue
    b. assert
    c. exhibit
    d. imitate

18. *morbid*
    a. cheerful
    b. strict
    c. fatal
    d. gloomy

19. *ominous*
    a. altogether
    b. hungry
    c. threatening
    d. disappearing

20. *ostracized*
    a. banished
    b. enrolled
    c. combined
    d. distracted

21. *patio*
    a. terrace
    b. Spanish food
    c. tower
    d. hinged box

22. *perceptible*
    a. advisable
    b. noticeable
    c. stunning
    d. slight

23. *poise*   a. gem   c. intelligence
                 b. composure   d. reflection

24. *premiere*   a. leader   c. youth
                 b. opening   d. winner
                    performance

25. *probation* a. connection   c. courage
                 b. decision   d. trial period

26. *reiterate* a. remember   c. warn
                 b. protest   d. repeat

27. *retrieve*   a. reconcile   c. combine
                 b. overlook   d. recover

28. *soliloquy* a. dock   c. separate
                 b. diamond   d. speech alone

29. *stamina*   a. endurance   c. startle
                 b. part of a flower d. a stone wall

30. *strategy*   a. planning   c. leveling
                 b. tiling   d. pitcher

31. *supercilious* a. high-ranking c. youthful
                    b. generous   d. haughty

32. *tawdry*   a. showy   c. bashful
                 b. gay   d. friendly

33. *vestige*   a. honor   c. inheritance
                 b. trace   d. secret

WORD LIST

The following list of 360 words has been selected from ninth-grade books. It should form the basis of your vocabulary study for the year. When you have mastered the exercises in this chapter, you will know most of these words.

abate	abstruse	addicted
abject	accessible	admonish
absolve	acclaim	adroit
abstain	acute	adversary
abstract	adage	advocate

affected
affront
agility
agitation
alien

aloof
allusion
amends
amiable
anarchy
animated
antagonize
apathy
apparition
appraisal

arbitrary
aroma
ascribe
assassin
assimilate
asterisk
atmosphere
augment
autonomy
aver

barbarism
benevolence
biographical
biped
bizarre
blithe
brusque
buoyant
cadence
calculation

caliber
callous
candid
centrifugal
chagrin
charlatan
chivalry
citadel
civility
cliché

clientele
climax
collaborate
comedy
commendable
commodious
competent
complement
compliance
comprehensive

confide
congeal
connive
connoisseur
contagious
controversy
cosmopolitan
culmination
cynic
debris

deduce
deficient
defile
defraud
demoralize

denounce
despot
destitute
detonate
dialogue

didactic
digress
diminish
dingy
discord
discreet
discrepancy
discrimination
disintegrate
dispatch

disperse
disrupt
dissect
dissent
docile
drastic
durable
dwindle
edifice
elegy

elite
embellish
emulate
encounter
epic
equation
equestrian
equilibrium
eradicate
erroneous

ethical
evacuate
exasperated
expedite
exploit
extol
extort
fallacy
falter
fantastic

farce
farcical
fervent
fictitious
figurative
filial
fissure
flaunt
formidable
fortitude

fossil
frenzied
futile
gallery
gaudy
gauntlet
geology
glean
glib
gloat

grotesquely
grueling
guise
habitat
hackneyed

haven
havoc
hectic
herald
heretic

hilarious
homicide
horde
hydraulic
idiomatic
imbibe
immaterial
immune
impose
impulsive

incessant
incise
inclination
incomprehensible
indelible
indolence
indomitable
indulgent
inevitable
infamous

infringe
ingenious
innovation
intact
intelligible
intentional
intercept
intricate
intrigue
invoke

irrelevant
jaunty
laconic
larceny
lax
lethal
liability
livid
ludicrous
luxurious

malinger
manifest
manipulate
meander
mediocre
melodramatic
menial
metaphor
mimic
monotonous

moor
morbid
mottled
murky
navigator
nether
nimble
nominal
nondescript
obsession

obtuse
officious
omen
ominous
opaque

opportune
oppressive
optimistic
orthodox
ostracized

palatial
panorama
paramount
passive
patio
patriarch
perceptible
perennial
peruse
pervade

pessimistic
plaintive
plot
poach
poignant
poise
ponderous
portend
portly
potency

potion
precedent
predatory
premature
premier
premiere
presume
probation
procrastinate
proficient

promenade
prospective
protagonist
prowess
pungent
quaint
radiate
rapt
ravenous
realistic

realm
reconcile
redress
reiterate
reluctant
repast
replica
repress
reprimand
reprisal

requisite
resilient
resourceful
retract
retrieve
rigorous
romantic
ruthless
sable
satirical

sector
sedentary
seethe
sequel
setting

shrew
simile
sinister
skeptical
slake

smug
soliloquy
solvent
somber
sordid
spacious
spurn
stamina
statute
stereotype

sterile
strategy
submission
subsequent
subversion
sundry
supercilious
surmount
susceptible
symbol

table d'hôte
tantalizing
tawdry
tawny
terra firma
terse
testimonial
theme
thwart
tragedy

transcribe

transpire

treatise

tripod

trite

trivial

turbulent

tutor

tycoon

ultimate

unkempt

urban

veneer

venerable

versatile

vestige

victual

virile

virtual

vogue

volatile

vulnerable

wan

wary

wistful

wrangle

wrest

wry

yearn

zodiac

PART SIX

Speaking
and
Listening

CHAPTER 20

Speaking Before Groups

Preparing for and Delivering Various Kinds of Speeches

As a student, you have already had some experience in speaking before your classmates, and you will have more in the years ahead. Besides participating in class discussions, you may take part in club meetings, make committee reports, announce events at assembly programs, and stir up enthusiasm at pep rallies.

The ability to speak easily and naturally will help you to succeed in school and later in a career. Speaking before groups is easy if you have some training and experience. In this chapter, you will learn how to handle some of the most common speech situations you will meet in school.

PREPARING A SPEECH [1]

20a. Choose an appropriate topic.

A good speech requires careful preparation. Trying to make a speech without planning it is like approaching a test

[1] Since preparing a speech is in many ways like preparing a composition, you will find additional, detailed suggestions for choosing a topic, organizing content, and so on, in Chapter 13, page 264.

442

in a new subject without studying for it. This section will guide you through the necessary steps in preparing a speech for delivery.

Sometimes the subject of your speech will be given to you, or you may be given a choice among several subjects. If the choice of topic is left to you, you should be guided by several principles:

(1) Your topic should be one about which you have firsthand information.

If your hobby is raising pigeons, talk about their care and breeding. If you have used a sailboat or motorboat, explain how to handle it. If you have gone on an overnight hike, tell about your experiences. A girl who attends dancing school might describe ballet positions. A boy who likes cars might explain how an automobile is put together. As a student once phrased it, "Speak in your own backyard."

When you talk from firsthand experience, you are not at a loss for ideas, you speak fluently, and you infect your listeners with your own enthusiasm. Your listeners will be attentive because they are aware that you know what you are talking about.

(2) Your topic should be one in which you have a genuine interest.

Suppose you are a skier who is curious about the short skis that are coming into use. All of your experience has been on conventional long skis. You are interested in knowing about the claimed advantages of short skis, about how they would feel in particular situations, about what kind of skiing they are best suited for. Preparing a talk about this subject on which you have some information, some questions, and some opinions, will certainly be interesting to you. Ideas about what to say and how to say it will come naturally to you because you care about the topic.

20a

(3) Your topic should be one that will interest your listeners.

Before deciding on your topic, ask yourself whether it will capture the attention of your audience. Consider the age, likes and dislikes, backgrounds, and special interests of your listeners. If you are speaking to young people of your own age, you can be fairly sure that what interests you will also interest them. A group of parents or other adults, however, might be more interested in your ideas about careers, recreation in your community, or school problems. If the group you are addressing has a special interest, such as sports, photography, cooking, or travel, choose a topic with that interest in mind.

Look at your proposed subject from your listeners' viewpoint. Once they know what your topic is, will they want to hear your speech?

● EXERCISE 1.   List five subjects which you feel competent to speak about because of your experience. In a sentence or two for each, explain the nature of your experience.

EXAMPLES   *How to Sail a Boat. My family has a fourteen-foot sailboat that I have been sailing for the past two years. I have received expert instruction in sailing from my father.*

Figure Skating. I have enjoyed ice skating since I was six years old. Last winter I spent an average of two hours daily practicing figure skating.

● EXERCISE 2.   List two topics which might appeal to each of the groups below.

1. your home-room class   4. French or Spanish club
2. science club   5. dramatic society
3. 4–H group

● EXERCISE 3.   Reflect on a speech you have recently heard, perhaps in a school assembly, in church, or on television. Discuss the following questions in class.

1. Was the speaker's information based on firsthand experience?
2. Did he show a genuine interest in his subject?
3. Was his subject interesting to his listeners? Why?

20b. Have a definite purpose when you speak.

Speaking without a purpose is like shooting a gun without aiming it. You may hit something—but probably not what you intended.

Aim your speech. Know beforehand *why* you are speaking. Your purpose may be

> to inform
> to convince
> to impress
> to entertain
> to move to action

Suppose, for example, you are going to speak to your English class on the topic of automobiles. What you say depends largely on your purpose.

If your purpose is *to inform*, you may discuss what a buyer should keep in mind before purchasing a second-hand car, the way a carburetor works, or the proper method of waxing or polishing a car.

If your purpose is *to convince*, you may discuss the advisability of equipping automobiles with safety belts and other protective devices.

If your purpose is *to impress*, you may compare the number of automobiles in this country with the number in other countries or tell about the unusual features that will probably appear in future cars.

If your purpose is *to entertain*, you may talk about amusing adventures you have had while touring with your family or friends.

If your purpose is *to move to action*, you may argue that a driver-training course should be included in your school curriculum and ask your listeners to sign a petition to the principal to that effect.

20b

After deciding on your topic, determine your purpose and always keep it in mind when preparing your talk.

● EXERCISE 4. Suppose you were asked to speak to your classmates on one of the topics listed below. Explain how the content of your talk would be affected by your purpose.

baseball   pollution
modern inventions   nonmedical use of drugs
school clubs   making something useful
Community Chest   earning money
modern music   my neighborhood

● EXERCISE 5. Analyze a speech you recently heard.

1. Did it have a definite purpose?
2. Was the purpose clearly stated?
3. Was everything the speaker said related to his purpose?
4. Did the speaker accomplish his purpose? (How do you know?)

20c. Gather material for your speech.

After you have settled on your topic and purpose, your next step is to gather material.

Do not go immediately to the library to consult reference books and magazine articles. This should be the final step in gathering material. If you read what others have written before you do your own exploring and thinking, your talk may lack originality. It may be a summary of what others have said rather than an expression of your own experiences and thoughts. Instead, follow these steps:

(1) Explore your own background.

What do you already know about your subject? You probably know more than you suspect. Examine your information and ideas. What do they suggest for further exploration?

(2) Observe.

Keep your eyes and ears open for material bearing upon your topic. You may learn from conversations, newspapers, or radio and television programs.

(3) Question.

Ask someone who knows a great deal about your topic to give you additional information. One of your parents, a neighbor, a service-station owner, or a local merchant may be an expert on your subject.

(4) Read.

After you have followed the three steps listed above, it is time to use the library. Consult encyclopedia articles, books, and magazines. Record pertinent information on note cards for easy reference.[1]

Always gather more material than you can use. A good speaker is an authority on his subject—he may use less than half of what he has at hand.

(5) Reflect.

The content of your speech should grow gradually. It cannot be prepared overnight. Choosing a subject well in advance of the scheduled speaking date will give you time to think about it, adding and discarding ideas. Jot down new thoughts as they occur to you. They will often come at odd moments—while you are walking to school, waiting for a bus, chatting with friends, dressing, and even doing your homework. This kind of preparation is a slow process, but it results in thorough knowledge of subject matter which, in turn, will contribute to self-confidence as you talk.

● EXERCISE 6. Select a topic for a three-minute talk to your English class. Make a list of the sources of information you intend to consult, using the following headings.

1. Your own experience (describe it)
2. Situations you may observe for pertinent information
3. Persons you are going to question, and what you will ask them
4. Books and periodicals (name of the book, magazine, or newspaper, title of chapter or article, page number)

20c

[1] See instructions on taking notes in Chapter 16, pages 345–46.

Use one of the topics listed below, or choose one of your own.

1. How young people can earn money
2. Are educational TV programs effective?
3. Why study Latin?
4. The man (or woman) I most admire
5. My hobby
6. Cats and cat lovers
7. Stock car races
8. Academic or vocational high school
9. The rewards of travel
10. Learning to type

20d. Arrange your material by preparing an outline.

Your final step in preparation is to arrange the material you have gathered. As in written compositions, it is important to find the right order for your ideas.

If you have jotted down your notes on index cards with each idea on a separate card, you can easily put them in sequence. Lay aside those that do not seem to fit logically into your plan. If it is apparent that your speech will be too long, you will have to decide which sections to exclude, and you will remove those cards.

Do not attempt to write your speech. Preparing an outline helps you arrive at the best arrangement of main and supporting ideas and fixes them in your memory. Later you can develop your wording from it.[1]

An outline for a short speech should usually cover only one side of a page and should include only your main points. The example on page 449 illustrates the form and content of an outline for a short speech.

[1] For a full discussion of outlining, see pages 278–81.

TRAINING A DOG

Purpose: To inform

I. The importance of training
   A. Value to dog
   B. Value to owner

II. Basic Training
   A. Housebreaking
   B. Walking on a leash
   C. Responding to owner's call

III. Advanced training
   A. Further training in obedience
   B. Training for hunting

IV. Things to avoid
   A. Coddling
   B. Overfeeding

● EXERCISE 7. Using the topic and the sources you chose for Exercise 6, prepare an outline for a three-minute speech.

20e. Prepare a provocative introduction and a conclusion that leaves your audience with the central idea of your talk.

Have you ever known what you want to say but wondered how to begin? You have probably heard many speeches that begin with a statement such as: "I want to say a few things about our baseball team this season," or, "My topic this afternoon is hobbies." Did you react with a mental yawn? A good speaker catches the audience's attention at the very beginning with something that will pique their interest.

Prepare your introduction carefully. Begin with an unusual fact or observation, a question, or even an exaggeration; then go on to develop your topic.

EXAMPLES   State champions! Is that too wild a dream for our baseball team this year?

20
d-e

Boxing, button collecting, book-binding, and beetles —all these are hobbies that some people enjoy. But I'm here to speak in praise of bowling.

A common problem for amateur speakers is knowing how to stop. They often drift to a halt weakly like a motorboat that has run out of gas. The conclusion is your last chance to drive home main ideas. It is important enough for you to prepare carefully.

You can conclude by summarizing the major points you have covered.

EXAMPLES   Our ball team should have a good season. Most of last year's players are back; we have some promising newcomers; the pitching staff is strong; and we have the best coach in Staunton County.

If you're looking for an interesting hobby, take up bowling. It's good exercise because it develops every muscle in the body. It's good fun because you can join our school bowling club. It's inexpensive because the local alley has a reduced rate for high school students. You may become a champion!

DELIVERING A SPEECH

If you have gone through the preparatory steps in the earlier part of this chapter, you are almost ready to deliver your speech. You may feel that you need some pointers.

20f. Overcome excessive nervousness.

Probably you feel somewhat nervous before beginning to speak before a group. You should! Nervousness is a sign that your body is keyed for action. Every good public speaker is on edge before he begins his address, even though he may have had years of experience in talking before groups. Experienced actors and actresses readily admit that they are tense before stepping on the stage.

What you must guard against is *excessive* nervousness which prevents free movement or coherent thinking.

Here are some practical suggestions for preventing stage fright.

(1) Know your subject thoroughly.

Begin your preparation well in advance of the day on which you are scheduled to speak. Mull over your topic, talk about it with your parents and friends, and read as much as you can about it. When you know your material thoroughly, you will gain self-confidence.

(2) Practice.

Rehearse your talk aloud, preferably before a full-length mirror. Do not try to memorize the speech. (You may, however, memorize the first and last sentences so that you can get off to a smooth start and finish gracefully.) Using your outline, "talk through it" several times to acquaint yourself with the sequence of ideas. Each time you practice, you will use different words; but such changes of phrasing are desirable because they give your speech a flavor of spontaneity. It is the ideas and the sequence that you want to fix firmly in your mind, not the exact words. Practice will increase your self-confidence, too.

(3) Keep your purpose in mind.

Forget about yourself. Think of what you want your listeners to believe, feel, or do. Concentrate on *why* you are speaking.

(4) Relax.

Yawn, breathe deeply, and let yourself go limp for a moment or two before you face your audience. These actions will reduce your tension.

(5) Stand, move about, and gesture naturally.

Stand easily erect, feet a few inches apart, weight mainly on the ball of one foot, shoulders level. There is no need to stand in one spot throughout a speech unless you are speak-

20f

ing into a fixed microphone. You may feel more relaxed if you move around a bit. Move, for example, when there is an important change in thought or when you want to emphasize a point. Take care, however, not to move about aimlessly or too frequently. Random movements distract listeners.

Gestures are not movements added to a speech; they are natural movements of the body impelled by an urge from within. You gesture when you converse with your friends, and they gesture when they speak with you. The next time you carry on a conversation, notice how much gesturing goes on.

Carry into public speaking this natural impulse to gesture. Show the size and shape of an object with your hands. Point to parts of an article, chart, or diagram if you are using one. It may be appropriate to draw a simple illustrative sketch on the chalkboard. Gesturing, like walking, relieves nervous tension. Of course, exaggerated gestures that call special attention to themselves should be avoided.

20g. Talk directly to your listeners.

Look at your audience. Let your gaze move smoothly over the group so that each member feels that you are talking directly to him. Remember that you are not reciting or exhibiting. You are communicating.

● EXERCISE 8. Deliver the three-minute speech for which you prepared in Exercises 6 and 7.

Pronunciation and Enunciation

When a speaker mispronounces or mumbles a word, the listener is distracted, his attention wanders from the thought to the pronunciation. Learning to pronounce and enunciate words correctly will be an asset in all your speaking, formal and informal.

20h. Learn to pronounce words correctly.

(1) Listen to good speakers.

Radio and television announcers, public speakers, actors and actresses, and teachers generally are acceptable models to imitate in pronunciation.

(2) Refer to the dictionary.

You should have a dictionary in your home so that you may readily check the pronunciation of unfamiliar words. If this is not possible, jot down any word that you are not sure how to pronounce, and look it up when you get to school.

● EXERCISE 9.   With the aid of a dictionary, learn the correct pronunciation of the following words.

absolutely	faucet	khaki
admirable	February	laboratory
alloy	final	orchestra
ally	finale	parliamentary
alternate	finance	particular
banquet	forehead	penalize
champion	formerly	positively
chastisement	gesture	recipe
column	grievous	romance
comfortable	hearth	salve
corps	hospitable	secretive
coupon	influence	solemnity
decade	interesting	usually

● EXERCISE 10.   Write ten sentences using words in Exercise 9. Try saying the sentences casually as you would in conversation, but be sure you pronounce the words correctly.

EXAMPLES   We decided in February to conduct our meetings according to parliamentary procedure.

Did the official penalize the champion?

20
g-h

(3) Do not omit sounds or syllables.

Careless speakers sometimes omit essential sounds. Pronounce each of the following words with particular attention to the sound represented by the bold-faced letter:

ac**c**ept	len**g**th	proba**b**ly
as**k**ed	lib**r**ary	reco**g**nize
exac**t**ly	pic**t**ure	stren**g**th

Be sure to include the sound of *h* when you pronounce these words:

hue	humane	humid
huge	humanity	humor
human	humble	humorous

Some speakers make the sound of words vague by leaving out a syllable. Although many of these words may drop a syllable in ordinary conversation, they should be given careful, but not exaggerated, pronunciation wherever you use them in public speaking.

accidentally	electric	history
actually	family	jewel
average	finally	mathematics
champion	generally	memory
chocolate	geography	mystery
company	giant	poetry
cruel	grocery	suppose

● EXERCISE 11. *Oral Drill.* Read the following sentences aloud, making sure you pronounce each word correctly.

1. Poetry is no longer a mystery to me.
2. History and geography are both concerned with humanity.
3. Where is the library?
4. Susie asked whether it is humid in the arctic.
5. I don't see the humor in this grocery list.
6. Bill generally whistles while he does his mathematics problems.
7. The mystery concerns the missing family diamonds.
8. This electric cord is exactly nine feet in length.
9. Mel has the strength of a giant.

10. The champion didn't recognize the humorous aspect of the picture.
11. Thank you; I shall accept your offer of chocolate.
12. I suppose Vivian upset the vase accidentally.
13. I have a different memory of that incident.
14. The company finally left on Saturday.
15. That practical joke was actually more cruel than humorous.
16. The population explosion is one of the most important questions facing humanity today.
17. Can you describe your ideal teacher exactly, Patricia?
18. How these human footprints got here is a mystery.
19. What is the average length of the antarctic summer?
20. I suppose you will want the television set on while I am studying.

(4) Do not add sounds or syllables.

Each of the following words has only one syllable.

bale	film	known
blown	gale	male
down	grown	realm
elm	helm	sale

Study the following words to be sure you do not add a syllable or a sound when you pronounce them.

athlete	grievous	lightning
burglar	hindrance	ticklish
chimney	idea	translate
draw	laundry	umbrella

(5) Do not transpose sounds.

There are some words in which sounds are often transposed: speakers may say, for example, *calvary* for *cavalry*, *modren* for *modern*. Be careful of the following:

cavalry	performance
children	perspiration
hundred	poinsettia
irrelevant	prescription
larynx	prodigy
modern	tragedy

● EXERCISE 12.   *Oral Drill*. Read the following sentences aloud, making sure you pronounce each word correctly.

1. That elm tree must have been blown down in the gale.
2. The lightning seemed to touch the chimney.
3. The Colemans have four male puppies for sale.
4. Paul hopes to make a name for himself in the realm of music.
5. Do you think in French, or do you translate each sentence?
6. Slight stature is no hindrance to some athletes.
7. Florence confessed that it was rather a ticklish situation.
8. Will my umbrella fit into your suitcase?
9. These bales of cotton came from Mississippi.
10. The burglar must have come down the fire escape.
11. What kind of film are you using?
12. How can an idea be more powerful than a weapon?
13. Maggie has a job in the laundry after school.
14. Jerry had not known that his carelessness would lead to such a grievous error.
15. The most experienced sailor should take the helm.
16. Given a pencil and a blank wall, any young child will be tempted to draw.
17. That little seedling has grown into a tree.
18. Most athletes are good in more than one sport.
19. Did you buy a red or a white poinsettia?
20. Your argument is true but irrelevant.
21. Is there likely to be a prodigy among a hundred children?
22. What is the role of the larynx in speech?
23. The importance of cavalry has diminished considerably in modern warfare.
24. Some of Shakespeare's greatest plays are tragedies.
25. Who said, "Genius is one percent inspiration and ninety-nine percent perspiration"?

20i. Improve your enunciation by sounding your words clearly.

Enunciation refers to distinctness of utterance. A speaker may pronounce a word correctly—that is, use correct stress and vowel quality—yet mumble or mouth it so that it cannot be heard clearly.

For clean-cut enunciation, vigorous lip, tongue, and jaw action is necessary. Practicing such old-fashioned nonsense sentences as the following helps develop clear enunciation.

Betty Botta bought a bit of butter.
"But," said Bet, "this butter's bitter.
If I put it in my batter,
It will make my batter bitter."
Prunes and prisms, prunes and prisms.
The big black bug bit the big black bear.
Truly rural, truly rural.
Tent tops and ten tops and ten dented tent tops.
Five wives wearily weave bright red rugs.
Theophilus Thistle, the successful thistle sifter, successfully sifted some thistles.
She sells seashells by the seashore.

A common fault among beginning speakers is to link each sentence with the one preceding by means of *and*. At the end of each sentence, stop! Begin each new sentence cleanly.

Another common fault is the use of *ur*. The repeated use of this sound between words or sentences is annoying. Avoid it.

● EXERCISE 13. People often make the mistake of substituting *n'* for *ng*, as, for example, *swimmin'* for *swimming*. List twenty words ending in *ng* and practice saying them singly and in sentences.

● EXERCISE 14. *Oral Drill.* The final consonant combinations in the following words are difficult to pronounce. Practice until you can say each word clearly and easily.

1. breadth	7. crafts	13. sects	19. twelfths
2. width	8. tufts	14. facts	20. months
3. hundredth	9. hyacinths	15. tracts	21. folds
4. lifts	10. lengths	16. mists	22. fields
5. wafts	11. respects	17. tests	23. builds
6. shifts	12. acts	18. fifths	24. adjusts

20i

25. masks	28. faiths	31. precepts	34. tastes
26. desks	29. myths	32. depths	35. asks
27. youths	30. accepts	33. precincts	36. tenths

● EXERCISE 15.   *Oral Drill.* Practice saying the following pairs of words, being careful not to substitute *d* for *t*, or *t* for *th*.

1. riding	writing	10. true	through
2. medal	metal	11. taught	thought
3. bidden	bitten	12. tinker	thinker
4. pedal	petal	13. boat	both
5. madder	matter	14. tent	tenth
6. padding	patting	15. tick	thick
7. beading	beating	16. tree	three
8. boding	boating	17. tow	throw
9. biding	biting	18. tie	thigh

KINDS OF SPEAKING SITUATIONS

You are called on to speak in many different circumstances, in and out of school. This chapter cannot possibly cover all speech situations. You have already studied some and have had experience in others. The pages that follow describe three kinds of speaking assignments that you should be prepared to fulfill.

Talking About an Experience

Since, obviously, one talks best about what he knows, beginning speakers are often asked to relate an experience or a personal narrative. You should learn to do this smoothly and entertainingly.

20j. Relate experiences that are unusual or otherwise interesting.

(1) Begin with action.

Long, explanatory openings are usually unnecessary and dull. Start in the middle of things. Give your listeners credit for being able to fill in the background.

When I awoke one night in camp and found a snake coiled at the foot of my bed, I was a bit upset.

I did not stop to think when I saw smoke pouring out of the window of my neighbor's house. I rushed to the phone and shouted, "I want to report a fire!"

Sauntering home from the movies late one night, I was startled when two men dashed out of a store and scrambled into a waiting car. Then I heard someone inside the store scream, "Help!"

(2) Use direct conversation.

The exact words of a speaker are more interesting and lively than an indirect statement. Compare these two versions of the same incident.

An old lady felt someone bump into her. When she perceived that it was a young man beside her, she asked if she could help him, noting that he seemed lost. He inquired why she thought he was lost. She replied that he was standing in her kitchen.

An old lady felt someone bump into her. When she perceived the figure beside her, she inquired, "Can I help you, young man? You seem to be lost."

"What makes you think I'm lost?" retorted the young man, bristling.

"Well," she replied gently, "you're in my kitchen."

(3) Maintain suspense.

Include details and episodes that keep your listeners in suspense. Lead to a climax. Do not reveal the ending too soon.

(4) Use action-packed verbs.

A good storyteller chooses verbs that are specific rather than general because they help a listener to see, feel, and hear.

GENERAL   Allen walked into the classroom.
SPECIFIC   Allen strolled [sidled, limped, burst, dashed, slouched] into the classroom.

20j

GENERAL   The jet rose into the sky.
SPECIFIC   The jet zoomed [roared, lurched, shot] into the sky.

● EXERCISE 16.   Briefly relate an unusual experience you have had or have heard about. It may be exciting, amusing, or both, but the incident or its outcome should be unusual. Be sure you begin with action, use conversation and specific verbs, and maintain suspense.

● EXERCISE 17.   Relate an unusual incident in the life of a famous man or woman. Use the library to get your facts; then retell the incident in your own words. The following list is suggestive only.

1. Dwight D. Eisenhower
2. Colonel Charles Lindbergh
3. Robin Hood
4. Admiral Richard Byrd
5. Lawrence of Arabia
6. Richard the Lion-hearted
7. Helen Keller
8. John Paul Jones
9. Socrates
10. Thomas Edison
11. Napoleon
12. Walter Schirra
13. Jacqueline Cochran
14. Tenzing Norgay
15. Eleanor Roosevelt
16. John F. Kennedy

● EXERCISE 18.   Tell the class about an unforgettable person you have met. Your listeners may want to know how you happened to meet him, what kind of person he is, and what his achievements are. Remember to avoid a long, explanatory beginning. Use direct rather than indirect quotations, and employ action-packed verbs.

Talking About Current Events

Current happenings of local, state, national, or international significance are suitable subjects for talks before groups. So, too, are events in the fields of business, science, music, art, sports, education, and literature.

20k. When speaking about current events, choose important happenings that are likely to affect the lives of your listeners.

Your talk should be more than a restatement of a news item. It should express a fresh and original viewpoint—your own.

A current-events talk may be divided into two parts: (1) a statement of the facts, (2) an interpretation of the facts.

Where can you obtain the facts? Accounts in reputable newspapers or news magazines provide a source of material. So do radio and television broadcasts. For background information consult histories, encyclopedias, and atlases in your school or local library.

You cannot expect, of course, to interpret fully all of the complex events of our complex world. Many brilliant analysts devote their careers to such matters. When you select a current event to talk about, keep a few guiding principles in mind:

(1) Choose a topic that is suitably limited in scope.

TOO BROAD	Trouble in the Middle East
SUITABLE	A Shooting Incident on the Morocco-Algeria Border
TOO BROAD	The Government's Farm Support Program
SUITABLE	A Question Facing Wheat Growers This Week

Do not select a topic about which you can do nothing but parrot what you have read. Choose one that has some significance for you and your listeners and about which you have done some thinking.

(2) Choose a topic about which you know enough to talk intelligently.

Many current happenings are so involved and so puzzling that there are honest differences of opinion about them. Thorough study often leaves one uncertain about what to think of an event he is observing. Do not feel that you *must*

20k

express an original opinion about your topic if you do not have one. Instead, show that you have thought about the event—and tell what some of your thoughts are.

For example, a girl may report on a state senator's speech in favor of converting a local wilderness area into a park. Without giving an opinion of her own on this proposal (for she may not have made up her mind), she can raise some questions that bear on the issue: How would a park affect the people who now live in the area? Has the senator ever visited the area himself? Is it suitable for use by the public? How would it be maintained? Her report will be a stimulating one even though her personal "interpretation" has been in the form of questions.

● EXERCISE 19.   Deliver a three-minute talk on an important current event. Prepare an outline to guide you when speaking.

Talking About Books, Movies, and Television Shows

Much of your time is spent in reading and in watching movies or television. Reporting on books and dramatic programs helps to sharpen your own appreciation of them and gives your listeners ideas and suggestions for their own entertainment.

201. A report on a book, movie, or television program should include a description of your subject and your estimate of it.

When you speak before a group about a book you have read, your purpose is to tell enough about it so that your listeners may decide for themselves whether they want to read it. A book report includes at least two elements: (1) a description of the plot or contents, (2) your evaluation.

When discussing fiction, do not reveal the entire plot, because by doing so you deny your listeners the pleasure of discovering the outcome for themselves. Tell just enough to whet interest. You may describe an exciting or amusing scene in detail or, if you wish, read it aloud when it is short, so that your listeners can judge for themselves whether the book has merit.

It is generally advisable to describe the appearance and traits of the main characters. Show how they act under certain circumstances, and indicate how they change during the course of the story.

In addition to giving the title and author and touching upon the plot and characters, discuss some of the following topics in your report. Do not try to include them all.

1. Setting (time and place)
2. Climax
3. Style (vocabulary, ease or difficulty of reading, narrative or descriptive skill)
4. Comparison with the motion-picture version
5. Comparison with other books by the same author
6. Comparison with other books by different authors dealing with the same subject
7. Humor (Illustrate by reading a few paragraphs aloud.)
8. An incident that reveals character
9. A brief account of the author's life
10. The theme

Your listeners will want to hear your opinion of the book. Do not be satisfied with a statement such as, "I enjoyed the book immensely" or "I thought the book was dull." Explain why you found it interesting or boring. Was it because of the style, plot, vocabulary, or setting? Was the story too fanciful or too realistic?

In reporting on nonfiction, consider such topics as

1. Title and author
2. Scope (What are the main topics?)
3. Style (Are the explanations interesting? clear?)
4. Usefulness (What useful information have you learned from reading it? Discuss an event, discovery, problem, or topic in detail.)

20 l

5. Your estimate of the book (Why did you find it interesting or dull?)

In reporting on a biography, discuss some of these points:

1. Title and author
2. The life, achievements, and personality of the subject of the biography
3. The obstacles he faced and overcame
4. Your reasons for admiring (or disliking) him
5. Your estimate of the book

The suggestions offered for book reports apply in large part to discussions about movies and television plays. There are, however, some aspects of a motion picture that seldom enter into a book review. For example:

1. Cast (Who played the leading roles? Were the actors well cast?)
2. Acting (Who gave the best performances? Was the acting natural and effective? In which scenes was the acting most memorable?)
3. Photography (color or black and white? artistic or ordinary?)
4. Settings (lavish? simple? appropriate?)
5. Costumes (attractive? authentic?)
6. Sound (clear? muffled?)
7. Distinctness (Was the actors' speech distinct? Was dialect used effectively?)
8. Comparison with novel (How did the motion picture differ from the novel of the same name? Were the changes justified?)

● EXERCISE 20.   Read and report orally to your class on a novel, biography, drama, or work of nonfiction which your teacher has approved in advance. Prepare an outline to guide you when speaking.

● EXERCISE 21.   Orally review a good movie or television play that you have recently seen.

CHAPTER 21

Listening

Sharpening Listening Skills

Why should you learn to listen? "I've been listening all my life," you may say, "and I don't need to be taught how to do it."

Nearly everyone can listen more effectively than he does. With training and practice you can become a better listener.

Each day you spend a large part of your time listening. You listen more than you speak, you speak more than you read, and you read more than you write. If you are an average student, you spend 57 percent of your day listening. (Nurses spend 43 percent; businessmen, 45 percent; dietitians, 63 percent.)

There is a difference between hearing and listening. Hearing is a *passive* process. You hear radio music or the noise of an air conditioner as you concentrate on your homework. You hear street noises as you converse with friends at home. You are aware of these sounds without making a conscious effort to hear them.

Listening is an *active* process. When you listen you must pay attention and make an effort to recall what is said. You have to think with the speaker, separate facts from opinions and the important from the trivial, and judge the value of what is said. You have to fight against distractions and other barriers to good listening.

Some people do not realize that they have an obligation

to listen courteously, even if a speaker is dull and uninteresting. Inattention is distracting not only to the speaker but also to other members of the audience. Furthermore, if you are not listening, you may miss hearing something of importance.

PURPOSEFUL LISTENING

When you can, have a reason for listening. Sometimes you may listen for information. At other times you may listen to stimulate your thinking, reinforce opinions you already hold, or improve your ability to use language more effectively. You often listen to radio and television programs for sheer enjoyment.

Some students fake attention. They pretend to listen while the teacher or a classmate speaks, but at the same time they direct their attention to something else. Do not fall into the habit of half-listening. If you have this fault, you can correct it by listening with a purpose. Know why you are listening and keep your purpose always in mind. Are you listening to become informed, to understand and follow directions, to improve your language skill, or to form a judgment?

21a. Keep in mind your purpose for listening.

(1) Listen to gain information.

Everyone forgets much of what he learns within an hour after learning it; forgetting sets in immediately after learning. To retain the important parts of what you hear, pay close attention to what is said and review it immediately. If you listen attentively, you will remember better.

● EXERCISE 1.   Compose five questions similar to the following. Read them aloud, pausing about five seconds between each question to allow your classmates time to jot down their answers. When you have finished, your classmates will check their answers to determine how accurately they have listened.

1. In the series of numbers *7–2–5–4–3*, the fourth number is ———.
2. In the list of words *in–on–up–at–of*, the third word is ———.
3. In the list of words *and–off–but–for–how*, the word beginning with *o* is ———.
4. In the announcement, "*Send your entries together with 25¢ to Music Contest, Post Office Box 119, New York, N.Y. 10006,*" the post office box number is ———.
5. In the statement, "*Ed and John will make the campfire, Joe and Tom will set up the tent, and Charlie will cook the food,*" what is Joe's job?

● EXERCISE 2. Read aloud ten names. Then ask your classmates to write as many of the names as they can recall.

● EXERCISE 3. Compose an explanation or announcement in which certain essential information is omitted. Read your announcement to the class. Your classmates will show their mental alertness by telling what information is missing.

EXAMPLE   "To make pancakes, put milk, egg, and shortening in a bowl. Mix lightly. Grease the griddle. Turn the pancakes when the edges look cooked and when the tops are covered with bubbles." [This statement omits mention of amounts, and of flour or pancake mix, and of pouring the batter onto the griddle.]

(2) Listen to instructions.

Everyone gives and receives oral instructions nearly every day. A businessman gives directions to his secretary; a foreman, to a new trainee; a home owner, to a carpenter; a housewife, to a delivery boy. Strangers give travel directions, husbands and wives give directions to each other, and so do parents and children. In school you often receive instructions from your teachers. It is important that you understand and remember them accurately. As you listen to instructions, follow the guides on the next page.

21a

a. Ask questions if you don't understand something.
b. Take notes if the instructions are long or complicated or if they are to be carried out at some later time.
c. Don't let your attention wander; you may miss an essential detail.

● EXERCISE 4. Describe your current English assignment. Does everyone in the class agree on its details? Would you say that the class listened well when the teacher made the assignment?

● EXERCISE 5. Orally give travel directions from school to your home. Call upon students to repeat your directions.

● EXERCISE 6. Describe how to do or make something, taking care that each step of the process is in correct order. Give your classmates a chance to ask questions before calling on them to repeat your instructions.

(3) Listen to understand questions and to find answers.

Have you ever given a wrong answer simply because you did not understand what you were asked and you were afraid to admit it? This may happen if you are only half listening. If you are not sure you understand a question, rephrase it in your own words or ask the speaker to repeat it before you attempt to answer. It is senseless to respond to something you do not understand.

A good listener not only *hears* questions but also *originates* them. Sometimes you listen to a speaker because you know he will tell you something you want to hear: he will answer some questions you have in mind. At other times questions come into your mind as you listen. In either case, if you focus on your purpose for listening—to learn the answer to certain questions—you will be alert and attentive. You may find yourself thinking, for example, "What does he mean by that?" or "What proof can he offer for that statement?" or "What are the disadvantages of his plan?" Listen to find out whether the speaker answers your unexpressed questions in the course of his talk. If he does not, ask them during the discussion period.

● EXERCISE 7. The following paragraphs are excerpts from an address by Albert Einstein to a graduating class of engineers and scientists. If you had been a member of his audience, what would have been your purpose in listening? What clue to the content of his talk does he give in the beginning? What question does Einstein raise? How does he answer it? What unstated question does he raise and *not* answer?

. . . I could sing a hymn of praise with the refrain of the splendid progress in applied science that we have already made, and the enormous further progress that you will bring about. We are indeed in the era and also in the native land of applied science. But it lies far from my thought to speak in this way. . . .

Why does this magnificent applied science, which saves work and makes life easier, bring us so little happiness? The simple answer runs: because we have not yet learned to make a sensible use of it. . . .

It is not enough that you should understand about applied science in order that your work may increase man's blessings. Concern for man himself and his fate must always form the chief interest of all technical endeavors, concern for the great unsolved problems of the organization of labor and the distribution of goods—in order that the creations of our mind shall be a blessing and not a curse to mankind.

● EXERCISE 8. Think of the most recent speech you have heard during a school assembly program. Tell what questions ran through your mind as you listened. Did the speaker answer them?

ACCURATE LISTENING

A reader who does not understand a printed thought can reread it. A listener who does not understand a spoken thought cannot always ask that it be repeated. Spoken words are sometimes hard to follow. They are "on the wing" and must be caught in flight. A few pointers will help you in your attempt to understand what you hear.

21b. Listen accurately.

There is no point in listening at all if you fail to understand the speaker's message. Listening for certain aspects of a talk will help you.

(1) Notice the structure of a talk or lecture.

A good speaker prepares an outline of a formal speech. He may keep this outline in front of him when he speaks, or he may commit it to memory. He may occasionally deviate from it, but in general he sticks to his prearranged plan. A good listener can discern the structure of a prepared talk. He will ask himself such questions as these:

What is the speaker's topic?
What are his main points?
What facts does he offer as proof?
What does he want me to feel, believe, or do?

To perceive a speaker's plan is not always easy. Making a mental outline as you listen or jotting down notes in the form of an outline may help you to follow the speaker's points.

(2) Listen for transitional words, phrases, and sentences.

A speaker will sometimes give an audience clues by telling what his main points will be, by signaling them with transitional devices, and by summarizing his message.

MAIN POINTS   I want to speak to you about George Washington as a surveyor, soldier, and President.

There are three reasons why I am opposed to high school fraternities and sororities.

TRANSITIONAL	Next . . .
DEVICES	In the second place . . .
	There is still another reason . . .
	In conclusion . . .
	Finally . . .
SUMMARIES	A high school education, therefore, is necessary if you want to lead a satisfying and useful life.
	I conclude as I began: Go to college to learn how to live and how to earn a living.

(3) Look for visual clues.

A listener responds to what he sees as well as to what he hears. A speaker's posture, gestures, and facial expressions may help your understanding. Do his gestures mark his main points? Does a shrug or other movement show what details can be forgotten? Also, pay attention to whatever aids a speaker gives in the form of chalkboard or props.

● EXERCISE 9. Borrow a book of speeches from the library. Ask a teacher or a classmate to read a short speech from it. The rest of the class should observe the structure of the speech, making a rough outline from notes that they take as they listen. When the outlines are compared, how closely do they resemble one another? Analyze the ways in which students were guided (or perhaps misled) to perceive the structure of the speech.

● EXERCISE 10. For this exercise the class should be divided into two groups. One group will view a telecast speech with the sound turned off. The other group will watch the same speech with the sound on. The first group will tell how much they learned by merely looking at the speaker. The second group will then be able to judge how much the first group missed. Of course, in order to get the most out of this kind of exercise, it is a good idea to have some knowledge of the topic of the speech.

21b

CRITICAL LISTENING

An intelligent listener thinks about what he hears. He is not satisfied with merely understanding a speaker; he weighs what the speaker says and evaluates the arguments that are given to support a topic before he comes to any conclusion.

21c. Evaluate what you hear.

As a listener, ask yourself:

What did the speaker say that was new to me?

What did he say that was helpful? Why was it helpful?

Did he get his information from firsthand experience? If not, from what source did he get it? Did it seem reliable?

Do I agree with what he said? Why or why not?

(1) Distinguish main ideas from details.

Facts are important as a foundation for ideas. If you try to recall all the facts a speaker mentions, however, you may miss the main point.

In the following paragraph, notice the detailed facts that are given. What is the main idea?

Cigarette smoking produces many harmful effects and shortens life. For almost four years the American Cancer Society studied approximately 200,000 men between the ages of fifty and sixty-nine. In that time 7,316 of the regular cigarette smokers died. During the same time 4,651 nonsmokers of the same age died. The difference of 2,665 can be regarded as the number of excess deaths associated with smoking. Most of the excess deaths resulted from coronary-artery disease. Some were caused by lung cancer and others by diseases of the arteries, bladder, and liver. The death rate from all causes was higher among smokers than nonsmokers.

● EXERCISE 11.   Compose a paragraph which states detailed facts to prove a point. Read your paragraph aloud and ask your classmates to repeat the main idea. To find your facts, use an encyclopedia, a science or history book, or some other reliable source.

(2) Distinguish facts from opinions.

A fact is something that can be proved to be true. An opinion is not provable; it represents someone's belief. Of the statements below, which are facts and which are opinions?

Water boils at 212° Fahrenheit.

Everyone should study a foreign language.

To find the area of a square, multiply the length of any two sides.

The discovery of America was the most important event in history.

My political party has the better candidate.

● EXERCISE 12. Analyze the following paragraphs, separating fact from opinion.

Until he was seven or eight, Dickens' education was supervised by his mother. Then for a short time he went with Fanny to a dame school over a dyer's shop . . . About 1821, when Dickens was nine, he was sent, along with Fanny, to William Giles' neighborhood academy. There he remained until he left Chatham some eighteen months later, and there he received almost half— and by far the better and more important half—of his formal education.

William Giles, then still in his twenties and just down from Oxford where he had taken a degree, was a humane and generous schoolmaster. Dickens came to him a "sensitive, thoughtful, feeble-bodied little boy, with an amount of experience as well as fancy unusual in such a child, and with a dangerous kind of wandering intelligence that a teacher might turn to good or evil, happiness or misery, as he directed it." Giles directed it well. He liked and encouraged Dickens, and he inducted him into the school's liberal curriculum and superior methods.[1]

[1] From "Dark Corners of the Mind: Dickens' Childhood Reading," by Harry Stone. *The Horn Book Magazine*, June 1963.

21c

(3) Watch out for propaganda devices.

Sometimes speakers attempt to persuade listeners by using propaganda devices. Among the most common such devices are the following:

Name-calling. This is a device by which a speaker attempts to defeat an opponent not by rational arguments but by calling him names or smearing his reputation. Mudslinging of this sort is not worthy of anyone. Do not repeat a smear, and do not believe it until the person under attack has had a full opportunity to reply or until you have examined the evidence.

Slogans. Propagandists know the value of a slogan. It is simple, catchy, and easily remembered. An involved train of thought is hard to follow; a series of arguments is hard to remember. A slogan makes thinking unnecessary. It *oversimplifies* by reducing a chain of arguments to a few words.

EXAMPLES   Ask the man who owns one.
All the news that's fit to print.
Two cars in every garage.
America for Americans.

Slogans play an important part in politics and advertising. When you hear a slogan, remember that it does not tell a complete story. Do not let it divert you from an examination of the issues.

The testimonial. Sometimes statements by well-known personalities are used to persuade you to vote a certain way, buy a certain product, or adopt a certain belief. Apply these questions to any testimonial:

Is the speaker an authority in the field? A renowned scientist, for example, should be heard with respect when he discusses scientific matters but with less confidence when he talks about music, art, or politics—subjects which possibly are outside his area of competence.

Is the speaker unbiased? Is he paid for his testimonial, or does he stand to gain in any other way by it? If so, there is a strong possibility of bias. At times it is difficult to discover bias. Knowing something about the speaker's background and reputation helps.

The bandwagon. Most people like to do what others are doing and believe as others believe. Propagandists know and capitalize on this human tendency.

"Everybody is joining our cause," they say. "Come along or you'll find yourself alone."

It requires will power and the ability to think for oneself to resist hopping on the bandwagon. Do not be fooled into joining a movement simply because others are doing it.

As a listener, you should be alert to the propagandist's art. Do not be misled by appeals to your emotions or by statements that have nothing to do with the issue.

● EXERCISE 13. Give an example of each of the preceding propaganda devices. You may, if you wish, select your examples from radio and television commercials and from newspaper and magazine advertisements. For each example, tell how an alert listener should respond.

PART SEVEN

Mechanics

Capital Letters

The Rules of Capitalization

In written or printed English, a capital letter at the beginning of a word not only serves as an important eye signal to the reader (indicating, for example, the beginning of a sentence) but also often marks a significant difference in meaning (for example, the difference between *march* and *March*). In your writing, then, you should use necessary capitals. Just as important, you should carefully avoid unneeded capitals. Learning the rules of capitalization in this chapter will help you develop this writing skill.

22a. Capitalize the first word in every sentence.

WRONG   the home economics teacher told us, "by doing a simple experiment, you can find out whether or not coffee contains chicory. sprinkle a small amount of coffee into a glass of ice water. the coffee grounds will stay on top of the water. if chicory is present, it will not float but will sink and color the water."

RIGHT   The home economics teacher told us, "By doing a simple experiment, you can find out whether or not coffee contains chicory. Sprinkle a small amount of coffee into a glass of ice water. The coffee grounds will stay on top of the water. If chicory is present, it will not float but will sink and color the water."

Traditionally, the first word of a line of poetry is capitalized.

EXAMPLE　A duck whom I happened to hear
　　　　　Was complaining quite sadly, "Oh, dear!
　　　　　　Our picnic's today,
　　　　　　But the weathermen say
　　　　　That the skies will be sunny and clear."

Some modern poets (E. E. Cummings, for example) do not follow this practice. They may capitalize only the first line, and sometimes not even that. In such cases, use capital letters as they are used in the copy of the poem from which you are quoting.

● EXERCISE 1.　Make a list of the ten words that should be capitalized in the following paragraph. Be sure to capitalize the words you list.

how boring the conversation was at our family reunion in fact, at the supper table, the conversation lulled me to sleep a hypochondriac, Uncle Max never stopped complaining about his hiccups he insisted that hiccups are infallible symptoms of heart trouble my aunt talked incessantly about dieting she told us the exact number of calories on our plates soon my cousin drowned my aunt out by repeating old jokes grandpa kept interrupting everyone to tell dreadfully familiar tales of the old days of course, these tales were wholly unrelated to heart ailments, calorie counting, and ancient jokes overcome by boredom, I could not stay awake.

22b. Capitalize the pronoun *I* and the interjection *O*.

Always capitalized, *O* is rarely used. Generally, it is reserved for invocations and is followed by the name of the person or thing being addressed. In your writing, you will probably find little opportunity to use *O*. You may, however, use the interjection *oh*, which is not capitalized unless it is the first word in a sentence.

EXAMPLES　The play was a hit, but oh, how frightened I was!
　　　　　"Exult O shores! and ring O bells!" is a line from
　　　　　Walt Whitman's poem "O Captain! My Captain!"

22
a-b

● EXERCISE 2. Number 1–10 on your paper. If an item is correct, write *C* after the appropriate number. If there are errors in the use of capitals, copy the item on your paper, inserting capitals where needed and omitting unnecessary capitals.

1. oh dear! i think i've lost my watch.
2. yesterday i learned the psalm which begins, "Bless the Lord, o my soul."
3. why shouldn't i paint the chair pink?
4. I think I'll pass the test tomorrow, but Oh, how I dread taking it!
5. In the poem "The Fool's Prayer," the jester pleads, "O Lord, be merciful to me, a fool!"
6. walking in the woods, i almost stepped on a snake, and Oh, was i frightened!
7. Oh, Ritchie! I've won a trip to Europe!
8. Please listen carefully while i read the answer i received.
9. oh, for pity's sake! i wish you would stop saying, "o Romeo, Romeo, wherefore art thou, Romeo?"
10. My favorite lines from the play are

> "see how she leans her cheek upon her hand.
> oh, that i were a glove upon that hand,
> that i might touch that cheek!"

22c. Capitalize proper nouns and proper adjectives.

As you study the words below, observe (1) the difference between a common noun and a proper noun and (2) the ways adjectives (called *proper adjectives*) may be formed from proper nouns.

COMMON NOUNS	PROPER NOUNS	PROPER ADJECTIVES
a philosopher	Plato	Platonic dialogue
a country	England	English customs
a leader	Abraham Lincoln	Lincolnlike simplicity
a queen	Queen Victoria	Victorian poetry

Common nouns name a class or group. For example, *teacher* and *student* are common nouns because they name one of a group of people. Common nouns are not capitalized unless they begin a sentence or a direct quotation or are included in a title (see page 488). Proper nouns, such as *Mrs. Hersey* and *Paul Donahue*, name *particular* people, places, or things. They are always capitalized.

Some proper names consist of more than one word. In these names, short prepositions (generally, fewer than five letters) and articles are not capitalized.

EXAMPLES Tomb of the Unknown Soldier
Society for the Prevention of Cruelty to Animals
Charles the Bold

Proper adjectives, adjectives formed from proper nouns, usually modify common nouns: *Spanish mackerel*. Sometimes, however, the proper adjective modifies a proper name (for example, *Victorian England*) or is part of a proper name (for example, *English Channel*).

◆ NOTE Proper nouns and adjectives sometimes lose their capitals through frequent usage; examples are *maverick* and *castile*.

● EXERCISE 3. Below is a list of common and proper nouns. For each proper noun, give its proper adjective. Use your dictionary if you wish. After the proper adjective, write an appropriate noun for the adjective to modify. For each common noun, give two proper nouns.

EXAMPLES 1. Mexico
1. *Mexican border*
2. city
2. *Chicago, New York*

1. France	4. Jefferson	7. pioneer	9. island
2. India	5. Spain	8. month	10. author
3. Hercules	6. continent		

(1) Capitalize the names of persons.

EXAMPLES Sandra   Bobby Joe Franklin
Miss Willis   Mr. Charles F. Skinner
Margaret Love   Aunt Jean and Uncle Gordon

22c

(2) Capitalize geographical names.

Towns, Cities   Georgetown, San Diego, Kansas City
Counties, Townships   Harrison County, Sheffield Township
States   Alaska, Florida, North Dakota, New Hampshire
Sections   the East, the North, the Southwest, the Middle West,
   New England

◆ NOTE   The words *north, west, southeast,* etc., are not capitalized when they indicate direction: *driving through the Northwest* but *traveling northwest; states in the South* but *south of town.*

Countries   the United States of America, Canada, New Zealand
Continents   North America, Asia, Europe, Africa
Islands   Philippine Islands, Long Island, the West Indies, the
   Isle of Palms
Mountains   Rocky Mountains, Mount McKinley, the Alps,
   the Mount of Olives
Bodies of Water   Pacific Ocean, Adriatic Sea, Red River, Lake
   of the Woods
Roads, Highways, Streets   Route 66, U.S.Highway 301, Pennsylvania Turnpike, Seneca Avenue, West Twenty-first
   Street, Walnut Drive
Parks   Yellowstone National Park, Cleburne State Park

◆ NOTE   In a hyphenated number, the second word begins with a small letter.

As you study the list above, notice that words like *City, Island, River, Street,* and *Park* are capitalized because they are part of the name. If words like these are not part of a proper name, they are common nouns and are therefore not capitalized. Compare the following lists.

PROPER NOUNS	COMMON NOUNS
life in New York City	life in a big city
Liberty Island	a faraway island
crossing the Spokane River	across the river
on State Street	on a narrow street
in Grant Park	in a state park

● EXERCISE 4.   Number 1–20 on your paper. In each of the following items you are to choose the correct one of the two forms. After the proper number on your paper, write the letter of the correct form (*a* or *b*).

1. a. His store is on Front Street in Burlington.
   b. His store is on front street in Burlington.
2. a. We crossed the Snake river.
   b. We crossed the Snake River.
3. a. He now lives in california.
   b. He now lives in California.
4. a. Did you fly over South America?
   b. Did you fly over south America?
5. a. He took a picture of Pikes peak.
   b. He took a picture of Pikes Peak.
6. a. City streets in the west are often wide.
   b. City streets in the West are often wide.
7. a. Yellowstone National Park has many geysers.
   b. Yellowstone national park has many geysers.
8. a. The city of Columbus is the capital of Ohio.
   b. The City of Columbus is the capital of Ohio.
9. a. The hurricane swept over the Gulf Of Mexico.
   b. The hurricane swept over the Gulf of Mexico.
10. a. Drive east on U.S. Highway 35.
    b. Drive East on U.S. highway 35.
11. a. We are proud of our State parks.
    b. We are proud of our state parks.
12. a. I live on Forty-Fifth Street.
    b. I live on Forty-fifth Street.
13. a. The headquarters are in Travis County.
    b. The headquarters are in Travis county.
14. a. The Vikings called the atlantic ocean the sea of darkness.
    b. The Vikings called the Atlantic Ocean the Sea of Darkness.
15. a. The states in the Midwest are referred to as the nation's breadbasket.
    b. The States in the midwest are referred to as the nation's breadbasket.
16. a. A three-lane Highway is dangerous.
    b. A three-lane highway is dangerous.
17. a. I have a map of the Hawaiian Islands.
    b. I have a map of the Hawaiian islands.

18. a. New York City is the largest city in the east.
    b. New York City is the largest city in the East.
19. a. The Great Salt Lake is near the Nevada border.
    b. The Great Salt lake is near the Nevada border.
20. a. His address is 2009 Bell Avenue.
    b. His address is 2009 Bell avenue.

● EXERCISE 5. Write a paragraph of about 100 words telling about a town or city that you know well. Give its exact location (the county, state, section of the country), and name some of its streets. Also tell about the points of interest—parks, dams, lakes, mountains—that your state is proud of. Be sure to capitalize all of the geographical names that you use in your description.

(3) Capitalize names of organizations, business firms, institutions, and government bodies.

Organizations American Red Cross, National Boxing Association, Boy Scouts of America

◆ NOTE The word *party* may be written either with or without a capital letter when it follows Republican or Democratic: *Republican party* or *Republican Party*.

Business firms Imperial Biscuit Company, Western Union, Academy Department Stores, Inc.

Institutions United States Naval Academy, Columbia University, Radcliffe College, Fairmont High School, Bellevue Hospital

◆ NOTE Do *not* capitalize words like *hotel*, *theater*, *college*, and *high school* unless they are part of a proper name.

Kenmore High School	a high school teacher
Waldorf-Astoria Hotel	a hotel in New York
Ritz Theater	to the theater

Government bodies Congress, Federal Bureau of Investigation, House of Representatives, State Department [Usage is divided on the capitalization of such words as *post office* and *courthouse*. You may write them either way unless the full name is given, when they must be capitalized: *Kearny Post Office, Victoria County Courthouse.*]

(4) Capitalize the names of historical events and periods, special events, and calendar items.

Historical events and periods   French Revolution, Boston Tea
Party, Middle Ages, World War II

Special events   Interscholastic Debate Tournament, Gulf Coast
Track and Field Championship, Parents' Day

Calendar items   Saturday, December, Fourth of July, Mother's
Day

◆ NOTE   Do not capitalize the names of seasons unless personified: *summer, winter, spring, autumn*, or *fall*, but *"Here is
Spring in her green dress."*

Names of seasons are, of course, capitalized when they are
part of the names of special events: *Winter Carnival, Spring
Festival.*

(5) Capitalize the names of nationalities, races, and religions.

Nationalities   Canadians, an American, a Greek

Races   Oriental, Negro

Religions   Christianity, a Baptist, Mormons, Moslems, Buddhists

(6) Capitalize the brand names of business products.

EXAMPLES   Fritos, Frigidaire, Chevrolet

◆ NOTE   Do not capitalize the noun that often follows a brand
name: *Chevrolet truck.*

(7) Capitalize the names of ships, planets, monuments, awards, and any other particular places, things, or events.

Ships, Trains   the *Mayflower*, the *Discovery*, the *Yankee Clipper*,
the *Silver Meteor*

Aircraft, Spacecraft, Missiles   F–105 *Thunderchief, Viscount,
Sigma VII*, Telstar

Planets, Stars   Mars, Jupiter, the Milky Way, the Dog Star

◆ NOTE   Except when listed with other planets or stars, *earth,
sun*, and *moon* are not capitalized.

Monuments, Memorials   Washington Monument, Lincoln Memorial

Buildings   Prudential Insurance Building, Rockefeller Center, Eiffel Tower

Awards   Purple Heart, Distinguished Service Cross, Masquers' Dramatic Medal, Key Club Achievement Award

● EXERCISE 6.   Copy the following, using capitals wherever needed.

1. mars and saturn
2. on monday, march 20
3. a theater on west forty-third street
4. a hospital in albany, new york
5. carson park, near jefferson high school
6. laddie boy dog food
7. the sinking of the *lusitania*
8. world war I
9. the class play on thursday night
10. columbia university
11. a negro spiritual
12. the union of soviet socialist republics
13. fuller brushes
14. on christmas eve
15. a presbyterian
16. new haven yacht club
17. ford motor company
18. cadillac limousine
19. french and indian war
20. the united states supreme court

● EXERCISE 7.   Correctly use each of the following in a sentence of your own.

1. high school
2. High School
3. hotel
4. Hotel
5. building
6. Building
7. earth
8. Earth
9. south
10. South

22d. Do *not* capitalize the names of school subjects, except languages and course names followed by a number.

EXAMPLES   Next year I will study a foreign language and will take general science, history, and algebra.

Presently I am taking English, Geography I, American History II, and home economics.

◆ NOTE   Do *not* capitalize the members of a class (*freshman, sophomore, junior, senior*) unless part of a proper noun: A *freshman* cannot attend the *Junior-Senior Banquet.*

● REVIEW EXERCISE A. Copy the following sentences, using capitals wherever needed.

1. to begin with, mr. ronson mentioned the fact that mercury and venus are closer to earth than jupiter is.
2. every freshman at jefferson high school knows he will take at least three years of english and one year of mathematics.
3. while in the city of washington, we saw the ford theater, where lincoln was shot.
4. a methodist, a baptist, and a roman catholic conducted an interesting panel discussion.
5. since I plan to study medicine at northwestern university, I'm taking latin and biology I.
6. after I had gone to the grocery store at the corner of thirty-first street and stonewall avenue, I stopped at the twin oaks lumber company, which is two blocks south of cooper avenue.
7. vacationing in the west, we saw electric peak, which is on the northern boundary of yellowstone national park; we also saw devil's tower, which is in northeastern wyoming.
8. later we drove along riverside drive and saw the lincoln memorial, which is on the banks of the potomac river in potomac park.
9. in the spring, usually the first saturday after easter, the women's missionary society, a baptist organization, gives a picnic for our class.
10. leaving ecuador, in south america, on a banana boat named *bonanza*, they went through the panama canal and sailed through the caribbean sea to nassau in the bahama islands.

22e. Capitalize titles.

(1) Capitalize the title of a person when it comes before a name.

EXAMPLES   President Gaines   Mrs. Morrison
              Principal Yates   Miss Collins
              Dr. Hughes   Professor Jackson

**22
d-e**

(2) Capitalize a title used alone or following a person's name only if it refers to a high official or to someone to whom you wish to show special respect.

EXAMPLES   Can you name England's Prime Minister, the Prince of Wales, and the Duke of York?

The General has written that he will be unable to attend.

I look forward to meeting the Judge. [special respect]

Andy Simons, president of our science club, announced that Marian had been elected secretary.

My brother Roger, a captain in the Marine Corps, is home on leave.

◆ NOTE   When a title is used alone in direct address, it is usually capitalized.

EXAMPLES   We are happy to see you, Doctor.

What is your decision, Superintendent?

Tell me, Coach, what are our chances?

(3) Capitalize words showing family relationship when used with a person's name but *not* when preceded by a possessive.

EXAMPLES   Aunt Mabel, Cousin Enid, Uncle Stanley

my mother, your father, Clifford's sister

EXCEPTION   When family-relationship words like *aunt* and *grandfather* are customarily thought of as part of a name, capitalize them even after a possessive noun or pronoun.

EXAMPLES   My Uncle Stanley lives in Ohio

You will like Kate's Grandmother Murray.

◆ NOTE   Words of family relationship may be capitalized or not when used in place of a person's name: I gave it to *Mother* or I gave it to *mother*.

(4) Capitalize the first word and all important words in titles of books, periodicals, poems, stories, movies, paintings, and other works of art.

Unimportant words in a title are *a, an, the,* and short prepositions and conjunctions (fewer than five letters). Of course, if the last word in the title is a short preposition, it is capitalized.

The words *a*, *an*, and *the* written before a title are capitalized only when they are part of a title: the *Saturday Review*, *The Education of Henry Adams*. Before the names of magazines and newspapers, *a*, *an*, and *the* are usually not capitalized in a composition: I was reading the *Denver Post*.

The Bible and the books of the Bible are always capitalized.

EXAMPLES *A Connecticut Yankee in King Arthur's Court*, *The Sea Around Us*, *My Name Is Aram* [books]

the *Ladies' Home Journal*, the *Riverton Gazette* [periodicals]

"The Charge of the Light Brigade" [poem]

"The Pit and the Pendulum" [story]

Odd Man Out, *The Great Escape*, *Lawrence of Arabia* [movies]

Mona Lisa, *Portrait in Gray and Black*, *The Thinker* [works of art]

Treaty of Paris, Declaration of Independence, Bill of Rights [historical documents]

"Age of Kings," "Twilight Zone," "Gunsmoke," "Music till Dawn" [television and radio programs]

"Missouri Waltz," "Love's Old Sweet Song," *The Marriage of Figaro*, "The Flight of the Bumblebee," Beethoven's *Ninth Symphony* [musical compositions]

(5) Capitalize words referring to the Deity.

EXAMPLE **God** and **His** universe

◆ NOTE The word *god*, when referring to the pagan deities of the ancients, is not capitalized: The Greek poet paid tribute to the god Zeus.

● EXERCISE 8. Number on your paper 1–10. If the capitalization among the following phrases and sentences is correct, write *C* (for *correct*) after the appropriate number on your paper. If the capitalization is wrong, write the correct form.

1. superintendent adams
2. "Home On The Range"
3. the *Reader's Digest*
4. elected president of her class
5. the president of the United States
6. among the pagan gods
7. My Aunt Clare taught me to respect god.
8. my cousin's mother
9. my father and Senator Hall
10. *the Mystery of Edwin Drood*

● EXERCISE 9.   Write two sentences of your own to illustrate each of the five rules for capitalizing titles. (You will have ten sentences in all.)

● REVIEW EXERCISE B.   Copy the following sentences, and use capitals wherever needed. In this exercise, apply all the rules you have learned in this chapter. Be prepared to give a reason for each capital that you use.

1. speaking to the seniors of lamar high school, mr. carter praised *the tyranny of words*, a book by stuart chase.
2. on the sunday before labor day, we drove as far as the murphy motel, a mile west of salem, virginia; the manager, mr. kelly, told us he was a member of the virginia tourist court association.
3. waiting for a city bus at the corner of twenty-first street and hemphill drive, we admired the westlake shirts in henson's window display.
4. father and his brother, my uncle julian, told me about rockefeller center and about the shops on fifth avenue in new york city.
5. professor massey studied at the library of congress and the folger shakespeare library during july and august.
6. althea gibson's autobiography, *I always wanted to be somebody*, was published by harper & row.
7. I especially like the photograph—made by pan american world airways—of mount mckinley, in alaska.
8. in his junior year at sheridan high school, uncle rufus studied latin, french, english, geometry, and art.

9. the reverend walker said that the gods of the pagans did not offer the promise of immortality that our god does.

10. after the texans so bravely fought against the forces of general santa anna in 1836, the alamo became famous as the shrine of texas liberty, a symbol of american freedom, like the statue of liberty.

● REVIEW EXERCISE C.   Copy the following, using capitals wherever needed.

1. dr. franklin n. morgan
2. taking chemistry II
3. traffic on a main street
4. *the adventures of huckleberry finn*
5. merry christmas, mayor.
6. in history class
7. an assignment in english
8. a problem in mathematics
9. a park in the west
10. a mexican town
11. the washington monument
12. north of kansas city
13. on highway 80
14. the secretary of state
15. early christians and jews
16. the old testament in the bible
17. last thanksgiving
18. "song of the open road"
19. the boston tea party
20. the milky way and the north star

Summary Style Sheet

NAMES OF PERSONS

Ellen Black	a girl I know
Mrs. Alfred E. Jones	a friend of the family
Mr. Stanley Fillmore	our family lawyer

GEOGRAPHICAL NAMES

Mexico City	a city in Mexico
Shetland County	a county in North Carolina
the Canary Islands	some islands in the Atlantic
Great Smoky Mountains	climbing mountains
Pacific Ocean	across the ocean
Sixth Street	a narrow street
Abilene State Park	a state park
in the East, North, Midwest	traveling east, north, west

ORGANIZATIONS, BUSINESS FIRMS, INSTITUTIONS, GOVERNMENT BODIES

Oakdale Garden Club	a club for gardeners
Safety First Moving Company	a company of movers
Rosedale High School	a small high school
Supreme Court	a traffic court
Department of Commerce	a department of government

HISTORICAL EVENTS AND PERIODS, SPECIAL EVENTS, CALENDAR ITEMS

War Between the States	a bitter war
Atomic Age	an age of progress
National Open Golf Tournament	a golf tournament
Labor Day	a national holiday
April, July, October, January	spring, summer, autumn, winter

NATIONALITIES, RACES, RELIGIONS

British	a nationality
Caucasians	a race
Roman Catholic	a religion
God and His universe	the gods of ancient Rome and myths about them

BRAND NAMES

Mercedes-Benz	a sports car
Coca-Cola	a cola drink

OTHER PARTICULAR PLACES, THINGS, EVENTS, AWARDS

Flying Cloud	a clipper ship
Metroliner	a streamlined train
Caravelle	a jet airplane
Polaris	a missile
North Star	a bright star
Earth, Mars, Jupiter, Saturn, Pluto	on the earth
Jefferson Memorial	a memorial to Jefferson

Washington Monument	a monument in Washington
Senior Class Picnic	a senior in high school
Congressional Medal of Honor	a medal for bravery

SPECIFIC COURSES, LANGUAGES

Chemistry I	my chemistry class
Spanish	a foreign language
United States History II	the history book

TITLES

Officer Wiley	a police officer
Hurry, Officer!	
the President of the United States	the president of the class
the Senator from West Virginia	a senator's duties
the King of Denmark	a king's subjects
Uncle Randolph	my favorite uncle
Harriett's Aunt Lucy	Harriett's aunt
The Last of the Mohicans	a novel
the New York Times	a daily newspaper
Holy Bible	a religious book

CHAPTER 23

End Marks and Commas

Periods, Question Marks, Exclamation Points, Commas

In speaking, you use voice inflections and pauses to make your meaning clear. In writing, marks of punctuation such as end marks and commas act as substitutes for these inflections and pauses.

Be sure to use proper marks of punctuation to make your meaning clear. If you learn the rules in this and in the following chapters, and apply these rules whenever you write, your compositions will not only be correct but also easier to understand.

END MARKS

End marks—periods, question marks, and exclamation points—indicate a writer's purpose. For instance, if a writer intends to state a fact, he uses a period to end his statement. (For a classification of sentences according to purpose, see Chapter 2, pages 66–68.)

23a. A statement is followed by a period.

Periods follow declarative sentences, sentences that make statements. Notice in the second example on page 495 that a declarative sentence containing an indirect question is followed by a period.

EXAMPLES   Columbus sailed west to reach the East. [declarative sentence]

George asked what was the matter.

23b. A question is followed by a question mark.

Use a question mark after interrogative sentences.

EXAMPLES   What if we should fail?
How can a fish drown?
Was the bus on time?
Where is it? There?

A direct question may have the form or word order of a declarative sentence. Since it *is* a question, however, it is followed by a question mark.

EXAMPLES   A fish can drown?
The bus was on time?

Be sure to distinguish between a declarative sentence which contains an indirect question and an interrogative sentence, which asks a direct question.

INDIRECT QUESTION   He asked me **what kept her away.** [declarative]

DIRECT QUESTION   What kept her away? [interrogative]

23c. An exclamation is followed by an exclamation point.

EXAMPLES   Ouch!
Wow! What a game!
Look out!

Sometimes declarative and interrogative sentences show such strong feeling that they are more like exclamations than statements or questions. If so, the exclamation point should be used instead of the period or question mark.

EXAMPLES   I simply cannot work this puzzle!
Can't you be quiet for a minute!

23d. An imperative sentence is followed by either a period or an exclamation point.

As with declarative and interrogative sentences, imperative sentences, particularly commands, may show strong feeling. In such cases, the exclamation point should be used. When an imperative sentence makes a request, it is generally followed by the period.

EXAMPLES   Close that door!
                          Please close that door.
                          Look at the clowns.

Sometimes, to be courteous, a writer will state a command or request in the form of a question. Because of the purpose, however, the sentence is really an imperative sentence and is therefore followed by a period or an exclamation point.

EXAMPLES   May I interrupt for a moment.
                          Will you stop that noise!

23e. An abbreviation is followed by a period.

EXAMPLES   A. E. Housman [Alfred Edward Housman]
                          Mr., Jr., Dr. [Mister, Junior, Doctor]
                          D.C., N.C. [District of Columbia, North Carolina]
                          B.C., A.D. [before Christ, *anno Domini*]
                          Ave., St., Rd. [Avenue, Street, Road]
                          lb., oz., in., ft., [pound or pounds, ounce or ounces, inch or inches, foot or feet]

If an abbreviation comes at the end of a statement, do not use an extra period as an end mark.

EXAMPLE   Mr. Faulkner has never been to Brooklyn, N.Y.
      BUT   Have you ever been to Brooklyn, N.Y.?

Some frequently used abbreviations, especially abbreviations of government agencies and international organizations, are correctly written without periods.

EXAMPLES   TV, IQ, FM, CBS, ROTC, USAF, UN, mph, rpm

When in doubt about whether to use periods, consult your dictionary.

● EXERCISE 1.   Copy the following sentences, inserting periods, question marks, or exclamation points.

1. What a score
2. What is the score
3. I asked what the score was
4. Caesar's troops invaded Britain in 54 BC
5. By AD 800 Baghdad was already an important city
6. Dr Jonas E Salk developed the first effective polio vaccine in 1955
7. Why is absolute zero theoretically the lowest temperature possible
8. Please explain why absolute zero is theoretically the lowest temperature possible
9. Is there a complete absence of heat when the temperature is absolute zero
10. Yippee   A color TV for my birthday

● EXERCISE 2.   Correctly using periods, question marks, and exclamation points, write ten sentences as directed below.

One sentence stating a fact
One sentence making a request
One exclamation
Two direct questions
Two declarative sentences containing indirect questions
One imperative sentence that does show strong feeling
One imperative sentence that does not show strong feeling
One courteous command in the form of a question

COMMAS

Like other marks of punctuation, commas are necessary for clear expression of ideas. As you read the following sentences aloud, notice how the placement of the comma affects the meaning of each sentence.

EXAMPLES   When your friends help, you stop working.
When your friends help you, stop working.

23
d-e

If you fail to use necessary commas, you may confuse your reader.

CONFUSING   My favorite cousins are Bonnie Gail Billy Joe Calvin Joan and Matt. [How many cousins?]

CLEAR   My favorite cousins are Bonnie Gail, Billy Joe, Calvin, Joan, and Matt.

The rules and exercises that follow will help you learn the correct use of commas.

23f. Use commas to separate items in a series.

Notice in the following examples that the number of commas in a series is only one less than the number of items in the series.

EXAMPLES   Students, teachers, parents, and visitors attended the picnic. [nouns]

The happy, carefree, enthusiastic picnickers thoroughly enjoyed the outing. [adjectives]

They swam, sunbathed, played games, ate, and chatted. [verbs]

They roamed over the hill, through the fields, down to the lake, and across the bridge. [prepositional phrases]

Suddenly a storm broke with a crashing of thunder, a flashing of lightning, and a downpouring of rain. [gerund phrases]

Those who had walked to the picnic, who had brought small children, who had no umbrellas or raincoats, or who had worn good clothes dashed to a nearby farmhouse. [subordinate clauses]

When the last two items in a series are joined by *and*, you may omit the comma before the *and* if the comma is not necessary to make the meaning clear.

CLEAR WITH COMMA OMITTED   Sugar, coffee and celery were on sale last Saturday.

NOT CLEAR WITH COMMA OMITTED We elected our class officers: president, vice-president, secretary and treasurer. [How many officers were elected, three or four? Does one person serve as secretary and treasurer, or are two people needed for separate jobs?]

CLEAR WITH COMMA INCLUDED We elected our class officers: president, vice-president, secretary, and treasurer.

Some writers prefer always to use the comma before the *and*, whether or not it is necessary for clarity. Follow your teacher's instructions on this point.

◆ NOTE Some words—such as *shoes and socks, rod and reel, shampoo and set*—are used in pairs and may be set off as one item in a series: *For supper we had ham and eggs, lettuce and tomatoes, and ice cream and cake.*

(1) If all items in a series are joined by *and* or *or*, do not use commas to separate them.

EXAMPLES I bought a tie and a shirt and a hat.
Hubert or Roy or Wallace can build the float.

(2) Independent clauses in a series are usually separated by semicolons. Short independent clauses, however, may be separated by commas.

EXAMPLES The wind blew furiously through the trees; lightning flashed across the sky; thunder boomed and rolled; rain poured down.

The wind blew, lightning flashed, thunder boomed, rain poured down.

23g. Use a comma to separate two or more adjectives preceding a noun.

EXAMPLE That is a rough, narrow, dangerous road.

When the last adjective in a series is thought of as part of the noun, the comma before the adjective is omitted.

EXAMPLES I collect foreign postage stamps.
A vain, talkative disc jockey annoys me.

23 f-g

Pairs of words like *postage stamp, disc jockey, car key, movie star, stock market,* and *living room* are considered as single units—as though the two words were one word, a compound noun. In the sentences above, *foreign* modifies the unit *postage stamp; vain* and *talkative* modify *disc jockey.*

A good test to determine whether the adjective and noun form a unit is to insert the word *and* between the adjectives. In the first sentence, *and* cannot be logically inserted: *foreign and postage stamps.* In the second sentence, *and* would be logical between the first two adjectives (*vain and talkative*) but not between the second and third (*talkative and disc*). If *and* fits sensibly between the adjectives, use a comma.

Another test is to change the order of the adjectives. *Talkative, vain disc jockey* would be correct, but not *postage foreign stamps* or *disc talkative jockey.* If the order of the adjectives cannot be reversed sensibly, no comma should be used.

● EXERCISE 3.   Number your paper 1–10. Copy each series below, inserting commas wherever needed.

EXAMPLE   1. Arnold caught bass catfish and perch.
    1. *bass, catfish, and perch*
        or
    1. *bass, catfish and perch*

1. George Washington Carver derived from the peanut such items as ink coffee beauty cream and pigments.
2. My little sister can read write add and multiply.
3. Sulfur is used for manufacturing matches plastics paper and insect sprays.
4. She fluttered her long curled dark eyelashes.
5. It was an unusual attractive floor lamp.
6. Mosquitoes hummed crickets chirped mockingbirds sang and frogs croaked.
7. A wise monkey is supposed to hear no evil see no evil and speak no evil.

8. On the surface of the moon are round deep craters and steep rugged mountains.
9. Do you want French dressing mayonnaise or vinegar on your salad?
10. Robert Browning says that youth is good that middle age is better and that old age is best.

● EXERCISE 4. Number your paper 1–10. Think of an appropriate series of words, phrases, or clauses for each blank below; then write each series, properly punctuated, after the corresponding number on your paper.

1. —— are among my classmates.
2. We noticed —— all along the highway.
3. The —— movie star enjoyed the extravagant publicity.
4. Our teacher said that ——.
5. I want —— for my birthday.
6. The —— autumn leaves are beautiful indeed.
7. You can make high grades by ——.
8. A —— girl stepped up to the box office.
9. Today symbols of success include ——.
10. A considerate person ——.

● EXERCISE 5. Write ten sentences, each one containing a correctly punctuated series, as follows:

Two sentences with a series of nouns
Two sentences with a series of verbs
Three sentences with adjectives in a series
One sentence with a series of subordinate clauses
Two sentences with a series of phrases

23h. Use a comma before *and*, *but*, *or*, *nor*, *for*, and *yet* when they join independent clauses.

A comma goes before a coordinating conjunction when a completed thought is on *both sides* of the conjunction. Do not be misled by compound verbs, which often make a sentence look as though it contains two independent clauses. Compare the structure of the two sentences on the following page.

23h

COMPOUND SENTENCE (two independent clauses)

Brian changed the oil, and Junior washed the car.

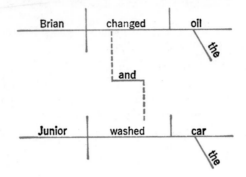

SIMPLE SENTENCE (one subject with a compound verb)

Brian changed the oil and washed the car.

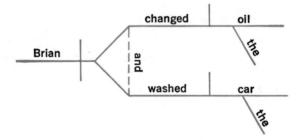

Study the following correctly punctuated compound sentences, noticing that independent clauses (with a subject *and* a verb) are on both sides of *and, but, or, nor, for,* and *yet.*

Into the garbage pail she flung the burned cake, **and** her mother helped her start another.

Everyone was at the game, **but** Quincy arrived an hour late.

Either the gift was lost in the mail, **or** he has forgotten to thank me.

He did not come to my birthday party, **nor** did he even bother to answer the invitation.

George Cooper will no longer sell magazine subscriptions to everyone in our neighborhood, **for** he has finally saved enough money for college.

The critics panned the play, **yet** it ran for six months.

◆ NOTE A comma always goes before *for* and *yet* joining two independent clauses. The comma may be omitted, however, before *and, but, or,* or *nor* when the independent clauses are very short and when there is no possibility of misunderstanding.

EXAMPLE The lights were off and the door was locked.

● EXERCISE 6. Many sentences in this exercise contain clauses joined by the conjunctions *and, but, or, nor, for, yet.* Do not copy the sentences. Number your paper 1–20. Decide where the commas should come, and write on your paper after the proper number the word preceding each comma; add the comma and the conjunction following it. If a sentence is correct as it is written, write *C* (for *correct*) after the proper number on your paper.

EXAMPLES 1. Beaumont led in the first inning by two runs but Houston was leading in the third inning by a score of six to two.
    1. *runs, but*
    2. Ethan whispered something to Philip and quickly left the stadium.
    2. *C*

1. The long drought that had crippled the farmers and ranchers finally ended for day after day the rain came down in sheets.
2. The beds of streams that had long been dry came to life and the caked soil became green with grass.
3. For a time the ranchers rejoiced for their cattle began to grow fat.
4. There was plenty of water now for crops and livestock yet the rains did not stop.
5. Small streams turned into raging rivers and the rivers became large lakes greedily engulfing the countryside.
6. Frightened sheep huddled on the hilltops and the carcasses of many fat cows floated down the rivers.

7. The levees broke and water flooded the towns.
8. A levee broke in my hometown and left six feet of water in the city square.
9. Not only were places of business ruined as merchandise floated out broken doors and windows but several persons were drowned when their houses were washed away.
10. Soon the American Red Cross set up first-aid stations near the town and provided food and clothes for the homeless.
11. Neighboring cities began to chip in with their relief dollars and merchants pledged twenty percent of their sales receipts for the Flood Fund.
12. The state legislature passed an emergency appropriation bill to help the flood victims and the national government came forward with assistance for the disaster area.
13. At last the weather became more merciful and settled down to normal.
14. The bright sun and dry winds came forth to challenge the angry streams and rivers.
15. The clean-up job took tremendous courage and hard work yet stores soon opened for business.
16. Squads of rescue workers helped ranchers to clear away debris and farmers to replant crops.
17. Civic organizations did not fail to anticipate a possible typhoid epidemic nor did they forget to combat the hordes of mosquitoes infesting the once-flooded area.
18. There were some tragic consequences of the deluge but the flood had good psychological effects.
19. Both farmers and ranchers could now hope for good crops and green pastures for the first time in seven years.
20. People laughed as they gave credit to the new governor for breaking the drought or they feigned dismay upon hearing someone mention the incoming "flood" of mail.

23i. Use a comma to set off nonessential clauses and nonessential participial phrases.

A nonessential (or nonrestrictive) clause or participial phrase adds information that is not necessary to the main idea in the sentence.

As you read the following sentences aloud, pause and lower your voice to indicate that each italicized clause or participial phrase is not essential to the basic meaning of the sentence.

NONESSENTIAL CLAUSES   Ellis Riley, **who often plays hooky,** should be expelled.

The National Bank and the Merchandise Mart, **which were firetraps,** were torn down.

I am very proud of my mother, **whose charm and talent impress everyone.**

NONESSENTIAL PHRASES   Senator Stewart, **hoping for a compromise,** began a filibuster.

Alice's Adventures in Wonderland, **written by Lewis Carroll,** has become a classic.

Each italicized clause or phrase above can be omitted because it is not essential to identify the word it modifies. For example, the first clause, *who often plays hooky,* does not identify Ellis Riley; neither does the first phrase, *hoping for a compromise,* identify Senator Stewart. Each of them may be omitted without affecting the meaning of the main idea: *Ellis Riley should be expelled; Senator Stewart began a filibuster.*

However, when a clause or phrase is necessary to the meaning of a sentence, or when it tells *which one,* the clause or phrase is *essential* (or *restrictive*), and commas are *not* used.

Notice how the meaning of each sentence below changes when the essential clause or phrase is omitted.

ESSENTIAL CLAUSES   Freshmen **who play hooky** should be expelled.

All buildings **which were firetraps** were torn down.

I'd like to throw every hat **that I buy on sale** into the garbage can.

23i

◆ NOTE An adjective clause beginning with *that* is usually essential.

ESSENTIAL PHRASES   Senators **hoping for a compromise** began a filibuster. [Not all senators; just the ones hoping for a compromise.]

A book **written by Lewis Carroll** has become a classic. [Not any book, but one by Lewis Carroll.]

● EXERCISE 7. Seven of the following sentences contain nonessential clauses; copy and properly punctuate these sentences. Three sentences are correct as they are written; for these, write *C* (for *correct*) after the proper number on your paper.

1. Daisy Maude Snyder who is my second cousin will visit me next week.
2. We take the *Shreveport Times* which has especially good editorials.
3. Highways that have eight lanes are built for speed and safety.
4. You should know my father who likes to tinker with anything mechanical.
5. All girls who cut their hair short look gawky.
6. Theophilus Snead who has a short haircut looks gawky.
7. I attend Cottonwood High School which has an enrollment of 368.
8. All contestants who answer this difficult question will receive a prize.
9. The hog-nosed snake which some people fear is not poisonous.
10. In *The Man of Feeling* which is a very sentimental story Harley who is overcome by his great devotion to the heroine falls dead upon hearing that his love is returned.

● EXERCISE 8. The following sentences contain participial phrases, some essential and some nonessential. If a sentence is correctly punctuated, write *C* (for *correct*) after the proper number on your paper. Copy the other sentences, punctuating them correctly.

1. All students, planning to attend the Student Council meeting, will be excused from class at two o'clock.
2. Louis Pasteur working hard in his laboratory took time out to treat people for rabies.
3. The fifty-story Civic Center, located on the corner of Main Street and Daniels Place, dominates the skyline of the city.
4. Every child, enrolling in school for the first time, must be vaccinated for smallpox.
5. Their youngest daughter loved by everyone is not at all spoiled.
6. Anyone seeing a suspicious character should notify the police.
7. A long-distance telephone call received on one's birthday is always welcome.
8. My left big toe, badly bruised by the blow, began to swell.
9. Miss Danby trying not to smile offered to help us put on the stage makeup.
10. The "House of Tiles" built in Mexico City during the sixteenth century is now famous as the "House of Sanborn."

● **EXERCISE 9.** Many of the following sentences contain nonessential clauses or participial phrases and therefore require commas. Some sentences, however, are correct. If a sentence is correctly punctuated, write *C* (for *correct*) after the proper number on your paper. If it is incorrect, copy on your paper the word preceding each comma and place the comma after it. Number your answers to agree with the number of the sentences.

EXAMPLES 1. The man who wrote the book is John Evans.
　　　　　1. *C*
　　　　　2. Carlton Ewell who wrote the book gave a talk.
　　　　　2. *Ewell, book,*

1. An adolescent likes to single out a hero who can dazzle the nation with his novel "brand" of crooning or acting.
2. This hero worship which adults sometimes say is a common "affliction" of teen-agers takes many forms.
3. For example, when Chauncey Crooner moans through a catchy ditty, his young audience reacting suitably to his sentimental singing swoons or gasps or faints.

4. During his reign which seldom lasts more than a year or two followers imitate his haircut or echo his coined expressions.

5. Soon, however, Two-Gun Gus from Gremlin Gulch blasting his way into the hearts of Saturday-night movie-goers steals the limelight from Chauncey who doesn't fake melodies on a broken-down banjo or wear a blue and red bandanna.

6. Within a few weeks, companies which specialize in "G.G.G. Bandannas" suddenly have a tremendous business.

7. Every young person who respects the latest fads wears a bandanna with the label "G.G.G." meaning "Gus, Gremlin Gulch."

8. Before long, Peery Musical Company performs a similar feat by manufacturing "Mi-Mi-Fa" banjos which have strings adjusted to the only notes Gus can play.

9. In time, though, even Gus must leave the stage to make room for someone who has patented a new brand of music that "sends" teen-agers.

10. In my opinion, the attention that young people pay to singing idols is more beneficial than harmful.

11. A youngster interested in novelty bandannas and banjos is not likely to be a statistic on the list of juvenile delinquents.

12. David Pierce who lives next door to me is learning music so that he can play the piano as his favorite movie star plays it.

13. When the movie star that he admires fades into a has-been, the boy will not lose interest in music.

14. My final point which seems very sane to me is that hero worship is a necessary part of growing up.

15. A person who hurriedly tries to bridge the gap between childhood and adulthood nearly always feels left out and unsuccessful.

16. The main reason which is a very simple one is that it takes several years to bridge this gap.

17. A typical adolescent being entirely too old to play hopscotch and far too young to vote or join the army thinks he is just marking time until he finally does grow up.

18. Looking around, this adolescent filled with restless ambition sees successful actors and crooners.

19. He finds for himself an idol that becomes a symbol for *Success* spelled with a capital letter.
20. "Someday," the youngster thinks to himself, "I may become the brightest star of all shining even more brilliantly than the one I now admire."

23j. Use a comma after certain introductory elements.

(1) Use a comma after words such as *well, yes, no, why,* etc., when they begin a sentence.

EXAMPLES   **No,** I have not answered her letter.

Why, surely you haven't forgotten already!

(2) Use a comma after an introductory participial phrase.

EXAMPLES   **Pausing for a moment in the doorway,** the teacher smiled at the class.

Frightened by the noise, the pigeons flew from the roof.

(3) Use a comma after a succession of introductory prepositional phrases.

EXAMPLES   **Near the gate at the end of the lane,** I watched the wild stallion race out of the corral.

In drawings by young children, proportions are often very inaccurate.

A short introductory prepositional phrase does not require a comma unless the comma is necessary to make the meaning clear.

EXAMPLES   **In this state** we have a sales tax.

In this state, taxes are comparatively high. [The comma is necessary to avoid reading *state taxes.*]

(4) Use a comma after an introductory adverb clause.

EXAMPLES   **After Alexander had hit the ball over the fence,** the crowd gave him a standing ovation.

Until we found the source of the fire, everyone was searching nervously through closets and wastebaskets.

23j

● Exercise 10. The sentences in this exercise contain introductory elements. Decide where commas should be used. Copy on your paper the word preceding each comma, and place a comma after it. Number your answers to accord with the number of the sentences. If a sentence does not require a comma, write *C* (for *correct*) after the appropriate number.

EXAMPLES   1. Known in China four thousand years ago falconry is an ancient sport.
1. *ago,*
2. Like a hawk a falcon has a crooked beak.
2. *C*

1. Although falconry is indeed an ancient art in America many men still enjoy this sport.
2. Having sharp claws and hooked beaks falcons are by nature good hunters.
3. Instead of using guns or other modern weapons some sportsmen capture and train falcons.
4. After learning to fly a female falcon is taken from the nest and tamed.
5. Until the falcon becomes accustomed to living around men it wears a hood.
6. Covering the eyes and most of the head this leather hood helps the hunter control the falcon.
7. When the falcon has the hood on the hunter carries the bird into a field.
8. In the field is the desired game.
9. When the hunter sees a crow or a pigeon and takes the hood off the falcon quickly attacks the game.
10. Besides a hood other implements are used in falconry.
11. Attached to the falcon's legs jesses are short leather strips with bells.
12. If a falcon should bring down game out of sight these jesses help the hunter find his bird.
13. During the hunt a falconer usually wears a heavy leather gauntlet.
14. When he is training a young falcon to hunt he also uses lures.
15. Used properly lures teach falcons to attack certain birds.

16. Containing pieces of meat and the wings of a bird the lures quickly attract falcons.
17. Within seconds a hungry falcon usually pounces upon the lure.
18. Yes falcons become trained hunters in a short time.
19. Since this trained hunter's speed and accuracy are tremendously effective guns are unnecessary.
20. In the field with a trained falcon hunters often use a dog to flush and retrieve the game.

23k. **Use commas to set off elements that interrupt the sentence.**

Two commas are used around an interrupting element—one before and one after.

EXAMPLE   He, of course, won't be there.

Sometimes an "interrupter" comes at the beginning or at the end of a sentence. In these cases, only one comma is needed.

EXAMPLES   Nevertheless, I think we should go.
I don't know why, however.

(1) Appositives and appositive phrases are usually set off by commas.

EXAMPLES   Everyone, **even his enemies,** respects him.

An extremely talented girl, Claudia Hunt deserves our praise.

I often play tennis, **a lively game.**

Sometimes an appositive is so closely related to the word preceding it that it should not be set off by commas. Such an appositive usually has no modifiers; that is, there is no appositive phrase.

EXAMPLES   my sister **Elizabeth**   **we girls**
the novelist **Jack London**   **us students**

● EXERCISE 11. Number your paper 1–20, and copy (1) the word preceding the appositive (if any), (2) the

23k

appositive or appositive phrase, and (3) the word following the appositive or appositive phrase (if any). Correctly punctuate the appositives; a few of them will not need any commas.

EXAMPLE 1. My brother Gregory discussed the brakes with Mr. Mays the owner of the garage and with Hiram the car dealer.
   1. *brother Gregory discussed*
      Mays, the owner of the garage, and
      Hiram, the car dealer

1. Yesterday at dawn my family was startled out of bed by an explosion the dying gasp of my Uncle Jasper's car. 2. Soon we heard loud voices those of our relatives. 3. Mamie my aunt asked, "Is this pretty house where your brother Maynard lives?" 4. Not waiting for an answer, she squealed, "Oh, won't they be surprised to see us their favorite relatives!"

5. Snorky my little cocker spaniel expressed our unhappy surprise by barking noisily at the intruders our uninvited and unexpected relatives. 6. Then High Voltage their Saint Bernard lumbered forward and tried to make breakfast out of Snorky. 7. Dad untangled the snarling animals and tied both of them Snorky and High Voltage in the backyard. 8. Mortal enemies the dogs spent the rest of the day growling and yapping at each other.

9. A minor incident that fight was only the beginning of the turmoil at our house. 10. Wilbur Uncle Jasper's youngest boy took an immediate fancy to a hand-painted vase a treasured heirloom and dashed it to smithereens against the kitchen cabinet. 11. While Aunt Mamie was apologizing for Wilbur, Uncle Jasper was chasing Sylvester his oldest boy. 12. Sylvester, in turn, was chasing my sister Beulah in order to cut her hair with Mother's best sewing scissors.

13. Just before I left the house a building that we used to call home Uncle Jasper said, "We're going to spend our vacation a full two weeks with you." 14. To be polite to these wild parasites, we have to stay home all day and play boring games especially canasta and checkers. 15. Even our bedtime formerly ten o'clock has changed to midnight. 16. Since Aunt Mamie

has insomnia a disease prohibiting sleep after 4 A.M. everybody gets up for an early breakfast. 17. My head aches when I think about the length of their visit a whole week and five long days.

18. A while ago, however, Mother a wonderful person smiled at my complaints. 19. "Take heart, Daniel my son," she said playfully. "Remember that every relative has his day. 20. Our day will come on a Thursday in November Thanksgiving when we'll drop in on *them!*"

● EXERCISE 12. Use each of the following items as an appositive in a sentence of your own. Be sure to use commas if necessary.

1. Linda
2. a nuisance
3. my neighbor
4. a good teacher
5. Austin and Victor
6. the life of the party
7. a girl sitting near me
8. the candidate to elect
9. a book for young people
10. the man that you should meet

(2) Words used in direct address are set off by commas.

EXAMPLES   That program, **Florence,** has been changed.
Miss Nelson, may I leave class early?
Please answer the doorbell, **Elsie.**

● EXERCISE 13. Copy and correctly punctuate the following sentences.

1. Do you remember Patty what Romeo's last name is?
2. Mr. Chairman I move that we adjourn.
3. Please let me go to the movies Dad.
4. Yes Miss O'Neill I shall be glad to help you.
5. What is the answer to the riddle my wise friend?

(3) Parenthetical expressions are set off by commas.

Parenthetical expressions are side remarks adding information or relating ideas. When writing, you should ordinarily use commas to set off parenthetical matter.[1]

[1] For the use of parentheses and dashes to set off parenthetical matter, see pages 559–60.

The following expressions are commonly used parenthetically: *consequently, however, moreover, nevertheless, therefore, after all, as a matter of fact, at any rate, for example, for instance, in fact, in my opinion, in the first place, of course, on the contrary, on the other hand, generally speaking, I believe* (*guess, know, hope, think, suppose*), *to tell the truth.*

EXAMPLES   He did not, **however,** keep his promise.
After all, I couldn't have known.
Men prefer dark suits in winter, **generally speaking.**

Some expressions may be used both parenthetically and not parenthetically. Compare the following pairs of correctly punctuated sentences; read the sentences aloud.

PARENTHETICAL	NOT PARENTHETICAL
However, did you do that?	**However** did you do that?
To tell the truth, he tries.	He tries **to tell the truth.**
Dad, **I think,** will approve.	**I think** Dad will approve.

◆ NOTE   A contrasting expression introduced by *not* is parenthetical and must be set off by commas.

EXAMPLE   It is the spirit of the giver, **not the gift,** that counts.

● EXERCISE 14.   Number your paper 1–10. Copy the following: (1) the word (if any) preceding each interrupter, (2) the interrupter itself, and (3) the word (if any) following it. Supply the necessary punctuation.

EXAMPLE   1. However your plan in my opinion might work.
   1. *However, your*
      plan, in my opinion, might

1. To tell the truth I have never seen a flying fish.
2. I do know however that some birds can swim.
3. No person of course can see everything in existence; everybody has to depend upon the word of authorities.
4. My father is I believe an authority about fish that can fly.
5. In fact he has seen a Catalina fish fly as high as twenty feet in the air.

6. Having large fins not wings this fish skips along the top of the water and then suddenly leaps skyward.
7. This fish generally speaking is about a foot or a foot and a half long.
8. There are other animals that fly without wings however.
9. Some squirrels for example can glide from one tree to another; they fly about at night not in the daytime.
10. On the contrary I am sticking to the truth; these squirrels use their tails as rudders and their skin as built-in parachutes.

● EXERCISE 15. Use each of the following items as a parenthetical or an interrupting element in a correctly punctuated sentence of your own.

EXAMPLE 1. our new coach
        1. *The main speaker was Mr. Wilkins, our new coach.*

1. the umpire	6. Michigan
2. for instance	7. my friend
3. well	8. no
4. as a matter of fact	9. I think
5. therefore	10. on the contrary

231. Use a comma in certain conventional situations.

(1) Use a comma to separate items in dates and addresses.

EXAMPLES   My family moved to Knoxville, Tennessee, on Monday, May 4, 1964.

On May 4, 1964, I changed my address to 645 Commerce Street, Knoxville, Tennessee 37902

Notice that no comma divides *May 4* (month and day) and *645 Commerce Street* (house number and street name) because each is considered one item. The ZIP code is not separated from the name of the state by a comma: Racine, Wisconsin 53401.

231

(2) Use a comma after the salutation of a friendly letter and after the closing of any letter.

EXAMPLES   Dear Aunt Edith,   Sincerely yours,
            My dear Cynthia,   Yours very truly,

(3) Use a comma after a name followed by *Jr., Sr., M.D.*, etc.

EXAMPLES   Allen Davis, Jr.   Ens. Charles Jay, U.S.N.
            Stanley Brown, M.D.   Myron K. Wilson, Sr.

● EXERCISE 16.   Copy and correctly punctuate any of the following sentences that need commas. If a sentence is correct as it stands, write *C* (for *correct*) after the proper number on your paper.

1. On Friday September 13 1973 I visited friends who live at 234 Oakdale Drive Birmingham Alabama   35223.
2. Were you in St. Louis during May or June in 1972?
3. This letter is addressed to Mr. M. K. Cranberry Jr. 4608 Cherry Blossom Lane Appleton Wisconsin   54911.
4. The Constitution of the United States was signed on September 17 1787 eleven years after the adoption of the Declaration of Independence on July 4 1776.
5. The letter ended, "Yours truly Henry H. Fleming M.D."

23m. Do not use unnecessary commas.

Too much punctuation is just as confusing as not enough punctuation. This is especially true of commas.

CONFUSING   Cora, hurt my feelings, and then, apologetically, said, she was cross, because of an aching, wisdom tooth.

CLEAR   Cora hurt my feelings and then apologetically said she was cross because of an aching wisdom tooth.

Have a *reason* (either a definite rule or a matter of meaning) for every comma or other mark of punctuation that you use. When there is no rule requiring punctuation and when the meaning of the sentence is clear without it, do not insert any punctuation mark.

Summary of Uses of the Comma

23f. Use commas to separate items in a series.
    (1) If all items in a series are joined by <u>and</u> or <u>or</u>, do not use commas to separate them.
    (2) Independent clauses in a series are usually separated by semicolons. Short independent clauses are sometimes separated by commas.

23g. Use a comma to separate two or more adjectives preceding a noun.

23h. Use a comma before <u>and, but, or, nor, for,</u> and <u>yet</u> when they join independent clauses.

23i. Use a comma to set off nonessential clauses and nonessential participial phrases.

23j. Use a comma after certain introductory elements.
    (1) Use a comma after words such as <u>well, yes, no, why,</u> etc., when they begin a sentence.
    (2) Use a comma after an introductory participial phrase.
    (3) Use a comma after a succession of introductory prepositional phrases.
    (4) Use a comma after an introductory adverb clause.

23k. Use commas to set off sentence interrupters.
    (1) Appositives and appositive phrases are usually set off by commas.
    (2) Words used in direct address are set off by commas.
    (3) Parenthetical expressions are set off by commas.

23 l. Use a comma in certain conventional situations.
    (1) Use a comma to separate items in dates and addresses.
    (2) Use a comma after the salutation of a friendly letter and after the closing of any letter.
    (3) Use a comma after a name followed by <u>Jr., Sr., Ph.D.,</u> etc.

23m. Do not use unnecessary commas.

● Review exercise A. Select from the following sentences all words which should be followed by a comma. List these words on your paper, placing a comma after each one. Number your answers according to sentences.

example   1. No Madge I did not talk to Mr. Huey the manager of the bookstore.
       1. *No, Madge, Huey,*

1. Looking for the lost car keys we searched under the car in the house on the porch and among the weeds.
2. Well I guess that Stan likes dates not prunes.
3. Among the synonyms are *humor wit sarcasm* and *irony*.
4. After we had placed an advertisement in the evening paper we found the owner of the puppy.
5. This letter which is dated July 14 1972 is addressed to Mr. Nicholas Walters Sr. R.F.D. 3 Culver City California 90230.
6. I sold three tickets Caleb sold four Jill sold ten and Myrna sold twelve.
7. About ten o'clock on the morning of Saturday February 23 we entered the city limits of Hartford Connecticut.
8. Michael you know of course that Archie hates teas receptions and formal dinners.
9. We left Moravia which is a resort town in New York and drove on to Owasco Lake which is near Syracuse.
10. Wanting to be noticed the baby jumped up and down in his crib and shook the railings and whimpered piteously.

● Review exercise B. Using the Summary of Uses of the Comma (page 517), write sentences of your own to illustrate the rules, as follows:

Three sentences illustrating rule 23f (including one illustrating each subrule)
Two sentences illustrating rule 23g
Three sentences illustrating rule 23h
Two sentences illustrating rule 23i, one containing a nonessential clause and the other containing a nonessential participial phrase
Four sentences illustrating rule 23j (one illustrating each subrule)

Three sentences illustrating rule 23k (one illustrating each sub-rule)

Three sentences illustrating rule 231 (one illustrating each sub-rule)

Write before each sentence the number of the rule it illustrates.

● REVIEW EXERCISE C. Copy the following sentences, inserting end marks and commas where necessary.

1. When Mr. Charles Chatham Jr. my geography teacher visited West Lafayette Indiana he toured the campus of Purdue University

2. Reading that book I learned that Ottawa not Montreal is the capital of Canada

3. Amos will you write to me at 237 Candona Drive Boulder Colorado   80303

4. That plant is I think a kind of cactus that is commonly called a prickly pear

5. Yes Acadia National Park which is on the Atlantic coast is only a short drive from Bangor Maine

6. In the second sentence on page 23 notice the lively vivid action verbs the introductory prepositional phrases and the two subordinate clauses

7. Ritchie leave the room shut the door and be quiet

8. Mrs. Hood assured me that she didn't mind my breaking the cup but I am going to see what I can do about finding her another one

9. Look out Jack That big black Doberman pinscher almost bit you

10. Oh didn't you know that on March 5 1970 my family left Reidsville North Carolina and moved to Highland Park a suburb of Chicago Illinois

CHAPTER 24

Semicolons and Colons

SEMICOLONS

A semicolon looks like what it is: part period and part comma. It says to the reader, "Stop here a little longer than you stop for a comma but not so long as you stop for a period."

Semicolons are used primarily in compound sentences. Since most writers depend largely upon simple and complex sentences to express their ideas, the semicolon is not often used. As you study the rules in this chapter regarding semicolons, follow the lead of professional writers; use the semicolon correctly and effectively but sparingly.

24a. Use a semicolon between independent clauses in a sentence if they are not joined by *and, but, or, nor, for, yet.*

Notice in the following pairs of sentences that the semicolon takes the place of the comma and the conjunction joining the independent clauses.

EXAMPLES   First I washed the dishes and swept the kitchen**, and** then I went to the grocery store.

First I washed the dishes and swept the kitchen **;** then I went to the grocery store.

> Lillian enjoys reading detective stories, **but** her brother prefers science fiction.

> Lillian enjoys reading detective stories; her brother prefers science fiction.

Similarly, a semicolon can take the place of a period between two complete thoughts (independent clauses) that are closely related.

EXAMPLE Warren listened attentively to the joke. His half smile gradually changed into an ear-to-ear grin. [two simple sentences]

Warren listened attentively to the joke; his half smile gradually changed into an ear-to-ear grin.

As you study the sentences below (taken from the works of professional writers), observe that each semicolon has a complete thought on *both* sides of it and that the two independent clauses are not joined by *and*, *but*, *or*, *nor*, *for*, or *yet*. Since the thoughts of the main clauses in each example sentence are very closely related, a semicolon is better than a period.

EXAMPLES

Making the vaccines more potent is probably not the answer; there would be a greater risk of more severe reactions to the inoculations themselves.

In one city a fur dealer was giving merchandise certificates as prizes in a radio contest; in another a sewing-machine distributor gave credit certificates to winners (and losers) of contest promotions.

A huge tie results; to break the tie entrants must pay another, often higher, fee and solve more difficult puzzles.

● EXERCISE 1. Read the following sentences and decide where semicolons may be used. Copy on your paper the following: (1) the word before each semicolon, (2) the semicolon itself, and (3) the word that comes after it. In some instances, you may prefer to use a period. If so, write the word before the period, the period itself, and the word (capitalized) following the period.

24a

EXAMPLES   1. The girls walked gracefully along the platform the crowd clapped, whistled, and sighed its approval.
   1. *platform; the*
   2. I'll never forget those bathing beauties by chance, Charles and I happened to be at Horton City Park last July 4, the day of the contest.
   2. *beauties. By*

1. Miss Hayes talked today about Anatole France's *The Man Who Married a Dumb Wife* the heroine of this play is extremely comical.
2. According to Miss Hayes, the hero in France's play married a girl who could not speak she had something wrong with her tongue and was physically unable to utter a word.
3. For a time all was peaceful in the household of the newlyweds before long, however, the husband grew lonely.
4. He longed to hear his wife's voice one day he decided to take her to a doctor to find out whether or not something could be done to get her to speak.
5. The doctor examined the young wife's mouth then he announced, "An operation may successfully free her tongue."
6. Overcome with joyful hope, the husband agreed to an immediate operation within a few days his wife had recovered and could speak as clearly as anyone else.
7. She could also speak longer and louder than her husband she soon began to scold and to nag and to gossip.
8. Morning, noon, and night she talked and talked and talked her poor husband, growing frantic, went back to see the doctor.
9. "Please, doctor," he pleaded, "perform another operation to shut her up I want her back as she used to be—a silent woman."
10. The doctor had only this to say: "I can't change her I can only recommend deafness for you."

24b. Use a semicolon between independent clauses joined by such words as *for example, for instance, that is, besides, accordingly, moreover,*

nevertheless, furthermore, otherwise, therefore,
however, consequently, instead, hence.

These words are often transitional expressions linking independent clauses. When used in this way, they are preceded
by a semicolon, not a comma. They are, however, usually
followed by a comma.

WRONG	Janet did as she was told, however, she grumbled un- graciously.
RIGHT	Janet did as she was told **; however,** she grumbled un- graciously.
WRONG	I did not go to the movies, instead, I worked on my project.
RIGHT	I did not go to the movies **; instead,** I worked on my project.

Caution: When the expressions listed in the rule appear
within a clause, not as a transition *between* clauses, they are
usually punctuated as interrupters (set off by commas). The
two clauses are still separated by a semicolon: *We are going*
ahead with plans for the picnic; everyone, **however,** *will*
not be able to attend.

24c. A semicolon (rather than a comma) may be
needed to separate the independent clauses of a
compound sentence if there are commas within
the clauses.

This use of the semicolon often helps to make a sentence
clear.

CONFUSING	She will invite Irene, Beth, and Eunice, and Graham will ask Leslie and Val.
CLEAR	She will invite Irene, Beth, and Eunice **;** and Graham will ask Leslie and Val.

CONFUSING After the fire, Lionel stood in the middle of the lot, now covered with charred debris, and, not tired and discouraged, he began to scrape through the ashes as if he were trying to uncover something of value.

CLEAR After the fire, Lionel stood in the middle of the lot, now covered with charred debris; and, not tired and discouraged, he began to scrape through the ashes as if he were trying to uncover something of value.

● EXERCISE 2. Follow the directions for Exercise 1 as you show where to use semicolons in the following sentences.

1. Traveling through the countryside last summer, we decided not to follow any schedule, for example, we took side roads if we found any that looked interesting.

2. One quiet road, many miles from the main highway, wound narrowly through the hills, at times it seemed to disappear altogether under the bushes growing along it.

3. As Dad steered the car carefully, the conversation that Mother and I had been having died out, impressed by the stillness of our surroundings, we became strangely silent.

4. There were no houses nearby, but, seeing the remains of a few old rock chimneys, we knew that someone must have lived here many years ago.

5. After traveling about ten miles along this road, we noticed a small, square area fenced around with iron rails, inside the fence, all overgrown with grass and wildflowers, were old graves.

6. A few of the graves, dating back to the early 1800's, had crude stone monuments with traces of names that the elements had not yet scratched out, but others, having only two stones marking the site, had no names.

7. As we looked at the little cemetery, we wondered what stories these people could have told about early settlements, about the hardships of pioneers, or about the terrors of the wilderness, perhaps they had lived through famines and blizzards and Indian raids.

8. The Comanches, according to our history books, had roamed

this lonely area, therefore, we assumed that some of these people had died during skirmishes.

9. We continued to stand there for some time, each of us deep in thought, finally Dad said, "Peace," and we walked slowly back to the car.

10. On the way back to the highway, we continued to be very quiet, furthermore, each of us seemed relieved when we finally drove into a gay, lively town.

24d. Use a semicolon between items in a series if the items contain commas.

EXAMPLES The examinations will be held on Wednesday, June 26; Thursday, June 27; and Friday, June 28.

There were two representatives from Pittsburgh, Pennsylvania; four from Buffalo, New York; and three from Cleveland, Ohio.

● EXERCISE 3. All of the following sentences contain items in a series. If the items should be separated by semicolons, copy the sentence, adding the needed semicolons. If a sentence needs no semicolons, write *C* (for *correct*) after the corresponding sentence number on your paper.

1. In the sixteenth century there were centers of learning in France, Italy, and Germany.

2. Western culture was enriched by centers of learning in Paris, France, Rome, Italy, and Mainz, Germany.

3. Before Cortez came to Mexico, the Aztecs had constructed dikes to irrigate cornfields, had made mirrors and razors out of stone, and had devised effective war weapons.

4. The Incas in Peru planted crops, such as corn, domesticated animals, such as the llama, and developed crafts, such as weaving.

5. Mr. Healy discussed the importance of men like Gutenberg, inventor of movable type, Galileo, inventor of the first complete astronomical telescope, and Newton, discoverer of the law of gravity.

● REVIEW EXERCISE A. Read the following sentences and decide where semicolons should be used. Do not copy the

24d

sentences. Instead, write on your paper the sentence number; after it, copy the word preceding the needed semicolon, write the semicolon, and then copy the word following the semicolon. If a sentence needs no semicolon, write *C* (for *correct*) after the appropriate number on your paper. (*Caution:* Remember that when a semicolon and quotation marks come together, the semicolon goes *outside* the quotation marks.)

EXAMPLE 1. Unfortunately, many superstitions are not dead they survive in our conversations and sometimes influence our behavior.

      1. *dead; they*

1. Our conversations frequently mirror old superstitions we "interpret" ordinary events strangely and illogically almost every day.
2. Generally speaking, these interpretations are virtual synonyms for events for example, *my burning ears* means "somebody is talking about me."
3. Other examples include *Friday 13*, "an unlucky day," *open umbrellas indoors*, "bad luck," and *gifts of knives*, "cut or severed friendships."
4. Many customs have their roots in superstitions for instance, when you cover your yawns with your hand, you are not only being polite but also paying respect to superstition.
5. Men used to think that horned devils sat in trees or on high buildings and passed the time of day by shooting poisoned arrows into the hearts of unfortunate persons walking below.
6. Since the air seemed to be infested with hordes of devils, many men believed that these imps would seize every opportunity to enter the body and corrupt the soul of a man.
7. To yawn was to create the opening that the devils were seeking a person who covered the yawn with his hand could stop the invisible invaders from entering his body.
8. When someone sneezes in our presence, we often say "Bless you" very quickly this custom is also based upon ancient lore about devils.
9. Although a sneeze is no more than a noisy spray of moisture, it seems to call for a special and an immediate blessing.

10. Long ago men believed that demons were continually trying to put spells on people however, when a person sneezed, he shook off the curse and thus deserved a blessing.

11. My friend Gloria often brags about something like never missing a word on a spelling test nevertheless, she then suddenly freezes with fearful anticipation of failure and adds quickly, "Knock on wood."

12. In order to be sure that she will make a perfect score on the next test, Gloria finds a piece of wood and knocks on it vigorously I do the same thing.

13. This custom hinges on an old idea that demons lived in trees and that they would occasionally help a person by bringing him good luck.

14. As Shakespeare's Iago tells us in plain language, a devil has to *appear* good at times otherwise he could not lure men away from goodness.

15. These tree-dwelling devils were not fools they knew how to use "good luck" for their own evil purposes.

16. They also expected men to perform certain rituals one of these was a kind of thanksgiving ceremony.

17. A man enjoying a run of good fortune was obligated to show his gratitude by knocking on a tree the devils living inside the tree not only heard the thank-you knocks but also extended the period of good luck.

18. After men had moved from the country to large cities, no tree was convenient therefore, any piece of wood became an appropriate substitute.

19. The superstitious fear of walking under a ladder is more sensible a ladder could fall and injure you.

20. I imagine that our grandchildren will go on knocking on wood, blessing a person who sneezes, and covering their yawning mouths but these customs are rather foolish actions for people living in an enlightened age.

● REVIEW EXERCISE B. Using semicolons and commas where appropriate, write two sentences of your own (ten sentences in all) to illustrate each of the patterns of punctuation on the next page.

1. PATTERN   Independent clause **;** independent clause.

   EXAMPLE   Gilbert made a touchdown during the last quarter; we won by a score of 6 to 0.

2. PATTERN   Independent clause **,** coordinating conjunction, independent clause.

   EXAMPLE   Gilbert made a touchdown during the last quarter, and we won by a score of 6 to 0.

3. PATTERN   Introductory element **,** independent clause **;** independent clause.

   EXAMPLE   During the last quarter of the game, Gilbert made a touchdown; we won by 6 to 0.

4. PATTERN   Independent clause **;** transitional word **,** independent clause.

   EXAMPLE   There was a scoreless tie at the beginning of the last quarter; however, Gilbert soon made a touchdown.

5. PATTERN   Independent clause with commas **;** coordinating conjunction, independent clause.

   EXAMPLE   Mary is bringing ham sandwiches, potato salad, and deviled eggs; and I am baking cookies and making lemonade.

COLONS

Generally, the colon is used to call the reader's attention to what comes next.

24e. Use a colon to mean "note what follows."

(1) Use a colon before a list of items, especially after expressions like *as follows* and *the following*.

EXAMPLES   The equipment that you will need is **as follows :** a light jacket, heavy boots, a rifle, several cartons of shells, and a sharp hunting knife.

That summer we traveled through **the following** states **:** Arkansas, Kentucky, Tennessee, North Carolina, and Virginia.

> The principal's desk was cluttered with all kinds of papers : unopened letters, absence reports, telephone messages, and unpaid bills.
>
> I have three hobbies : sewing, cooking, and painting.

In the last two examples, the items before which the colon is used are appositives. If a word has a list of appositives following it, the colon is used to make the sentence clear.

◆ NOTE When a list follows immediately after a verb or preposition, do not use a colon.

WRONG My three hobbies are: sewing, cooking, and painting.

RIGHT My three hobbies are sewing, cooking, and painting.

WRONG That summer we traveled through: Arkansas, Kentucky, Tennessee, North Carolina, and Virginia.

RIGHT That summer we traveled through Arkansas, Kentucky, Tennessee, North Carolina, and Virginia.

(2) Use a colon before a long, formal statement or quotation.

EXAMPLE Horace Mann had this to say about dealing with those who disagree with you : "Do not think of knocking out another person's brains because he differs in opinion from you. It would be as rational to knock yourself on the head because you differ from yourself ten years ago."

24f. Use a colon in certain conventional situations.

(1) Use a colon between the hour and the minute when you write the time.

EXAMPLES 7 : 30 A.M.   3 : 15 P.M.

(2) Use a colon between chapter and verse in referring to passages from the Bible.

EXAMPLES Genesis 27 : 28   Ruth 1 : 16

24
e-f

(3) Use a colon after the salutation of a business letter.

EXAMPLES   Dear Sir :   Dear Mr. Roberts :
            Gentlemen :   Dear Professor Stanton :

● EXERCISE 4. Number your paper 1–10. Decide where colons should appear in the following sentences. If a sentence does not need a colon, write *C* (for *correct*) after its number. If a colon is required after a word, copy the word and write a colon after it. If a colon is needed to divide numbers, copy the numbers and add the needed colon.

EXAMPLE   1. At 9 01 A.M., Miss Blake wrote on the board this line from Kipling's speech "Words are the most powerful drug used by mankind."
           1. *9:01*
              speech:

1. Reading Proverbs 3 13, the minister supported his main point with the following quotation "Happy is the man that findeth wisdom, and the man that getteth understanding."
2. In science class we have to learn the meaning of the following words *amphibian*, *chromosome*, *neutron*, *oxidation*, and *vertebrate*.
3. Miss Thompson invited Alden, Richard, and Sammy.
4. The farmer explained the uses of the various parts of the plow landslide, clevis, jointer, and beam.
5. Experts can identify a fingerprint by observing the nature of the following arches, whorls, loops, and composites.
6. At 10 45 the teacher closed the lesson by reading Exodus 20 12 "Honor thy father and thy mother, that thy days may be long upon the land which the Lord thy God giveth thee."
7. At 8 20 the agent told us that the 6 10 train would not arrive before 9 15 P.M.
8. Along the midway were several kinds of rides a roller coaster, a whip, two merry-go-rounds, and a Ferris wheel.
9. There were sandwiches, cold drinks, and candy on our television tables.
10. At an airport I like to listen to the many noises motors roaring before takeoff, loudspeakers announcing departures and

arrivals, passengers dropping quarters into insurance machines, telephones ringing at every counter, and skycaps greeting incoming passengers.

● REVIEW EXERCISE C.   Using commas, semicolons, and colons, copy and correctly punctuate the following sentences.

1. A scrawny friendly stray dog wandered out onto the field and the umpire stopped the game temporarily.
2. Because they do not conduct electricity the following materials can be used as insulators rubber glass cloth and plastics.
3. There are only three primary colors in painting red blue and yellow.
4. Other colors are mixtures of primary colors for instance purple is a mixture of red and blue.
5. The ten-gallon hat of the cowboy was used as a protection from the sun a dipper for water and a pan for washing his hands and leather chaps protected him from thorny bushes.
6. The minister began his sermon by quoting these two verses from the Bible Matthew 23 37 and John 16 27.
7. In his speech to the Sock and Buskin our dramatic club Mr. Henry Stevenson Jr. quoted from several Shakespearean plays *Romeo and Juliet The Tempest Macbeth* and *Julius Caesar.*
8. Captain James Cook explored much of the Pacific Ocean he found the Hawaiian Islands in 1778.
9. From 1851 to 1864 the United States had four Presidents Millard Fillmore a Whig from New York Franklin Pierce a Democrat from New Hampshire James Buchanan a Democrat from Pennsylvania and Abraham Lincoln a Republican from Illinois.
10. From 1 15 to 1 50 P.M. I was so sleepy that my mind wandered completely tuning out the lesson I rested my head on my right palm and let my eyelids sag to half-mast.

CHAPTER 25

Italics and Quotation Marks

ITALICS

Italics are printed letters that lean to the right, *like this*. When you write or type, you indicate italics by underlining the words you want italicized. If your composition were to be printed, the typesetter would set the underlined words in italics. For example, if you type

Daniel Defoe wrote Robinson Crusoe.

the sentence would be printed like this:

Daniel Defoe wrote *Robinson Crusoe.*

25a. Use underlining (italics) for titles of books, plays, movies, periodicals, works of art, long musical compositions, ships, and so on.

EXAMPLES   Great Expectations [a novel]
Romeo and Juliet [a book-length play]
St. Louis Post Dispatch [a newspaper]
Reader's Digest [a magazine]
Madame Butterfly [an opera]
Haydn's Surprise Symphony [a long musical composition]
Venus de Milo [a statue]
Flying Cloud [a ship]
Spirit of St. Louis [a plane]

The words *a*, *an*, and *the*, written before a title, are italicized only when they are part of the title. Before the names of newspapers and magazines, however, they are not italicized, even if they are capitalized on the front page of the newspaper or on the cover of the magazine.

EXAMPLES   I am reading Hemingway's *The Old Man and the Sea*.
             In the museum we saw Rodin's statue *The Thinker*.
             My father subscribes to the *Wall Street Journal* and
             the *Atlantic*.

Magazine articles, chapter headings, and titles of short poems, short stories, and short musical compositions, when referred to in a composition, should be placed in quotation marks, not italicized. See page 540 for this rule.

25b. Use underlining (italics) for words, letters, and figures referred to as such and for foreign words.

EXAMPLES   The word <u>existence</u> has three e's.
             Because my <u>7</u> looked like a <u>9</u>, I lost five points on
             the math test.
             Is your knowledge of foreign expressions limited to
             <u>faux pas</u> and <u>bon voyage</u>?

● EXERCISE 1.   List on your paper all words and word groups in the following sentences which should be italicized; underline each. Before each word or word group, write the number of the sentence in which it appears.

1. Christopher Columbus and his crew sailed on three ships: the Santa Maria, the Niña, and the Pinta.
2. Some foreign phrases, like faux pas and qui vive, can often express ideas more clearly than English words can.
3. I just got back my book report on Wade's book The Boy Who Dared.
4. The margin is full of red ink saying that William Penn's last name has two n's, that the word hunky-dory does not ad-

**25
a-b**

equately describe the author's style, and that I should always cross my t's and dot my i's.

5. After her long lecture Miss Reece asked me to comment on the popularity of Handel's Messiah and of Mozart's opera The Marriage of Figaro.

6. Since I was reading an article in the March issue of the Reader's Digest, I did not hear her lecture on musicians.

7. I had, however, just learned two new words, reverberate and venerable; therefore, I solemnly answered, "Their venerable melodies have reverberated through the centuries."

8. Upon hearing my learned comment, Adrian, who had been reading the Chicago Tribune, dropped his newspaper in amazement.

9. Stunned by my reply, Miss Reece began to stammer something about Michelangelo and the beauties of his works of art, such as his Kneeling Angel and his David.

10. After the bell had rung, she told us to become familiar with such books as Lives of the Composers and Art Through the Ages.

QUOTATION MARKS

When writing a composition, you may wish to report the exact words of a conversation, to copy a passage from a book, or to refer to the title of a song or magazine article. You should, therefore, learn how to use quotation marks correctly.

25c. Use quotation marks to enclose a direct quotation—a person's exact words.

EXAMPLES   Owen said, "The last feature has started."
"Let's go for a swim," suggested Dan.

Do not use quotation marks for *indirect* quotations.

DIRECT QUOTATION   Jacqueline said, "I am going to Trenton on Saturday." [the speaker's exact words]

INDIRECT QUOTATION   Jacqueline said that she was going to Trenton on Saturday. [not the speaker's exact words]

Caution: Be sure to place quotation marks at both the beginning and the end of a direct quotation.

WRONG   He whispered, "Please don't tell the coach.

RIGHT   He whispered, "Please don't tell the coach."

25d. A direct quotation begins with a capital letter.

EXAMPLE   According to Albert Einstein, "Imagination is more important than knowledge."

Miss March said, "All of Unit 7 and the first chapter in Unit 8." [Although this is not a sentence, it is apparently Miss March's complete remark.]

EXCEPTION   If the direct quotation is obviously a fragment, it may begin with a small letter.

EXAMPLE   Are our ideals, as Scott says, mere "statues of snow" that soon melt? [The quotation is obviously only a part of Scott's remark.]

25e. When a quoted sentence is divided into two parts by an interrupting expression such as *he said* or *Mother asked,* the second part begins with a small letter.

EXAMPLES   "I believe," he said, "that Francis is telling only part of the truth."

"I'm sorry," I replied, "but I can't possibly go to your party."

If the second part of the quotation is a new sentence, a period (not a comma) follows the interrupting expression; and the second part begins with a capital letter.

EXAMPLE   "A folk ballad usually has many stanzas," explained the teacher. "Each stanza has four lines."

Caution: Remember that an interrupting expression is not a part of a quotation and therefore should not be inside quotation marks.

25
c-e

WRONG   "Please don't tell me, I said, how the movie ends."

RIGHT   "Please don't tell me," I said, "how the movie ends." [Two pairs of quotation marks are needed for the broken quotation.]

When two or more sentences are quoted together, use only one set of quotation marks.

WRONG   Joseph said, "In the spring I like to work in the yard." "I hate to wash windows and mop floors."

RIGHT   Joseph said, "In the spring I like to work in the yard. I hate to wash windows and mop floors."

25f. A direct quotation is set off from the rest of the sentence by commas or by a question mark or exclamation point.

EXAMPLES   Margaret announced, "I really must be going," then stayed for another hour.

The crowd yelled, "Hold that line!" as the visiting team threatened to score.

25g. Other marks of punctuation when used with quotation marks are placed according to the following rules:

(1) Commas and periods are always placed inside closing quotation marks.

EXAMPLES   "I haven't seen the movie," remarked Jeannette, "but I understand it's excellent."

As I feared, Miss Watkins announced, "Close your books for a pop quiz."

He read aloud "The Bells," a poem by Edgar Allan Poe.

(2) Colons and semicolons are always placed outside closing quotation marks.

EXAMPLES   Socrates once said, "As for me, all I know is that I know nothing"; I wonder why everyone thinks he was such a wise man.

The following aviators received medals of honor for "service beyond the call of duty": Wilfred Grant, Jacob Glasgow, and Hugh Dumas.

(3) Question marks and exclamation points are placed inside the closing quotation marks if the quotation is a question or an exclamation; otherwise, they are placed outside.

EXAMPLES   "Is the pain unbearable?" the dentist asked as I squirmed and grunted.

"Not yet!" I exclaimed. "But it could be after you start drilling!"

Is his motto still, "Stay in the game and pitch"?

How I laughed when he called me a "budding genius"!

● EXERCISE 2.   Number your paper 1–10. If a sentence below contains an indirect quotation, change it to a direct quotation, correctly punctuated. If a sentence contains a direct quotation, change it to an indirect quotation, correctly punctuated.

EXAMPLES   1. Mr. Anderson said that he would pay me well.
1. *Mr. Anderson said, "I will pay you well."*
2. "What's the trouble?" she asked.
2. *She asked what the trouble was.*

1. My brother said that he would miss the rehearsal.
2. "What is your excuse?" asked the principal.
3. "Sam," asked Claudette, "why aren't you playing football this year?"
4. The thief finally admitted that he stole the furs.
5. I told Dad that I needed fifteen dollars.
6. "How is it possible?" asked my teacher.
7. Bill yelled that the score was tied again.
8. Granddad says two rings around the moon mean rain within two days.
9. Jim said he thought he could win.
10. "That," Miss Turner confessed facetiously, "is the first mistake I've made in ten years."

**25
f-g**

25h. When you write dialogue (two or more persons having a conversation), begin a new paragraph every time the speaker changes.

EXAMPLE

"You have just come down?" said Mr. Drummle, edging me a little away with his shoulder.

"Yes," said I, edging *him* a little away with *my* shoulder.

"Beastly place," said Drummle. "Your part of the country, I think?"

"Yes," I assented. "I am told it's very like your Shropshire."

"Not in the least like it," said Drummle.[1]

● EXERCISE 3. Write a page of dialogue that will show your ability to use quotation marks correctly. Perhaps you would like to retell a favorite anecdote in your own words and let the dialogue of the speakers carry the action forward. Better still, report the exact words of a real conversation that will entertain your classmates. You can get ideas for interesting dialogues if you will remember definite situations—for example, arguing about a play on the baseball diamond, apologizing for a social blunder, trying to make an escape from a determined salesman, or mistaking a stranger for an old friend.

25i. When a quoted passage consists of more than one paragraph, put quotation marks at the beginning of each paragraph and at the end of the entire passage. Do not put quotation marks after any paragraph but the last.

EXAMPLE

"Our landlord had a tolerable good house and clean furniture, and yet we could not be tempted to lodge in it. We chose rather to lie in the open field, for fear of growing too tender.... The truth of it is, we took so much pleasure in that natural kind of

[1] From *Great Expectations* by Charles Dickens.

lodging that I think at the foot of the account mankind are great losers by the luxury of feather beds and warm apartments.

"The curiosity of beholding so new and withal so sweet a method of encamping brought one of the senators . . . to make us a midnight visit. But he was so very clamorous in his commendations of it that the sentinel, not seeing his quality, either through his habit or behavior, had like to have treated him roughly.

"After excusing the unreasonableness of his visit, . . . he swore he was so taken with our lodging that he would set fire to his house as soon as he got home and teach his wife and children to lie, like us, in the open field." [1]

25j. Use single quotation marks to enclose a quotation within a quotation.

EXAMPLES   Exasperated, Joanne reported, "Then he remarked innocently, 'I was only trying to help.'"

Mr. Hull answered, "The phrase 'world enough and time' is from one of Andrew Marvell's poems."

"Why did you shout 'Ouch!'?" I asked.

"Did you hear me ask 'Where's the money?'" he inquired.

● EXERCISE 4.   Write eight sentences of your own, as instructed below.

Two quoted sentences, each interrupted by an expression such as *I said*

One sentence containing a quoted fragment or part of a sentence

Two sentences, each containing an indirect quotation

One sentence containing a quoted question

One interrogatory sentence ending with a quotation that is not a question

One sentence containing a quotation within a quotation

25
h-j

From *A History of the Dividing Line* by William Byrd (1728).

● REVIEW EXERCISE A.   The dialogue below is designed to test your ability to use quotation marks and the other marks of punctuation used with quotation marks. As you copy the dialogue on your paper and insert quotation marks and other necessary punctuation, be sure to start a new paragraph with each change of speaker. If you have difficulty working out this exercise, reread the dialogue under rule 25h.

Those are odd sounds coming from Junior's room observed Dad, laying aside the evening paper. One! we heard Junior say firmly. Yeow squalled Hey Bag, our cat. Two snapped Junior. Yeow! Yeow squawked the cat. What on earth can be going on in there with Junior counting and the cat yelling Yeow Mother asked as she and Dad eased toward the door of Junior's room. That's fine, Hey Bag. Now count to three, demanded Junior, simultaneously pinching the tail of the sputtering cat three times. Son! Stop that this instant exclaimed Dad, his every other word punctuated by Yeow from the counting cat. Junior leaped to his feet and stroked the cat gently. School's out, Hey Bag! Come on, and I'll rob my piggy bank to get you some liver. Of all things! Dad continued to scold. Later that night, after hearing Dad's lecture, Junior promised, I'll never do it again, Pop. Never! Then, as a kind of afterthought, he added, Do you suppose Hey Bag and I can get a job with the circus when I grow up?

25k. Use quotation marks to enclose titles of articles, short stories, poems, songs, chapters, and other parts of books or periodicals.

EXAMPLES   Review Chapter 24, "Your Inborn Behavior."

The title of the article, "What Every Adolescent Should Know," caught my attention.

I have not read "More Alarms by Night," though I have read many other short stories by Thurber.

Do you really think that "The Raven" is Poe's best poem?

Dad was singing "On Top of Old Smoky."

Remember that long, book-length poems and long musical compositions are italicized, not quoted. (See page 532.)

EXAMPLES   He assigned Chapter VIII, "The Food You Need," beginning on page 125 of *Your Health and Safety*.

Have you read the short story called "The Ambitious Guest" in Nathaniel Hawthorne's book *Twice-Told Tales?*

"Figures—Freckles—Foresight," an article in *Good Housekeeping*, is interesting.

You may wonder how to decide whether to italicize a title or to put it in quotation marks. In general, you italicize the title of a book-length poem, one long enough to be published in a separate volume. Such poems are usually divided into titled or numbered sections—cantos, parts, books, etc. Examples are Milton's *Paradise Lost*, Tennyson's *Idylls of the King*, and Longfellow's *Evangeline*.

Long musical compositions, the titles of which should be italicized, include operas, symphonies, ballets, oratorios, and concertos.

EXAMPLES   In my report on Samuel Taylor Coleridge, I plan to quote from *Lyrical Ballads*, from Part VII of *The Rime of the Ancient Mariner*, and from the second stanza of "Kubla Khan."

Miss Hurley sang "The Last Rose of Summer" from the opera *Martha*.

My favorite song is "Tonight" from *West Side Story*.

● REVIEW EXERCISE B.   Copy the following, correctly using italics and quotation marks.

1. At the party Ellen sang I Could Have Danced All Night, from the Broadway musical My Fair Lady.
2. The Latin term summa cum laude appeared on the valedictorian's diploma.

25 k

3. I have never seen the opera Carmen, said Roberta, but I have often heard the Toreador Song.

4. After reading Dickens' A Christmas Carol, I wrote an essay entitled Scrooge Sees Ghosts; but at one point I omitted the final e in the word Scrooge.

5. My favorite story by Arthur Conan Doyle is The Adventure of the Dying Detective, which is included in the anthology The Complete Sherlock Holmes.

6. The New York World-Telegram and Sun, in reviewing the ballet Swan Lake, stated, Last night's performance was the highlight of the season.

7. Have you ever seen the play Our Town, asked Marian. If not, you should certainly see the production by the senior class next Friday.

8. Mr. Meyers announced, Since you students did so well in today's discussion of Shakespeare's Henry V, I will assign no homework; needless to say, this news delighted me.

9. Oh, look! exclaimed Fred as we looked through the old magazines. This 1963 issue of Life has an article entitled Loch Ness Secret Solved.

10. Miss Charles asked, What did the Nurse mean when she exclaimed, Ah, welladay!?

● REVIEW EXERCISE C.   This exercise covers all marks of punctuation that you have studied so far. Copy and correctly punctuate the following sentences.

1. In 1831 a man named Michael Faraday my history teacher began experimented with a magnet and a copper disk

2. Oh I read about Faraday in the book You and Science Hector muttered

3. Faraday's important discovery continued Mr McCall is described in yesterday's assignment

4. I then remembered the chapter entitled Science Is Applied to Industry and Agriculture

5. Was it Michael Faraday who wrote I have at last succeeded in magnetizing and electrifying a ray of light

6. When I said that Faraday turned magnetism into electricity Mr McCall exclaimed Good for you Jonathan

7. I thought sir Ada interrupted that Faraday invented the radio
8. The radio in 1831 Hector asked in astonishment
9. No the radio came in the early twentieth century Mr McCall went on Ada Faraday's linking of light and electricity did lead to the radio Faraday however invented the dynamo not the radio
10. Although it's true that a dynamo is a universally recognized symbol of power Mr McCall concluded I quote exact words from your textbook The dynamo does not itself create power but changes the power of heat or falling water into electricity

CHAPTER 26

Apostrophes

Possessive Case, Contractions, Plurals

Apostrophes are necessary for expressing meaning clearly in written English. For instance, the difference in meaning between *shell* and *she'll* or *shed* and *she'd* is indicated in writing by the apostrophe (and, of course, the context in which the word appears).

If you sometimes forget to use apostrophes, or if you use them incorrectly, the rules in this chapter will prove helpful.

26a. To form the possessive case of a singular noun, add an apostrophe and an *s*.

The possessive case of a noun or pronoun shows ownership or relationship. The nouns and pronouns in bold-faced type below are in the possessive case.

OWNERSHIP   I borrowed **Murray's** mitt.

                Dad's boat needs painting.

                Have you seen **my** scrapbook?

RELATIONSHIP   **Lydia's** cousin is in town.

                Cleaning the garage was a **day's** work.

                I appreciate **your** sending the gift.

EXAMPLES   Dad's car   a hard day's work
                   Ned's baseball   this morning's paper
                   the governor's speech   a quarter's worth
                   Mr. Jones's briefcase   a dollar's worth

EXCEPTION   Many writers use only the apostrophe in forming the possessive case of a noun ending in *s*. Otherwise, pronunciation would be difficult in some cases: *Ulysses' strategy*, not *Ulysses's strategy*. Generally, you should use the apostrophe and the *s* unless there is such a pronunciation problem.

● EXERCISE 1.   Form the possessive case of each of the following singular words. After each possessive word, write an appropriate noun.

EXAMPLE   1. Carol
            1. *Carol's idea*

1. dime   3. child   5. friend   7. Aunt Margaret   9. Eloise
2. week   4. cousin 6. Ruth   8. fox   10. Mr. Ross

26b. To form the possessive case of a plural noun ending in s, add only the apostrophe.

EXAMPLES   both boys' behavior   families' efforts
                   two weeks' vacation   knives' edges
                   five dollars' worth   heroes' stories

Most plural nouns do end in *s*. Some nouns, however, form their plurals somewhat irregularly. (See page 577.) To form the possessive case of a plural noun that does not end in *s*, add an apostrophe and an *s*.

EXAMPLES   mice's tracks   women's gloves   teeth's cavities

● EXERCISE 2.   Write the possessive case of each of these plural words.

1. policemen   4. galaxies   7. novels   9. geese
2. magazines   5. deer   8. dictionaries   10. children
3. people   6. quarters

Caution: Do not use an apostrophe to form the *plural* of a noun. Remember that the apostrophe shows ownership or relationship; it is nearly always followed by a noun.

26
a-b

WRONG   Two girls' forgot their coats.

RIGHT   Two girls forgot their coats. [simple plural]

RIGHT   Two **girls'** coats are hanging in the hall. [The apostrophe shows that the coats belong to the two girls.]

● EXERCISE 3.   Revise the following phrases by using the possessive case.

EXAMPLE   1. the meetings of the athletes

1. *the athletes' meetings*

1. a lunch for girls
2. absences of students
3. the shoes for men
4. salaries of teachers
5. textbook for sophomores
6. duty of the voters
7. food for invalids
8. the work of actors
9. uniforms for nurses
10. spirit of the players

Summary

The following examples illustrate rules 26a and 26b:

SINGU-LAR	SINGULAR POSSESSIVE	PLURAL	PLURAL POSSESSIVE
friend	friend's home	friends	friends' homes
month	month's work	months	two months' work
dollar	dollar's worth	dollars	three dollars' worth
enemy	enemy's attack	enemies	enemies' attack
box	box's lid	boxes	boxes' lids
thief	thief's loot	thieves	thieves' loot
woman	woman's purse	women	women's purses
sheep	sheep's wool	sheep	sheep's wool
ox	ox's yoke	oxen	oxen's yoke

26c. Possessive personal pronouns do not require an apostrophe.

Possessive personal pronouns are

my, mine   our, ours
your, yours   their, theirs
his, her, hers, its

Caution: The possessive form of *who* is *whose*, not *who's* (meaning "who is"). Similarly, do not write *it's* (meaning "it is") for *its*, or *they're* (meaning "they are") for *their*.

My, your, her, its, our, and *their* are used before a noun. *Mine, yours, hers, ours,* and *theirs,* on the other hand, are never used before a noun; they are used as subjects, complements, or objects in sentences. *His* may be used in either way.

EXAMPLES   That is **my** book. That book is **mine.**
               Her answer was correct. **Hers** was the correct answer.
               Sandra has **your** hat. Sandra has a hat of **yours.**
               Janet has **our** tickets; Sally has **theirs.**
               Here is **his** report. Here is a report of **his.**

26d. Indefinite pronouns in the possessive case require an apostrophe and *s*.

EXAMPLES   everyone**'s** ideas   neither**'s** fault
               somebody**'s** pencil   another**'s** answer

● EXERCISE 4.   Number 1–10 on your paper. Choose the correct word in parentheses, and write it after the corresponding number.

1. The mistake is probably (ours, our's).
2. (Who's, Whose) dog is that?
3. (Yours, Your's) is more appropriate than mine.
4. Were (anyone's, anyones') overshoes left in the cloakroom yesterday?
5. That old car of (their's, theirs) has two flat tires.
6. The team was proud of (its, it's) good sportsmanship.
7. (Everybodys, Everybody's, Everybodys') suggestions will be considered.
8. Mrs. Parker, (who's, whose) husband is a senator, takes part in all the campaigns.
9. (Eithers, Either's, Eithers') costume may win the prize.
10. (Ones, One's, Ones') emotions should not take the place of careful judgment.

● REVIEW EXERCISE A.   Using the words listed below, make four columns on your paper. Head the columns *Singular, Singular Possessive, Plural,* and *Plural Possessive,* and write those forms of each word. Add a suitable noun to fol-

**26
c-d**

low each word in the possessive case. If you do not know how to spell the plural form of any of these words, use your dictionary.

1. cousin	3. salmon	5. guard	7. jockey	9. umpire
2. lady	4. doctor	6. milkman	8. dollar	10. he

● REVIEW EXERCISE B.   Some of the words in each of the following sentences are incorrect. After the number of each sentence, write correctly the incorrect words in the sentence.

EXAMPLE   1. Marie's mother is one of the judge's in the Art Museums' contest.

　　　　　1. *judges, Museum's*

1. Mrs. Macmillan, my best friends mother, belongs to the Womens' Literary Club.
2. Who's turn is it to read aloud Alfred Noye's poem "The Highwayman"?
3. Freds' father gave him ten dollar's worth of hockey equipment.
4. The firemens' actions held the damage in yesterdays' fire to a minimum.
5. Everybodys' suggestions seem better than our's.
6. The childrens' report cards were signed by all their teachers'.
7. In six month's time, those student's behavior has greatly improved.
8. Mr. Smiths' banquet honored his employees' wives.
9. One of Archimedes' achievements was the theory that explains a levers' mechanics.
10. My oldest sisters' twin daughters say that the new reading room is a favorite meeting place of their's.

26e. In compound words, names of organizations and business firms, and words showing joint possession, only the last word is possessive in form.

Compound words　　school **board's** decision
　　　　　　　　　nobody **else's** business
　　　　　　　　　mother-in-**law's** house
　　　　　　　　　secretary-**treasurer's** report

Organizations	American Medical Association's endorsement
Business firms	Wizard Freight Company's moving vans
Joint possession	Bess and Marie's room
	parents and teachers' aims
	Abbott, Clark, and North's address

EXCEPTION   When one of the words showing joint possession is a pronoun, both words must be made possessive in form: **Marie's and my room** [not *Marie and my room*].

◆ NOTE   Use the *of* phrase to avoid awkward possessive forms.

AWKWARD   the manager of the Greenville Appliance Center's daughter

BETTER   the daughter of the manager of the Greenville Appliance Center

AWKWARD   the Society for the Prevention of Cruelty to Animals' advertisement

BETTER   the advertisement of the Society for the Prevention of Cruelty to Animals

26f. When two or more persons possess something individually, each of their names is possessive in form.

EXAMPLES   **Mrs. Wheeler's** and **Mrs. Stuart's** children [the children of two different mothers]

Eddie's and **Gwen's** shoes [individual, not joint, possession]

● EXERCISE 5.   Revise the following phrases by using the possessive case.

EXAMPLE   1. the boat owned by Silas and Evan
        1. *Silas and Evan's boat*

1. the secret of Alison and Mary
2. the policy of Procter and Gamble
3. the feet of Allan and Jerome
4. letters written by the editor-in-chief
5. the secrets of everybody else

**26
e-f**

6. the cooking of his sister-in-law
7. the party given by Acme Life Insurance Company
8. the car belonging to Mr. Montgomery and the one owned by Mr. Osborn
9. the equipment shared by Leslie and me
10. the employees of the Kurtz Novelty Corporation

● REVIEW EXERCISE C. Copy and correctly punctuate the following phrases. If a phrase does not need an apostrophe, write *C* (for *correct*) after its number on your paper.

1. Vincents car keys
2. the keys to the car
3. a freshmans ideas
4. the firemens dance
5. an hours drive
6. forty cents worth
7. worth forty cents
8. letters from friends
9. several friends advice
10. Sandy and Erwins bicycle
11. a months salary
12. last weeks *Post*
13. six weeks vacation
14. Jessicas and Beryls posters
15. Randolph Companys sale
16. the boys at school
17. childrens wisdom
18. from the mouths of babes
19. in two years time
20. suggestions of theirs

● REVIEW EXERCISE D. From the following sentences, list in order on your paper all words requiring apostrophes, and insert the apostrophes. After each word, write the thing possessed or related. Number your list by sentences.

1. One Saturday afternoon, coming out of Millers Shoe Store on my way to Hardin and Crawfords Cafe, I saw two little boys selling the next mornings paper. 2. One boys name was Monroe, and the others name was Cleve.

3. "Read tomorrows news tonight!" yelled Monroe. 4. "Read all about Colorados blizzard, the Mayors operation, the high schools championship swimmers, and the Charity Funds progress!" 5. All the while, Cleve was silently watching the suns disappearance behind dark clouds overhead; he made no effort to catch a customers attention. 6. Monroes yelling, however, was not getting much better results than Cleves silence; neither boy had sold one cents worth of the Cloverville Publishing Companys newspapers. 7. In fact, everyone rushed past the two boys newsstand as though both deaf and blind.

8. Angry because of his partners attitude, Monroe scolded, "Cleve, are you going back to Mr. Longs office without selling any of the companys papers? 9. A mans job out here is to advertise each days news and to sell at least three dollars worth in an hours time." 10. Cleves face was still turned upward; he seemed indifferent to his friends anxiety.

11. Walking back and forth, Monroe waved his papers under cab drivers noses and pedestrians chins. 12. Trying to get the peoples interest, he bellowed, "Read about your citys crime wave! Robbery at Rich and Thompsons stationery store! Arson in Baileys hardware store! 13. Buy your childrens favorite comics—Dick Tracys adventures, Supermans victories, Dennis the Menaces crazy doings, Pogos wise words!" 14. The boys words sold only thirty cents worth of news; no one cared about "tomorrows news tonight."

15. In a few minutes time it began to rain, and Monroes hopes for good sales completely vanished. 16. But Cleves hopes were high! 17. Dashing forward, he had in an instant every passerbys full attention. 18. "Step right this way, folks!" he barked. "Umbrellas for sale! Buy yourselves fifteen cents worth of umbrella. 19. These eight sections of Sundays paper can cover your heads!" 20. In ten minutes time Monroe and Cleves newsstand had sold all its papers, and two very wet little boys were happily racing toward Mr. Longs office.

26g. Use an apostrophe to show where letters or numbers have been omitted in a contraction.

A contraction is a shortened form of a word or figure (*can't* for *cannot*, *'64* for *1964*) or of a group of words (*he'll* for *he will*, *let's* for *let us*, *o'clock* for *of the clock*). Contractions are used chiefly in conversation and in informal writing. The apostrophes in contractions indicate where letters have been left out.

EXAMPLES   He is not here.   He isn't here.
            You are right.   You're right.
            Marian is late.   Marian's late.
            She has gone home.   She's gone home.
            I had forgotten.   I'd forgotten.

26g

Ordinarily, the word *not* is shortened to *n't* and added to a verb without any change in the spelling of the verb:

is not	isn't	were not	weren't
are not	aren't	has not	hasn't
does not	doesn't	have not	haven't
do not	don't	had not	hadn't
did not	didn't	would not	wouldn't
was not	wasn't	should not	shouldn't

EXCEPTIONS   will not   won't
              cannot   can't

Remember: do not confuse contractions with possessive pronouns. Study the following lists.

CONTRACTIONS	POSSESSIVE PRONOUNS
Who's playing? [*Who is*]	**Whose** play is it?
It's growing. [*It is*]	Watch **its** growth.
You're the boss. [*You are*]	**Your** boss telephoned.
There's a fish. [*There is*]	That fish is **theirs.**
They're white cats. [*They are*]	**Their** cats are white.

● EXERCISE 6.   Write ten sentences of your own, using correctly each of the words listed below.

1. it's
2. you're
3. their
4. who's
5. your
6. there
7. whose
8. its
9. they're
10. theirs

● EXERCISE 7.   Number 1–10 on your paper. If a sentence below has a contraction without an apostrophe, copy the contraction and add a correctly placed apostrophe. If a sentence is correct as it stands, write *C* after the number.

1. Well be there on time.
2. Well, be there on time.
3. Didnt you know that?
4. "Schools out!" he yelled.
5. Schools were notified.
6. He lets us win.
7. Lets win this game.
8. Its four oclock.
9. Whos calling, please?
10. The gold rush was in 49.

● EXERCISE 8. Number 1–10 on your paper. Choose the correct word in parentheses, and write it after the corresponding number.

1. (*It's*, *Its*) is a contraction of *it is* or *it has*.
2. (It's, Its) been lost for months.
3. (*Who's*, *Whose*) is a contraction of *who is* or *who has*.
4. (Who's, Whose) that beautiful girl?
5. (Who's, Whose) bracelet is this?
6. (Your, You're) my best friend.
7. (There, Their, They're) not very happy.
8. Our speaker is Dr. Morgan, (whose, who's) just returned from France.
9. (Theirs, There's) no time like the present.
10. I think that (theirs, there's) is the best exhibit.

26h. Use the apostrophe and *s* to form the plural of letters, numbers, and signs, and of words referred to as words.

EXAMPLES The word *grammar* has two *r*'s, two *a*'s, and two *m*'s.

Grades on this test ran from the low 70's to the upper 90's.

Circling the *&*'s in my composition, the teacher said to spell out all *and*'s.

● EXERCISE 9. Number 1–10 on your paper. Correctly form the plural of each of the following italicized items:

1. learning his *ABC*
2. cross your *t*
3. no *if* about it
4. + and −
5. *p* and *q*
6. writing *Z*
7. to pronounce the *r*
8. the early *1960*
9. no *6* or *7* in the answer
10. his *oh* and *ah*

● REVIEW EXERCISE E. List in order the words that require apostrophes in the sentences below. Be sure that you insert the apostrophes exactly where omissions occur in contractions and after the *s* in possessives of plural words. Number your list by sentences.

26h

1. Im still working on todays assignment. 2. After two hours of hard work, Im not through revising it, although I have taken time to dot my *i*s and cross my *t*s. 3. Now Ill need to go back and strike out some *and*s and *so*s. 4. If Id followed my English teachers instruction, Id have added some action verbs to replace too many weak *were*s. 5. Its a job to write a composition on "My Familys Most Remarkable Character."

6. My papers purpose is to describe my mothers main characteristics. 7. To begin with, shes remarkably unselfish as she looks after her two boys needs and helps solve her husbands problems. 8. Its not easy at our home to keep everything going along smoothly, but shes always on the job. 9. If the boys fireworks on July 4 or their ball games in the backyard bring in dozens of complaints, shell manage somehow to restore the neighborhoods peace.

10. The other day a neighbor, whose blatant voice on the telephone would have frightened anybody elses parent, couldnt ruffle my mothers feathers a bit. 11. He stormed, "Those boys wont let a mans wife get even a few minutes rest!"

12. "Oh, Mr. Newton," Mother answered sweetly, "I hope you havent finished your lunch. Why, its barely twelve oclock. 13. Id just started over to take you a piece of coconut cake that Ive made according to your mother-in-laws favorite recipe. 14. Ill be over in five seconds time." 15. Naturally, this neighbors objections were quickly squelched by Mothers kindness.

16. An honor graduate of Central State College in the class of 47, Mothers known for her ability to concentrate. She also, however, has a one-track mind. 17. An incident that occurred in the summer of 63 will illustrate this part of my mothers character. 18. One day, after working all day at Brown and Kendalls Bakery, she had to drive to the airport within forty-five minutes. 19. Driving over loose gravel on the dark highway, Mother didnt think about anything except, "Its almost time for my nephews plane to arrive." 20. When the car hit a pile of gravel and suddenly swerved into a ditch, narrowly missing a telephone pole, Mothers only comment was this: "I didnt remember to put the steak out to thaw, and Im wondering whether or not my sisters boy will eat last nights meat loaf."

CHAPTER 27

Other Marks of Punctuation

Hyphens, Dashes, Parentheses

HYPHENS

As you know, some compound words are hyphenated (*attorney-general*); some are written as one word (*carport*); some are written as two or more words (*real estate*). As our language grows, new compound words enter the vocabulary, bringing writers the problem of choosing the correct form.

Whenever you need to know whether a word is hyphenated, consult your dictionary. In addition, learn to use the hyphen in the following situations.

27a. Use a hyphen to divide a word at the end of a line.

If you will look at the right margins of pages in this book, you will see that hyphens are often used to divide words at the ends of lines. *A word must always be divided between syllables.*

WRONG   He spoke, but it was obvious that he didn't recognize me.

RIGHT   He spoke, but it was obvious that he didn't recognize me.

27a

If you need to divide a word and are not sure about its syllables, look it up in your dictionary. Keep in mind these rules for syllable division:

1. Since words are divisible between syllables only, do not divide one-syllable words.

WRONG	Do you know how much that big tackle weighs?
RIGHT	Do you know how much that big tackle weighs?
RIGHT	Do you know how much that big tackle weighs?

2. You should try to avoid dividing capitalized words.

WRONG	Roger's uncle works at the Smithsonian Institution.
RIGHT	Roger's uncle works at the Smithsonian Institution.

3. If a word is already hyphenated, divide it *only* at a hyphen.

WRONG	Tonight I am going to meet my new brother-in-law.
RIGHT	Tonight I am going to meet my new brother-in-law.

4. Do not divide a word so that one letter stands alone.

WRONG	My dog hates to be left alone during the day.
RIGHT	My dog hates to be left alone during the day.

● EXERCISE 1.   Suppose that you are considering dividing the following words at the ends of lines. If necessary, check your dictionary for the proper syllabication. Then copy each word and use a hyphen to indicate where you would make the division. If a word should *not* be divided, write "carry forward" after the corresponding number on your paper.

EXAMPLES   1. monument
          1. *monu-ment (or mon-ument)*
          2. month
          2. *carry forward*

1. swimming	8. Indo-Chinese	15. hyphen
2. method	9. unhappy	16. strength
3. panorama	10. whose	17. cameo
4. special	11. questionnaire	18. traction
5. impartial	12. spectacular	19. galaxy
6. inside	13. Vera	20. oboe
7. French	14. cross-reference	

27b. Use a hyphen with compound numbers from twenty-one to ninety-nine and with fractions used as adjectives.

EXAMPLES   thirty-five students
a two-thirds majority [but *two thirds* of the votes]

27c. Use a hyphen with the prefixes *ex-*, *self-*, *all-*, and with the suffix *-elect*, and with all prefixes before a proper noun or proper adjective.

EXAMPLES   ex-champion   mid-September
self-confident   trans-Pacific
all-star   anti-Communist
President-elect   pre-Revolutionary

● EXERCISE 2. In the following sentences, ten hyphens are needed. List the words that should be hyphenated, correctly punctuated, on your paper.

1. The exstudents hoped that the proposal would pass by a two thirds majority.
2. About three fourths of the club members are under twenty one years of age.
3. The expresident told us about events that took place during the preRenaissance era.
4. An all American quarterback last year, Mac boasts of being a self made star.
5. December and January have thirty one days; but February has only twenty eight, except during leap year, when it has twenty nine.

27
b-c

DASHES

As you have learned, many words and phrases are used *parenthetically*. That is, they break into the main thought; they are explanations, qualifications, or just "side remarks." They do not affect the grammatical construction of the sentences in which they occur.

Most parenthetical elements are set off by commas (see page 513) or parentheses (see page 560). Sometimes, however, words or phrases or clauses used parenthetically may demand a stronger separation. In some such cases, you use a dash.

27d. Use a dash to indicate an abrupt break in thought.

EXAMPLES   Stephens—Mr. Stephens, I mean—was waiting for me in his office.

Jason Stowe—his nickname is "Peanuts"—has moved into my neighborhood.

"Then what—what shall I say?" Sara faltered.

"I hope—" Audrey began and then stopped.

● EXERCISE 3. Copy the following sentences (adapted from the work of professional writers who used the dash correctly and effectively) and insert dashes where they are appropriate.

1. "It it's not right," he stammered.
2. Suddenly and don't ask me how it happened the conviction came to me that he was right.
3. My sister's engagement this is supposed to be a secret will be announced Sunday.
4. The climate there winters sometimes last for eight months will be quite a change from Florida.
5. The valedictorian that is, the student having the highest average will receive a special award.

PARENTHESES

Parentheses are used to set off parenthetical elements that serve as explanations or qualifications. Since parentheses are *enclosing* marks, they are used in pairs.

27e. Use parentheses to enclose matter which is added to a sentence but is not considered of major importance.

EXAMPLES Next Monday night (of course, I'll see you before then) we will meet at the stadium.

During the Middle Ages (from about A.D. 500 to A.D. 1500), Moslems and Vikings invaded Europe.

Mrs. Clement Nelson (formerly Miss Valerie Kirk) was the guest of honor.

North Carolina's Senator Jordan (Democrat) led the debate on the proposal.

There are several poems by Walter de la Mare (1873–1956) in this book.

As you see from the examples above, the material enclosed in parentheses may range from a single word or number to a short sentence. In the first example, the sentence in parentheses is part of the main sentence. Sometimes an entire sentence, standing alone, can be placed in parentheses.

EXAMPLE Correct the spelling errors in these sentences. (Do not write in your book.)

Notice that the period for the enclosed sentence is placed inside the parentheses. Punctuation marks are used within parentheses when they belong with the parenthetical matter, as above. Do not, however, place a punctuation mark within parentheses if it belongs to the sentence as a whole.

EXAMPLES We plan to rehearse at least twenty hours (probably longer); moreover, we must know our parts before the first rehearsal.

In general, follow the two rules at the top of the next page when you are considering using parentheses.

27 d-e

1. Always be sure that any material enclosed in parentheses may be omitted without changing the basic meaning and construction of the sentence.

2. Commas, dashes, and parentheses are frequently interchangeable, especially for setting off incidental words or phrases. Commas are more common than dashes; dashes are more common than parentheses.

● EXERCISE 4. Decide where parentheses may be used in the following sentences (adapted from the works of professional writers who used parentheses). Copy the sentences, including the parentheses and punctuating the parenthetical elements correctly.

EXAMPLE 1. These three powers formed the Triple Entente which means "triple understanding."

  1. *These three powers formed the Triple Entente (which means "triple understanding").*

1. Bake the meat in a very hot oven 450° F. for about forty minutes.
2. For shallow containers, buy Oasis a spongelike, moisture-retaining block from a florist.
3. Around her neck she wore a shabby furpiece whether mink, muskrat, or alley cat I could not determine.
4. Having learned something do not eat old turtles I was now determined to explore the whole subject.
5. From Clement Moore's "'Twas the Night Before Christmas" which is a perennial favorite with young children to the second chapter of St. Luke which is for all ages, the poetry of Christmas is gay and rich in meaning.
6. He frets about the heavy expenses of being on the tour $15,000 a year.
7. A sperm whale the kind Moby Dick was grows to eighty feet.
8. The architect later he designed the Woolworth Tower in New York became dissatisfied and threatened to sue.
9. I am only against the phony or in a kinder term the irrational liberal.
10. The game State vs. Eastern was nothing but an endless series of ineffectual charges at midfield.

● REVIEW EXERCISE A. Copy the following sentences, and punctuate them by using hyphens, dashes, or parentheses. (Do not add commas in this exercise.) When you have a choice between dashes and parentheses, be prepared to give a reason for the choice you make.

EXAMPLE   1. In my history book there are several maps see page 716, for example that clearly show the proximity of Cuba to the United States.

          1. *In my history book there are several maps (see page 716, for example) that clearly show the proximity of Cuba to the United States.*

1. During the next ten years 1954–1964 my father worked for Throckmorton Brothers, Inc.

2. Senator Varner Republican, New York voted against the proposal; nevertheless, it passed by the required two thirds majority.

3. In March of 1963, the best friend of the wheat growers rain paid no visits to the all important farmlands of the Middle West.

4. The ex president of the club he always seemed too self confident and all knowing was fond of quoting Shakespeare in any situation.

5. These symptoms dizziness, headaches, fever often indicate the beginning of an infectious disease.

6. One of my New Year's resolutions to do my homework on time has been difficult to keep.

7. Twenty seven members of the Glee Club lucky people! have been invited to sing at the Governor's Ball.

8. Stephen either Stephen or his twin Stewart will doubtless make the All State team this year.

9. I am definitely going to the beach probably in mid July and I can hardly wait!

10. In "The Secret Sharer," Joseph Conrad 1857–1924 links Leggatt to Cain with the phrase "a fugitive and a vagabond." See Genesis 4:14.

● REVIEW EXERCISE B. This exercise covers capitalization and all marks of punctuation (Chapters 22–27). Copy and correctly punctuate the following sentences, using capitals where necessary. You may divide sentences if you wish.

1. Our forefathers men like washington jefferson and lincoln fought for these rights life liberty and the pursuit of happiness

2. Rod evans sailing over the last hurdle easily won the race roger evans his brother came in a slow second

3. Hurrah shouted Winston I knew youd make it Rod When are you heading for the olympics your father said last night my son rod is going to be all american this year

4. Rosemary is knitting her first sweater a pink soft wool one with no sleeves whatever according to directions in the May 65 issue of seventeen magazine

5. Well he does I believe still live at 268 fairway lane des moines iowa   50318

6. Fathers day comes on the third sunday in june mothers day comes on the second sunday in may

7. George dreams of working at the brookhaven national laboratory at upton new york

8. Ive carefully studied chapter 23 end marks and commas in our textbook english grammar and composition as well as the other chapters on punctuation therefore I use commas for appositives and for series quotation marks to enclose titles of chapters and semicolons to separate main clauses not joined by and but or nor for or yet

9. Jimson weed was named after jamestown virginia and wisteria was named after caspar wistar 1696–1752 an anatomist

10. A devilfish doesnt have a forked tail and a sand dollar wont buy a chocolate soda or a ticket to the play junior miss but an electric eel can shock you

Spelling

Improving Your Spelling

No one is a born speller. Everybody must work to learn to spell words correctly. If you really want to improve your spelling, you can do so by making a sustained effort. No one else can do this for you. The suggestions and rules in this chapter are designed to help you help yourself to learn to spell better.

GOOD SPELLING HABITS

As you read the italicized rules below, keep in mind that these are not merely rules to be learned now and forgotten later. They are suggestions for forming good habits that will help you spell words now and in the future, in school and out of school.

1. Keep a list of your spelling errors.

Whenever you misspell a word, find out immediately what the correct spelling is. Then list the word on a special page in your notebook. Although this does take time, it will not in the long run take as much time as you would use later trying to learn the same word after you had misspelled it for years.

One way to record your words is to prepare a spelling page with four columns. In the first column, correctly spell the word you missed. (Never enter a misspelled word on your spelling page.) In the second column, write the word again, this time divided into syllables and accented. In the third column, write the word once more, circling the spot that gives you trouble. In the fourth column, give the reason for your mistake, or set down any comment that will help you to learn the word.

EXAMPLE

probably	prob′a·bly	probably	Pronounce correctly.
usually	u′su·al·ly	usually	*usual* + *ly* (Study rule 28d.)
tragedy	trag′e·dy	tragedy	Keep *g* and *d* straight; *tragedy* has *raged* in it.

2. Use the dictionary as a spelling aid.

In order to keep an accurate word list (the only kind of any value), you will need to look up your misspelled words in the dictionary. Don't guess about the correct spelling. (You have already guessed and missed; another guess may lead to a further distortion of it. Play safe; use your dictionary.) The very experience of looking up the word helps you to fix it in your mind so that you will remember it longer.

3. Learn to spell by syllables.

A syllable is a word part which can be pronounced by itself. For instance, the word *thor′ough* has two syllables; the word *sep′a·rate* has three syllables; the word *par·tic′-u·lar* has four syllables.

When you divide a long word into its syllables, you make a number of shorter parts out of it. Since short words are easy to spell, you make spelling easier. The word *superintendent*, for example, is a long word that may prove hard to spell unless you divide it into syllables. Then it becomes much easier: *su·per·in·ten·dent*.

● EXERCISE 1. Look up the following words in your dictionary, and divide each one into syllables. Pronounce each syllable correctly, and learn to spell the word by syllables. Be prepared to make a perfect score on a spelling test on these words.

1. representative
2. fascinate
3. candidate
4. temperature
5. apparent
6. similar
7. benefit
8. definition
9. acquaintance
10. awkward

4. Avoid mispronunciations that lead to spelling errors.

Since you often spell words according to the way you pronounce them, mispronunciation causes misspelling. For instance, if you say *mis·chie′vi·ous* instead of *mis′chie·vous*, you will spell the word incorrectly by adding an extra syllable.

● EXERCISE 2. *Oral Drill.* After carefully studying the correct pronunciations in parentheses below, read each word aloud three times, stressing the correct pronunciation of the italicized letters. Be prepared to spell these words from dictation.

1. at*h*lete (ath′lēt)
2. chil*dren* (chil′drən)
3. drow*ned* (dround)
4. *es*cape (ə·scāp′, e·scāp′)
5. every*body* (ev′rē·bod′ē)
6. iden*t*ity (ī·den′tə·tē)
7. in*tro*duce (in′trə·do͞os′, –dyo͞os′)
8. j*u*st (just)
9. lib*ra*ry (li′brer·ē, –brə·rē)
10. ligh*tn*ing (līt′ning)
11. p*er*haps (pər·haps′)
12. p*re*fer (pri·fûr′)
13. pro*ba*bly (prob′ə·blē)
14. quiet (kwī′ət)
15. rec*o*gnize (rek′əg·nīz)
16. s*ur*prise (sər·prīz′)
17. tha*n* (t̶han)
18. the*n* (t̶hen)
19. um*br*ella (um·brel′ə)
20. us*ual*ly (yo͞o′zho͞o·əl·ē)

5. Revise your papers to avoid careless spelling errors.

Although rereading takes only a few minutes, it makes a great difference in the correctness of your work. As you find and revise your spelling errors, be sure to eliminate all botchy handwriting. When you carelessly dot closed *e*'s, make your *o*'s look like *a*'s and your *g*'s like *q*'s, or hurriedly write over letters, you will make twice as many spelling errors as you would if you were more careful about your handwriting. Remember, too, that careless mistakes in handwriting can distort your meaning. For instance, an un-dotted *i* looks like an *e*, and an uncrossed *t* may be inter-preted as an *l*. There is a big difference between the mean-ing of *foot* and *fool*, for example.

6. *To master the spelling of a word, pronounce it, study it, and write it.*

When you are trying to learn how to spell a word, first *pronounce the word*, noting its syllables. As you know, think-ing of a word syllable by syllable makes the spelling easier.

Second, *study the word*, noticing especially any letters which might make the spelling hard. Notice, for example, that *doctor* has two *o*'s, that *where* has *here* in it, and that *across* has only one *c*, being composed of two little words: *a + cross*.

Third, *write the word*. Spelling is of use only in writing. The movement of your hand in making the letters will help to fix the spelling in your mind.

● EXERCISE 3.   To gain practice in looking at and in writ-ing commonly misspelled words, copy each of the following words; carefully observe the italicized silent letters as you write. Then have a friend dictate the words to you (or your teacher may wish to do this in class).

1. ans*w*er	9. mor*t*gage	17. me*a*nt
2. a*w*kward	10. condem*n*	18. *aisle*
3. *w*hole	11. col*um*n	19. toni*gh*t
4. to*w*ard	12. r*h*ythm	20. disciplin*e*
5. *k*no*w*, *k*new	13. su*b*tle	21. sur*e*ly
6. *k*no*w*ledge	14. use*d* to	22. tho*ugh*
7. writ*t*en	15. befor*e*	23. thro*ugh*
8. of*t*en	16. inste*a*d	24. nin*e*ty

7. *Learn lists of commonly misspelled words.*

Most spelling errors made by students are made in rela-tively few frequently written words. Lists of such words appear on pages 589–92.

● Exercise 4.   If you miss any of the little words in the following list, you will make a serious error in spelling. Although many of these words may look easy to you, study each one carefully. If you misspell any word, put it on your spelling list.

across	color	hoping	speak
again	coming	laid	speech
all right	country	later	straight
almost	dear	likely	surely
always	doesn't	making	tear
among	eager	many	thing
any	early	minute	think
began	February	none	through
belief	forty	off	tired
bigger	friend	once	together
built	grammar	paid	truly
business	guess	raise	Tuesday
busy	half	really	very
buy	having	safety	wear
can't	heard	shoes	Wednesday

8. Learn to spell by association.

Make any kind of association that will help you to remember a difficult word. For example, the word *earnest* has two words in it, *ear* and *nest; delivery* has *liver.* You can link rhyming words, putting an easy word with a hard one: *ear, hear; truly, unruly; loose, noose.*

● Exercise 5.   Find the words within words in order to fix in your memory the correct spelling.

EXAMPLE   1. laboratory
            1. *Laboratory has both labor and rat.*

1. bulletin	5. opportunity	9. attacked	13. handkerchief
2. ninety	6. courteous	10. attention	14. apologize
3. meant	7. explanation	11. excellent	15. permanent
4. copies	8. immediately	12. apparent	16. conscience

SPELLING RULES

Although most spelling is learned by memorizing words, you can "figure out" the correct spelling of many words after you have mastered the rules given on the following pages.

ie and ei

28a. Write *ie* when the sound is long *e*, except after *c*.

EXAMPLES	achieve	deceit	receive
	believe	field	relief
	brief	grief	shield
	ceiling	niece	thief
	chief	piece	yield

EXCEPTIONS   either, leisure, neither, seize, weird

Write *ei* when the sound is not long *e*, especially when the sound is long *a*.

EXAMPLES	neighbor	counterfeit
	rein	foreign
	reign	forfeit
	veil	height
	weigh	heir

EXCEPTIONS   friend, mischief, kerchief

● EXERCISE 6.   Write the following words, supplying the missing letters (*e* and *i*) in the correct order. In class, be prepared to explain how the rule applies to each word. When you have determined the correct answers, memorize the list.

1. f...ld	6. bel...ve	11. w...ght	16. ...ther
2. p...ce	7. rec...ve	12. rel...f	17. n...ther
3. f...nd	8. conc...ve	13. conc...t	18. dec...ve
4. ch...f	9. fr...ght	14. ach...ve	19. s...ze
5. c...ling	10. h...ght	15. pr...st	20. r...gn

–cede, –ceed, and –sede

28b. **Only one English word ends in *–sede*— *supersede*; only three words end in *–ceed*—*exceed*, *proceed*, and *succeed*; all other words of similar sound end in *–cede*.**

EXAMPLES precede recede secede
     intercede concede accede

Adding Prefixes and Suffixes

A *prefix* is one or more letters or syllables added to the beginning of a word to change its meaning.

28c. **When a prefix is added to a word, the spelling of the word itself remains the same.**

Take, for example, the word *do*. By adding the prefixes *un–* or *over–*, you have the words *undo* and *overdo*. The spelling of the word *do* does not change. Study the following examples:

il + literate = illiterate   dis + approve = disapprove
in + numerable = innumerable mis + step = misstep
im + mortal = immortal   re + organize = reorganize
un + certain = uncertain   over + rule = overrule

A *suffix* is one or more letters or syllables added to the end of a word to change its meaning.

28d. **When the suffixes *–ness* and *–ly* are added to a word, the spelling of the word itself is not changed.**

EXAMPLES

sure + ly = surely useful + ness = usefulness
real + ly = really   polite + ness = politeness
usual + ly = usually stubborn + ness = stubbornness

EXCEPTIONS Words ending in *y* usually change the *y* to *i* before *–ness* and *–ly:* empty—emptiness; easy—easily.

**28
a-d**

One-syllable adjectives ending in *y*, however, generally follow rule 28d: *dry—dryness; sly—slyly*.

True and *due* drop the final *e* before *–ly: truly, duly*.

● Exercise 7. Number 1–20 on your paper. Correctly spell each word below as you add the prefix or suffix indicated.

1. un + necessary	11. occasional + ly
2. re + commend	12. keen + ness
3. plain + ness	13. cleanly + ness
4. actual + ly	14. mis + spell
5. il + legal	15. over + run
6. im + mature	16. mean + ness
7. real + ly	17. practical + ly
8. sure + ly	18. dis + appearance
9. dis + appear	19. in + adequate
10. dis + solve	20. dis + ease

● Exercise 8. Number 1–10 on your paper. First, correctly add the suffix *–ly* to these words: *hungry, true, necessary, noisy, sleepy*. Then add the suffix *–ness* to *tardy, happy, saucy, flighty, heavy*.

28e. Drop the final *e* before a suffix beginning with a vowel.

EXAMPLES

hope + ing = hoping	fame + ous = famous
care + ing = caring	imagine + ary = imaginary
share + ing = sharing	admire + ation = admiration
love + able = lovable	force + ible = forcible

EXCEPTIONS 1. mile + age = mileage

2. The final *e* is kept in some words to avoid confusion with other words.

    dyeing and *dying, singeing* and *singing*

3. The final *e* is kept in words ending in *ce* or *ge* to retain the soft sound.

    peaceable, noticeable, advantageous

● EXERCISE 9. Write correctly the words formed as indicated.

1. become + ing
2. guide + ance
3. continue + ous
4. surprise + ed
5. shine + ing

6. ridicule + ous
7. please + ant
8. believe + ing
9. courage + ous
10. determine + ation

28f. Keep the final *e* before a suffix beginning with a consonant.

EXAMPLES

nine + ty = ninety
hope + ful = hopeful
care + less = careless

entire + ly = entirely
awe + some = awesome
pave + ment = pavement

EXCEPTIONS

due + ly = duly
true + ly = truly
whole + ly = wholly
acknowledge + ment
  = acknowledgment

nine + th = ninth
awe + ful = awful
argue + ment = argument
judge + ment = judgment

● EXERCISE 10. Apply rules 28e and 28f as you add each designated suffix, and decide whether or not to keep or drop the final *e*. (In this exercise there are no exceptions to the rules.)

1. announce + ment
2. use + age
3. treasure + er
4. imagine + ary
5. definite + ly
6. care + ful
7. sincere + ly
8. write + ing
9. virtue + ous
10. desire + able

11. white + ness
12. revere + ent
13. sure + ly
14. hope + less
15. arrange + ment
16. have + ing
17. complete + ly
18. safe + ty
19. lose + ing
20. nine + ty

**28
e-f**

28g. With words ending in *y* preceded by a consonant, change the *y* to *i* before any suffix not beginning with *i*.

EXAMPLES

fifty + eth = fiftieth	beautify + ing = beautifying
lazy + ness = laziness	terrify + ing = terrifying
worry + ed = worried	worry + ing = worrying
mystery + ous = mysterious	verify + ing = verifying
hasty + ly = hastily	imply + ing = implying

EXCEPTIONS　(1) some one-syllable words:

shy + ness = shyness
spry + ly = spryly
sky + ward = skyward

(2) *lady* and *baby* with suffixes: *ladylike, ladyship; babyhood*

Observe that words ending in *y* preceded by a vowel usually do not change their spelling before a suffix:

joy + ful = joyful
array + ed = arrayed
boy + hood = boyhood

● EXERCISE 11.　Apply rule 28g as you add each designated suffix and decide whether or not to change the final *y* to *i*. (In this exercise, there are no exceptions to the rule.)

1. extraordinary + ly
2. gratify + ing
3. modify + cation
4. try + ing
5. ally + ance
6. cry + ing
7. necessary + ly
8. fortify + cation
9. deny + al
10. carry + ed
11. glorify + ed
12. secretary + al
13. purify + ing
14. apply + cation
15. defy + ant
16. likely + hood
17. satisfy + ed
18. supply + er
19. rely + able
20. ply + ant
21. amplify + er
22. certify + cate
23. comply + ing
24. merry + ment
25. multiply + cation

28h. Double the final consonant before a suffix that begins with a vowel if both of the following conditions exist:

(1) the word has only one syllable or is accented on the last syllable

(2) the word ends in a single consonant preceded by a single vowel.

EXAMPLES

drop + ing = dropping   occur + ence = occurrence
plan + ed = planned   propel + er = propeller
sit + ing = sitting   control + ed = controlled

If both of these conditions do not exist, the final consonant is not doubled before a suffix:

jump + ed = jumped
appear + ance = appearance
tunnel + ing = tunneling
travel + er = traveler

● EXERCISE 12. Apply rule 28h as you add each designated suffix.

1. run + er
2. defer + ed
3. swim + ing
4. begin + er
5. expel + ed
6. control + ed
7. hot + est
8. flirt + ing
9. permit + ed
10. compel + ing
11. expect + ation
12. open + ing
13. inform + ed
14. number + ing
15. hit + er
16. travel + ing
17. riot + ous
18. exist + ence
19. color + ation
20. stop + age

● REVIEW EXERCISE A. All of the following words are spelled correctly, according to rule. Number 1–20 on your paper. After the appropriate number, write the number of the rule that applies to the correctly spelled word.

28
g-h

EXAMPLE 1. *niece 28 A*

1. receive	8. dissatisfy	15. unnecessary
2. concede	9. forlornness	16. improvement
3. hoping	10. tiresome	17. inquiring
4. immortal	11. forfeit	18. capitalization
5. eight	12. definitely	19. forbidden
6. defenseless	13. serenity	20. merciless
7. thief	14. patrolled	

The Plural of Nouns

Changing a singular noun to a plural noun sometimes presents problems. The rules on the following pages will help you solve these problems.

28i. Observe the rules for spelling the plural of nouns.

(1) The regular way to form the plural of a noun is to add an s.

SINGULAR	boat	nickel	teacher	house
PLURAL	boats	nickels	teachers	houses

(2) The plural of nouns ending in s, x, z, ch, or sh is formed by adding es.

The addition of *es* to the words below makes them pronounceable because of the extra syllable *es* creates.

SINGULAR	glass	box	waltz	beach	dish	Mr. Jones
PLURAL	glasses	boxes	waltzes	beaches	dishes	the Joneses

● EXERCISE 13. Correctly write the plural of each of the following words:

1. guess	6. cafeteria
2. ax	7. watch
3. tongue	8. branch
4. wall	9. speech
5. dollar	10. amateur

(3) The plural of nouns ending in *y* preceded by a *consonant* is formed by changing the *y* to *i* and adding *es*.

SINGULAR   sky   army   story   baby
PLURAL   skies   armies   stories   babies
EXCEPTION   Plurals of proper nouns: *the Hardys, the Carys.*

(4) The plural of nouns ending in *y* preceded by a *vowel* is formed by adding an *s*.

SINGULAR   delay   key   boy   guy
PLURAL   delays   keys   boys   guys

● EXERCISE 14.   Write the plural of the following words:

1. lady   5. butterfly   8. quantity
2. relay   6. ally   9. day
3. donkey   7. lullaby   10. jalopy
4. copy

(5) The plural of some nouns ending in *f* or *fe* is formed by changing the *f* to *v* and adding *s* or *es*.

As you study the formation of the plurals in the following words, notice the way the words are pronounced.

SINGULAR   roof   belief   leaf   wife   calf
PLURAL   roofs   beliefs   leaves   wives   calves

● EXERCISE 15.   Write the plural of each of these words:

1. thief   4. knife
2. chef   5. giraffe
3. life

(6) The plural of nouns ending in *o* preceded by a vowel is formed by adding *s*; the plural of nouns ending in *o* preceded by a consonant is formed by adding *es*.

SINGULAR   radio   rodeo   echo   hero   tomato   Negro
PLURAL   radios   rodeos   echoes   heroes   tomatoes   Negroes

28
i

EXCEPTIONS   Nouns ending in *o* preceded by a consonant and *referring to music* form the plural by adding *s*.

SINGULAR   alto   solo   piano
PLURAL   altos   solos   pianos

● EXERCISE 16.   Write the plurals of these nouns:

1. shampoo   4. hobo
2. soprano   5. veto
3. torpedo

(7) The plural of a few nouns is formed in irregular ways.

SINGULAR   foot   man   ox   mouse   child   tooth
PLURAL   feet   men   oxen   mice   children   teeth

(8) The plural of compound nouns written as one word is formed by adding *s* or *es*.

SINGULAR   spoonful   leftover   smashup   icebox   spyglass
PLURAL   spoonfuls   leftovers   smashups   iceboxes   spyglasses

(9) The plural of compound nouns consisting of a noun plus a modifier is formed by making the noun plural.

SINGULAR   brother-in-law   attorney at law   notary public
PLURAL   brothers-in-law   attorneys at law   notaries public

(10) Some nouns are the same in the singular and the plural.

SINGULAR AND PLURAL   deer, trout, Japanese, sheep

● EXERCISE 17.   Write the plural form of the following words:

1. woman   6. armful
2. ox   7. mouse
3. foot   8. man-of-war
4. son-in-law   9. deer
5. maid of honor   10. Chinese

(11) The plural of some foreign words is formed as in the original language.

SINGULAR	crisis	datum	analysis	alumnus
PLURAL	crises	data	analyses	alumni

◆ NOTE   A few words taken from a foreign language have an alternate plural form, regularly formed as in English: *appendix: appendices* or *appendixes*. Sometimes the English plural is the preferred one; the plural of *formula* is preferably *formulas*, not *formulae*. Consult your dictionary to determine the preferred spelling of the plural of such words.

(12) The plural of numbers, letters, signs, and words considered as words is formed by adding an apostrophe and *s*.

EXAMPLES   Put the *g*'s and the *6*'s in the second column.
Change the *&*'s to *and*'s.

● REVIEW EXERCISE B.   Try to make a perfect score on this exercise, which covers the rules for forming the plural of nouns. Number your paper 1–30, and write the plural form of each of the following nouns. After each one, write the number of the subrule that applies.

1. shelf
2. paper
3. gas
4. joy
5. echo
6. radio
7. cuff
8. elf
9. solo
10. woman
11. trout
12. hero
13. library
14. church
15. *A*
16. lieutenant colonel
17. handful
18. handkerchief
19. Negro
20. index
21. *13*
22. ox
23. maid of honor
24. Chinese
25. armful
26. roof
27. trio
28. history
29. man-of-war
30. potato

WORDS OFTEN CONFUSED

If you will master both the meaning and the spelling of the words in the lists on the following pages, you can eliminate many errors in your compositions. Study only a few at a time, and really master them.

advice	[noun] *counsel* He gave me some excellent *advice*.
advise	[verb] *to give advice* He *advised* me to finish high school.
all ready	[pronoun plus adjective] *everyone ready* When he arrived, we were *all ready* to go.
already	[adverb] *previously* Henry has *already* gone.
affect	[verb] *to influence* What he said did not *affect* my final decision.
effect	[verb] *to accomplish;* [noun] *consequence* or *result* The governor has *effected* many changes during his administration. The *effect* of these changes has been most beneficial.
all right	[This is the only acceptable spelling. Although it is in the dictionary, the spelling *alright* has not yet come into good usage.]
all together	*everyone in the same place* When we were *all together*, we opened the gifts.
altogether	*entirely* He was *altogether* wrong.
brake	*stopping device* The *brakes* on Dad's car are good.
break	*shatter, sever* A last straw *breaks* a camel's back.

capital   [noun] *city* or *money used by business;* [adjective]
               punishable by death or *of major importance* or
               excellent
               Raleigh is the *capital* of North Carolina.
               Mr. Dawson will need more *capital* to modernize
               his equipment.
               Treason is a *capital* crime.
               He made a *capital* error in preparing the report.
               This is a *capital* detective story.

capitol   [noun] *building; statehouse*
               In Raleigh, the *capitol* is on Fayetteville Street.

choose   [used for present and future tense] *select*
               You may *choose* your own partner.

chose   [past tense—rhymes with *hose*]
               Yesterday she voluntarily *chose* to take a nap
               after lunch.

coarse   *rough, crude*
               The *coarse* material is very durable.
               He never uses *coarse* language.

course   *path of action or progress; unit of study; track or*
               way; also used with *of* to mean *as was to be*
               expected
               The airplane lost its *course* in the storm.
               I am taking a *course* in algebra.
               He is at the golf *course.*
               Of *course,* you have met Elmer.

● EXERCISE 18.   Number your paper 1–20. Write after the
proper number the correct one of the words given in parentheses in the sentences below.

1. Betty has (all ready, already) handed in her paper.
2. (All right, Alright), I'll mow the lawn now.
3. What was the coach's (advice, advise) to you players at half
   time?
4. Are you taking a (coarse, course) in sewing?

5. This poison is supposed to have a deadly (affect, effect).
6. Last night we (choose, chose) our leader.
7. He did not, of (coarse, course), remember me.
8. The mechanic adjusted the (brakes, breaks).
9. You should have known that Sacramento, not Los Angeles, is the (capital, capitol) of California.
10. You can (choose, chose) your own music.
11. They were (all together, altogether) at Thanksgiving.
12. The newspaper strike seriously (affected, effected) sales in department stores.
13. I'm sure that the baby will be (all right, alright).
14. His (coarse, course) manners offended everyone.
15. A fragile piece of china (brakes, breaks) easily.
16. The beautiful (capital, capitol) of our state is built of limestone and marble.
17. May we (choose, chose) between a dance and a picnic?
18. He was not (all together, altogether) satisfied.
19. Are they (all ready, already) to go now?
20. In *Hamlet*, Polonius gives the following (advice, advise) to his son Laertes: "This above all: to thine own self be true."

● EXERCISE 19.   Write twenty original sentences correctly using the seventeen words you have just studied. Use each word at least once.

complement   *something that completes or makes perfect; to complete or make perfect*

  Linking verbs are followed by subject *complements*.

  The office now has a full *complement* of personnel.

  The yellow rug *complemented* the warm-looking room.

compliment   *a remark that says something flattering about a person; to say something flattering*

  I was not impressed by his flowery *compliments*.

  I must *compliment* you on that lovely flower arrangement.

consul	*the representative of a foreign country* The French *consul* was guest of honor at the banquet.
council	*a group called together to accomplish a job* The city *council* will debate the proposed bond issue tonight.
councilor	*a member of a council* At the council meeting Father plans to introduce Dr. Watkins, the new *councilor*.
counsel	*advice; the giving of advice* I am deeply grateful for your *counsel*.
counselor	*one who gives advice* I do not think I am qualified to act as your *counselor*.

des'ert	*a dry region* Be sure to fill the gas tank before you start across the *desert*.
desert'	*to leave* He *deserted* his comrades.
dessert'	*the final course of a meal* What do you plan to have for *dessert?*

● EXERCISE 20. Number your paper 1–10, and write the correct one of the words in parentheses after the appropriate number.

1. Congress appropriated funds for a new irrigation project in the (desert, dessert).
2. The Security (Consul, Council, Counsel) of the United Nations consists of eleven members.
3. The new hat will effectively (complement, compliment) my fall outfit.
4. Besides teaching English, Miss Patton also serves as (councilor, counselor) of the Y-Teens.
5. With my brother away at college, our house seems (deserted, desserted).

6. You should pay more attention to your father's (consul, council, counsel).

7. I passed on your charming (complement, compliment) to Isabel.

8. At their meeting, all the members of the city (council, counsel) agreed that the tax proposal was unworkable.

9. Baked Alaska is my favorite (desert, dessert).

10. In the opera *Madame Butterfly*, Sharpless is the American (consul, counsel) in Japan.

● EXERCISE 21.   Write ten original sentences, each using one of the words you have just studied.

---

formally   *properly, according to strict rules*
Should he be *formally* introduced?

formerly   *previously, in the past*
The new consul was *formerly* a member of Congress.

---

hear   *to receive sounds through the ears*
Did you *hear* the President's speech?

here   *this place*
Come *here*, Rover.

---

its   [possessive of *it*]
The bird stopped *its* singing.

it's   *it is*
It's an easy problem.

---

lead   [present tense, pronounced lēd] *to go first*
I'll *lead* the way.

led   [past tense of *lead*]
Last week he *led* us to victory.

lead   [pronounced led] *a heavy metal;* also *graphite* in a pencil
The *lead* on my line was too heavy for the cork.

loose	[rhymes with *noose*] *free, not close together*
	The string on the package is too *loose*.
	The car swerved out of the *loose* gravel.
lose	[pronounced lo͞oz] *to suffer loss*
	Do not *lose* our lunch money.

moral	having to do with *good* or *right;* also *a lesson of conduct*
	It is a *moral* question.
	These fables all have a *moral*.
morale	*mental condition, spirit*
	The *morale* of the citizens is low.

passed	[verb, past tense of *pass*]
	He *passed* us in the corridor.
past	[noun or adjective or preposition]
	I didn't inquire about his *past*.
	Her *past* experience got her the job.
	I went *past* the house.

peace	opposite of *strife*
	After the long war, *peace* was welcome.
piece	*a part of something*
	Do you care for a *piece* of pie?

● EXERCISE 22. Number your paper 1–20. Write after the proper number the correct one of the words given in parentheses in the sentences below.

1. Sitting in the back row, we could hardly (here, hear) the speaker.
2. The class is proud of (its, it's) progress.
3. The commander praised the division's high (morale, moral).
4. It is already (passed, past) nine o'clock.
5. Facing defeat, he did not (lose, loose) courage.
6. The searchers hoped that the dog would (lead, led) them to the lost boy.
7. Mother told us to stay (hear, here).

8. The hard-driving fullback (led, lead) the team to victory.
9. I have more interest in my work than I (formally, formerly) had.
10. Molly (passed, past) all her examinations.
11. We couldn't decide what the (moral, morale) of the story was.
12. I like a pencil that has soft (led, lead).
13. Everyone was (formally, formerly) dressed at the dance.
14. (It's, Its) too late to catch the early train.
15. There Ben found true (peace, piece) of mind.
16. June shouted, "I'll give you a (peace, piece) of my mind!"
17. When my shoelace came (lose, loose), I tripped and fell.
18. Mrs. Hogan just (past, passed) me in the hall.
19. This (peace, piece) of chicken is bony.
20. Clara never seems to (lose, loose) her temper.

● EXERCISE 23. Write twenty original sentences correctly using the words you have just studied. Use each word at least once.

---

plain	*not fancy;* also *a flat area of land;* also *clear* Nancy wears very *plain* clothes. The storm lashed the western *plains.* He made his point of view *plain.*
plane	*a flat surface, a level;* also *a tool;* also *an airplane* Are you taking *plane* geometry? The debate was conducted on a high *plane.* Martin made the wood smooth by using a *plane.* The *plane* arrived at the airport on time.

---

principal	*head of a school;* also, as an adjective, *main* or *most important* Ted had a long talk with the *principal.* Winning is not our *principal* goal.
principle	*a rule of conduct;* also *a law* or *a main fact* We live by certain *principles.* They don't know the first *principles* of physics.

quiet	*silent, still* The library should be a *quiet* place.
quite	*to a great extent or degree; completely* My little brother is *quite* clever for his age. I *quite* understand your reasons for not attending.

shone	[past tense of *shine*] The sun *shone* this morning.
shown	*revealed* Bob has not *shown* me his scrapbook.

stationary	*in a fixed position* The chairs were not *stationary*.
stationery	*writing paper* Use white *stationery* for business letters.

than	[a conjunction, used for comparisons] Jimmy enjoys swimming more *than* golfing.
then	[an adverb or conjunction indicating *at that time* or *next*] I polished my shoes; *then* I combed my hair. Did you know Barbara *then?*

their	[possessive of *they*] The boys gave *their* opinions.
there	*a place* [also used to begin a sentence (see page 43)] I'll be *there* on time. *There* aren't any cookies left.
they're	*they are* *They're* at the station now.

● EXERCISE 24.   Number your paper 1–20. Write the correct one of the words in parentheses after the corresponding number.

1. Please be as (quiet, quite) as possible in the corridors.
2. Mr. Carver is the (principal, principle) of our school.
3. The last reel of the movie was not (shone, shown).
4. The bleachers didn't seem very (stationary, stationery).

5. He said that not paying debts is against his (principals, principles).
6. Dr. Palmer was (quiet, quite) pleased with the results of the experiment.
7. That night the big moon (shone, shown) brightly.
8. Did you buy a box of blue (stationary, stationery)?
9. (Than, Then) he erased the board and started over.
10. Joe knows how to use a (plain, plane) in his shop.
11. Your (principal, principle) problem is learning to spell.
12. What did you do (than, then)?
13. A lone cowboy was crossing the (plain, plane).
14. Do you still live (their, they're, there)?
15. Alice has mastered the basic (principals, principles) of grammar.
16. Do you drink your coffee (plain, plane) or with cream and sugar?
17. I can work much faster (than, then) he can.
18. All of the freshmen invited (their, there, they're) parents to the party.
19. (Their, There, They're) coming here tomorrow.
20. (Their, There) are two *s*'s in *omission* and in *possible*.
21. No matter what game you are playing, do not let your opponent know your (principal, principle) objectives.
22. Two years ago my father bought a (stationary, stationery) store.
23. This summer my mother has decided that I am going to improve myself rather (than, then) enjoy myself.
24. (Their, There, They're) books are still here.
25. As we landed, we saw the wide, green (plain, plane) below.

● EXERCISE 25.   Write twenty original sentences correctly using the words you have just studied. Use each word at least once.

---

threw	*hurled*
	Freddy *threw* three balls.
through	*in at one side and out at the opposite side*
	The fire truck raced *through* the heavy traffic.

to	[a preposition; also part of the infinitive form of a verb] She told us *to clean* the windows. [infinitive] She has gone *to the store.* [prepositional phrase]
too	[adverb] *also; more than enough* I like polo, and Ted does, *too.* He was *too* tired to think clearly.
two	*one + one* I noticed *two* packages on the sofa.

waist	*the middle part of the body* This dress is too large in the *waist.*
waste	*unused material;* also, *to squander* During the war, children collected *waste* fats. Please do not *waste* money on that.

weak	*feeble; lacking force;* opposite of *strong* Grandmother is too *weak* to walk yet. We could not hear his *weak* voice.
week	*seven days* Dad has been gone a *week.*

weather	*conditions outdoors* [no *h* sound] The *weather* suddenly changed.
whether	indicates alternative or doubt [pronounce the *h*] She didn't know *whether* or not to enter the contest.

who's	*who is, who has* I can't imagine *who's* at the door now. *Who's* been marking in my book?
whose	[possessive of *who*] *Whose* bicycle is this?

your	[possessive of *you*] What is *your* idea?
you're	*you are* Joe, *you're* the best friend I have.

● EXERCISE 26.　Number your paper 1–20. Write after the proper number the correct one of the words given in parentheses in the sentences below.

1. The (weather, whether) in Mexico City was pleasant.
2. Dad (threw, through) the skates into my closet.
3. Sally is going to the concert. Are you going, (to, too, two)?
4. Next (weak, week) the Bears will play the Packers.
5. We were in Boston a (weak, week).
6. The ball crashed (threw, through) the window.
7. Those children are (to, too, two) tired to study.
8. (Your, You're) trying too hard, Tommy.
9. (To, Too, Two) of the puppies are brown.
10. I don't remember (weather, whether) I signed the check or not.
11. I became (weak, week) in the knees when she announced my entrance.
12. (Your, You're) sleeve is torn.
13. Each majorette wore a gold sash around her (waist, waste).
14. (Whose, Who's) bat is it?
15. Tell me (weather, whether) or not we won.
16. The water seeped (threw, through) the basement window.
17. (Whose, Who's) going to be first?
18. I forgot (to, too, two) address the envelope.
19. You should not consider this a (waist, waste) of time.
20. I couldn't decide (weather, whether) or not to agree.

● REVIEW EXERCISE C.　Write a sentence correctly using each of the following words.

1. your	8. weak	15. its	22. their
2. who's	9. moral	16. there	23. whether
3. to	10. chose	17. then	24. lead
4. waist	11. breaks	18. stationary	25. piece
5. through	12. you're	19. principle	
6. week	13. too	20. plain	
7. loose	14. whose	21. shown	

● REVIEW EXERCISE D.　Number your paper 1–20. After the appropriate number, write the correctly spelled word in parentheses in the phrases on the next page.

1. a (brief, breif) talk
2. (neither, niether) one
3. (course, coarse) cloth
4. three (solos, soloes)
5. now and (then, than)
6. more (then, than) that
7. going (threw, through)
8. a few (weeks, weaks)
9. (surely, surly) on time
10. many (Negros, Negroes)
11. on the (cieling, ceiling)
12. two (copies, copys)
13. (loosing, losing) weight
14. some good (advice, advise)
15. four (cupsful, cupfuls)
16. may (choose, chose)
17. chocolate cake for (desert, dessert)
18. driving (passed, past) the theater
19. (to, too) energetic
20. (weather, whether) or not to stay

50 SPELLING DEMONS

Here are fifty simple words which cause many people trouble. It is wise to be aware of them. You will learn them most easily if you study them five at a time.

ache	cough	guess	once	tired
again	could	half	ready	tonight
always	country	hour	said	trouble
answer	doctor	instead	says	wear
blue	does	knew	shoes	where
built	don't	know	since	which
busy	early	laid	sugar	whole
buy	easy	meant	sure	women
can't	every	minute	tear	won't
color	friend	often	though	write

300 SPELLING WORDS

absence	acquaintance	apology
absolutely	actually	apparent
acceptance	administration	appearance
accidentally	affectionate	approach
accommodate	agriculture	approval
accompany	amateur	arguing
accomplish	ambassador	argument
accurate	analysis	assurance
accustomed	analyze '	attendance
achievement	anticipate	authority

available
basically
beginning
believe
benefit
benefited
boundary
Britain
calendar
campaign

capital
category
certificate
characteristic
chief
circuit
circumstance
civilization
column
commissioner

committees
comparison
competent
competition
conceivable
conception
confidential
conscience
conscious
consistency

constitution
continuous
control
cooperate
corporation
correspondence
criticism

criticize
cylinder
debtor

decision
definite
definition
deny
description
despise
diameter
disappearance
disappointment
discipline

disgusted
distinction
distinguished
dominant
duplicate
economic
efficiency
eighth
elaborate
eligible

embarrass
emergency
employee
encouraging
environment
equipped
essential
evidently
exaggerate
exceedingly

excellent
excessive
excitable

exercise
existence
expense
extraordinary
fascinating
fatal
favorably

fictitious
financier
flourish
fraternity
frequent
further
glimpse
glorious
grabbed
gracious

graduating
grammar
gross
gymnasium
happiness
hasten
heavily
hindrance
humorous
hungrily

hypocrisy
hypocrite
icy
ignorance
imagination
immediately
immense
incidentally
indicate
indispensable

inevitable

innocence

inquiry

insurance

intelligence

interfere

interpretation

interrupt

investigation

judgment

knowledge

leisure

lengthen

lieutenant

likelihood

liveliness

loneliness

magazine

maneuver

marriage

marvelous

mechanical

medieval

merchandise

minimum

mortgage

multitude

muscle

mutual

narrative

naturally

necessary

Negroes

niece

noticeable

obligation

obstacle

occasionally

occurrence

offense

official

omit

operations

opportunity

oppose

optimism

orchestra

organization

originally

paid

paradise

parallel

particularly

peasant

peculiar

percentage

performance

personal

personality

perspiration

persuade

petition

philosopher

picnic

planning

pleasant

policies

politician

possess

possibility

practically

precede

precisely

preferred

prejudice

preparation

pressure

primitive

privilege

probably

procedure

proceed

professor

proportion

psychology

publicity

pursuit

qualities

quantities

readily

reasonably

receipt

recognize

recommendation

referring

regretting

reign

relieve

remembrance

removal

renewal

repetition

representative

requirement

residence

resistance

responsibility

restaurant

rhythm

ridiculous

sacrifice
satire
satisfied
scarcely
scheme
scholarship
scissors
senate
sensibility
separate

sergeant
several
shepherd
sheriff
similar
skis
solemn

sophomore
source
specific

sponsor
straighten
substantial
substitute
subtle
succeed
successful
sufficient
summary
superior

suppress
surprise
survey

suspense
suspicion
temperament
tendency
thorough
transferring
tremendous

truly
unanimous
unfortunately
unnecessary
urgent
useful
using
vacancies
vacuum
varies

Manuscript Form

Standards for Written Work

A *manuscript* is any typewritten or handwritten composition, as distinguished from a printed document. In your school work this year and the years ahead, you will be writing more and more manuscripts. You should learn now to follow correct form for your written work.

29a. Follow accepted standards in preparing manuscripts.

Your teacher will find it easier to read and evaluate your papers if they are properly prepared. There is no single correct way to prepare a paper, but the rules below are widely used and accepted. Follow them unless your teacher requests you to do otherwise.

1. Use lined composition paper or, if you type, white paper 8½ by 11 inches in size.

2. Write only on one side of a sheet of paper.

3. Write in blue, black, or blue-black ink, or typewrite. If you type, double-space the lines.

4. Leave a margin of about two inches at the top of a page and margins of about one inch at the sides and bottom. The left-hand margin must be straight; the right-hand margin should be as straight as you can make it.

5. Indent the first line of each paragraph about one-half inch from the left margin.

29
a

6. Write your name, the class, and the date on the first page. Follow your teacher's instructions in the placement of these items. You may put them on three separate lines in the upper right-hand corner of the sheet, or write them in one line across the top of the page. Either way, they should begin about one inch down from the top of the page.

7. If your paper has a title, write it in the center of the first line. Skip a line between the title and the first line of your composition. (Double-space twice if you are typing.)

8. If the paper is more than one page in length, number the pages after the first, placing the number in the center of the line, about one-half inch down from the top.

9. Write legibly and neatly. If you are using unlined paper, try to keep the lines straight. Form your letters carefully, so that *n*'s do not look like *u*'s, *a*'s like *o*'s, and so on. Dot the *i*'s and cross the *t*'s. If you are typing, do not strike over letters or cross out words. If you have to erase, do it neatly.

29b. Learn the rules for using abbreviations.

In most of your writing, you should spell out words rather than abbreviate them. A few abbreviations, however, are commonly used.

The following abbreviations are acceptable when they are used before or after a name: *Mr.*, *Mrs.*, *Dr.*, *Jr.*, and *Sr.* If they do not accompany a name, spell out the words instead of using the abbreviations.

EXAMPLES   Mr. Casey   Dr. Macmillan
              Mrs. Murphy   George C. White, Sr.

              I have an appointment with our family doctor.
              The junior class is giving a picnic for the seniors.

The abbreviations A.M. (*ante meridiem*—"before noon"), P.M. (*post meridiem*—"after noon"), A.D. (*anno Domini*—"in the year of our Lord"), and B.C. (before Christ) are acceptable when they are used with numbers.

EXAMPLES   The party is scheduled to begin at 7:30 P.M.

Octavian (63 B.C.–A.D. 14) is now known as **Augustus Caesar**. [Notice that the abbreviation A.D. precedes the number, and B.C. follows it.]

Abbreviations for organizations are acceptable if they are generally known.

EXAMPLES   My father gave up his weekly swim at the **YMCA** to attend the **PTA** meeting.

I am reading a book about the **FBI**; Margaret plans a report on a booklet published by the **UN**. [Abbreviations for government agencies are usually written without periods.]

29c. Learn the rules for writing numbers.

Numbers of more than two words should be written in numerals, not words. If, however, you are writing several numbers, some of them one word and some more than one, write them all the same way. Always spell out a number that begins a sentence.

EXAMPLES   Jack has sold **257** magazine subscriptions.

Mother has canned **thirty-seven** quarts of peaches.

I have only **five** days in which to write **seven** reports.

There are **563** students in the freshman class, **327** in the sophomore class, **143** in the junior class, and **98** in the senior class.

One thousand five hundred band members attended the annual State Contest Festival.

Write out numbers like *seventh*, *fifty-third*, and so on. If they are used with a month, however, it is customary to use numerals only.

EXAMPLES   My brother graduated **second** [not 2nd] in his class at the Naval Academy.

School closes on **June 6** [or the sixth of June; not June 6th].

29
b·c

29d. Learn the rules for dividing words at the end of a line.

Sometimes you do not have room to write all of a long word at the end of a line. It may look better to start the word on the next line; however, if doing that would leave a very uneven right-hand margin, you should divide the word, using a hyphen after the first part. Learn the rules for dividing words (see pages 555–56). Remember that you should try to avoid dividing words if possible. Usually a slightly irregular margin looks better than a hyphenated word.

29e. Learn the standard correction symbols.

In correcting your papers, your teacher may use some or all of the symbols given below. If you memorize these symbols, you will understand at once what is wrong in your paper. If you are not sure how to correct your error, use the index of this book to find the section that you need to review.

ms	error in manuscript form or neatness
cap	error in use of capital letter
p	error in punctuation
sp	error in spelling
frag	sentence fragment
r-s	run-on sentence
ss	error in sentence structure
k	awkward sentence or passage
nc	not clear
ref	unclear reference of pronoun
gr	error in grammar
w	error in word choice
¶	Begin a new paragraph here.
t	error in tense
∧	You have omitted something.

Making Writing Interesting: Words and Their Use

Making Writing Interesting: Words and Their Use

Writers, who are constantly working and playing with words, develop a deep respect for them. They know that whether their writing is interesting or uninteresting, clear or unclear, depends largely on the words they choose.

Writers enjoy studying words. They become fascinated by the characteristics words possess. They know that words may be noisy or quiet, beautiful or ugly, hard or soft, fresh or tired, calm or emotional, kind or cruel, formal or informal, general or specific.

Writers are aware, too, of the interesting histories of words—their origins, their changing forms, and their shifting meanings. As a young person interested in improving your writing, you can hardly do better than to cultivate the same strong interest in words that the experienced writer has.

The purposes of this chapter are, first, to try to arouse your curiosity about words and, second, to show you how an understanding of words and their ways can help you to write more interestingly.

THE SOUNDS OF WORDS—ONOMATOPOEIA

Some words have sounds that reflect their meaning. These are words that have the sound of what they refer to. For example, the word *bubbling* has the sound made by a boiling liquid. The formation of words that imitate natural sounds, as *bubbling* does, is called onomatopoeia (on′·ə·mat′·ə·pē′·ə).

The following words are examples of onomatopoeia: *buzz, clang, creak, groan, hiss, jangle, rattle, scratch, splash, thud.*

In writing certain kinds of description, writers find onomatopoetic words very useful. The American poet Amy Lowell, in writing a prose description of the bombardment of a French town during World War I, chose words for the effect of their sounds. Read aloud the following passage from "The Bombardment," emphasizing the sound words. You will find at least five examples of onomatopoeia. Notice also the poet's use of rhyme in this prose passage.

> Slowly, without force, the rain drops into the city. It stops a moment on the carved head of St. John, then slides on again, slipping and trickling over his stone cloak. It splashes from the lead conduit of a gargoyle, and falls from it in turmoil on the stones in the Cathedral square. Where are the people, and why does the fretted steeple sweep about in the sky? Boom! The sound swings against the rain. Boom again! After it, only water rushing in the gutters, and the turmoil from the spout of the gargoyle. Silence. Ripples and mutters. Boom! [1]

● EXERCISE 1.   Prepare a list of at least ten onomatopoetic words not included in the list at the top of the page or in the Amy Lowell selection. Compare your list with those lists made by your classmates.

SOUND AND MEANING

Even when they are not onomatopoetic, word sounds often seem to reflect a word's meaning. The sounds of the words *alone*, *lonely*, and *loneliness*, for example, seem to suggest the feelings they refer to. No one knows exactly how or why certain sounds or combinations of sounds came to acquire certain meanings, except, of course, for words of

[1] From "The Bombardment" from *Men, Women, Ghosts* by Amy Lowell. Reprinted by permission of Houghton Mifflin Company.

onomatopoetic origin. Still it is interesting to notice the way word sounds, like the sound of *lonely*, do seem to suggest certain feelings. Is it possible that a made-up word, a meaningless word, can just by its sound suggest a meaning?

● EXERCISE 2. Below is a list of five made-up words. Copy the list and after each word write the feeling it suggests to you, such as sadness, weariness, happiness, fear, loneliness.

1. siskilally
2. lornsorge
3. lumbergast
4. limmitypippiny
5. mogandroapal

Probably no one would insist that a general idea, such as sadness, has a particular sound, or that sounds in themselves are happy or sad. As a result of our experiences with words, however, we do find it hard to imagine that a word of an entirely different sound from a familiar word can mean the same thing. Here is a sentence containing the word *solemn*. "Throughout the funeral everyone was depressingly solemn." Now substitute for *solemn* the nonsense word *mippy*. "Throughout the funeral everyone was depressingly mippy." Does *mippy* convey the feeling of depression? Now try another nonsense word, *gorlornal*. "Throughout the funeral everyone was depressingly gorlornal." Do you think the sound of *gorlornal* fits the meaning of the sentence better than *mippy*?

● EXERCISE 3. Make up five nonsense words whose sounds suggest specific feelings to you. Ask your classmates what feelings your "words" suggest to them. What conclusion are you able to draw concerning the relationship between the sound of a word and the feeling it inspires?

Skillful writers, especially poets, sometimes choose words for the effect of their sound as well as for their meaning.

Edgar Allan Poe said that when he was searching for a sorrowful word to use over and over as a refrain in his poem "The Raven," he chose the word *nevermore* because both its meaning and its sound are sad.

In his melancholy poem *Ulalume*, Poe showed clearly his remarkable ability to select just the right word for the effect he wanted. He wished to create an effect of mystery and sorrow with overtones of death, which brings the greatest sorrow we know. Read the following stanza aloud, noting the skillful use of sorrowful sounds.

> The skies they were ashen and sober;
> The leaves they were crispèd and sere—
> The leaves they were withering and sere:
> It was night, in the lonesome October
> Of my most immemorial year;
> It was hard by the dim lake of Auber,
> In the misty mid region of Weir—
> It was down by the dank tarn of Auber,
> In the ghoul-haunted woodland of Weir.

BEAUTY IN WORDS

The following paragraph expresses the pleasure one man finds in words.

I like fat, buttery words, such as ooze, turpitude, glutinous, toady. I like solemn, angular, creaky words, such as strait-laced, cantankerous, pecuniary, valedictory. I like spurious, gold-plated, black-is-white words, such as gentlefolk, mortician, free-lancer, mistress. I like crunchy, brittle, crackly words, such as splinter, grapple, jostle, crusty. I like suave *v* words, such as Svengali, svelte, bravura, verve. I like sullen, crabbed, scowling words, such as skulk, glower, scabby, churl. I like words such as trickery, tucker, genteel, and horrid. I like pretty-pretty, flowered, endimanche [1] words, such as elegant, halcyon, Elysium,

[1] *Endimanche* is a French adjective meaning "put on Sunday clothes."

artiste. I like wormy, squirmy, mealy words, such as crawl, blubber, squeal, drip. I like sniggly, chuckling words, such as cowlick, gurgle, bubble, and burp. I like words.[1]

Is there such a thing as a beautiful word or an ugly word? Some writers think there is. When asked to list what he considered the ten most beautiful words in the language, Wilfred Funk, a famous lexicographer, listed the following: *dawn, hush, lullaby, murmuring, tranquil, mist, luminous, chimes, golden, melody.* Saying these words aloud, you may react to them as Mr. Funk did and find them beautiful. Are their sounds beautiful, regardless of their meaning? Note that five of them contain the letter *l*, whose sound Mr. Funk apparently thought beautiful.

Fannie Hurst, an American novelist, offered six words as her candidates for the most beautiful: *serenity, beauty, mercy, peace, vitality, madonna.* To what extent do you think Miss Hurst was affected by the sounds and to what extent was she affected by the meaning of these words? Note, incidentally, that there is only one *l* in the words she suggested. H. L. Mencken, linguist and essayist, once said he thought *cellar door* to be a most beautiful expression. Certainly he was judging entirely by sound!

● EXERCISE 4. Select, from the words given above, the five you consider the most beautiful. Then add five words of your own choice to the list. Compare your choices with those of your classmates.

● EXERCISE 5. List ten words you consider the ugliest words you know. You may wish to begin with *ugly* itself.

While the sounds of most words are unrelated to the meanings of the words, some words, as you have seen, do reveal a close relationship between sound and meaning. We

---

[1] This paragraph, written by Alec Phare and quoted in *The Wolfe Magazine of Letters*, was reprinted in *Reader's Digest* of June 1949. Used by permission of The Reader's Digest.

become so accustomed to this relationship that the sound of a word actually seems to suggest the meaning. When we write, we may increase the power of our writing by choosing words whose sound and meaning both work for us.

WORD HISTORIES—DERIVATION

No aspect of word study is more fascinating to word lovers than word histories. Tracing the history of a word to find out its origin and how it came to mean what it means today is an interesting study called etymology. Scholars engaged in this study are etymologists. The etymologist can trace a word back to what he calls its origin. That is, he can tell us whether in the beginning it was a Greek or Latin or English (Anglo-Saxon) word or a word from some other language. He can show us that many of our words are a combination of two or more ancient words. He can show us how a word's meaning has changed during its history. The etymologist can explain changes in the spelling and pronunciation of the word over the centuries, and he can give us the approximate times when the word took on additional meanings.

What the etymologist cannot do, of course, is explain the great mystery of all word origins. This is the mystery of how or why certain sounds came to represent certain things or ideas. A word is merely a symbol representing the thing or the idea. The origins of some words like *bang* or *crack* are easy to explain because the sounds of these words are onomatopoetic. Other words, like our noun *bear*, can be traced back to the Anglo-Saxons, who gave the word *bera* to this animal; but this does not explain why the Anglo-Saxons chose to give this particular name to this particular beast. It is usually impossible for the etymologist to explain why one symbol, one sound, was originally chosen to represent a particular idea or thing.

Sources of English Words

Words come into the language in many ways from many different sources. Some come from the names of persons. The sandwich acquired its name from John Montague, fourth Earl of Sandwich, who invented the sandwich in the eighteenth century. Some words are derived from myths. Our word *volcano* comes from Vulcan, Roman god of fire, whose fiery forge was said to be deep in a mountain. Words are derived from the names of places: *china* dishes; *damask* napkins, from Damascus. Some words are combinations of two or more words—*airplane*, *basketball*, *telecast* (television and broadcast). Etymologically, *television* derives from the Greek word *tele*, meaning *far*, plus the Latin word *videre*, meaning *to see*. *Broadcast* derives from the Anglo-Saxon word *brād*, meaning wide or extended in breadth, plus the Old Norse word *kasta*, meaning *to throw*.

The English language has been vastly enriched by words borrowed from other languages. Approximately 50 percent of English words are Latin in origin, including words that came from the Latin-based languages—French, Italian, and Spanish; 25 percent are Anglo-Saxon; 15 percent, Greek; 10 percent, all other languages. One can find English words that were borrowed from nearly every major language in the world. Here are a few familiar examples of words borrowed from other languages:

tepee	Dakota Indian
memoir	French
myth	Greek
piano	Italian
cigar	Spanish
kindergarten	German
yacht	Dutch
ski	Norwegian
alcohol	Arabic
pajama	Persian

● EXERCISE 6.   Using a dictionary that gives derivations, look up and record the language from which English borrowed each of the following words: *balcony, cargo, climax, cosmetic, slogan, succotash, wagon, waltz, kimono, tea.*

A great many English words are combinations of roots and prefixes from Latin and Greek. *Television,* mentioned above, is one example. You will find other examples on pages 429 to 432. On pages 432 to 434 you will find examples of words with interesting histories, and a list of common expressions that English borrowed from other languages.

● EXERCISE 7.   Select one of the following words, look up its origin—the interesting story behind it—and report to the class: *titanic, macadam, maverick, guillotine, utopian, braille, corduroy, limousine, pedagogue, quixotic, bonfire, curfew.*

NEW WORDS

A living language like English is constantly acquiring new words. Many words familiar to you were unknown when your parents were your age. New words, mostly nouns, come into the language as man's knowledge increases. The new words are formed in about the same ways that words have always been formed. Sometimes they are coined from appropriate roots and prefixes from the Latin and Greek: *astronaut*—space traveler (*astro*—star + *naut*—sailor; literally, star sailor). Sometimes they are combinations: *bloodmobile*. Occasionally a new word is formed from the first letters of words in a descriptive phrase: *scuba*—*s*elf-contained *u*nderwater *b*reathing *a*pparatus.

The language changes and grows also when old words are used in new ways so that they acquire new meanings. You learned earlier that our word *bear* was originally the Anglo-Saxon word *bera,* the Anglo-Saxon name for this animal. The dictionary now lists these additional meanings for *bear:*

(1) a gruff, ill-mannered, clumsy person; (2) a speculator, especially one in the stock exchange, who seeks to depress prices or who sells in the belief that a decline in prices is likely.

● EXERCISE 8.   The following words are old words that have distinctly new meanings. From your own knowledge or with the help of the dictionary, explain the new meanings of these words.

1. satellite	6. cool
2. pad	7. computer
3. rock	8. hip
4. beam	9. rumble
5. platter	10. swing

● EXERCISE 9.   Explain the method by which each of the following relatively new words was formed. Use your dictionary.

1. sit-in	6. stereophonic
2. skydiving	7. blitz
3. laser	8. cybernetics
4. Medicare	9. finalize
5. cosmonaut	10. antibiotic

You know that a word may be used as more than one part of speech. The word *cash*, for example, may be used as a noun: "She paid in cash"; as a verb: "Please cash this check"; and as an adjective: "He made a cash payment." A common kind of language change occurs when a word becomes accepted in use as a different part of speech. *Contact* was once used only as a noun. Today it is commonly used as a verb: "Contact me in the morning," and as an adjective: "contact cement."

In these ways, then, a living language constantly grows and changes. As knowledge expands and life changes, so does language grow and change; new words come into the language, and old words take on new meanings.

THE DENOTATIVE AND CONNOTATIVE MEANINGS OF WORDS

As you know, a word may have many different meanings. The noun *ring*, for example, has such varied meanings as a band worn around a finger, a roped-off area for boxing, and a telephone call. These literal meanings of a word are its denotative meanings. In addition to their denotative meanings, many words have connotative meanings. The connotative meanings are meanings that may be associated with the word by a reader or listener. They are meanings that the word suggests beyond its denotative meanings.

The words *statesman* and *politician*, for example, may have the same denotative meaning—one who is skilled in the science of government or politics. In their connotative meanings, however, the words are different. When you refer to an elected government official as a statesman, you honor him. When you refer to him as a politician, you may be insulting him, for the word *politician* has unfavorable connotations for many people. It suggests an ambitious person who is more concerned with his own selfish interests than with the needs of the people he represents.

Usually the connotations of a word stir our feelings, and we react to the word emotionally. The words *capitalist* and *capitalism*, although they have clear, technical, denotative meanings, might arouse strong antagonistic feelings in Russia, which has a communistic rather than a capitalistic society. Similarly, the words *communist* and *communism* might arouse antagonistic feelings in the United States, which has a capitalistic society. When a writer or public speaker uses the words *capitalism* and *communism*, he may be using them more for their connotative meaning than for their denotative meaning.

● EXERCISE 10.   The words in each group below are, to a degree, similar in their denotative meaning, but vastly different in their connotative meanings. List the words in each group in descending order according to the favorableness of their connotations; that is, put the word with the most favorable connotation first and the word with the most unfavorable connotation last. Opinions will differ.

1. thin, skinny, gawky, slender, lanky
2. defeat, edge-out, swamp, beat, overrun
3. conceited, vain, arrogant, cocky, self-confident
4. informer, stool pigeon, tattletale, spy, undercover agent
5. tight, thrifty, stingy, frugal, economical

As you may have discovered, words through their connotative meanings may affect people differently. Some words, like *motherhood, friendship, freedom, home, peace,* will have favorable connotations for almost everyone, but other words will cause widely varying reactions. A person's reactions to a word are determined by his experience and knowledge. Your reaction to *Nazi* will be negative because of your knowledge of history. Your reaction to *Yankee* probably depends on whether you were born in the South or in New England.

● EXERCISE 11.   Read the following list of words and give your immediate reaction, as negative, affirmative, or neutral. Be prepared to explain in class the reasons for your reactions. Ask your parents for their reactions to the words.

1. snake
2. dentist
3. chocolate
4. labor union
5. Republican
6. Frenchman
7. welfare
8. millionaire
9. teacher
10. breakfast

● EXERCISE 12.   Distinguish between the connotations of the words in each of the following pairs. The denotative meanings of the paired words are similar. Their connotative meanings may prove to be quite different.

1. dog, cur
2. idealist, dreamer
3. rare, half-cooked
4. determined, obstinate
5. fastidious, fussy
6. used, second-hand
7. graveyard, memorial park
8. job, chore
9. cook, chef
10. boat, yacht

LOADED WORDS

Closely related to the fact that words have important connotative meanings is the deliberate use by a writer of words that will prejudice the reader for or against something. Words that reveal the writer's opinion and tend to prejudice the reader for or against something are called loaded words.

● EXERCISE 13.   Both of the following descriptions of the same teacher contain loaded words. Read the two descriptions; the first is loaded against the teacher, and the second is in her favor. Make a list of the loaded words in the first selection; then beside each word write the corresponding loaded word from the second selection.

> Miss Carter ruled her third-grade prisoners with an iron hand. She demanded order at all times, and she got it. Exuberant boys and girls, fresh and excited from playground games, were abruptly squelched by an angry stare or a growled threat. Her towering, angular figure loomed over the class like a vengeful god. Had we known how to do so, we would have escaped from her in panic.

> Miss Carter handled her third-grade pupils with a firm hand. She expected order at all times, and her pupils gave it to her. Exuberant boys and girls, fresh and excited from playground games, were soon calmed by a shake of her head or a whispered warning. Her tall, statuesque figure hovered over us and added to our sense of security. We thought of Miss Carter as our guardian angel.

FORMAL WORDS AND INFORMAL WORDS

You know the meanings of the word *formal* and its opposite *informal*. You know that a party may be formal or informal. You hear references to formal clothes and informal clothes. A class or a meeting may be conducted formally or informally. Reports and essays may be written in a formal style or in an informal style. Hence there is formal English and informal English. You use informal English far more than you use formal English, but as you grow older and become better educated, you will find more use for formal English.

Although high school students seldom have occasion to speak or write the most formal English, they do have to learn that different situations call for different kinds of English. If you were speaking to a class of fourth-graders, you would naturally use different words from those you would use when speaking to a meeting of the Parent-Teachers Association, although you might be saying about the same thing to both groups. A report given in class or at a student council meeting or a talk delivered before the school assembly would require more formal English than would a conversation with friends or family. In fact, informal English is often called conversational English.

Most words may be used in both formal and informal situations, but some words are usually avoided in a formal piece of writing or a formal speech. For example, slang, because it is extremely informal, would not be used on a formal occasion, and would be used sparingly in class and in the writing done for school courses. In social conversation and in a friendly letter, you would probably use slang freely.

Slang

Slang consists of new words, or old words in new uses, that are adopted because they seem clever and colorful and show that the user is up-to-date, or, to use an informal phrase, "in the know." High school students are especially fond of slang and ingenious at inventing it. Sometimes a slang word becomes so completely acceptable that it is no longer slang but good informal English. Most slang words, however, live a short life. The popular slang of ten years ago would seem old-fashioned today. Only slang that lasts gets into the dictionary, where it is usually clearly labeled as slang. The following words, when used with the given meanings, are all marked *slang* in the *Standard College Dictionary*:

corny: trite, banal, sentimental, unsophisticated
to goof off: to waste time, loaf
lousy: contemptible, foul, mean, worthless
neat: wonderful, splendid
screwball: an unconventional or erratic person
square: one not conversant with the latest trends or fads
sourpuss: a person with a sullen, peevish expression or character
stinker: an unpleasant, disgusting, or irritating person

While slang is sometimes effective in informal talk, it is less effective in formal writing because it is too general and stale. A reader finds it almost meaningless. When you write, you usually have time to choose words that are more specific and more meaningful than slang.

● EXERCISE 14.   The following words were popular slang at the time this chapter was written. How many are still in use? Write a definition of each word whose slang meaning is familiar to you, and use the word in a sentence.

1. hung up
2. kooky
3. cop out
4. teenybopper
5. way out
6. gung-ho
7. a dope
8. groovy
9. swinger
10. drag

Slang, then, is a kind of language that is so informal that it is rarely used in writing.

Degrees of Formality Among Synonyms

A synonym is a word that means almost the same thing as another word. *Huge* and *immense* are synonyms. But among some synonyms there are degrees of formality. The words in the following pairs of synonyms would be acceptable in any kind of writing, but notice the difference in the degree of their formality. Are there differences also in their connotative meanings?

> necktie, cravat
> stealthily, surreptitiously
> write, inscribe
> murder, homicide
> commonplace, banal
> kind, beneficent
> nosy, inquisitive
> unbelievable, incredible
> small, diminutive
> exclude, ostracize

Appropriate Words

When you write, choose words that are appropriate to the kind of writing the situation calls for. A ninth-grade writer should not strain to use fancy words. Using a carefully high-toned vocabulary may annoy your reader, who will realize that you are putting on airs. On the other hand, you should not use language as informal as slang in serious compositions, where it is inappropriate.

To understand how inappropriate words will affect the tone of a report, read the following opening paragraph of a book report. List the words that you consider too informal to be appropriate in a serious book report and, after each, write a more formal word, one that will maintain the serious tone of the report. You should list at least five.

The Fixer by Bernard Malamud is a novel about the dirty tricks pulled on a Jew by anti-Semitic Russians before the Reds took over Russia in 1917. Yakov Bok, an unsuccessful Jewish repairman, or fixer, gets pinched for living under a false name in a part of Kiev where Jews were not allowed to live. The cops accuse him of a recent murder of a Russian boy, and then cook up false evidence against him. Although Yakov is completely innocent, he is put away in solitary confinement for over three years before his case comes to trial. During these years he is starved, frozen, beaten, poisoned, chained, and, in general, treated worse than a dog. Displaying amazing strength of character, he repeatedly refuses to sign a confession and is finally brought to trial. As Yakov is on his way to court in the paddy-wagon, Mr. Malamud ends his story. The reader can only guess whether Yakov was acquitted or sent to Siberia for life.

● EXERCISE 15.   The following are excerpts from a *Life* magazine article "Let Your Kids Alone" by Robert Paul Smith. The author wisely chose to write in a very informal style. Study the word choice and the conversational manner of each excerpt. Then rewrite it in a more formal style. Your rewritten version may not be so effective as Mr. Smith's, but the exercise will make clear to you the difference between formal and informal writing.

1. Big Brother, in this case, is all the parents who cannot refrain from poking their snoots into a world where they have no business to be, into the whole wonderful world of a kid, which is wonderful precisely because there are no grown-ups in it.

2. Although Big Brother has organized every league known to man and issued a rule book therefor, he has not yet put out a mimeographed sheet of instructions on watching squirrels. There are no books on how to be a lousy right fielder (it came to me natural), and in no book does it say that when you go to make a tackle, of course you shut your eyes and lie about it later. No doubt these books are being written.

3. The real point is that this kind of jazz doesn't fool anyone but the parents. The kids know that any grown-up who gets down on all fours and makes mudpies with them is either a spy or a fool.

4. Last year I wrote a book which suggested, in the mildest possible ways, that if people remembered what a nuisance grown-ups were when they were

kids, perhaps now that they were in turn presumably grown-ups, they might like to get off the kids' backs.[1]

TIRED WORDS

When a writer refers to a word as "tired," he means that the word has been used so much and so thoughtlessly that it has lost much of its meaning and its effectiveness. So-called tired words like *nice, swell, wonderful,* and *great* are common in conversation; they are, however, not exact enough to be effective in writing. When a friend asks you what kind of time you had at a party, you may use any one of those words to convey the idea that you enjoyed the party. However, if, again, you were writing a serious book report, you would be telling your reader little if you simply characterized the book as nice or swell or wonderful. These words have been so much used and so loosely used that they are almost without real meaning.

Another name for a tired word or a tired expression is *cliché* (klē·shā′). Clichés may be single words or they may be expressions containing more than one word. Among the most common clichés are comparisons—tired comparisons: busy as a bee, clear as crystal, quick as a flash, white as a sheet, fat as a pig, straight as an arrow, thin as a rail. Not all clichés are comparisons: few and far between, accidents will happen, gala occasion, fair sex, last but not least.

Good writers avoid clichés in any form—tired words, tired comparisons, or other tired expressions.

● EXERCISE 16.   Prepare a list of five tired words, five tired comparisons, and five tired expressions that are not comparisons. Do not include in your list any of the words or expressions used as examples above. Compare your list with those of your classmates. Combining lists, you should have a large collection of expressions to avoid whenever you write.

[1] From "Let Your Kids Alone" by Robert Paul Smith from *Life* Magazine, January 27, 1958. Copyright © 1958 by Robert Paul Smith. Reprinted by permission of Monica McCall, Inc.

GENERAL WORDS AND SPECIFIC WORDS

Good writing is specific, not general or vague. It is specific in both its content and its language. If, for example, you begin a paragraph with the statement "Students are not helping to keep the school corridors neat and clean," you should devote the rest of the paragraph to giving specific evidence to support your beginning statement. You will give specific examples that show how cluttered and dirty the corridors are.

Language is specific when its words are clear and definite in meaning, not hazy and general. For example, in describing an encounter with a dog, you would not be content simply to say that a dog came across the street toward you. Such a statement, with its very general words *dog*, *came*, and *street*, does not give the reader a clear picture. If you tell the kind of dog and the manner in which he came, and give a more specific idea of the street, your description will be much clearer.

A huge Irish setter, its feathered tail swinging from side to side, bounded toward me through the heavy traffic on Branch Boulevard.

This picture has been made more vivid in two ways. First, the words *dog* and *came* have been changed to *Irish setter* and *bounded*. Second, specific details have been added —the tail swinging and the traffic. Naming the street will help anyone who is familiar with Branch Boulevard to picture the scene.

● EXERCISE 17.   Arrange the words in each of the following lists in descending order of general to specific; that is, put the most general word first, the most specific word last.

1. dog, animal, creature, golden retriever
2. foreigner, man, person, Italian
3. building, edifice, office building, skyscraper
4. roast, main dish, food, meat
5. lineman, young man, guard, football player, athlete

● EXERCISE 18.   Write the following words in a column and, after each, write three more specific synonyms: 1. enclosure 2. bird 3. cried 4. spoke 5. walked 6. church 7. athlete 8. vehicle 9. structure 10. field

● EXERCISE 19.   Rewrite each of the following sentences, substituting specific words and specific details for the general, vague words so that your reader will understand more clearly what you are trying to say.

1. A man came into the room and spoke to the teacher.
2. His summer home on a beach faced the water.
3. She grew up in poverty in a city slum.
4. A defensive player stopped the play.
5. From a vantage point we were watching the game.

SUMMARY

You have learned that, when you write, you must make a great many decisions. You must decide which word out of the many available to you will best say what you want to say. In choosing a word, you should understand its connotative as well as its denotative meaning. You should choose words that are appropriate to the situation—formal or informal. You should avoid slang except in the most informal kind of writing. You should avoid tired words and expressions—clichés. You should choose the specific word, avoiding the general word. Above all, remember this: When you write, you have time to choose your words carefully. Take time! Do not just write down unthinkingly the first, or even the second word, that comes to you. The more time you spend on word choice the more effective your writing will be.

Composition Assignment—Specific Verbs

To demonstrate your ability to select from the many words available the one word that will be most specific and most effective, write a composition in which you describe a scene that is full of action. The verb is the key word in any description of action. Your verbs must convey clearly to the reader the action you want him to see. They must be specific.

In preparation for your composition, work through the following exercises.

I

In each of the following sentences the verbs have been omitted. Select for each sentence a verb or verbs that will clearly show the picture you have in mind. Write the verbs in order, numbering them according to the sentence number. Exchange papers with your classmates. Discuss the relative effectiveness of the many verbs suggested.

   a. Mr. McDougal was ——ing his new power mower across the front lawn.

   b. Late again, John —— through the classroom door, —— across the back of the room, and —— into his seat.

   c. When the period bell ——, every door along the deserted corridor —— open, and the thundering herd —— forth.

   d. Shielding his eyes from the sun, the right fielder —— forward, then —— abruptly, and with his bare hand outstretched, —— into the air, and —— the ball for the final out.

   e. Balancing in the bow of the rocking skiff, Barry and John —— each other, —— awkwardly, and —— overboard with a resounding splash.

II

The verb in each of the following sentences is vague and commonplace. It does not give as clear a picture as a more carefully selected specific verb can. After the proper sentence number, write a more specific verb that will make the picture clear as you see it. Compare your choices with those of your classmates.

1. He *hit* the ball over the fence.
2. He *ate* all the cake that was left.
3. She *called* for help.
4. The car *came* to a halt.
5. A trailer truck, its horn blaring, *went* past us down the hill.

III

In the following paragraph John Steinbeck tells what happened when, with his usually mild-mannered poodle Charley beside him in the car, he encountered a bear in Yellowstone Park. As you read, note how specific the verbs are.

> Less than a mile from the entrance I saw a bear beside the road, and it ambled out as though to flag me down. Instantly a change came over Charley. He shrieked with rage. His lips flared, showing wicked teeth that have some trouble with a dog biscuit. He screeched insults at the bear, which hearing, the bear reared up and seemed to me to overtop the car. Frantically I rolled the windows shut and, swinging quickly to the left, grazed the animal, then scuttled on while Charley raved and ranted beside me, describing in detail what he would do to that bear if he could get at him. I was never so astonished in my life.[1]

IV

Visualize someone in action and write a one-sentence description similar to those in Part I on page 618 in which you make the picture vivid by using specific verbs.

V

Now you are ready to write a full-length description (about 150 words) of an action-filled scene with which you are familiar. Before you write, take plenty of time to visualize the scene in all its details. Decide what you are going to include. Decide from what viewpoint you are going to watch the scene. You will be judged in this composition by your success in selecting effective verbs.

[1] From *Travels with Charley: In Search of America* by John Steinbeck. Copyright © 1961, 1962 by The Curtis Publishing Co., Inc. Copyright © 1962 by John Steinbeck. Reprinted by permission of The Viking Press, Inc.

If you need suggestions, the following may be helpful. Crowd scenes are good for an assignment of this kind because they provide many different actions to describe.

> The cafeteria at lunchtime
> The gym during an exciting basketball game
> The stadium at game time
> The school parking lot after school
> The beach or pool on a hot day
> A busy intersection at rush hour
> A riot or mob scene
> A county fair
> A public park on a weekend afternoon

You need not, however, use a crowd scene. You may prefer to describe an experience in which you performed or watched others perform many specific actions: a hike, a fishing exploit, a skiing or sailing experience, a storm, a time when you witnessed a frightening or exciting thing.

Tab Key Index

SUPPLEMENT

Making Writing Interesting: Words and Their Use

CORRECTION SYMBOLS

ms	error in manuscript form or neatness
cap	error in use of capital letters
p	error in punctuation
sp	error in spelling
frag	sentence fragment
ss	error in sentence structure
k	awkward sentence
nc	not clear
rs	run-on sentence
gr	error in grammar
w	error in word choice
¶	You should have begun a new paragraph here.
t	error in tense
∧	You have omitted something.

Index

627

CONTINUED ON BACK END PAPER

SPEAKING AND LISTENING

MECHANICS